Deploy Containers on AWS

With EC2, ECS, and EKS

Shimon Ifrah

Apress®

Deploy Containers on AWS: With EC2, ECS, and EKS

Shimon Ifrah
Melbourne, VIC, Australia

ISBN-13 (pbk): 978-1-4842-5100-3   ISBN-13 (electronic): 978-1-4842-5101-0
https://doi.org/10.1007/978-1-4842-5101-0

Managing Director, Apress Media LLC: Welmoed Spahr
Acquisitions Editor: Celestin Suresh John
Development Editor: Siddhi Chavan
Coordinating Editor: Aditee Mirashi

Cover designed by eStudioCalamar

Cover image designed by Freepik

Distributed to the book trade worldwide by Springer Science+Business Media New York, 233 Spring Street, 6th Floor, New York, NY 10013. Phone 1-800-SPRINGER, fax (201) 348-4505, e-mail orders-ny@springer-sbm.com, or visit www.springeronline.com. Apress Media, LLC is a California LLC and the sole member (owner) is Springer Science + Business Media Finance Inc (SSBM Finance Inc). SSBM Finance Inc is a **Delaware** corporation.

For information on translations, please e-mail rights@apress.com, or visit www.apress.com/rights-permissions.

Apress titles may be purchased in bulk for academic, corporate, or promotional use. eBook versions and licenses are also available for most. For more information, reference our Print and eBook Bulk Sales web page at www.apress.com/bulk-sales.

Any source code or other supplementary material referenced by the author in this book is available to readers on GitHub via the book's product page, located at www.apress.com/978-1-4842-5100-3. For more detailed information, please visit www.apress.com/source-code.

Printed on acid-free paper

Table of Contents

About the Author xi

About the Technical Reviewers xiii

Acknowledgments xv

Introduction xvii

Chapter 1: Getting Started with Containers on Amazon AWS 1

    Setting Up Your Amazon AWS Container Environment 2

        Installing Docker Desktop 2

        Signing Up for an Amazon AWS Account 12

        Using AWS CLI 13

        Using Visual Studio Code 26

    Understanding Key Concepts of Containers on Amazon AWS 37

        Elastic Container Registry 38

        Elastic Container Service 38

        Elastic Kubernetes Service 39

    Running Containers on Amazon AWS 40

    Summary 40

Chapter 2: Storing, Managing, and Deploying Docker Container Images
with Amazon ECR 41

    ECR Pricing 42

        Free Tier Account and ECR 43

    Setting Up Amazon ECR 43

        Creating an IAM Account 43

        Using Multifactor Authentication 50

        Creating an Access Key for AWS CLI 50

        Creating an ECR Repository 51

Pushing Docker Images to Amazon ECR 54

    Noting the ECR URI 54

    Building an Image 55

    Tagging the Image 57

    Authenticating to AWS ECR 57

    Pushing the Image 58

    Publishing Images from Visual Studio 2017 to AWS ECR 59

Pulling Images from Amazon ECR 61

    Authenticating to ECR 62

    Pulling an Image from ECR 62

Managing and Securing Amazon ECR 63

    Creating Lifecycle Policies 63

    Adding Tags 69

    Cost and Usage Report 71

    Creating an S3 Storage Bucket 73

    Creating a Report 74

    Viewing Reports 79

    Deleting Images 80

Summary 81

Chapter 3: Deploying Containerized Applications with Amazon ECS 83

Setting Up Amazon ECS 84

    ECS Fargate Introduction 84

    ECS EC2 Cluster Introduction 84

    ECS Cluster 85

    Task Definitions 85

    ECS Services 86

Using Amazon Fargate and an ECS EC2 Cluster to Deploy Containers 86

    Fargate 86

    EC2 87

    Virtual Private Cloud 87

    Deploying the Container with ECS Fargate and ECR 87

Creating, Managing, and Scaling an Amazon ECS Cluster 101

    Creating an ECS EC2 Cluster 101

    Creating a Task Definition for an ECS EC2 Cluster.. 105

    Creating a Task 108

    Scaling Tasks and Clusters.. 112

    Scaling Task Definitions 112

    Scaling an ECS EC2 Cluster 113

Monitoring and Managing Amazon ECS 116

    AWS CloudWatch 116

    Managing AWS ECS with AWS CLI 118

    Using ECS CLI 118

    Installing AWS ECS CLI on Windows 10 118

    Installing AWS ECS CLI on macOS 122

    Installing AWS ECS CLI on Linux 122

    Using ECS CLI 122

    Using AWS CLI 124

    Running Windows Containers on an AWS ECS Cluster 125

Summary.. 133

Chapter 4: Deploy a Containerized Application with Amazon EKS 135

Getting Started with Amazon EKS 136

    Kubernetes Building Blocks.. 137

    Kubernetes Architecture 138

Setting Up AKS 139

    Installing kubectl on Windows.. 140

    Installing kubectl on Mac 144

    Installing kubectl on Linux.. 144

Installing AWS IAM Authenticator for Kubernetes 145

    Installing AWS IAM Authenticator on Linux.. 145

    Installing AWS IAM Authenticator on macOS 145

    Installing AWS IAM Authenticator on Windows 146

    Creating the EKS Service Role.. 147

Setting Up and Configuring Amazon EKS Networking..148

    Creating a VPC and Security Group 148

    Creating an EKS Cluster..150

    Creating a kubectl Configuration File 152

    Creating an EC2 Key Pair..152

    Creating a Worker Node..153

    Joining the Worker Node EKS Cluster..156

    Deploying the Application..158

Deploying the Kubernetes Web UI 159

Managing and Securing the EKS Cluster 165

    Using CoreDNS 168

    Using Useful Kubectl Commands 168

    Using AWS CLI 170

    Adding Worker Nodes 171

    Understanding the EKS Service Limits 173

Summary..173

Chapter 5: Installing a Docker Host on an Amazon EC2 Instance 175

Installing a Docker Host on a Linux EC2 Virtual Machine..176

    Setting Up a Linux Instance as a Docker Container Host 176

Installing a Docker Host on a Windows Server Virtual Machine..185

Deploying, Managing, and Running Containers on an Amazon EC2 VM 193

    Updating Docker on Windows Server 193

    Downloading Images 195

    Deploying Containers..198

    Deleting Containers 200

    Deleting Multiple Containers 201

    Modifying a Security Group on an EC2 Host..202

    Managing Storage Volumes 207

Summary..211

Chapter 6: Securing Your Containerized Environment................................ 213

Protecting Your Service Accounts on Amazon AWS Container Services 214

    Using IAM Groups 215

    Granting Least Privileges.. 216

    Using Policies 217

    Reviewing Policies and Policy Usage 224

    Using a Password Policy.. 225

    Setting Up Multifactor Authentication for Root Accounts 227

    Setting Up IAM Roles 228

Protecting Your Code and Deployments 230

    Rotating Security Keys 230

    Creating a Trail.. 232

Protecting Your Containers and Container Host on Amazon EC2 235

    Using AWS CloudWatch 235

    Customizing the Navigation Menu.. 236

    Getting Started with CloudWatch 238

    Using CloudWatch Dashboards... 239

    Configuring Billing Alerts... 243

    Using AWS Config 247

Using AWS Web Application Firewall.. 249

    Exploring WAF Pricing... 250

    Configuring WAF 250

Summary... 254

Chapter 7: Scaling the AWS EKS, ECS, and ECR Containerized Environments 255

Creating an EKS Cluster... 256

    Creating an EKS IAM Role... 256

    Creating a VPC 257

    Creating the Cluster... 259

    Creating a Configuration File 262

    Creating a Worker Node... 263

Scaling Amazon EKS 268

    Scaling Down.. 272

Scaling Amazon ECS 273

    Scaling the ECS Fargate Service 273

    Scaling a Task Definition 276

    Scaling an ECS Cluster 278

    Scaling a Task Definition with an ECS Cluster.. 279

Scaling Amazon ECR 280

    Creating an ECR Repository in a Different Region... 281

Updating the EKS Cluster Version 283

    Scaling the Docker Container Host.. 286

Summary.. 288

Chapter 8: Monitoring Your Containerized Environment 289

Monitoring an Amazon EKS Cluster.. 290

    Installing the Kubernetes Web UI (Dashboard) 290

    Installing Heapster... 290

    Installing influxdb 291

    Creating a Heapster Cluster Role 292

    Creating an EKS-Admin Service Account 293

    Retrieving an Authentication Token 295

    Opening a Dashboard 295

    Monitoring EKS.. 296

    Monitoring Pods 297

    Monitoring Nodes 298

    Using CloudWatch.. 300

    Creating a New CloudWatch Dashboard.. 302

Monitoring Container Instances on Amazon ECS 307

    Viewing ECS Fargate Container Logs 310

Monitoring Amazon ECR Performance 313

    Using ECR Commands 314

Monitoring the Docker Container Host 314

    Creating an Alarm 316

Summary 318

Chapter 9: Backing Up and Restoring Your Containers and Hosts on Amazon AWS 319

Backing Up and Restoring Amazon EC2 Container Hosts 320

    Understanding EBS Snapshots 320

    Taking an EBS Snapshot (Backup) 320

    Taking an EC2 Snapshot 323

    Restoring an EC2 Instance 327

Backing Up and Restoring ECS Fargate Containers 332

Backing Up Your Amazon EKS Configuration 334

Using AWS Backup 335

Summary 337

Chapter 10: Troubleshooting Amazon AWS Containerized Solutions 339

Dealing with Common Issues 339

Troubleshooting Amazon EKS 340

    Troubleshooting Availability Issues 340

    Troubleshooting Performance Issues 340

Troubleshooting Amazon ECS Operations 347

    Using AWS ECS CLI 348

Troubleshooting Amazon ECR Registries 351

    Using the ECR Management Console 351

    Using AWS CLI 352

Troubleshooting Amazon EC2 Container Hosts 354

    Using AWS CLI EC2 355

Summary 358

Index 359

About the Author

Shimon Ifrah is an IT professional and author with 15 years of experience working for the largest IT companies in the world. His experience with AWS started 12 years ago with the first infrastructure-as-a-service cloud service and evolved from there to more complex services on the AWS platform. Over the years, Shimon has helped many organizations to migrate their services to AWS and manage them according to AWS best practices. Shimon has authored many training videos and blog posts about IT management.

Shimon also earned the following professional certifications: CCNA, MCSA, MCSE, MCTS X 6, MCTIP:SA, and MCITP:EA.

About the Technical Reviewers

Navin Sabharwal is an innovator, thought leader, author, and consultant in the areas of AI and machine learning, cloud computing, public cloud, private cloud, containerization, big data analytics, streaming analytics, IT automation, AIOps, Splunk, DevOps, and DevSecOps.

Navin is currently working with HCL Technologies as a practice lead for various technology areas. He has authored several best-selling books including *Cloud Capacity Management*, *Automation through Chef Opscode*, and *Practical MongoDB*, all from Apress.

Anindita Basak is a cloud architect and DevOps engineer. With more than a decade of experience, she helps enterprises to enable their digital transformation journey empowered with multicloud, DevOps, advanced analytics, and AI. She co-authored the books *Stream Analytics with Microsoft Azure* and *Hands-on Machine Learning with Azure* and was a technical reviewer of seven books on Azure along with two video courses on Azure data analytics. She also has worked extensively on AWS Infra, DevOps, and analytics.

Acknowledgments

I would like to thank my beloved family for all the support they gave me during the writing stage of the book, which took six months; without your support and love, I wouldn't have been able to do it.

Introduction

Writing a book about AWS is a complex task because AWS has more than 100 cloud services! In fact, most of the services have enough depth to be covered in a full book on its own.

When I took on the task of writing this book, I wanted to stay focused and deliver a book that covered AWS container services only, and I believe I have managed to do that.

This book covers the main container services in AWS.

- Amazon Elastic Container Registry (Amazon ECR)

- Amazon Elastic Container Service (Amazon ECS)

- Amazon Elastic Kubernetes Service (Amazon EKS)

- EC2 Docker container host

This book is for people who don't have a lot of knowledge of AWS as well as people who have experience working with Azure who want to learn AWS. You don't need to be a developer to read this book because the objective is to learn how to deploy and manage the services and not to use an application development lifecycle approach.

I have designed this book in a way that any person with working experience in IT and with a little prior AWS background can pick it up and get started with AWS container services.

- The first five chapters cover each service in-depth. The hands-on examples will teach you how to deploy the service and run Linux and Windows containers using the AWS management console or the AWS CLI.

- The last five chapters focus on securing your users and your code, backing up and recovering your data, and scaling each service using AWS best practices.

This book is also for beginners, engineers, and architects who want to get started with AWS containers using a step-by-step approach while gaining hands-on experience.

To use this book, you will need to know how to use Docker and run containers on Docker Desktop or Docker Engine on Windows Server or Linux.

The most complex parts in this book are about the Amazon Elastic Kubernetes Service, specifically where I show how to set up and deploy an EKS cluster and worker nodes.

I recommend you follow the steps in the EKS chapters without skipping anything as each step is needed to complete the next one and deploy the EKS cluster and worker nodes.

You can also use AWS Free Tier to reduce some of the costs of running AWS services; however, some of the AWS container services are not covered under the Free Tier offering.

When I started to work on this book with my publisher in late 2018, I wanted to write a book that would

- Be focused on AWS container services only

- Be as practical and hands-on as possible

In other words, my goal was to write a book that covered all the Amazon AWS container services from a hands-on perspective while being practical and easy to understand.

Many AWS books use an application development lifecycle approach in AWS; however, with that approach, the reader can get lost in the code and miss the primary purpose of learning the fundamentals.

In this book, I focused on each container service offering, covering it from the ground up. You'll learn how to do the following with each container service:

- **Learn**: You'll learn the basics of each service and its requirements.

- **Deploy**: You'll deploy the service in AWS using a step-by-step approach and see examples.

- **Scale**: You'll scale the service capacity using AWS best practices.

- **Manage**: You'll manage and secure the service using AWS best practices.

This approach allows you to focus on the task on hand and learn how to deploy containers on AWS, and it gives you all the tools needed to deploy a single container or multiple containers on a large scale.

You'll gain valuable knowledge and experience with this approach to learning, deploying, scaling, and managing containers on AWS.

CHAPTER 1

Getting Started with Containers on Amazon AWS

In this chapter, I'll show you how to set up your local environment on Windows 10, Linux Ubuntu, and macOS. I'll also show you how to set up your Amazon AWS account and Amazon CLI, which will set you up for success from the beginning.

If you already have Docker, an AWS account, and AWS CLI installed and configured on your local machine, you can skip parts of this chapter and start with the "Introducing Git and GitHub" section. Without a proper setup and the right tools to manage your AWS containerized environment, you won't be able to get far with your deployment and configuration.

Cloud computing is based on using the right tools, structure, and processes to provide services and infrastructure; therefore, it is essential to follow the technical requirements of this chapter and the entire book. Case in point: AWS is a cloud platform that runs and lives in the cloud, and to move your code and applications to AWS, you need the right tools installed on your machine. By using the tools covered in this chapter, you will be able to develop, test, and upload your containerized application to AWS in a seamless and secure manner.

To follow the exercises in this book, you need to install the following tools:

- Docker Desktop (Community Edition)
- Amazon AWS CLI
- Amazon Linux container image
- Visual Studio Code

You'll also need to set up a new Amazon AWS subscription or use an existing one.

1

© Shimon Ifrah 2019
S. Ifrah, *Deploy Containers on AWS*, https://doi.org/10.1007/978-1-4842-5101-0_1

Tip   Make sure your local tools are always up-to-date and running the latest version.

Setting Up Your Amazon AWS Container Environment

In this section, you'll learn how to set up the basic tools and services you'll need to run containers on Amazon AWS. The first tool I'll discuss is Docker Desktop, which enables you to develop containers on your local machine and ship them to Amazon AWS.

Installing Docker Desktop

In this section, I'll show you how to install Docker on the following platforms:

- Windows 10

- Ubuntu

- macOS

Without Docker installed on your machine, you will be not able to build, test, and deploy a containerized application to Amazon AWS or other cloud platforms.

For containerized applications to work on Amazon AWS, they must work 100 percent in your local environment (Windows or Linux). Therefore, I strongly recommend you thoroughly test any application you containerize because once you deploy the application to Amazon AWS, there is no way to modify it unless you modify the image on your local machine and push it back to AWS.

If you find a bug in your application, you need to fix the application in the local environment, repackage it, upload it to AWS as a new image, and redeploy it to a new container instance. This process can take 30 minutes minimum for a straightforward, single-tier application, and for more complex applications, it can take a few hours or in extreme cases days.

Installing Docker Desktop on Windows 10

To get started, I'll start by showing how to install Docker Desktop on a Windows 10 1809 machine; however, this also works on the 1709 and 1803 builds.

Before installing Docker Desktop on a Windows machine, you'll need the following:

- Window 10 64-bit physical machine or a virtual machine

- Windows 10 1607 and above update

- Enabled virtualization in the BIOS

- Minimum 4GB of RAM

- Local admin rights on the machine

To install Docker Desktop for Windows, you'll need to visit the Docker Hub web site (shown in Figure 1-1) using the following URL and download the installation file:

```
https://hub.docker.com/editions/community/docker-ce-desktop-windows
```

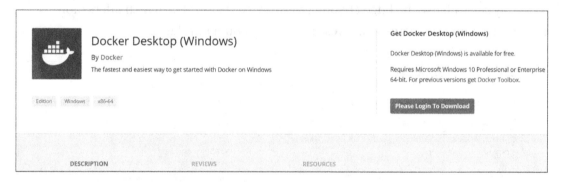

Figure 1-1. *Downloading Docker Desktop (Windows)*

When the download has completed and you have all the prerequisites, you can start the installation, as shown in Figure 1-2.

Tip   Always download and install the latest version build for better performance and up-to-date bug fixes.

Figure 1-2. *Selecting the Docker version*

On the installation page, you have the option to select the Docker channel you want to use.

In my case, I'll use the Edge channel, as shown in Figure 1-3, which offers more advanced features, the latest bug fixes, and more frequent updates.

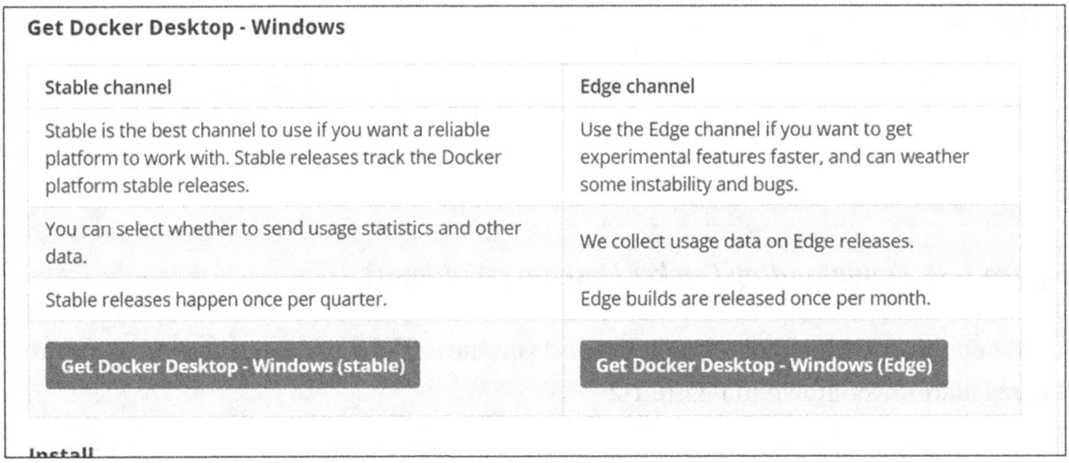

Get Docker Desktop - Windows

Stable channel	Edge channel
Stable is the best channel to use if you want a reliable platform to work with. Stable releases track the Docker platform stable releases.	Use the Edge channel if you want to get experimental features faster, and can weather some instability and bugs.
You can select whether to send usage statistics and other data.	We collect usage data on Edge releases.
Stable releases happen once per quarter.	Edge builds are released once per month.
Get Docker Desktop - Windows (stable)	Get Docker Desktop - Windows (Edge)

Install

Figure 1-3. *Selecting the Docker channel*

To install Docker, double-click the installer and follow the installation prompts, as shown in Figure 1-4.

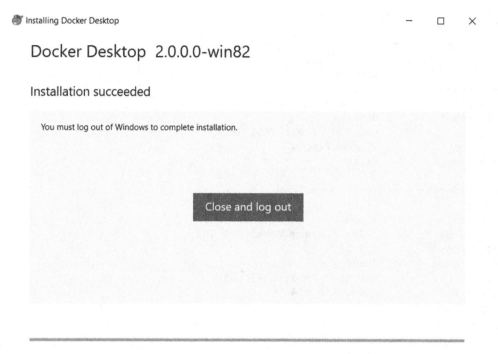

Figure 1-4. *Docker install screen*

Once Docker is installed, you are ready to start using it on a Windows 10 machine.

Personally, I like to use PowerShell Core 6 as my command-line utility, but you can also use the command prompt (`cmd.exe`) to manage Docker.

In this book, I'll also use Visual Studio Code as my command-line tool; however, for simple commands I like to use PowerShell.

Tip   By default, PowerShell 5.1 is installed on Windows 10. To download PowerShell Core 6.1, visit `https://github.com/PowerShell/PowerShell`.

To check that I have installed the correct version, I'll type the following `docker` command, as shown in Figure 1-5:

```
docker version
```

```
🔲 Administrator: PowerShell 6 (x64)
PS C:\> docker version
Client: Docker Engine - Community
 Version:           18.09.0
 API version:       1.39
 Go version:        go1.10.4
 Git commit:        4d60db4
 Built:             Wed Nov  7 00:47:51 2018
 OS/Arch:           windows/amd64
 Experimental:      false

Server: Docker Engine - Community
 Engine:
  Version:          18.09.0
  API version:      1.39 (minimum version 1.24)
  Go version:       go1.10.4
  Git commit:       4d60db4
  Built:            Wed Nov  7 00:56:41 2018
  OS/Arch:          windows/amd64
  Experimental:     true
PS C:\>
PS C:\>
```

Figure 1-5. *The docker version command*

Tip   Don't forget that the Docker CLI is case sensitive.

Running Docker on a Virtual Machine with Nested Virtualization

If you need to install Docker on a Windows 10 or Linux virtual machine using Microsoft Hyper-V, there is an extra configuration you will need to complete before installing Docker on a virtual machine.

For Docker to work on a virtual machine guest, you need to enable nested virtualization on the virtual machine on which you are going to install Docker.

Before you enable nested virtualization on a virtual machine, you need to meet the following requirements:

- Dynamic memory disabled on the virtual machine

- Windows 10 Professional or Enterprise version 1607 and above

- Two vCPU cores

- A minimum of 2GB of RAM assigned to the VM (I recommend you use 4GB)

To enable nested virtualization, shut down the virtual machine, as shown in Figure 1-6.

Tip   PowerShell Core 6 is not capable of managing Hyper-V using PowerShell cmdlets. For Hyper-V PowerShell management, please use the default PowerShell client that comes with Windows 10.

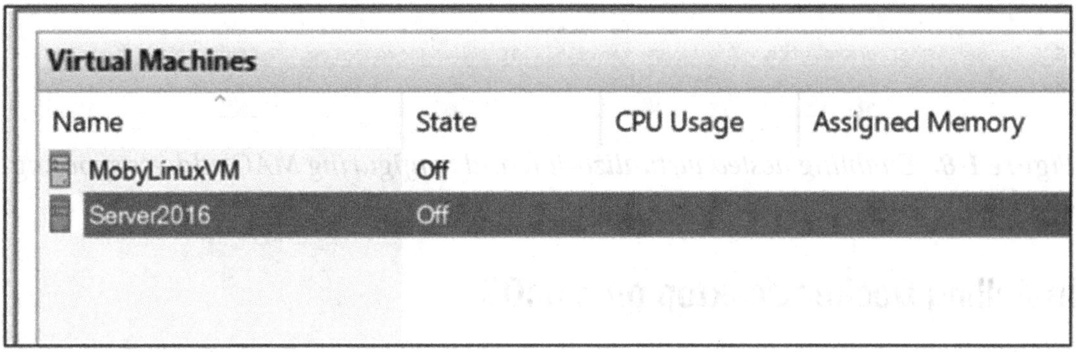

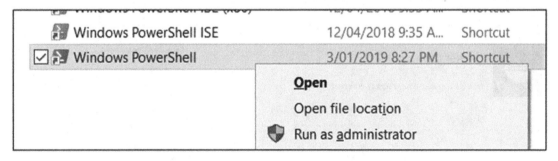

Figure 1-6. *Hyper-V virtual machines*

When the machine is turned off, open the installed PowerShell 5.1 console, right-click the PowerShell icon, and select "Run as administrator," as shown in Figure 1-7.

Figure 1-7. *PowerShell "Run as administrator" menu*

From the PowerShell console, run the following two cmdlets that enable nested virtualization and configure MAC address spoofing on the VM virtual network card, as shown in Figure 1-8.

```
Set-VMProcessor -VMName server2016 -ExposeVirtualizationExtensions $true

Get-VMNetworkAdapter -VMName server2016| Set-VMNetworkAdapter
-MacAddressSpoofing On
```

```
Administrator: Windows PowerShell
PS C:\> Set-VMProcessor -VMName server2016 -ExposeVirtualizationExtensions $true
PS C:\> Get-VMNetworkAdapter -VMName server2016| Set-VMNetworkAdapter -MacAddressSpoofing On
PS C:\>
```

Figure 1-8. *Enabling nested virtualization and configuring MAC address spoofing cmdlets*

Installing Docker Desktop on macOS

Installing Docker on macOS is as straightforward as installing it on Windows. To get started with Docker on macOS, use the following link to download the installer:

https://hub.docker.com/editions/community/docker-ce-desktop-mac

You also have the option here to use the Edge channel for more updates and advanced features, as shown in Figure 1-9.

Figure 1-9. *Downloading Docker for Mac*

When the download process is completed, double-click the downloaded `Docker.dmg` file and drag it to the Applications folder, as shown in Figure 1-10.

Figure 1-10. *Installing Docker for Mac*

When you complete the installation, double-click the Docker icon to start it; the icon appears in the status bar.

Installing Docker on Linux

For Linux installation, I have an Ubuntu 18.10 server running inside a virtual machine on my Windows 10 Hyper-V host, which I will turn into a container host.

The requirements to run Docker on Ubuntu are as follows:

- Ubuntu version 14.04 and above

- 64-bit version

- Two CPU cores

- 2GB RAM (minimum)

The first step in the process is to shut down the virtual machine and run the same Hyper-V commands as I ran on the Windows 10 VM.

The commands enable nested virtualization on the Ubuntu machine and allow me to turn it into a container host, as shown in Figure 1-11.

Server2016	Off			
UbuntuDocker	Running	12%	3000 MB	00:00:04

Figure 1-11. *Hyper-V Linux container host*

When the virtual machine is turned off, I will run the following two lines of code, as shown in Figure 1-12, and then turn the virtual machine back on:

Set-VMProcessor -VMName ubuntudocker -ExposeVirtualizationExtensions $true

Get-VMNetworkAdapter -VMName ubuntudocker| Set-VMNetworkAdapter
-MacAddressSpoofing On

```
PS C:\WINDOWS\system32> Set-VMProcessor -VMName ubuntudocker -ExposeVirtualizationExtensions $true
PS C:\WINDOWS\system32> Get-VMNetworkAdapter -VMName ubuntudocker| Set-VMNetworkAdapter -MacAddressSpoofing On
PS C:\WINDOWS\system32>
```

Figure 1-12. *PowerShell cmdlets*

Once the virtual machine is online, log in to it.

Then you can start with updating the package repository using the following command, as shown in Figure 1-13:

sudo apt-get update

```
vmadmin@ubuntudocker:~$ sudo apt-get update
[sudo] password for vmadmin:
Hit:1 http://archive.ubuntu.com/ubuntu cosmic InRelease
Get:2 http://archive.ubuntu.com/ubuntu cosmic-updates InRelease [83.2 kB]
Get:3 http://archive.ubuntu.com/ubuntu cosmic-backports InRelease [74.6 kB]
Get:4 http://archive.ubuntu.com/ubuntu cosmic-security InRelease [83.2 kB]
Get:5 http://archive.ubuntu.com/ubuntu cosmic/main Translation-en [513 kB]
Get:6 http://archive.ubuntu.com/ubuntu cosmic/restricted Translation-en [3,888 B]
Get:7 http://archive.ubuntu.com/ubuntu cosmic/universe Translation-en [5,063 kB]
30% [7 Translation-en 118 kB/5,063 kB 2%]_
```

Figure 1-13. *Linux update command*

To download and install Docker, run the following command, as shown Figure 1-14, which starts the installation process (and which will take a couple of minutes):

Sudo apt install docker.io

```
vmadmin@ubuntudocker:~$ sudo apt install docker.io
Reading package lists... Done
Building dependency tree
Reading state information... Done
The following additional packages will be installed:
  bridge-utils cgroupfs-mount dns-root-data dnsmasq-base libltdl7 pigz ubuntu-fan
Suggested packages:
  ifupdown aufs-tools debootstrap docker-doc rinse zfs-fuse | zfsutils
The following NEW packages will be installed:
  bridge-utils cgroupfs-mount dns-root-data dnsmasq-base docker.io libltdl7 pigz ubuntu-fan
0 upgraded, 8 newly installed, 0 to remove and 61 not upgraded.
Need to get 40.7 MB of archives.
After this operation, 199 MB of additional disk space will be used.
Do you want to continue? [Y/n]
```

Figure 1-14. *Installing Docker*

When the installation is completed, you'll be able to run any Docker command.

To test that Docker is up and running on my Ubuntu virtual machine, go ahead and spin up a container using the following command, as shown in Figure 1-15:

```
sudo docker run hello-world
```

```
vmadmin@ubuntudocker:~$ sudo docker run hello-world
Unable to find image 'hello-world:latest' locally
latest: Pulling from library/hello-world
1b930d010525: Pull complete
Digest: sha256:2557e3c07ed1e38f26e389462d03ed943586f744621577a99efb77324b0fe535
Status: Downloaded newer image for hello-world:latest

Hello from Docker!
This message shows that your installation appears to be working correctly.

To generate this message, Docker took the following steps:
 1. The Docker client contacted the Docker daemon.
 2. The Docker daemon pulled the "hello-world" image from the Docker Hub.
    (amd64)
 3. The Docker daemon created a new container from that image which runs the
    executable that produces the output you are currently reading.
 4. The Docker daemon streamed that output to the Docker client, which sent it
    to your terminal.

To try something more ambitious, you can run an Ubuntu container with:
 $ docker run -it ubuntu bash
```

Figure 1-15. *Running the hello-world container*

As you can see, Docker is now up and running, and my environment is ready.

Signing Up for an Amazon AWS Account

To run containers on Amazon AWS, you need an AWS account, and in this section, I'll show you how to sign up for an AWS account.

As of this writing, Amazon AWS offers a Free Tier account for 12 months for new members. The Free Tier account is a great way to start working and learning AWS because it offers all the core services for free with usage limitations.

These are the benefits of the Free Tier account:

- 750 hours per month of an Amazon EC2 Linux (micro t2) virtual machine

- 5GB of Amazon S3 cloud storage

- 750 hours of the Amazon Relational Database Service (RDS)

- 1 million API calls per month using Amazon API Gateway

- 50GB data transfer out and 2000,000 HTTP and HTTPS requests of Amazon CloudFront, which is an AWS content delivery network (CDN) with a global reach

- 750 hours a month of Amazon ElastiCache, which offers Redis and Memcached, which help improve the performance of data stores

- 15GB data transfer out across all Amazon AWS services

This list shows only the primary services. However, many more services are available for free for 12 months under the Free Tier offering.

I recommend you visit the Free Tier URL at `https://aws.amazon.com/free/` and review the services available.

To sign up for the Free Tier account, you must set up a new account because existing accounts cannot enjoy the offering. To sign up, visit `https://aws.amazon.com/free/` and click Create Free Account, as shown in Figure 1-16. Fill in the details and provide the credit card details so that AWS can charge in case you go over the Free Tier limit or use services that are not under the Free Tier package.

I recommend that you don't create multiple Free Tier accounts because you can easily forget about them and run free services that eventually expire and start to incur a cost.

Figure 1-16. Creating an AWS Free Tier account

Using AWS CLI

Now that your Amazon AWS Free Tier account is up and running, you can set up the Amazon AWS Command Line Interface (CLI), which offers command-line shell management instead of using a browser for AWS service management.

With AWS CLI, you can manage multiple environments, automate deployments, schedule tasks, and manage resources using AWS API access. Administrators and developers can develop scripts that create, update, and delete resources on the fly in seconds compared to minutes. I like to use AWS CLI to create a development environment that uses multiple services and then delete the environment using a single command.

With AWS CLI, you can keep your AWS environment clean, speed up provisioning time, and keep your costs under control. However, the main benefit is time because with AWS CLI you can spin up a fully functioning AWS environment with multiple services in less than five minutes that could take an hour to set up using a browser.

Tip   I recommend you develop a script library with automated tasks you write once and use multiple times because a good script library can save you hours every month.

My advice for AWS CLI is if you do a task more than once, automate the process as much as you can.

AWS CLI is available on all major operating systems, meaning Linux, macOS, and Windows. In the next section, I will show you how to install it.

Amazon AWS also offers developers the option to develop applications using the AWS Software Development Kit (SDK) to tap into AWS services easily. To view the AWS CLI source code and fork it or copy it from GitHub, visit the following URL:

```
https://github.com/aws/aws-cli
```

You can also join the AWS CLI community and take part in the development and release of AWS CLI by providing feedback and using new beta releases.

Tip   Always download the latest version of AWS CLI.

Installing AWS CLI on Windows 10

To download AWS CLI, browse to the following URL and download the installation file, as shown in Figure 1-17:

```
https://aws.amazon.com/cli/
```

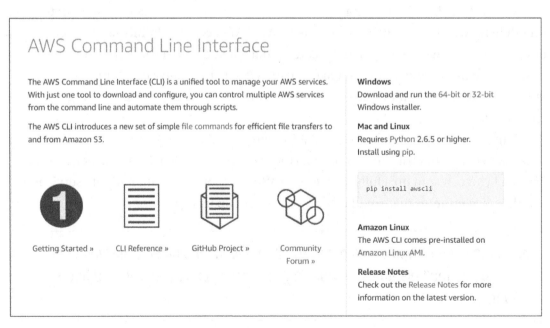

Figure 1-17. *Downloading AWS CLI*

It is recommended that you download the 64-bit version of AWS CLI, and if you need to deploy the tool to multiple machines using Microsoft SSCM or Intune, you can use the MSI file to deploy it automatically without user intervention.

To install AWS CLI, double-click the AWSCLI64PY3.msi file and follow the prompts, as shown in Figure 1-18.

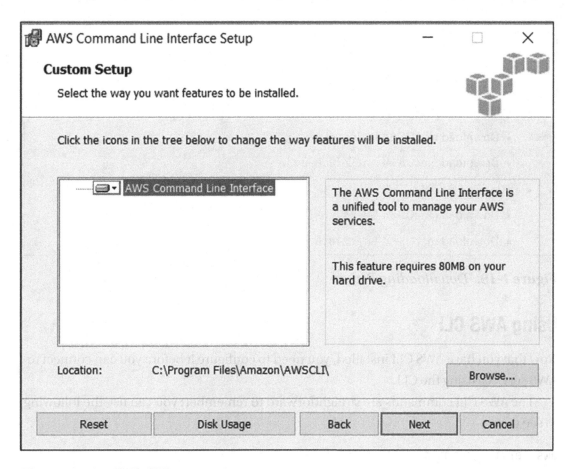

Figure 1-18. AWS CLI setup

Installing AWS CLI on Linux and macOS

To install AWS CLI on Linux and macOS, you need to have Python 2.6.5 or above installed on your machine. To install Python on Linux, run the following commands:

```
sudo apt update
```

```
sudo apt install python3-pip
```

To install Python on a macOS machine, browse to `https://www.python.org/downloads/mac-osx/` and download the installation file, as shown in Figure 1-19.

Python Releases for Mac OS X

- Latest Python 3 Release - Python 3.7.2
- Latest Python 2 Release - Python 2.7.15

- Python 3.7.2 - 2018-12-24
    - Download macOS 64-bit installer
    - Download macOS 64-bit/32-bit installer
- Python 3.6.8 - 2018-12-24
    - Download macOS 64-bit installer
    - Download macOS 64-bit/32-bit installer

Figure 1-19. *Downloading Python*

Using AWS CLI

Now that you have AWS CLI installed, you need to configure it before you can connect to AWS services using the CLI.

The AWS CLI commands are straightforward to remember; you can use the following to see them:

```
aws service command
```

For example, to work with an AWS S3 storage account, you can use the following command:

```
aws s3 ls
```

The previous command displays all the S3 account details.

To use the `help` command option, type the following:

```
 Aws command help
```

For example, you can use the `help` option with the `s3` command (as shown in Figure 1-20).

```
aws s3 help
```

In the figure you can see that the `help` option provides detailed output and the options for how to use the `s3` command. If you try it, you'll get a detailed description of how to copy a file from a local machine to an Amazon AWS S3 storage bucket without using a browser.

I know many AWS administrators who do all their AWS management and deployment tasks from the CLI and do not use a browser at all. More management options are available from the CLI compared to the browser.

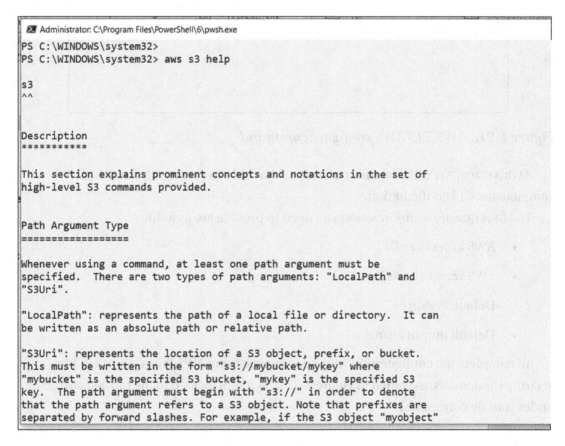

Figure 1-20. *AWS CLI S3 help command*

Configuring AWS CLI

Before you can start using AWS CLI, you need to configure it and make sure the connection to AWS is secure and safe and no one can compromise it.

To secure the communication to AWS, Amazon requires that incoming connections are cryptographically signed, and before you connect to AWS, you need to run the CLI configuration wizard.

To run the configuration wizard, from the AWS CLI screen you type the following command (as shown in Figure 1-21):

```
aws configure
```

```
PS C:\WINDOWS\system32> aws configure
AWS Access Key ID [None]:
```

Figure 1-21. *AWS CLI AWS configure command*

At this stage, AWS CLI asks four questions that help to secure the client and to complete the CLI configuration.

The four questions/information you need to provide are as follows:

- AWS access key ID

- AWS secret access key

- Default region

- Default output format

To complete the configuration, you need to access the AWS Portal and click My Security Credentials, as shown in Figure 1-22 (the menu located in the top-left corner under your display name).

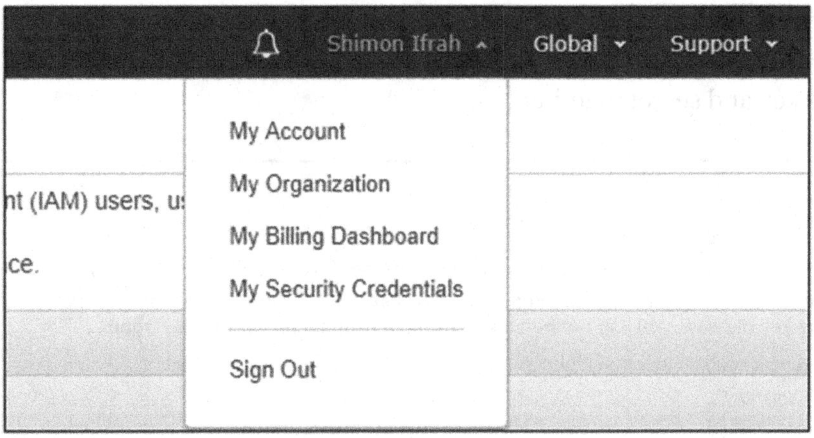

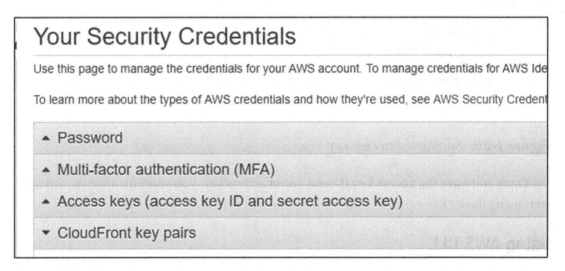

Figure 1-22. *My security credentials*

From the Your Security Credentials page, select "Access keys (access key ID and secret access key)," as shown in Figure 1-23.

Your Security Credentials

Use this page to manage the credentials for your AWS account. To manage credentials for AWS Ide

To learn more about the types of AWS credentials and how they're used, see AWS Security Creden

▲ Password

▲ Multi-factor authentication (MFA)

▲ Access keys (access key ID and secret access key)

▼ CloudFront key pairs

Figure 1-23. *Access keys*

In the "Access keys" menu, click the Create New Access Key button, as shown Figure 1-24.

Figure 1-24. *Creating a new access key*

At this stage, the security key is ready, and you have the option to download it and save it in a secure location or click the Show Access Key, as shown in Figure 1-25, which displays the key and secret together.

Figure 1-25. *Downloading the access key*

You should download the key file and save it in a secure location, as shown in Figure 1-26.

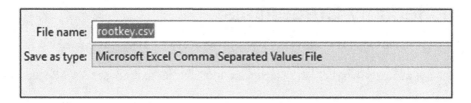

Figure 1-26. *Saving the access key*

Once you have the access key ID and secret access key, you can finish the wizard and start using the CLI.

Using AWS CLI

In this section, you'll learn how to use the AWS CLI to create a resource in AWS without accessing the AWS Portal.

I will start with a basic command that displays all the available regions in AWS capable of running an EC2 instance. In the output windows, as shown in Figure 1-27, I also use the option to control the display output, which in my case is a table.

The output is easy to understand and much quicker to load and display information compared to the AWS Portal.

```
aws ec2 describe-regions --output table
```

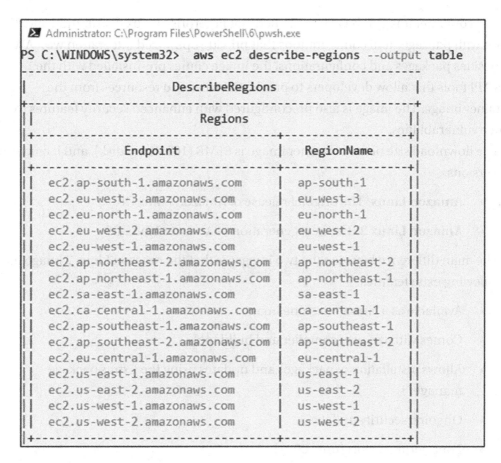

Figure 1-27. *Viewing AWS EC2 regions*

AWS CLI offers access to all the Amazon AWS container services, and the following are the CLI commands to access them:

- Amazon Elastic Container Registry (ECR): `aws ecr`

- Amazon Elastic Container Service (Amazon ECS): `aws ecs`

- Amazon Elastic Container Service for Kubernetes (Amazon EKS): `aws eks`

These services are the core container services on Amazon AWS, and I will talk more about them in great detail in the upcoming sections.

The next tool I will show how to use when working with AWS container services is the Amazon Linux container image.

The container image is based on the Red Hat Enterprise Linux distribution and comes with packages and configurations that provide optimized integration with AWS.

Besides packages and configurations, the image comes pre-installed with the AWS API tools that allow developers to provide services and resources from the container image. The image is also preconfigured with enhanced security features to reduce vulnerabilities.

The download size of the container image is 61MB (162Mb on disk), and it comes in two versions.

- **Amazon Linux**: The original release of Amazon Linux OS

- **Amazon Linux 2**: The next generation of Amazon Linux OS

The main difference between the two images is that the Amazon Linux 2 image has the following extra features:

- Available as a virtual machine image

- Comes with the new compiler and build tools

- Allows installation of packages and updates using the Extras package manager

- Ongoing security updates

- Long-term support (until 2023)

Using the Linux 2 Extras package manager, administrators and developers can install the latest updates using the following command and not the yum tool:

```
amazon-linux-extras install python
```

Both images come with long-term support (LTE) for five years, allowing you to develop your solutions using the image and know that AWS will provide security and bug fixes for many years.

I recommend you use the Amazon Linux 2 version, which is the next generation of Amazon Linux and considered to be more secure, stable, and optimized to run on Amazon AWS.

Downloading an Amazon Linux Container Image

To download the Amazon Linux container image, I will use my local Docker client and show you how you can download both versions.

To download Amazon Linux version 2, use the following Docker command:

```
docker pull amazonlinux:2
```

To download the Amazon Linux version 1, use the following command (shown in Figure 1-28):

```
docker pull amazonlinux
```

```
amazonlinux     2          2467e0b1e917     6 weeks ago     162MB
amazonlinux     latest     2467e0b1e917     6 weeks ago     162MB
```

Figure 1-28. *Amazon Linux image*

For more information about all the available tags, visit the Docker Hub URL, listed here:

```
https://hub.docker.com/_/amazonlinux/
```

Now that you have the image installed, you can deploy a container with the Amazon Linux container image.

To run a container of the AWS Linux 2 image with bash and delete the container when exiting, use the following command:

```
docker run --rm -it amazonlinux:2 bash
```

By default, the image comes with 105 packages installed, which gives you the perfect development and deployment environment without needing to add more packages.

To view and count all the available images, from inside the container run the following command (as shown in Figure 1-29):

```
yum list installed
```

```
bash-4.2# yum list installed
Loaded plugins: ovl, priorities
Installed Packages
amazon-linux-extras.noarch                          1.6.4-1.amzn2
basesystem.noarch                                   10.0-7.amzn2.0.1
bash.x86_64                                          4.2.46-30.amzn2
bzip2-libs.x86_64                                    1.0.6-13.amzn2.0.2
ca-certificates.noarch                              2018.2.22-70.0.amzn2
chkconfig.x86_64                                     1.7.4-1.amzn2.0.2
coreutils.x86_64                                     8.22-21.amzn2
cpio.x86_64                                          2.11-27.amzn2
curl.x86_64                                          7.55.1-12.amzn2.0.6
cyrus-sasl-lib.x86_64                               2.1.26-23.amzn2
diffutils.x86_64                                    3.3-4.amzn2.0.2
elfutils-libelf.x86_64                             0.170-4.amzn2
```

Figure 1-29. *Installed packages*

To count the number of packages installed, use the following command (shown in Figure 1-30):

```
yum list installed | wc -l
```

```
bash-4.2# yum list installed | wc -l
105
bash-4.2#
```

Figure 1-30. *Number of yum packages*

In the Amazon Linux 2 image, you can find tools such as bash, Python, OpenLDAP, curl, and many more.

To view the image OS release, use the following line:

```
cat /etc/os-release
```

To check the version of Amazon Linux 2, use the following line:

```
cat /etc/system-release
```

To check the image version details, use the following line:

```
cat /etc/image-id
```

To use the Amazon Linux 2 Extras package manager and download the packages directory into the image, you can use the following command, as shown in Figure 1-31, which will show you a list of all the available packages (also known as *topics*):

```
amazon-linux-extras list
```

```
bash-4.2# amazon-linux-extras list
  0  ansible2              available    [ =2.4.2  =2.4.6 ]
  2  httpd_modules         available    [ =1.0 ]
  3  memcached1.5          available    [ =1.5.1 ]
  4  nginx1.12             available    [ =1.12.2 ]
  5  postgresql9.6         available    [ =9.6.6  =9.6.8 ]
  6  postgresql10          available    [ =10 ]
  8  redis4.0              available    [ =4.0.5  =4.0.10 ]
  9  R3.4                  available    [ =3.4.3 ]
 10  rust1                 available    \
       [ =1.22.1  =1.26.0  =1.26.1  =1.27.2  =1.31.0 ]
 11  vim                   available    [ =8 0 ]
```

Figure 1-31. *Amazon Extras list*

I'll go ahead and install the Nginx 1.12 web server role using the following command (Figure 1-32):

```
sudo amazon-linux-extras install nginx1.12
```

```
bash-4.2# amazon-linux-extras install nginx1.12
Installing nginx
Loaded plugins: ovl, priorities
```

Figure 1-32. *Installing Nginx*

Once installed, the package appears as installed, as shown in Figure 1-33, and the counter of my installed packages has climbed to 189.

```
Complete!
 0  ansible2              available    [ =2.4.2  =2.4.6 ]
 2  httpd_modules         available    [ =1.0 ]
 3  memcached1.5          available    [ =1.5.1 ]
 4  nginx1.12=latest      enabled      [ =1.12.2 ]
 5  postgresql9.6         available    [ =9.6.6  =9.6.8 ]
```

Figure 1-33. *Nginx installed*

After running the following package count command (shown in Figure 1-34), you can see that I have an extra 84 packages.

```
bash-4.2# yum list installed | wc -l
189
bash-4.2#
```

Figure 1-34. *List of installed packages after installing Nginx*

Using Visual Studio Code

In the previous sections of this chapter, I showed how to do the following tasks:

- Install Docker on Windows 10, Linux, and macOS

- Install and configure AWS CLI on Windows 10, Linux, and macOS

- Download and run the Amazon Linux and Amazon Linux 2 container images

- Run basic commands inside the Amazon Linux images

The next tool you need is an integrated development editor (IDE) that will help you develop Docker files and manage your containers on the local machine.

Visual Studio Code (VS Code) is a free, cross-platform IDE designed, developed, and maintained by Microsoft that gives you a code editor, debugger, and many extensions that allow you to be more efficient and productive.

Under the hood, VS Code runs on Node.JS, and it is fast, light, and easy to use.

One of my favorite extensions is the Docker Container plug-in that allows you to manage containers and images directly from VS Code.

This feature saves me hours every month in cleanup efforts of my environment and helps me keep my Docker host light and clean from unused images and containers.

The update cycle and feature release cycle of VS Code are fast, and Microsoft also offers a special insider version that releases features and bug fixes almost every day.

In this book, I will use the regular (stable) version with the Docker extension.

Installing Visual Studio Code

To get started and download Visual Studio Code, visit the following URL: `https://code.visualstudio.com/`.

If you want to download the insider version of VS Code, please use `https://code.visualstudio.com/insiders/`.

In this case, both versions work with what you will do in this book; however, for stability reasons, I am using the stable VS Code version and not the insider version.

From the web site (shown in Figure 1-35), download the version for your OS and follow the installation prompts.

Figure 1-35. *VS Code home page*

Installing the Docker Extension for VS Code

To download the popular Docker extension for VS Code, click the Extensions icon and search for *Docker*. Click Install and Reload to restart VS Code with the extension, as shown in Figure 1-36.

Figure 1-36. *Docker extension for VS Code*

Once the extension is installed, you will see the Docker icon (shown in Figure 1-37) on the left side of VS Code with all the images, containers, and registries you have in your local environment.

Figure 1-37. *Docker registries*

With VS Code, you can delete an image, stop it, and connect to a container from the command prompt using a single click without typing Docker commands.

VS Code is also useful for the following:

- Creating and deploying new containers

- Debugging deployed containers

- Running a DockerFile

- Building custom images

Introducing Git and GitHub

Another tool I recommend you use is Git/GitHub. Git is an open source version control system that tracks changes in software code, scripts, and files by allowing multiple developers to use the same source code and track changes.

Git was created in 2005 to help with the development of the Linux kernel and is currently maintained and supported as free and open source software.

GitHub is a web and cloud-based hosting service for version control using Git, and on June 2018, Microsoft acquired GitHub for $7.5 billion and made many of the paid features free for use for individual developers.

The main feature that is now free in GitHub is the option for an individual to create unlimited private repositories to store private code. Private repositories compared to public ones are not shared with anyone and are password protected.

Using Git, developers can create code repositories and upload the code to GitHub. From the GitHub portal, they can assign permissions and manage access to team members who download the code, commit changes, and upload the code to the repository when completing their development, allowing other developers to pick up from where they finished while maintaining one source code.

To download Git and install it, please visit `https://git-scm.com/` (shown in Figure 1-38).

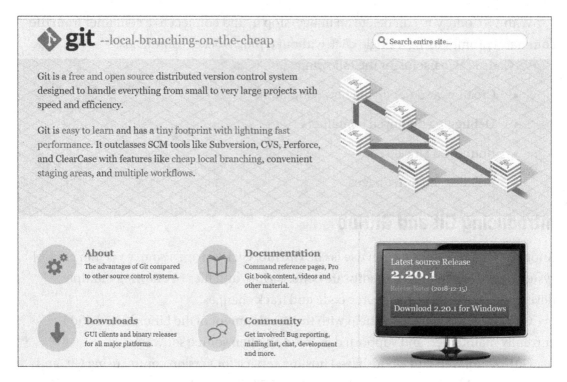

Figure 1-38. *Git home page*

To sign up for a free GitHub account, visit the following URL (shown in Figure 1-39):

`https://github.com`.

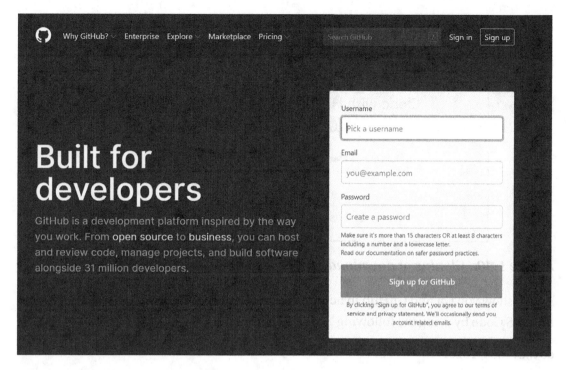

Figure 1-39. *GitHub home page*

Additional reading   Git offers a free Apress book at `https://git-scm.com/book/en/v2`.

Using GitHub

You can create private or public repositories on GitHub using a web browser, or you can use the Git command-line tool, which is faster.

To clone a public repository, you can use the following `git` command, which clones the ASP.NET Core repository. Alternatively, you can use a web browser to download the code.

```
git clone https://github.com/aspnet/AspNetCore.git
```

To use a web browser, click "Clone or download," as shown in Figure 1-40.

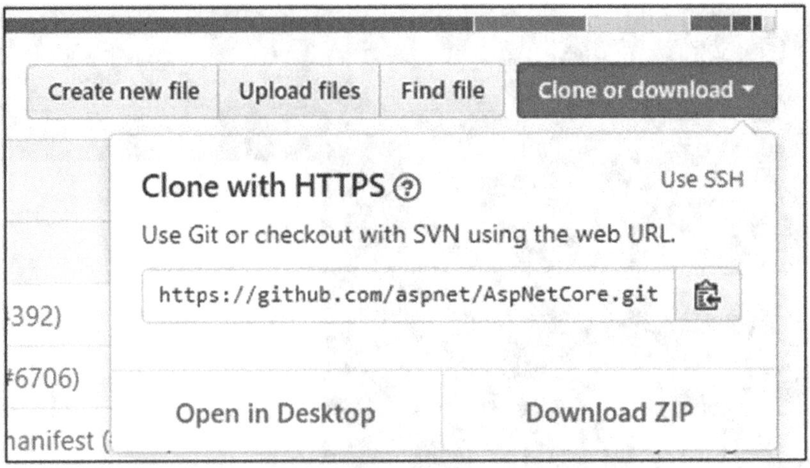

Figure 1-40. *Cloning or downloading a repository*

To show you Git and GitHub in action, I'll now create an ASP.Core project directly from VS Code by using the following .NET CLI command (as shown in Figure 1-41):

```
dotnet new razor
```

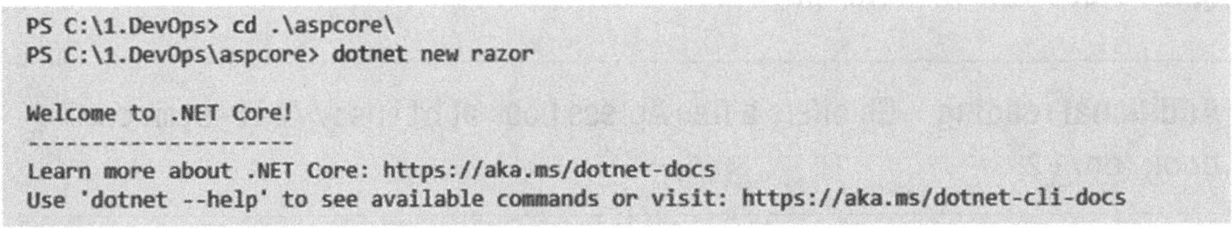

```
PS C:\1.DevOps> cd .\aspcore\
PS C:\1.DevOps\aspcore> dotnet new razor

Welcome to .NET Core!
---------------------
Learn more about .NET Core: https://aka.ms/dotnet-docs
Use 'dotnet --help' to see available commands or visit: https://aka.ms/dotnet-cli-docs
```

Figure 1-41. *Creating ASP.NET Core razor app using the command line*

After the ASP.NET Core project is ready, I'll access it from the command line and create a repository on my computer with the following commands (shown in Figure 1-42):

```
git init
git add .
git commit -m 'Initial version'
```

```
PROBLEMS   OUTPUT   DEBUG CONSOLE   TERMINAL

PS C:\1.DevOps\aspcore> git init
Initialized empty Git repository in C:/1.DevOps/aspcore/.git/
PS C:\1.DevOps\aspcore> git add .
PS C:\1.DevOps\aspcore> git commit -m 'Initial version'
[master (root-commit) 7356be2] Initial version
 Committer: Shimon Ifrah <Shimon.Ifrah@reece.com.au>
Your name and email address were configured automatically based
on your username and hostname. Please check that they are accurate.
You can suppress this message by setting them explicitly. Run the
following command and follow the instructions in your editor to edit
your configuration file:

    git config --global --edit

After doing this, you may fix the identity used for this commit with:

    git commit --amend --reset-author

 57 files changed, 48012 insertions(+)
```

Figure 1-42. *The git init command*

After the initial commit, all the files are added to the repository and are under version control.

If I add more files or modify existing ones, I'll need to use the following command to add them again and commit the changes. To add a single file to the repository, I'll use the following command:

```
git add deploy.cs
```

To commit the changes to Git, I'll commit again, as shown here:

```
git commit -m 'add deploy.cs.'
```

Moreover, to see all the commits and changes, I'll use the following command:

```
git show
```

Next, I'll delete a few files and use the following command to add all the changes:

```
Git add .
```

I'll commit the changes using the following command (Figure 1-43):

```
Git commit -m 'deleted 2 files'
```

```
2 files changed, 14 deletions(-)
delete mode 100644 aspcore.csproj
delete mode 100644 build.cs
```

Figure 1-43. *Deleting files*

When I run the `git show` command, Git shows me the content of the deleted file (shown in Figure 1-44).

```
diff --git a/aspcore.csproj b/aspcore.csproj
deleted file mode 100644
index cdc2717..0000000
--- a/aspcore.csproj
+++ /dev/null
@@ -1,14 +0,0 @@
-<Project Sdk="Microsoft.NET.Sdk.Web">

-  <PropertyGroup>
-    <TargetFramework>netcoreapp2.2</TargetFramework>
-    <AspNetCoreHostingModel>InProcess</AspNetCoreHostingModel>
-  </PropertyGroup>


-  <ItemGroup>
-    <PackageReference Include="Microsoft.AspNetCore.App"/>
-    <PackageReference Include="Microsoft.AspNetCore.Razor.Design" Version="2.2.0" PrivateAssets="All" />
-  </ItemGroup>

-</Project>
diff --git a/build.cs b/build.cs
deleted file mode 100644
index e69de29..0000000
```

Figure 1-44. *Running the git show command*

To upload my repository to GitHub, I'll start by creating a repository, as shown in Figure 1-45, from the GitHub web site, and then I'll make it private. I'll also take note of the repository URL.

Figure 1-45. *Creating a new repository*

From the Git command line, I'll set my global user account using the following line (optional):

```
git config --global user.email "email@example.com"
```

Using the repository URL from the previous step, I will issue the following commands:

```
git remote add origin https://github.com/username/name.git
git push -u origin master
```

At this stage, a pop-up screen appears and asks for authentication (shown in Figure 1-46). I'll use my GitHub username and password.

Tip It is recommended that you enable two-factor authentication on your GitHub account by going to Settings and Security.

On the GitHub login page, I'll enter my GitHub username and password.

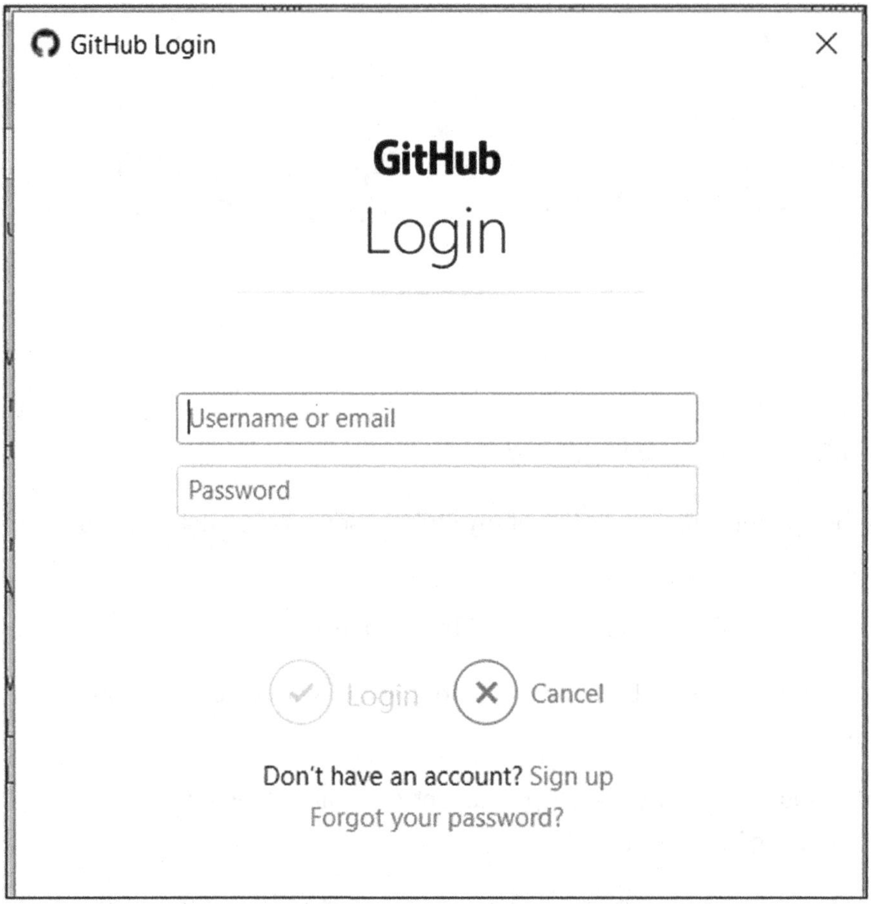

Figure 1-46. *Logging in to GitHub*

Once I'm authenticated to GitHub, Git will upload all the files to the remote repository, as shown in Figure 1-47.

```
Enumerating objects: 84, done.
Counting objects: 100% (84/84), done.
Delta compression using up to 8 threads
Compressing objects: 100% (79/79), done.
Writing objects: 100% (84/84), 716.36 KiB | 4.78 MiB/s, done.
Total 84 (delta 15), reused 0 (delta 0)
```

Figure 1-47. *Uploading files to GitHub*

After a few seconds, I will be able to view and access my code from the GitHub web site, as shown in Figure 1-48.

Figure 1-48. *Viewing uploaded files*

Tip   Never use GitHub to store sensitive information such as passwords, API keys, or credit card numbers.

Understanding Key Concepts of Containers on Amazon AWS

Now that your local environment is fully deployed and configured, you are ready to explore some of the key concepts of running containers inside Amazon AWS. The Amazon AWS infrastructure offers a hosting platform for running your containerized applications.

Amazon AWS offers the following three core services that allow you to run containerized applications:

- **Amazon Elastic Container Registry (ECR)**: Managed Docker container registry

- **Amazon Elastic Container Service (ECS)**: Container orchestration service

- **Amazon Elastic Kubernetes Service (EKS)**: AWS-managed Kubernetes cluster

Elastic Container Registry

The Amazon Elastic Container Registry provides a fully managed Docker container registry that is available from anywhere in the world and that is fast, secure, and fully scalable.

With ECR, developers can deploy, store, and manage Docker containers from local machines, the AWS container host, a Keurbenetes cluster, or any container orchestration service on AWS, Azure, or Google Cloud. ECR is available from anywhere and on any platform just like the Docker Hub public container registry.

The main difference between the Docker Hub container registry and ECR is that AWS ECR is a private registry available only to users you give access to. ECR comes with many security features that allow you to lock down access to the registry and images stored inside the repository. In addition, ECR is fully integrated with ECS and EKS, allowing you to deploy containers using ECR-hosted images. Amazon ECR fully supports the Docker Registry API and allows you to use Docker CLI commands such as push, pull, list, and tag without breaking your code while accessing ECR from any Docker environment. ECR container images are stored inside an Amazon S3 storage bucket with fully redundant storage across multiple AWS regions. You can also integrate ECR with third-party tools like CI/DC pipelines.

In the following chapters, I will show you how to work with and secure your images with ECR and other services on AWS.

To view all the available ECR commands using AWS CLI, use the following command:

```
aws ecr help
```

Elastic Container Service

To run containers in the cloud, you need a service that extracts all of the complexity of managing servers, storage, networking, and security and allows you to deploy containers.

You can do that with the Amazon Elastic Container Service. ECS is a highly scalable and powerful container orchestration service that supports Docker containers.

With ECS, you can do the following:

- Deploy containers you have developed on your local environment using Docker

- Make containers accessible from anywhere with no downtime and complex configurations

- Secure your containers using the built-in security infrastructure of AWS

To view all the available ECS commands using AWS CLI, use the following command:

```
aws ecs help
```

Elastic Kubernetes Service

Let's say you have a large containerized environment with 200+ containers in a complicated configuration where you need a high level of control over the entire lifecycle process of containers and the performance of the applications.

In cases like this, AWS gives you the option to run a Kubernetes cluster with great control and at the same time extract many of the underlying management and configuration. Amazon Elastic Container Service for Kubernetes gives you a managed Kubernetes cluster up and running on AWS in minutes without any complicated configuration, at an attractive price point.

EKS is based on Kubernetes and offers the following points:

- Open source container orchestration system that was developed by Google

- Maintained by the Cloud Native Computing Foundation

- The number-one container orchestration system for automated deployment and scaling of containerized applications

AWS maintains a network of Kubernetes management infrastructure across the globe that eliminates a single point of failure.

With EKS you don't need to manage the master Kubernetes servers or patch them; instead, AWS looks after the master servers and gives you control over the worker nodes. By default, all the communication between the EKS master and worker nodes is encrypted and secure.

The primary use cases of EKS are as follows:

- Microservices applications

- Batch processing

- Front-end applications

- Hybrid deployments between on-premises infrastructure and the cloud

AWS gives you the option to initiate the installation of new updates without needing to manage the update process.

You can also use the optimized Amazon Machine Image (AMI) that has drivers for GPU-enabled EC2 instances for more advanced workloads such as machine learning, financial analytics, and video transcoding.

Running Containers on Amazon AWS

To run containers on AWS, you need to meet a few requirements, and if you have followed this chapter so far, you are almost ready to run your first container, which I'll show how to do in the next chapters.

Running containers on Amazon AWS is not just a "tick the box" exercise or a complicated one either; it is a structured process that involves preparation and planning.

So far, I have shown you how to set up your local environment with Docker, an AWS account, and AWS CLI, and in the next chapter, I'll show you how to set up ECR.

Summary

In this chapter, I showed you how to get started running containers on AWS core container services like ECR, ECS, and EKS. You should now have the following tools and services installed and configured:

- AWS account (normal or Free Tier account)

- Docker Desktop installed on your local machine

- AWS CLI installed and configured using the `aws configure` command

- VS Code installed on your machine

- An understanding of how to use Git and GitHub

I also covered the following AWS container services: ECR, ECS, and EKS.

In the next chapter, you will start working with the Amazon Elastic Container Registry service.

CHAPTER 2

Storing, Managing, and Deploying Docker Container Images with Amazon ECR

In this chapter, you will get started with AWS Elastic Container Registry (ECR) and learn how to do the following:

- Create an Amazon ECR repository

- Connect to AWS ECR using Azure CLI

- Push and pull Docker images to ECR

- Manage ECR lifecycle policies

Amazon Elastic Container Registry is a fully managed Docker container registry hosted on the Amazon AWS data centers. The ECR service is secure, reliable, and scalable, allowing you to grow your applications and services without worrying about capacity and security.

Amazon ECR comes with a few main components you should know about to help you understand it better.

Table 2-1 lists all the ECR components.

© Shimon Ifrah 2019

S. Ifrah, *Deploy Containers on AWS*, https://doi.org/10.1007/978-1-4842-5101-0_2

Table 2-1. *ECR Components*

Components	Description
Registry	The registry is the primary logical resource that holds all the images.
Authorization token	The registry authentication mechanism secures the registry and allows access to authenticated users only.
Repository	The repository contains the Docker images.
Repository policy	Policies control access and lifecycles.
Images	Container images are used with the Docker `push` and `pull` commands.

Using these five components, AWS gives you the tools and policies to manage your registry while keeping the images safe and accessible 24/7 from any location.

Amazon ECR comes with a few limits you should know about in case you are planning to hyperscale the service. Currently, ECR has a limit of 1,000 repositories per region and 1,000 images per repository, which is very high and probably enough for 99.9 percent of AWS customers. Make sure you understand these limitations. Based on these two numbers, you can host 1 million container images per region in AWS.

The next number you should know about is the number of pull and push requests you can run per second, per region, and per account, which is 200 sustained requests and a burst of 400. AWS uses the same maximum number of layers per image, which is 127 layers and 100 tags per image.

ECR Pricing

The Amazon ECR pricing structure is straightforward and based on usage; it doesn't have any up-front costs.

Specifically, the ECR pricing is based on storage usage, meaning that you pay only for the amount of data that is stored in your repositories and the data transfer out to the Internet.

Free Tier Account and ECR

If you are using a Free Tier AWS account, you get 500MB of free storage for your repositories and 1GB of data transfer over the Internet. I usually use the data transfer to download my images using the `docker pull` command.

Please note that all uploads using `docker push` are free.

Setting Up Amazon ECR

Amazon AWS best practices recommend that you create a new user account using the AWS Identity and Access Management (IAM) console for ECR management and administration.

Tip   Because ECR requires authentication to the service every time you use it, you should not use your AWS root account to do it. Instead, use a less privileged account.

Creating an IAM Account

The first step in the ECR setup process is to create an account that you will use for AWS container management that is separate from your AWS root account. AWS recommends you create an IAM account for each user and never give your root account details to anyone.

When you create IAM accounts and groups, please follow these recommendations:

- When creating new users, make sure you give them access only to the resources they need to do their work and not more.

- When users no longer need access to resources on AWS, revoke their access or reduce their permissions level.

- Use groups when assigning permissions and reduce the need to set up permissions for each user.

- When assigning permissions to groups, try to align the groups with the job role; for example, developers need access to ECR and ECS but not to billing.

- Try always to grant the least privilege and grant only the required permissions groups need to perform their tasks.

If you are not sure how to get started with groups and permissions, start with AWS managed policies, which are stand-alone policies created by AWS that define permissions based on common roles that fit many use cases and job functions.

To create a new IAM account, log in to the AWS Portal; from the Services menu, select Security, Identify, & Compliance and click IAM.

In the IAM menu, click Users and then click the "Add user" button, as shown in Figure 2-1.

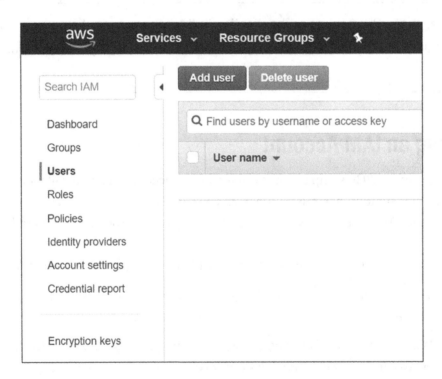

Figure 2-1. *IAM users*

On the "Set user details" page, enter the username (in my case, I'm using **administrator**), select "AWS Management Console access" for the access type, select "Autogenerated password," and Click Next: Permissions, as shown in Figure 2-2.

Tip   It is recommended that you assign permissions to groups, not users.

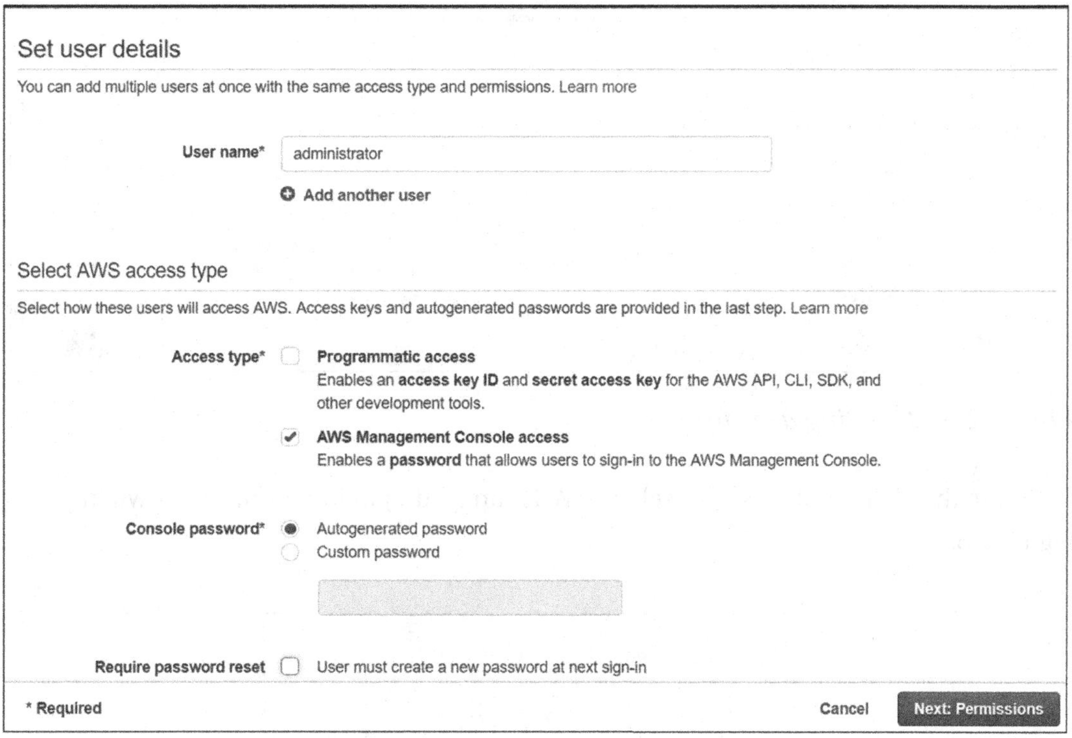

Figure 2-2. *Setting up the user details*

On the "Set Permissions" page, select "Add user to group" and click "Create group," as shown in Figure 2-3.

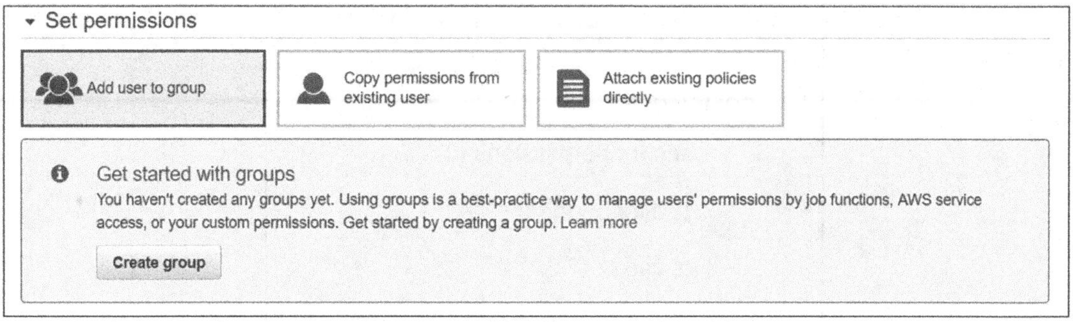

Figure 2-3. *Setting permissions*

On the "Create group" page, type **Administrators**, as shown in Figure 2-4.

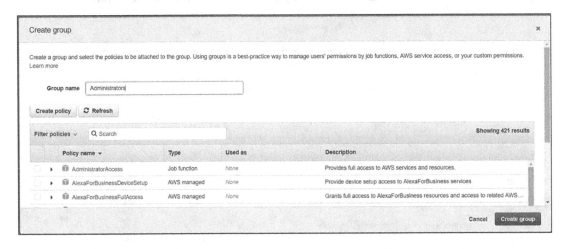

Figure 2-4. *Creating a group*

From the "Filter policies" list, select "AWS managed - job function," as shown in Figure 2-5.

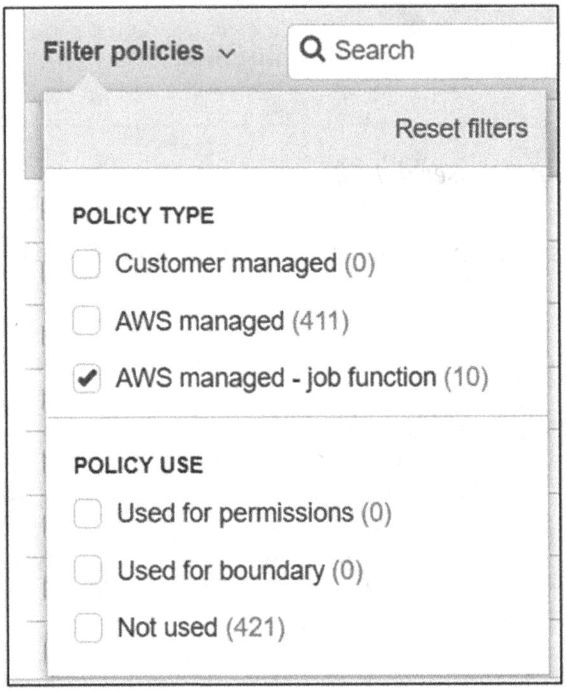

Figure 2-5. *Managed policies*

On the filtered results page, select AdministratorAccess and click "Create a group," as shown in Figure 2-6.

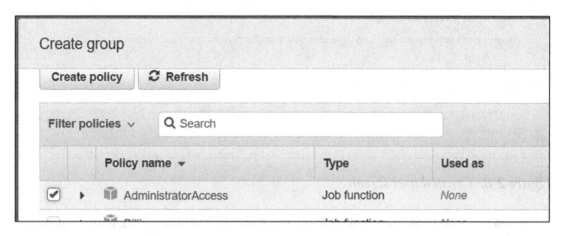

Figure 2-6. *Creating a group*

Your group should look like Figure 2-7.

Q Search		Showing 1 result
Group ▾	Attached policies	
☑ Administrators	AdministratorAccess	

Figure 2-7. *IAM administrators group*

Once the group setup is completed, click Next: Tags and add metadata tags to the account if needed. Click Next: Review to finish setting up the account and group. Review the account details and click "Create the user" when you are ready.

On the Success page, copy the sign-in URL and password to test the login, as shown in Figure 2-8.

Figure 2-8. *Created user screen*

When I click the link, AWS redirects me to a different AWS login URL with an account ID, IAM username, and password.

If you look closely, at the bottom of the page, there is an option to sign in using a root account.

To log in, I use the account ID, which was populated automatically by the URL and IAM username, which in my case is Administrator. The secure password was autogenerated for me, as shown in Figure 2-9.

Tip   If you don't remember the URL, you can use the regular AWS login page and type an account ID. You can also change the account ID with a name alias if you prefer to use a name and not numbers.

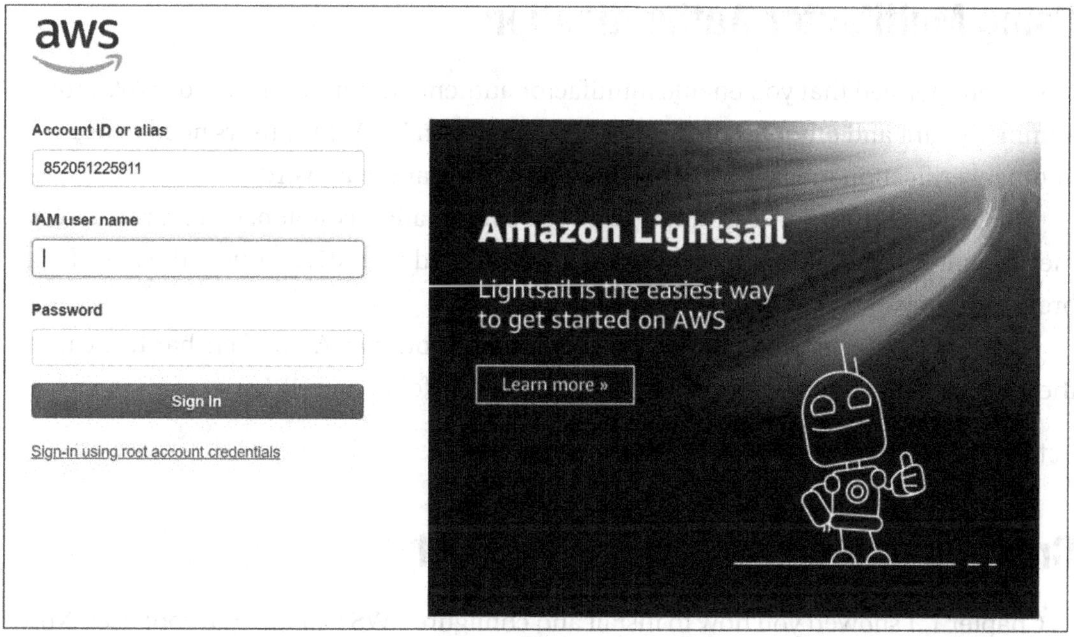

Figure 2-9. *AWS login screen using account ID*

After providing the correct login ID, the AWS Portal opens and allows me to start setting up my AWS environment, as shown in Figure 2-10.

Figure 2-10. *AWS services*

Using Multifactor Authentication

It is recommended that you enable multifactor authentication (MFA) on your AWS root admin account and other administrator accounts. With MFA, IAM users need to use another verification method on top of their username and password.

MFA ensures that if a username/password combination is stolen, no one can access the account without the extra verification. It's been said that MFA reduces the risk of breaking into your account by 80 percent.

AWS MFA is free when you use your own device; however, AWS offers hardware in the form of a YubiKey. For more information, visit the following URL:

`https://aws.amazon.com/iam/details/mfa/`

Creating an Access Key for AWS CLI

In Chapter 1, I showed you how to install and configure AWS CLI for your root user. Now, you are going to use a similar process to create an access key for your IAM Administrator account.

From the portal, click Services ➤ Security, Identify, & Compliance ➤ IAM ➤ Users.

In the user list, click Administrator and click the "Security credentials" tab, as shown in Figure 2-11.

Permissions	Groups (1)	Tags	Security credentials	Access Advisor
Sign-in credentials				

Figure 2-11. *Sign-in credentials*

On the "Security credentials" page, click "Create access key" and copy the two values listed on the screen. These values are the access key ID and the secret access key, as shown in Figure 2-12.

Tip   Keep both keys in a secure place.

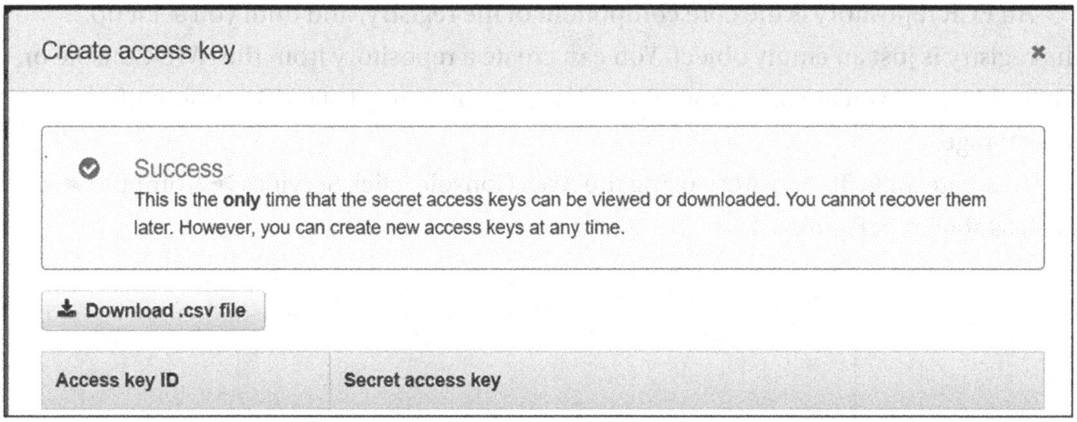

Create access key   ✕

⊘   Success
    This is the **only** time that the secret access keys can be viewed or downloaded. You cannot recover them
    later. However, you can create new access keys at any time.

⬇ Download .csv file

Access key ID   Secret access key

Figure 2-12. *Creating an access key*

Now that you have the two security keys, you can configure AWS CLI to use them.

To configure AWS CLI, I open my PowerShell console and type the following
command, as shown in Figure 2-13:

```
aws configure
```

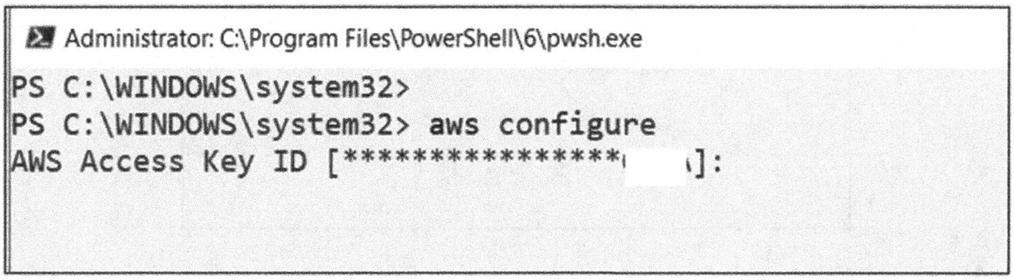

⬛ Administrator: C:\Program Files\PowerShell\6\pwsh.exe

```
PS C:\WINDOWS\system32>
PS C:\WINDOWS\system32> aws configure
AWS Access Key ID [****************    ]:
```

Figure 2-13. *The aws configure command*

Because I configured it in Chapter 1, I need to retype the new keys and go through
the wizard again. At the end of the wizard, my AWS CLI is ready to be used with my new
IAM account.

Creating an ECR Repository

Now that you have your IAM account and AWS CLI configured, you can create your
first repository. By default, all AWS accounts come with an ECR registry that has no cost
attached to it and is not active until you create a repository.

An ECR repository is the core component of the registry, and until you set it up, the registry is just an empty object. You can create a repository from the AWS Console or AWS CLI, and if you are using your Free Tier account, you get 500MB a month of free storage.

To create an ECR repository using the AWS Console, click Services ➤ Compute ➤ ECR, as shown in Figure 2-14.

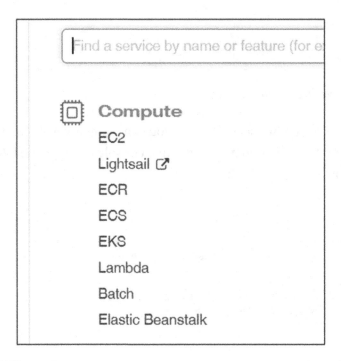

Figure 2-14. *ECR service*

Tip   For ECR pricing information, visit the URL `https://aws.amazon.com/ecr/pricing/`.

On the ECR page, fill in the details of the new repository by naming it and clicking "Create repository," as shown in Figure 2-15.

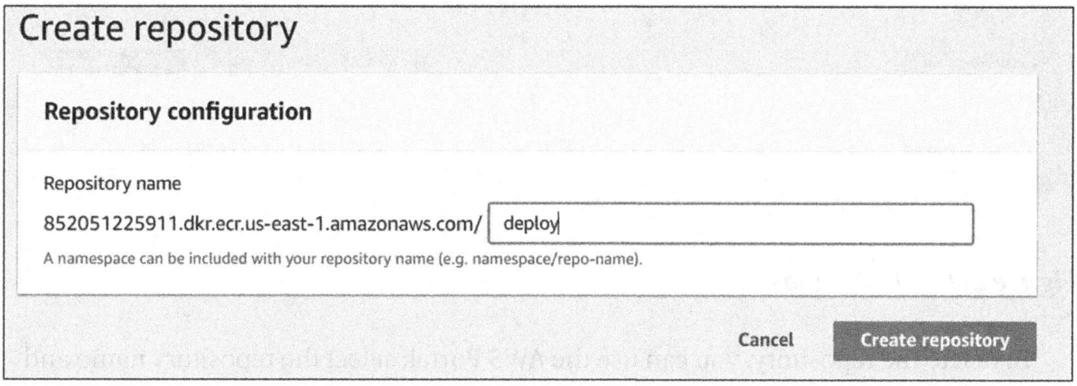

Create repository

Repository configuration

Repository name

852051225911.dkr.ecr.us-east-1.amazonaws.com/ | deploy

A namespace can be included with your repository name (e.g. namespace/repo-name).

Cancel   **Create repository**

Figure 2-15. *Creating a repository*

To use AWS CLI to create the repository, use the following command, as shown in Figure 2-16:

```
aws ecr create-repository --repository-name deploy
```

```
Administrator: C:\Program Files\PowerShell\6\pwsh.exe
PS C:\WINDOWS\system32>
PS C:\WINDOWS\system32> aws ecr create-repository --repository-name deploy
{
    "repository": {
        "repositoryArn": "arn:aws:ecr:us-west-1:852051225911:repository/deploy",
        "registryId": "852051225911",
        "repositoryName": "deploy",
        "repositoryUri": "852051225911.dkr.ecr.us-west-1.amazonaws.com/deploy",
        "createdAt": 1547954185.0
    }
}
PS C:\WINDOWS\system32>
```

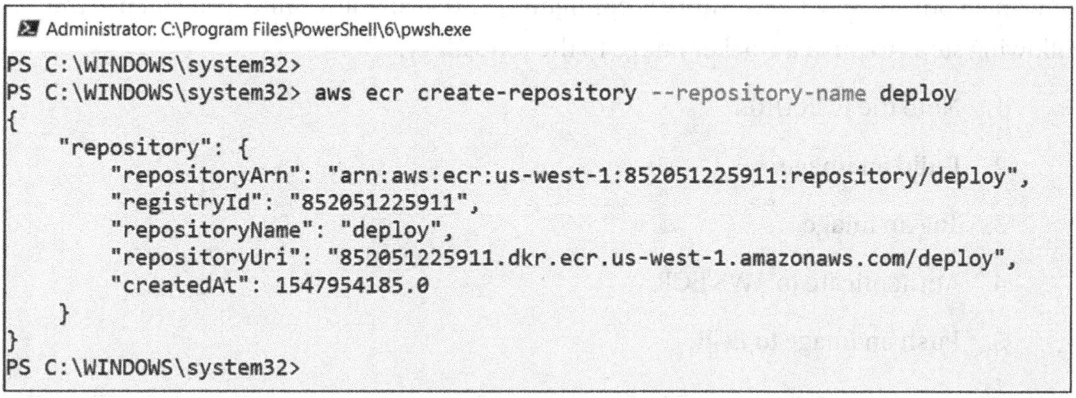

Figure 2-16. *Creating an ECR repository using AWS CLI*

If you log in to the portal, you'll see your new repository and the address to access it, as shown in Figure 2-17.

Figure 2-17. *ECR repository*

To delete the repository, you can use the AWS Portal; select the repository name and click the Delete button at the top-right corner.

You can also use the following command to delete it using AWS CLI:

```
aws ecr  delete-repository  --repository-name deploy
```

Pushing Docker Images to Amazon ECR

Now that your AWS ECR repository is configured and available online, you can use the following steps to push a Docker image to the repository:

1. Note the ECR URL.

2. Build an image.

3. Tag an image.

4. Authenticate to AWS ECR.

5. Push an image to ECR.

Tip   Before you upload your first image to ECR, make sure you are running the latest version of Docker Desktop and AWS CLI.

Noting the ECR URI

The first thing you need to do before starting is to write down the repository URI from the AWS Portal. In my case, the URL is as follows:

```
852051225911.dkr.ecr.us-west-1.amazonaws.com/deploy
```

You will find the URI in the AWS Portal under ECR ➤ Repositories. Use the copy icon to copy the URI to the clipboard, as shown in Figure 2-18.

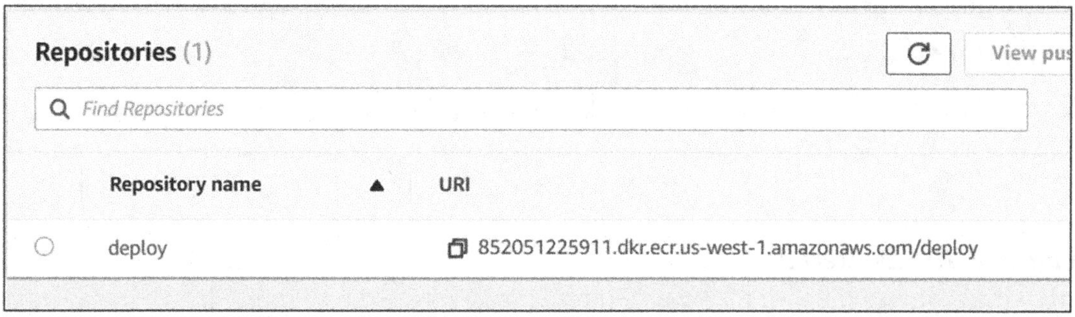

Figure 2-18. *Copying the ECR repository's URI*

Building an Image

Next, I'll use Visual Studio Code to view all the images I have on my computer using the following Docker command:

```
docker images
```

I can also use the docker build command to build an image from a DockerFile. If you need to build an image using a DockerFile, the following code shows how. As shown in Figure 2-19, I have a Dockerfile that installs Nginx on an Amazon Linux 2 container image, exposes port 8080, and configures the Nginx service to start when the container starts.

```
FROM amazonlinux:2
RUN amazon-linux-extras install nginx1.12
EXPOSE  8080
CMD ["nginx", "-g", "daemon off;"]
```

```
FROM amazonlinux:2|
RUN amazon-linux-extras install nginx1.12
EXPOSE  8080
CMD ["nginx", "-g", "daemon off;"]
```

Figure 2-19. *DockerFile*

After I save the file, I'll run the following docker build command and name the image awsnginx, as shown in Figure 2-20:

```
docker build --tag awsnginx  .
```

```
PS C:\1.DevOps\docker\AWSbuild1> docker build --tag awsnginx  .
Sending build context to Docker daemon  2.048kB
Step 1/4 : FROM amazonlinux:2
 ---> 2467e0b1e917
Step 2/4 : RUN amazon-linux-extras install nginx1.12
 ---> Running in a8763137b0ec
Loaded plugins: ovl, priorities
Cleaning repos: amzn2-core amzn2extra-nginx1.12
0 metadata files removed
0 sqlite files removed
```

Figure 2-20. *Docker build process*

When the build process is completed, I can start and run a container using the image. The following is the docker run command I'll use:

```
docker run --rm -it -p 8080:80/tcp awsnginx:latest bash
```

If I open my browser using https://localhost:127.0.0.1:8080, I'll see the Nginx default home page, as shown Figure 2-21.

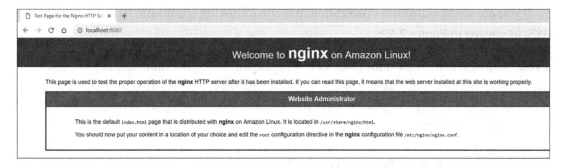

Figure 2-21. *"Welcome to nginx" screen*

Tagging the Image

The next action you need to take is to tag the image you want to push to ECR.

Tip   Make sure you use your URI and not the address in the following code:
`docker tag amazonlinux:2 852051225911.dkr.ecr.us-west-1.amazonaws.com/deploy:amazonlinux2`

Authenticating to AWS ECR

Now that you image is tagged, you need to authenticate to the ECR service from AWS CLI. To authenticate to ECR from Linux or macOS, I'll use the following command:

`aws ecr get-login --region us-west-1  --no-include-email`

In the previous command, I am requesting a security authentication token that is valid for 12 hours to a specific ECR registry.

I'm also specifying the AWS region the repository is located it; however, if you configured your AWS CLI to use a specific region (like in this book's examples), you don't have to use the region option.

Tip   To find your AWS region type, use the `aws configure` command in the AWS CLI console.

If you are using Windows PowerShell, use the following command to authenticate to AWS, as shown in Figure 2-22:

```
Invoke-Expression -Command (aws ecr get-login --no-include-email)
```

```
PS C:\1.DevOps\AWS> Invoke-Expression -Command (aws ecr get-login --no-include-email)
WARNING! Using --password via the CLI is insecure. Use --password-stdin.
Login Succeeded
```

Figure 2-22. *Authenticating to AWS ECR*

Pushing the Image

At this stage, you are ready to upload/push your image to AWS using the following command, as shown in Figure 2-23:

```
docker push 852051225911.dkr.ecr.us-west-1.amazonaws.com/
deploy:amazonlinux2
```

```
PS C:\1.DevOps\AWS> Invoke-Expression -Command (aws ecr get-login --no-include-email)
WARNING! Using --password via the CLI is insecure. Use --password-stdin.
Login Succeeded
PS C:\1.DevOps\AWS>  docker push 852051225911.dkr.ecr.us-west-1.amazonaws.com/deploy:amazonlinux2
The push refers to repository [852051225911.dkr.ecr.us-west-1.amazonaws.com/deploy]
9022126e4f14: Pushing [===>                                    ]  9.761MB/162.1MB
```

Figure 2-23. *Pushing the image*

Depending on the size of the image and your Internet connection, the image will be uploaded to ECR, and once ready, you can issue the following command, which displays all the images in the repository, as shown in Figure 2-24:

```
aws ecr list-images --repository-name deploy
```

```
PS C:\1.DevOps\AWS> aws ecr list-images --repository-name deploy
{
    "imageIds": [
        {
            "imageDigest": "sha256:fe1f25a3ebb2a736c04ea3a522b1eff9c315539604a534d519c787b277e94b9e",
            "imageTag": "amazonlinux2"
        }
    ]
}
PS C:\1.DevOps\AWS>
```

Figure 2-24. *Listing the ECR images*

You can also view the image in the AWS ECR portal, as shown in Figure 2-25.

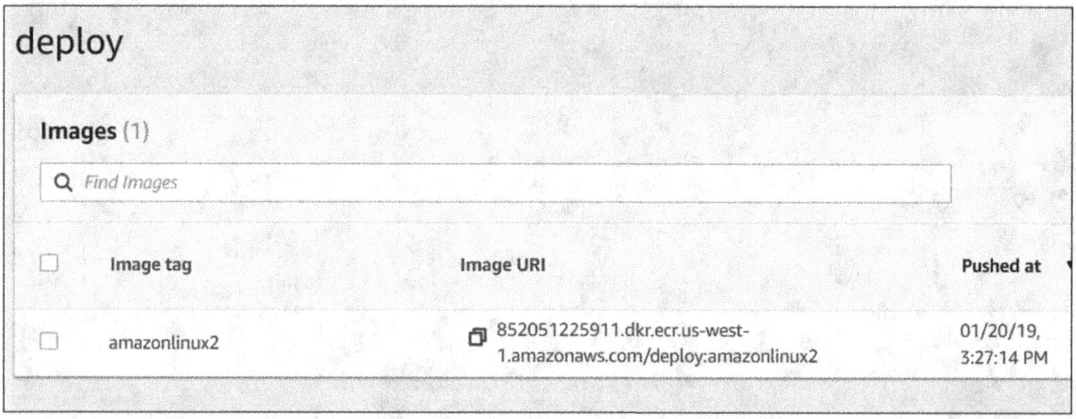

Figure 2-25. *ECR management console*

To delete a Docker image from ECR, select the image using the box at the left and click the Delete button at the top-right corner to delete it, as shown in Figure 2-26.

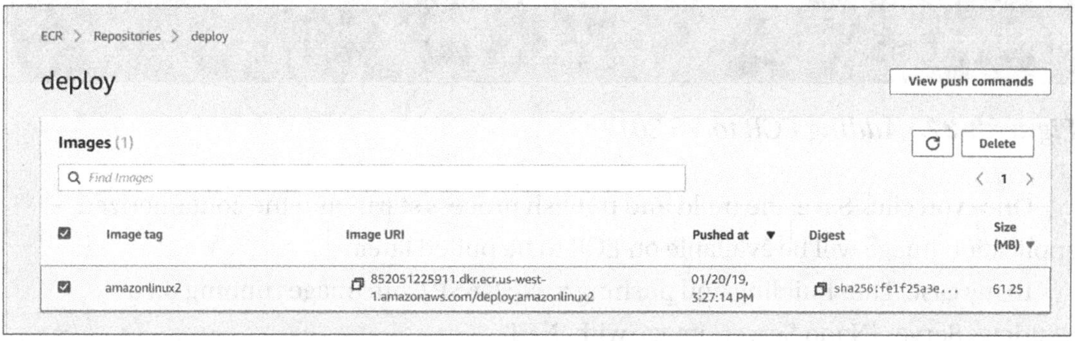

Figure 2-26. *Deleting an image*

Publishing Images from Visual Studio 2017 to AWS ECR

If you are using Visual Studio 2017 to develop or build containerized applications, you can use the built-in publishing tools to push images directly from VS to ECR.

To push an image from Visual Studio 2017, you need to open a containerized application and, from the Solution Explorer, right-click your project and choose Publish.

On the "Pick a publish target" page, select the Custom container registry option and fill in the URI address, username, and password, as shown in Figure 2-27.

59

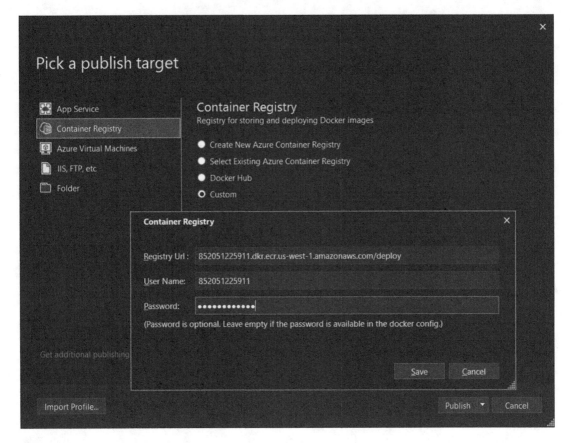

Figure 2-27. *Adding ECR to VS 2017*

Once you click Save, the build and publish process starts, and the containerized application image will be available on ECR to be pulled later.

In my case, I am building and pushing a .NET ASP Core image running on a Windows Server [Nano Server] image with .NET.

The publishing process can take an hour because VS 2017 needs to rerun the Dockerfile and build, verify, and push the image to ECR, as shown in Figure 2-28.

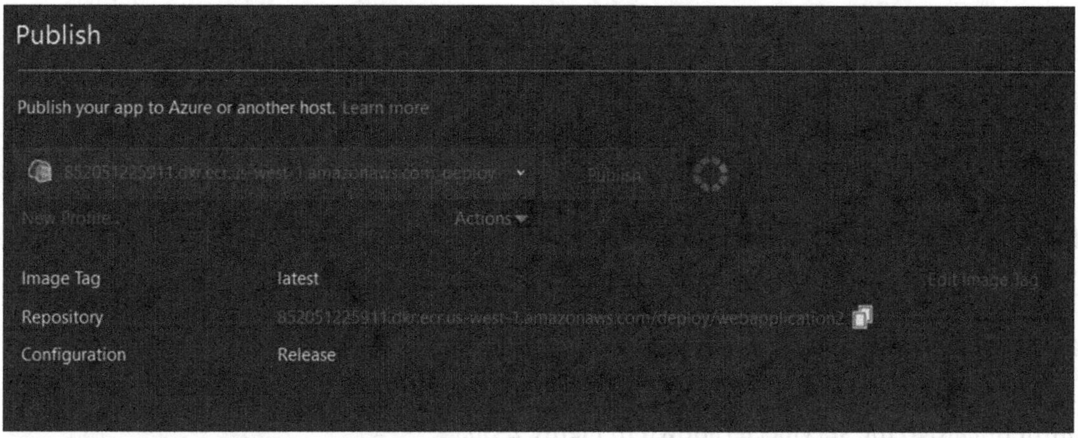

Figure 2-28. *Publishing an image*

Note   As of this writing, VS Code doesn't have a similar tool to upload images to ECR.

Pulling Images from Amazon ECR

In the previous section, you learned everything about pushing an image to ECR, including building an image and uploading it to ECR from a Docker client and Visual Studio 2017.

In this section, I'll show you how to pull images from ECR from anywhere and deploy them on your local machine. Before you start this process, note the image URL; you can find the image URL in the AWS Portal under ECR, as shown in Figure 2-29.

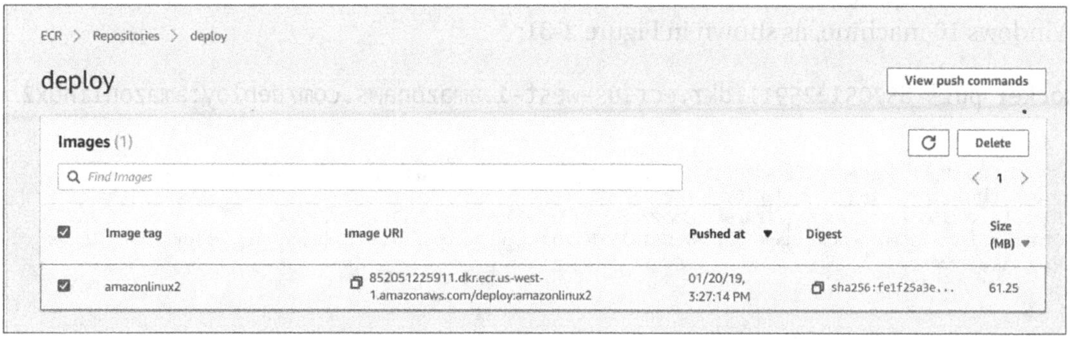

Figure 2-29. *ECR repository*

The process of pulling an image from ECR is as follows:

1. Authenticate to ECR.

2. Use a docker pull request to download an image.

Authenticating to ECR

The first step of pulling an image from ECR is to log in to ECR using AWS CLI and to authenticate using an access key.

You can use the following PowerShell command on a Windows 10 machine to authenticate to the service, as shown in Figure 2-30:

```
Invoke-Expression -Command (aws ecr get-login --no-include-email)
```

```
PS C:\1.DevOps> Invoke-Expression -Command (aws ecr get-login --no-include-email)
```

Figure 2-30. *Authenticating to ECR*

If you are on a Linux or macOS machine, you need to use the following command to authenticate to ECR, as shown in Figure 2-31:

```
aws ecr get-login --region us-west-1 --no-include-email
```

Pulling an Image from ECR

After successfully authenticating to the service, the only thing that is left to do is to use the docker pull command with the image URL.

In the following command, I am pulling my amazonlinux2 container image to my Windows 10 machine, as shown in Figure 2-31:

```
docker pull 852051225911.dkr.ecr.us-west-1.amazonaws.com/deploy:amazonlinux2
```

```
PS C:\1.DevOps> docker pull 852051225911.dkr.ecr.us-west-1.amazonaws.com/deploy:amazonlinux2
amazonlinux2: Pulling from deploy
Digest: sha256:fe1f25a3ebb2a736c04ea3a522b1eff9c315539604a534d519c787b277e94b9e
Status: Downloaded newer image for 852051225911.dkr.ecr.us-west-1.amazonaws.com/deploy:amazonlinux2
PS C:\1.DevOps> []
```

Figure 2-31. *The docker pull command*

Note   You can find the image URL in the AWS Portal.

As you saw in this section, pushing images to ECR and pulling images from ECR are not complicated processes; however, the main step you need to pay attention to is the authentication part, which is needed to create the connection to ECR and secure the download process.

Managing and Securing Amazon ECR

In this section, I go over all the management tasks you need to know about when working with Amazon Elastic Registry (ECR).

While in the previous two sections you learned how to configure, upload, and download your images to/from ECR, which are essential tasks, you must also know how to administer ECR. Many administrators and developers often neglect these management and housekeeping tasks, which are also essential.

Creating Lifecycle Policies

AWS ECR lifecycle policies allow developers and administrators to manage container images using specific rules that automatically help with the following tasks:

Lifecycles can help with the following tasks:

- Delete old images based on criteria you define such as image age and size

- Manage the number of active images

The policies and rules use preconfigured tags that are attached to images and based on the tags apply policies.

Creating a Lifecycle Policy

To get started with lifecycle policies, I'll show how to create a new test policy first. Note that only after I am happy with the preview result do I move it to become active.

To get started, log in to the AWS Portal, click ECR, and on the ECR page click the repository to which you want to apply the policy.

In the left menu, click Lifecycle Policy, as shown in Figure 2-32. In the top-left menu, click "Create rule."

Figure 2-32. *ECR menu*

On the Policy page, click "Edit test rules" to create a test rule and test it before actually running it, as shown in Figure 2-33.

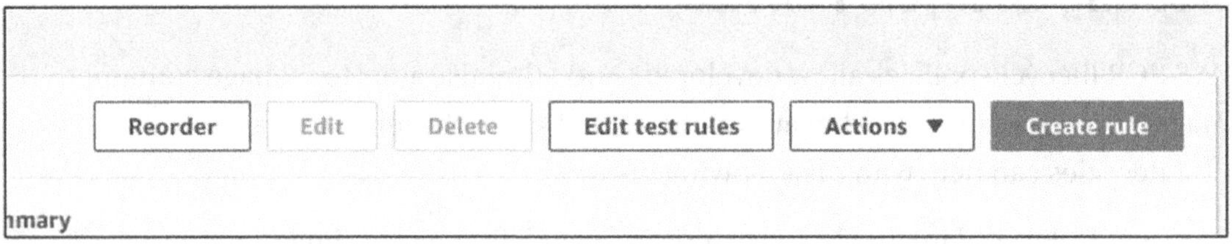

Figure 2-33. *Edit Test Rule*

In the test menu, click "Create rule" to configure the rule, as shown in Figure 2-34.

Figure 2-34. *Create Rule*

In Figure 2-35, you can see that AWS offers many options to control images. It also offers a "Rule priority" option in case you have multiple rules. You can also apply the rules to images with the following status:

- Tagged

- Untagged

- Any

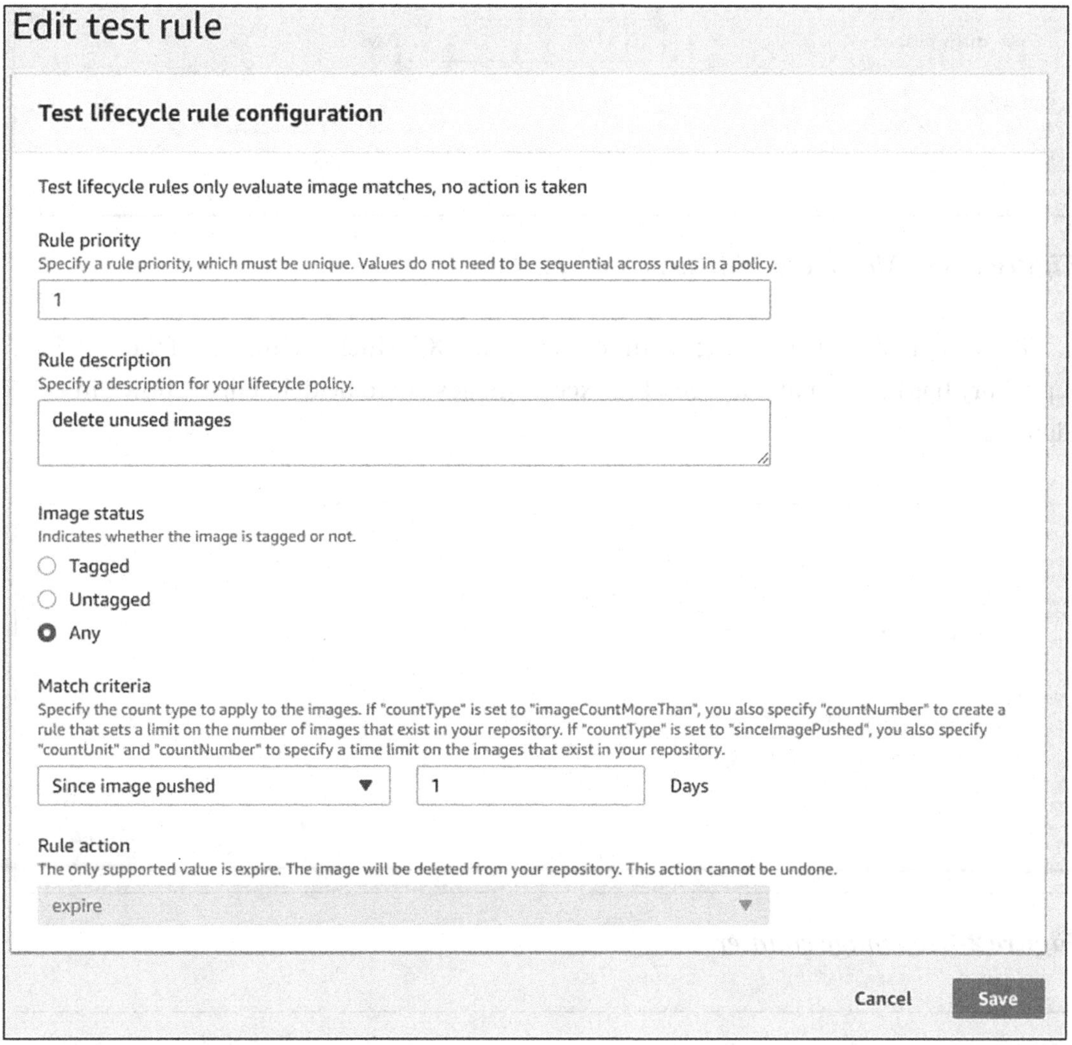

Edit test rule

Test lifecycle rule configuration

Test lifecycle rules only evaluate image matches, no action is taken

Rule priority
Specify a rule priority, which must be unique. Values do not need to be sequential across rules in a policy.

```
1
```

Rule description
Specify a description for your lifecycle policy.

```
delete unused images
```

Image status
Indicates whether the image is tagged or not.

○ Tagged
○ Untagged
● Any

Match criteria
Specify the count type to apply to the images. If "countType" is set to "imageCountMoreThan", you also specify "countNumber" to create a rule that sets a limit on the number of images that exist in your repository. If "countType" is set to "sinceImagePushed", you also specify "countUnit" and "countNumber" to specify a time limit on the images that exist in your repository.

| Since image pushed ▼ | 1 | Days |

Rule action
The only supported value is expire. The image will be deleted from your repository. This action cannot be undone.

```
expire                                              ▼
```

Cancel   Save

Figure 2-35. *Editing the test rule*

In the "Match criteria" section, you can decide when to delete an image based on specific criteria you define.

Currently, ECR offers two options. The first option is "Since image pushed X Days," which means that once X number of days have passed, the image will be deleted, as shown in Figure 2-36.

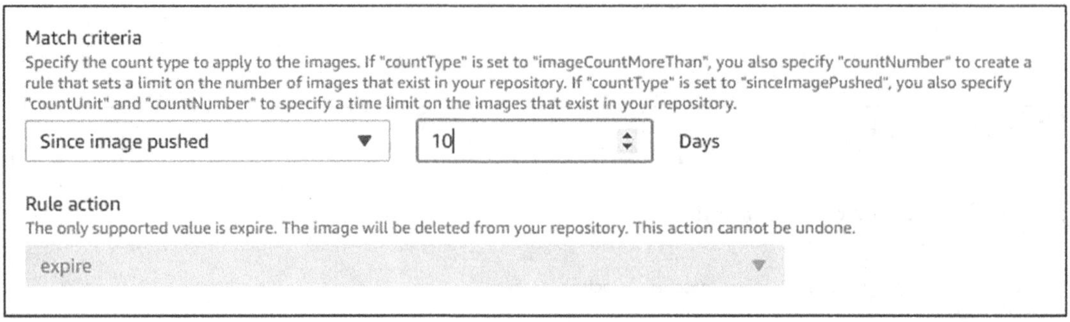

Figure 2-36. *Match criteria, days since pushed*

The second criteria is "Image counter more than X," which means that if the repository has more than X images, the excess images are to be deleted, as shown in Figure 2-37.

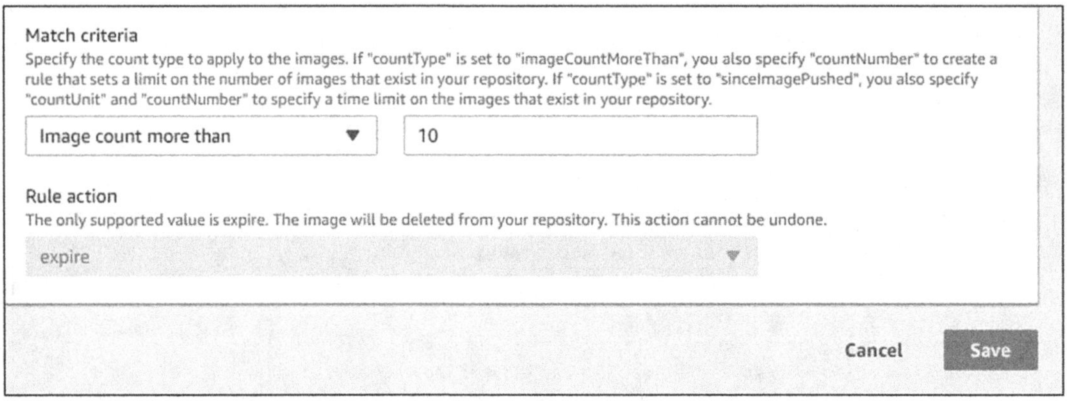

Figure 2-37. *Image counter*

Note   Once a lifecycle policy deletes an image, the image cannot be recovered.

Testing Lifecycle Policies

Once you are happy with the rule, you can click Save to continue to the preview stage to see a preview of what will be deleted as a result of the rule.

Specifically, to run a preview and see the results, select the rule and click "Save and run test," as shown in Figure 2-38.

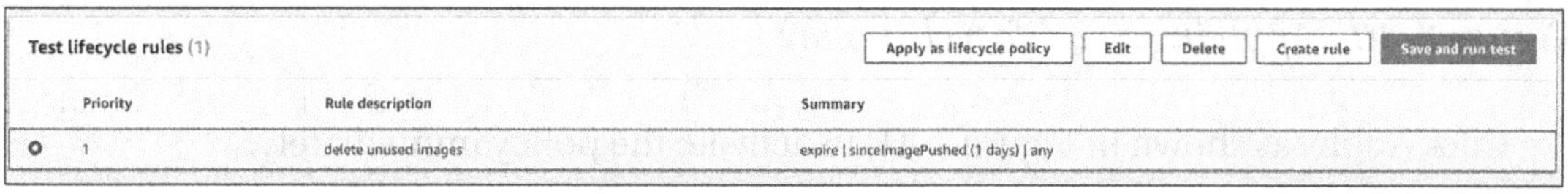

Test lifecycle rules (1)   Apply as lifecycle policy   Edit   Delete   Create rule   Save and run test

	Priority	Rule description	Summary
○	1	delete unused images	expire | sinceImagePushed (1 days) | any

Figure 2-38. *Saving and testing*

After a few minutes, the results will show up in the lower panel; in my case, I have one image that is going to be deleted, as shown in Figure 2-39.

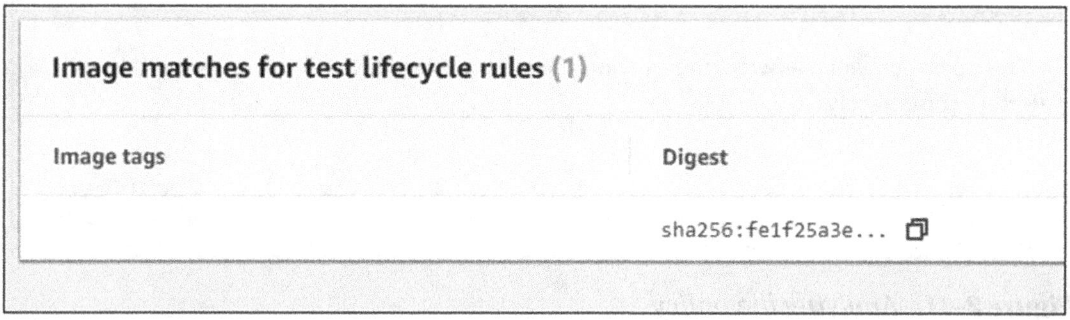

Image matches for test lifecycle rules (1)

Image tags	Digest
	sha256:fe1f25a3e...

Figure 2-39. *Image matches*

Applying the Policy

If you are happy with the results, click "Apply as lifecycle policy," as shown in Figure 2-40, which activates the policy and applies it within 24 hours.

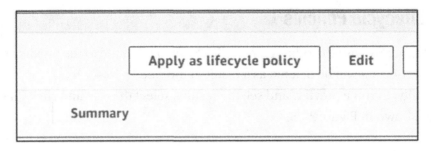

Figure 2-40. *Applying as a lifecycle policy*

Click Apply, as shown in Figure 2-41, to activate the policy immediately.

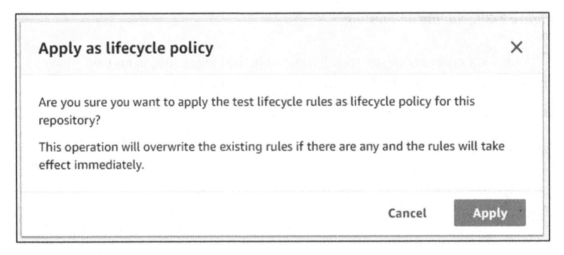

Figure 2-41. *Applying the policy*

View Results

After you click Apply, the policy goes into effect, and when it runs, you will see the message shown in Figure 2-42 on the lifecycle policy page.

Figure 2-42. *Viewing the results*

The "Lifecycle events history" page shows the task that removed an image as a result of the policy, as shown in Figure 2-43.

Lifecycle events history		
Q		
Completed at	▼	**Message**
2019-01-23T06:25:23.000Z		PolicyExecutionEvent | 1 images affected

Figure 2-43. *Event history*

Adding Tags

Tagging is another ECR feature that allows you to manage your repositories by assigning metadata to every repository in the form of a tag. A *tag* is a label that contains two types of information, a name and a value; the latest is optional, and once applied to a repository, it allows you to define ownership for billing purposes or just for reporting.

You can add, rename, and delete tags using AWS CLI or the AWS management portal without impacting the operation of ECR or the images hosted on it.

Tags have the following limitations:

- Up to 50 tags per repository

- 128 maximum key length

- Must be case sensitive

- Cannot use a prefix that starts with aws:

As I mentioned, tagging resources for billing purposes is the primary use case for tagging because it allows businesses to assign a cost to different business groups and to assign costs to projects.

To tag a repository, click the repository you need to tag.

In Figure 2-44, you can see my repository called deploy.

Figure 2-44. *ECR repositories*

From the Amazon ECR menu (shown in Figure 2-45), click Tags to access the Tags menu.

Figure 2-45. *Tags*

To add a tag to a repository, click the "Add tags" button, as shown in Figure 2-46.

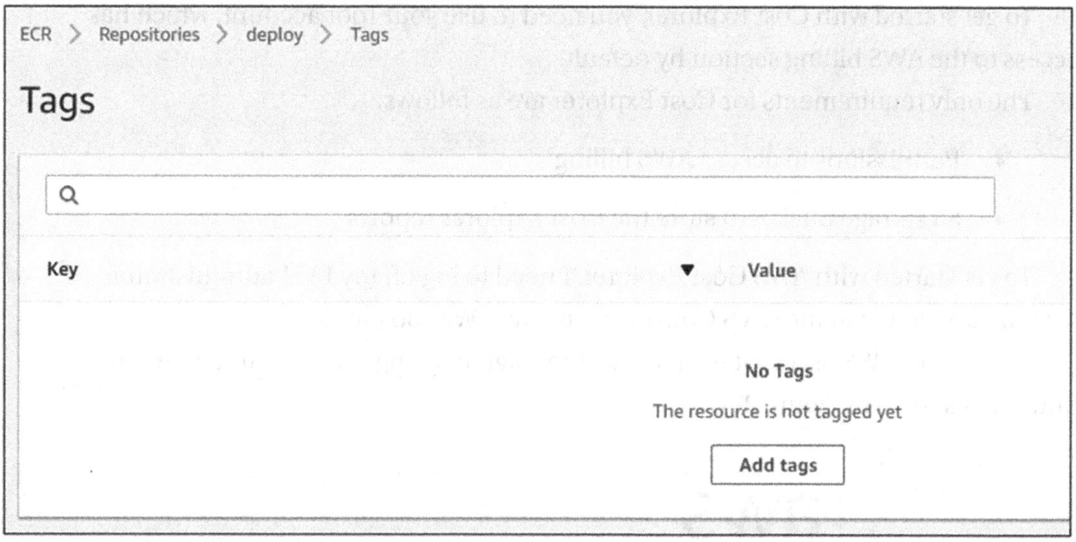

Figure 2-46. *Tags page*

In the new Tags menu, type the name of the tag, and if needed, use the Value option to add a value, as shown in Figure 2-47.

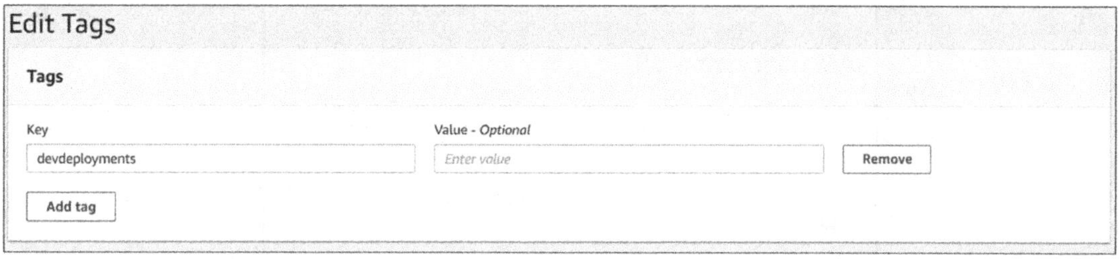

Figure 2-47. *Editing tags*

Cost and Usage Report

Knowing how to manage ECR is good, but what if you need to review and understand how much you spend on hosting your images on ECR? For that reason, AWS offers a free reporting tool called Cost Explorer, which allows you to review and analyze the cost of ECR.

Cost Explorer offers the ability to review data from the last 13 months and forecast how much you are likely to spend in the next three months. With Cost Explorer, you can identify the resources and areas you are spending a lot of money on and understand how you can reduce costs and increase efficiency. Cost Explorer shows the usage for ECR repository based on tags, which is why it is essential to use tagging in ECR.

To get started with Cost Explorer, you need to use your root account, which has access to the AWS billing section by default.

The only requirements for Cost Explorer are as follows:

- Permissions to access AWS billing

- S3 storage bucket to store the Cost Explorer reports

To get started with AWS Cost Explorer, I need to log off my IAM administrator account and log in to the AWS Console using my AWS root account.

To log in to AWS as a root user, I click the "Sign in using root account credentials" button, as shown in Figure 2-48.

Account ID or alias

852051225911

IAM user name

Password

Sign In

Sign-in using root account credentials

Figure 2-48. *Logging in to AWS*

Creating an S3 Storage Bucket

To create an S3 Storage bucket, use the following steps: on the AWS Services page, click S3 under the Storage section and click "Create bucket."

In the "Create bucket" wizard, fill in the details and follow the prompts to complete the creation process. In Figure 2-49 you can see how the wizard looks.

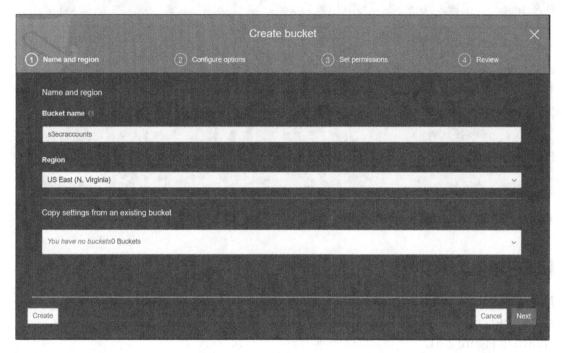

Figure 2-49. *Creating a bucket*

You can also customize some of the security permission settings, as shown in Figure 2-50.

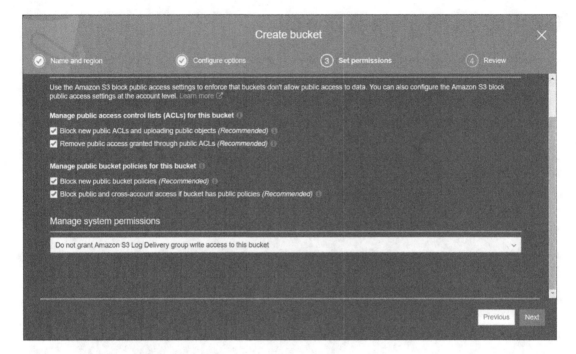

Figure 2-50. Setting permissions

Creating a Report

Now that you have a storage account to store your Cost Explorer reports, you can go ahead and create a report. From the AWS Services page, click AWS Cost Explorer, as shown in Figure 2-51.

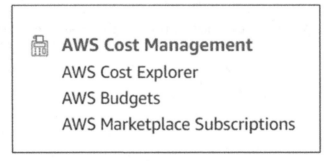

Figure 2-51. AWS Cost Explorer

On the Welcome to Cost Explorer screen, click the Enable Cost Explorer button, as shown in Figure 2-52.

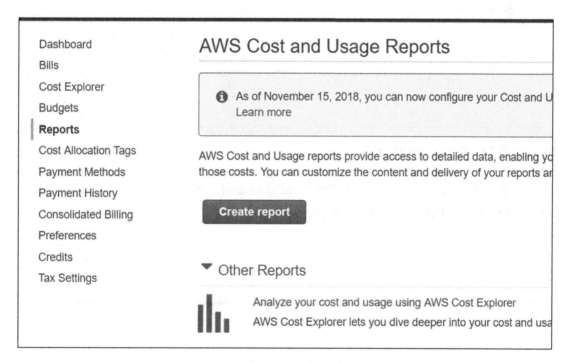

Figure 2-52. Enabling Cost Explorer

Once you enable Cost Explorer, return to the billing console, click Reports, and click "Create report," as shown in Figure 2-53.

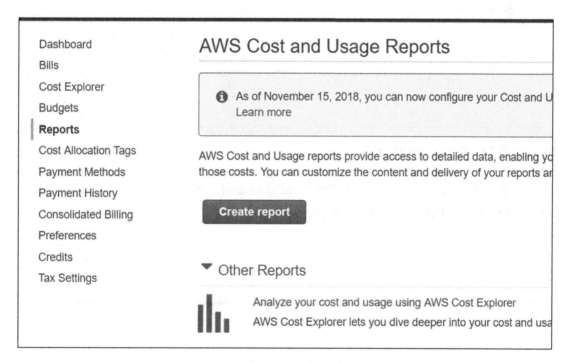

Figure 2-53. AWS cost and usage reports

On the AWS Cost Usage Report page, click "Create report" to start the process of generating a report by filling in all the needed information, as shown in Figure 2-54.

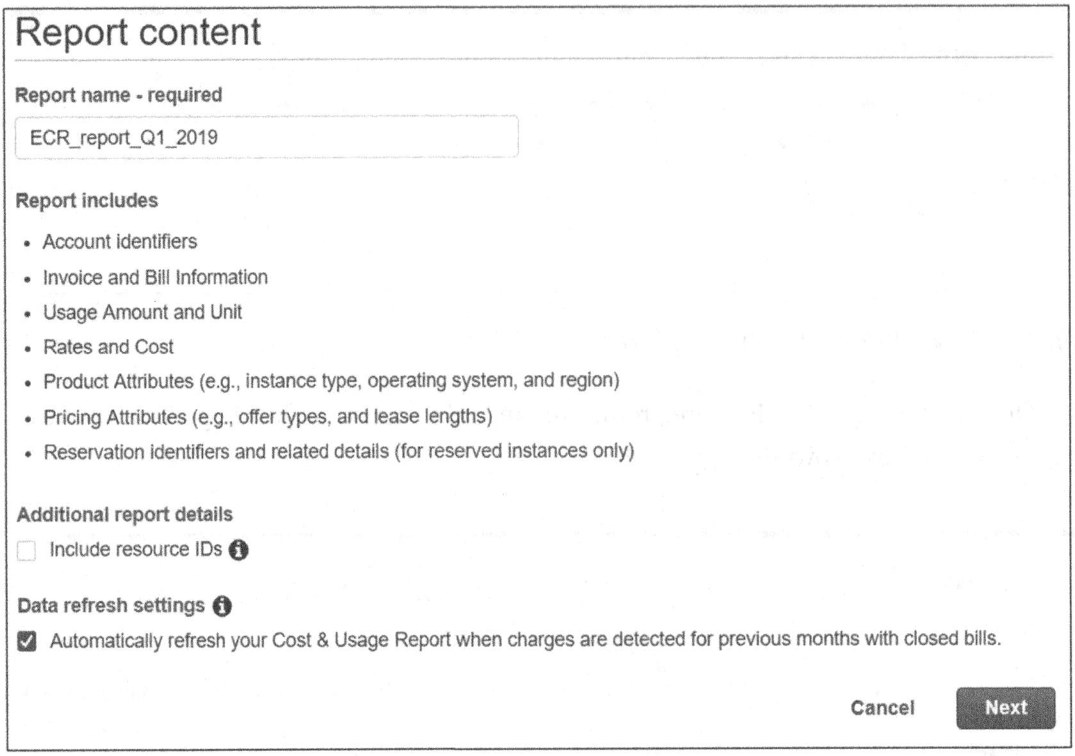

Report content

Report name - required

ECR_report_Q1_2019

Report includes

- Account identifiers
- Invoice and Bill Information
- Usage Amount and Unit
- Rates and Cost
- Product Attributes (e.g., instance type, operating system, and region)
- Pricing Attributes (e.g., offer types, and lease lengths)
- Reservation identifiers and related details (for reserved instances only)

Additional report details

☐ Include resource IDs ⓘ

Data refresh settings ⓘ

☑ Automatically refresh your Cost & Usage Report when charges are detected for previous months with closed bills.

Cancel   Next

Figure 2-54. *Report content*

On the "Delivery options" page, click Configure under the S3 bucket title and select the storage account you created in the previous section, as shown in Figure 2-55.

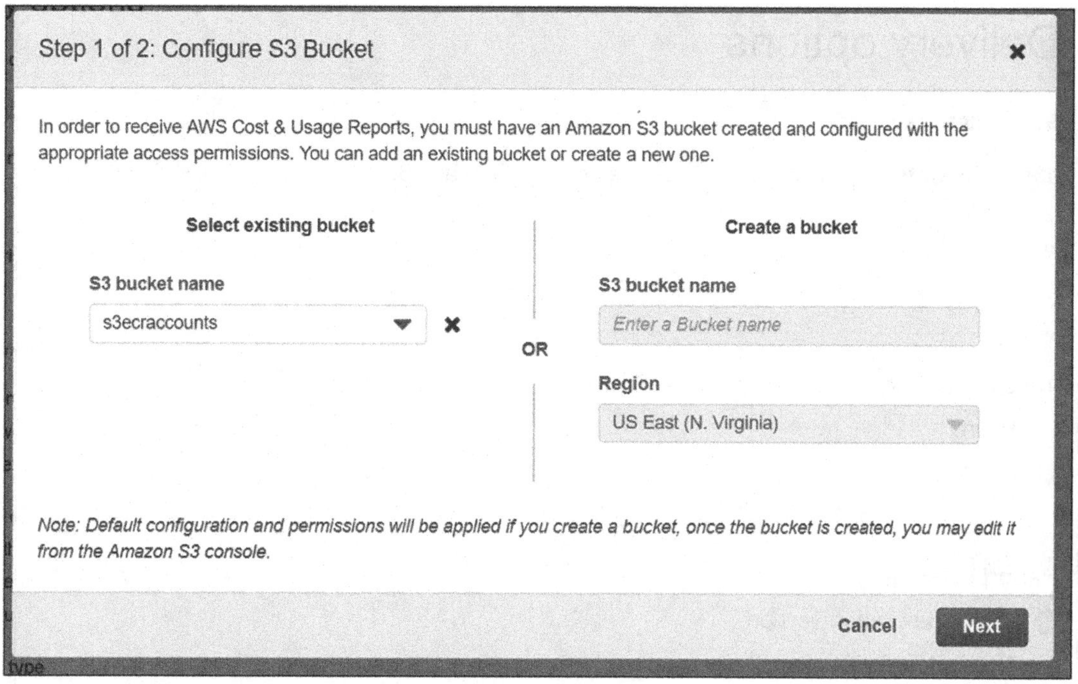

Step 1 of 2: Configure S3 Bucket   ✖

In order to receive AWS Cost & Usage Reports, you must have an Amazon S3 bucket created and configured with the appropriate access permissions. You can add an existing bucket or create a new one.

Select existing bucket		Create a bucket

S3 bucket name

| s3ecraccounts ▼ ✖ | OR | S3 bucket name |

Enter a Bucket name

Region

US East (N. Virginia) ▼

Note: Default configuration and permissions will be applied if you create a bucket, once the bucket is created, you may edit it from the Amazon S3 console.

Cancel   Next

Figure 2-55. *Configuring the S3 bucket*

After selecting the storage account, make sure a green check mark appears next to the S3 bucket section, as shown in Figure 2-56. Complete the report options, such as how often you want the report to be generated and the versioning information, as shown in Figure 2-56.

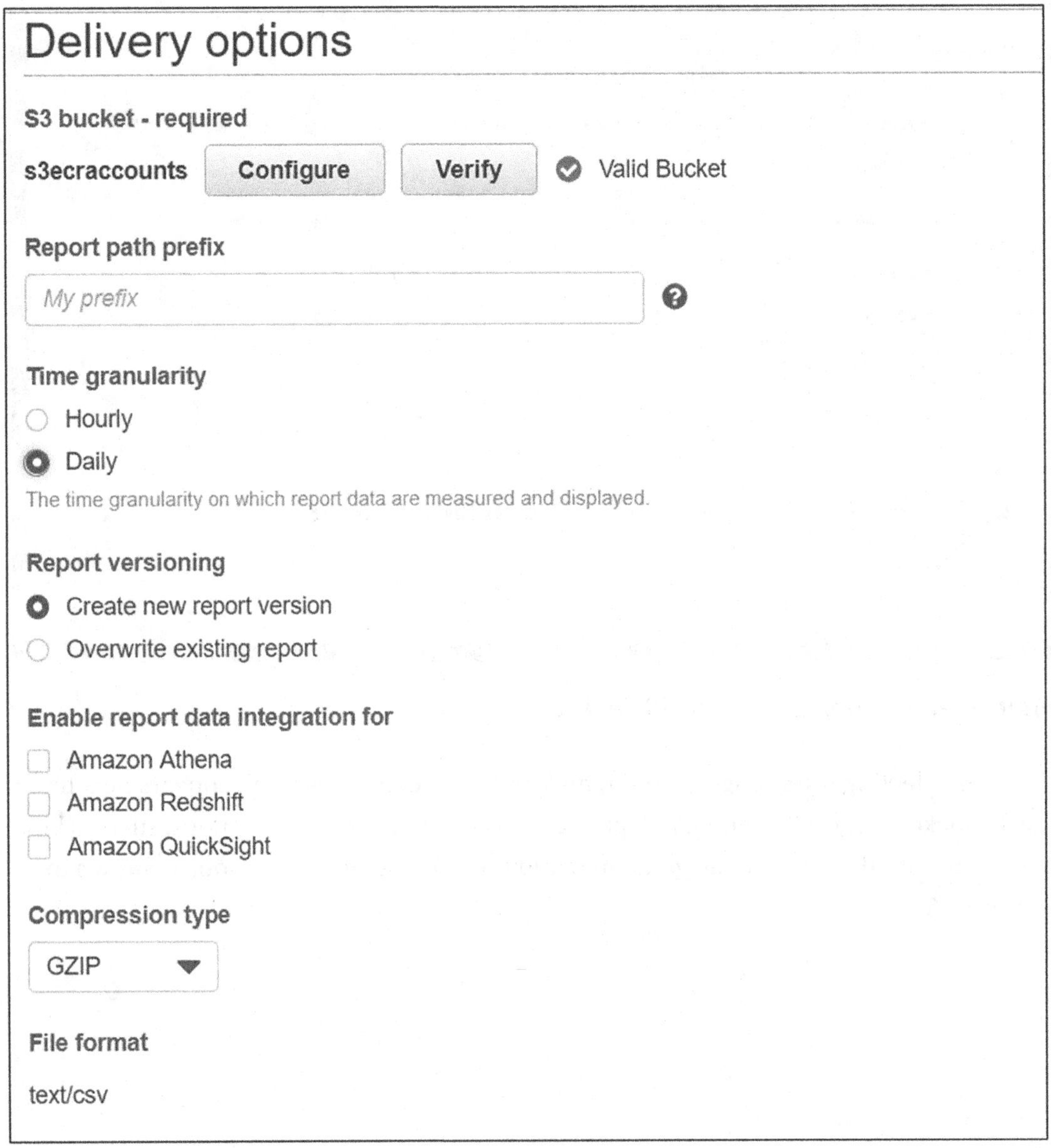

Delivery options

S3 bucket - required

s3ecraccounts   [**Configure**]   [**Verify**]   ✓ Valid Bucket

Report path prefix

| My prefix | ❓ |

Time granularity

○ Hourly

◉ Daily

The time granularity on which report data are measured and displayed.

Report versioning

◉ Create new report version

○ Overwrite existing report

Enable report data integration for

☐ Amazon Athena

☐ Amazon Redshift

☐ Amazon QuickSight

Compression type

| GZIP   ▼ |

File format

text/csv

Figure 2-56. *Delivery options*

If you followed all the steps, the report and a message telling you that the report was created successfully will appear on the AWS Cost and Usage Reports page, as shown in Figure 2-57.

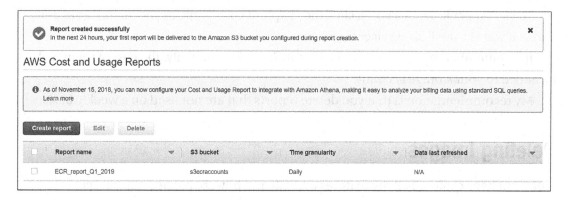

Figure 2-57. *Report created successfully*

Note   It takes 24 hours for a new report to be generated.

Viewing Reports

Within 24 hours AWS generates the first report, and you will see it in the AWS Cost Explorer, as shown in Figure 2-58.

Figure 2-58. *AWS Cost Explorer with report*

To view specific service costs, click the "Explore costs" link, as shown in Figure 2-58, and you will see the ECR service usage.

Just remember that if your reports are configured to run daily, the cost of them will be added to your storage account.

My recommendation is that you delete reports that are not used on a weekly basis.

Deleting Images

Since you have explored all the features on ECR and how to manage it from a cost perspective using AWS Cost Explorer, I'll now show how to delete images manually using the ECR console or using AWS CLI.

As always, you can use either of the two; sometimes it is much easier to use the web console rather than the AWS CLI tool.

To delete an image from the AWS Console, open ECR from the Services page, select the repository the image is located in, and select the box next to the image. Use the Delete button to delete it, as shown in Figure 2-59.

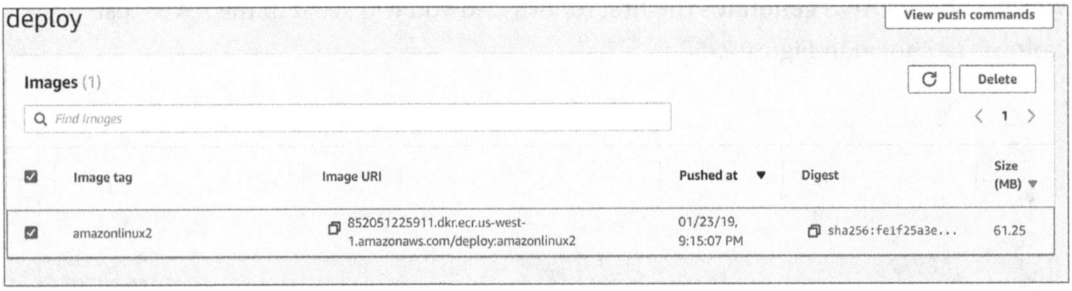

Figure 2-59. Deleting an image

To use AWS CLI to delete an image, start by logging into AWS ECR using the following command on Windows:

Invoke-Expression -Command (aws ecr get-login --no-include-email)

If you are on macOS or Linux, use the following command to log in:

aws ecr get-login --region us-west-1 --no-include-email

To view all the images in a repository called deploy, I'll use the following command:

aws ecr list-images --repository-name deploy

Now that I have the list of all the images inside my repository, I can use the following command and simply delete an image, as shown in Figure 2-60:

```
aws ecr batch-delete-image --repository-name deploy --image-ids
imageTag=amazonlinux2
```

```
PS C:\1.DevOps> aws ecr batch-delete-image --repository-name deploy --image-ids imageTag=amazonlinux2
{
    "imageIds": [
        {
            "imageDigest": "sha256:fe1f25a3ebb2a736c04ea3a522b1eff9c315539604a534d519c787b277e94b9e",
            "imageTag": "amazonlinux2"
        }
    ],
    "failures": []
```

Figure 2-60. *Deleting an image using AWS CLI*

Summary

In this chapter, you looked at the process of creating an Amazon AWS Elastic Registry repository from scratch. You created a repository, pushed an Amazon Linux 2 container image, and managed it using lifecycle policies.

You also used the docker pull command to download, or *pull*, an image from your ECR repository directly to your computer. To keep the costs under control, I covered the process of using AWS Cost Explorer and creating an S3 storage bucket to store them. In addition, I showed you how to delete an image from a repository using the AWS management console and using AWS CLI.

My recommendation in this chapter is that you keep a set of commands in a handy location where you can easily copy and paste them. Some of the commands are too long to remember, and you will use them all the time when managing ECR.

If you are planning a large ECR deployment, please remember that ECR has limits like 1,000 images per repository. If you get to a point where you have 20+ images stored in ECR, I recommend you use the lifecycle rules to manage your images and automate housekeeping tasks.

Finally, if you decide to use AWS Cost Explorer in a large organization, use the ECR tagging feature to tag your images for billing purposes.

In the next chapter, I'll show how to use Amazon Elastic Container Service (ECS) to deploy, manage, and scale containers on AWS.

CHAPTER 3

Deploying Containerized Applications with Amazon ECS

In this chapter, I will show you how to set up Amazon Elastic Container Service (ECS) and how to deploy services and containers to ECS.

ECS is a service that allows organizations, developers, and administrators to run containers in AWS without installing and configuring servers, networks, and storage. With ECS, you can deploy containers in minutes, and if you are already using ECR as your container registry, the process can be done in seconds.

ECS allows you to scale your containers from 1 to 100 using a single click, without worrying about the underlying infrastructure. With ECS, you can run Linux and Windows containers across many data centers and AWS regions.

In this chapter, I'll cover the following topics:

- How to set up and configure Amazon ECS

- When to use ECS Fargate or an EC2 cluster to run containers

- How to create ECS services using Fargate and EC2 clusters

- How to scale ECS tasks and services

- How to use AWS CloudWatch to monitor ECS

- How to install and use ECS CLI on all operating system platforms

- How to run Windows Server containers on AWS ECS EC2 clusters

© Shimon Ifrah 2019
S. Ifrah, *Deploy Containers on AWS*, https://doi.org/10.1007/978-1-4842-5101-0_3

Setting Up Amazon ECS

To get started with ECS, there are a few concepts you must understand when you deploy your services.

These are the four critical items in ECS you need to know:

- ECS clusters

- Task definitions

- Tasks

- ECS services

ECS Fargate Introduction

AWS ECS Fargate is a compute engine for deploying containers without needing to configure too many services. Specifically, Fargate makes the process of deploying containerized applications simple because you don't need to provision servers, storage, and other infrastructure.

The only thing you need to do is provide AWS Fargate with a container image and deploying it as a service or a single task (container) to ECS. In addition, if you followed Chapter 2 and are using ECR, you can connect the two services and run your containers using an ECR stored image.

ECS was first released in 2017 and now is the recommended deployment method for most containerized applications.

ECS EC2 Cluster Introduction

An AWS ECS EC2 cluster is the "old" deployment method of containers on AWS and considered more complicated, as you will see later in this chapter.

With ECS EC2, you need to provision EC2 instances that will run Docker; act as your container hosts; and manage storage, firewalls, and networking.

The setup time/effort to get an ECS EC2 cluster up and running is about ten times more than running ECS Fargate.

Tip   I recommend you use an ECS EC2 cluster over Fargate if you have very specific requirements.

As of this writing, you can't run Windows containers on ECS Fargate and can run them only on ECS EC2 clusters, as you will see later in this book.

ECS Cluster

An ECS cluster is a logical unit of core services and tasks that form the ECS cluster; once the cluster is configured, containers can be deployed to it using task definitions. The cluster type defines which type of containers you can run, Linux or Windows.

You can also define in which region your cluster will run and if you will use a Fargate or EC2 launch type. The difference between the two services is explained later in this chapter.

You can have multiple clusters; for example, you can have Production, Test, and Development clusters, or you can have a Windows cluster for Windows containers and a Linux cluster for Linux containers.

If needed, you can scale your cluster up or down using the ECS instances menu. You can also delete the cluster if you no longer need it.

Task Definitions

To run a Docker container in ECS, you need a task definition that defines which image to use in the container, how much memory and CPU the container will use, the launch type (Fargate or EC2), networking options (the subnet and security group), logging options, the commands to run, and the volumes to use.

As you can see, the task definitions are important because they control the deployment type.

Tasks

If you need to run a single container without load balancing and more advanced features, ECS tasks can get the job done.

Tasks are designed to help you deploy single containers; if you need a more advanced feature such as multiple containers, you use the next type of service, which is an ECS service.

ECS Services

To run a group of containers in ECS with multiple instances and load balancing, you create a service from a task definition and run your containers. An ECS service completes the process and deploys your container or containers.

Figure 3-1 shows the three core services that are needed to deploy containers into ECS. It is essential you remember these three services, as you will need to follow the sequence of executing them.

Tasks are also important; however, they are limited and not likely to be used in large or production environments.

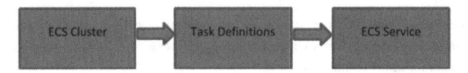

Figure 3-1. *Three core services*

In an existing ECS cluster, you only need to create a task definition and a service to run your containers.

Note   You can create task definitions without an existing ECS cluster.

Using Amazon Fargate and an ECS EC2 Cluster to Deploy Containers

Amazon ECS offers two container launch types, shown here:

- Fargate
- EC2

Fargate

Amazon Fargate allows you to run containers without worrying about container hosts and other related infrastructure. AWS manages the underlying hosts, updates, and networking.

Fargate is the recommended deployment method in AWS and will be suitable for most use cases; it was released in December 2017 and is currently recommended for most deployment scenarios.

Note   As of March 2019, you can't run Windows containers on ECS Fargate.

EC2

The EC2 launch type gives you control and lets you manage the ECS cluster. In this case, ECS deploys the EC2 cluster for you, and you take care of managing the cluster.

In most cases, it is not recommended that you use EC2; however, in some deployments, when there is a need for more control and advanced features, you can use the EC2 launch type.

Virtual Private Cloud

Amazon Virtual Private Cloud (VPC) allows you to configure a private network if you are managing your network in an on-premises environment. VPC has all the features that you will use in a traditional network, such as subnets, default gateways, firewalls, and layer 3 routing.

With VPC, you can control inbound and outbound traffic to VPC using the same tools you would on your on-premises network.

Deploying the Container with ECS Fargate and ECR

To deploy your first container on ECS Fargate, open the AWS management console and click ECS ➤ Task Definitions.

To create your first task definition, click the Create new Task Definition button, as shown in Figure 3-2.

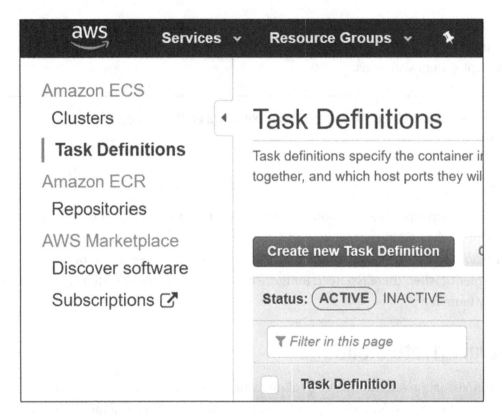

Figure 3-2.   *Creating a new task definition*

On the "Select launch type compatibility" page, select Fargate, as shown in Figure 3-3, and click Next.

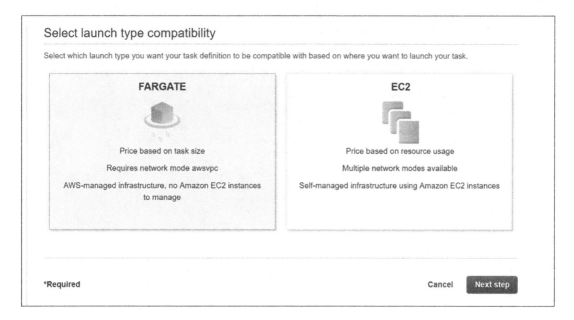

Figure 3-3. *Selecting the ECS launch type*

On the task definition page, fill in the details starting with the name and task size, which is very important. The task size is the actual amount of resources the container or containers will use. Make sure you spec your task with enough resources, but if needed, you can always modify the task definition later.

In Figure 3-4 and Figure 3-5, you can see the name configuration task and the task size of the test definition.

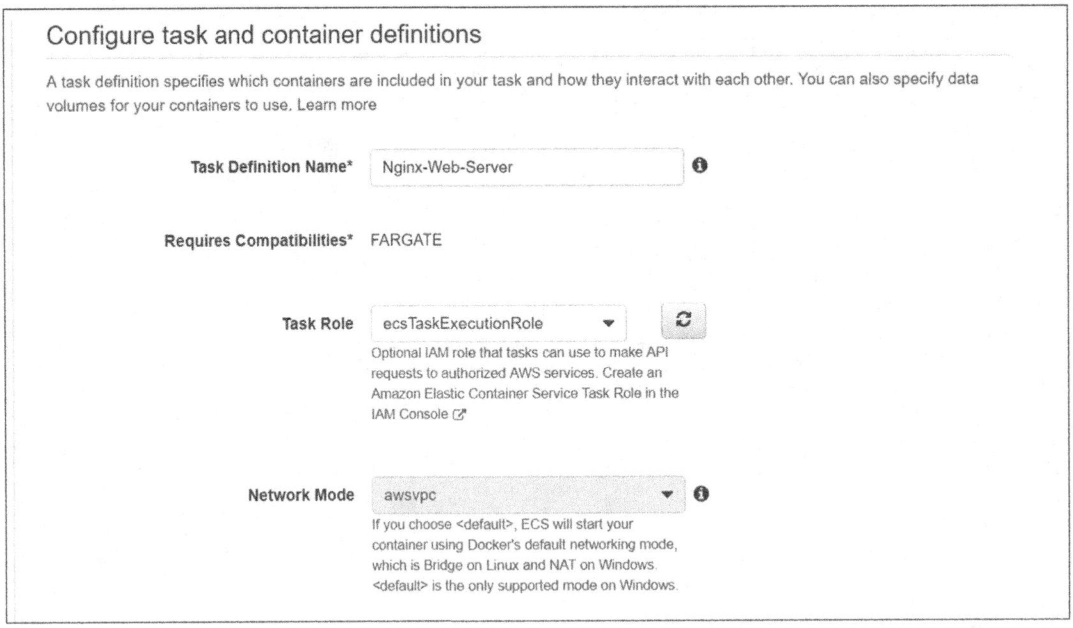

Figure 3-4. *Configuring task and container definitions*

In Figure 3-5, you can see the task size memory and CPU configuration options.

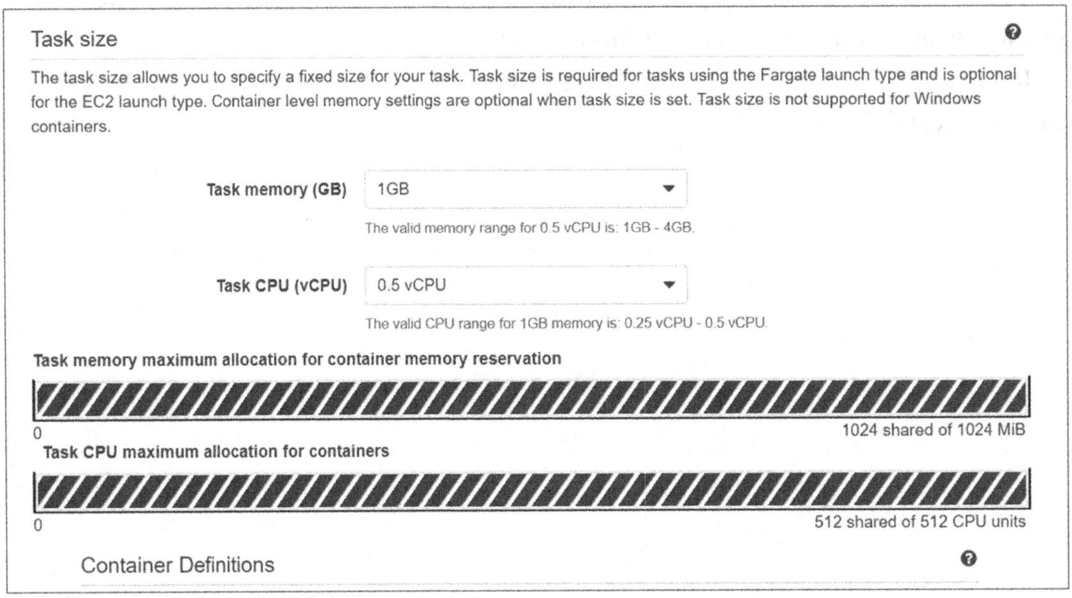

Figure 3-5. *Setting the task size*

In the last stage of the wizard, you define your container image, as shown in Figure 3-6.

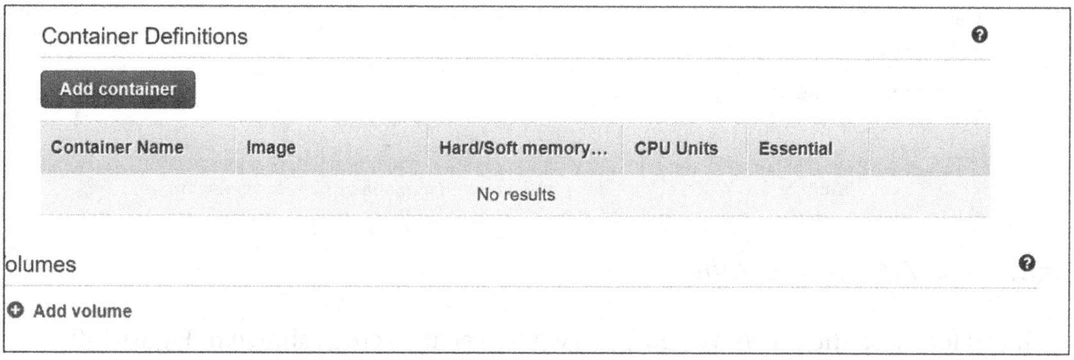

Figure 3-6. *Defining a container*

For this task, I will use my Nginx container image stored on Amazon ECR. To use it, I need to copy the image URL from the Images page, as shown in Figure 3-7. (You may recall this image repository, which I used in Chapter 2.)

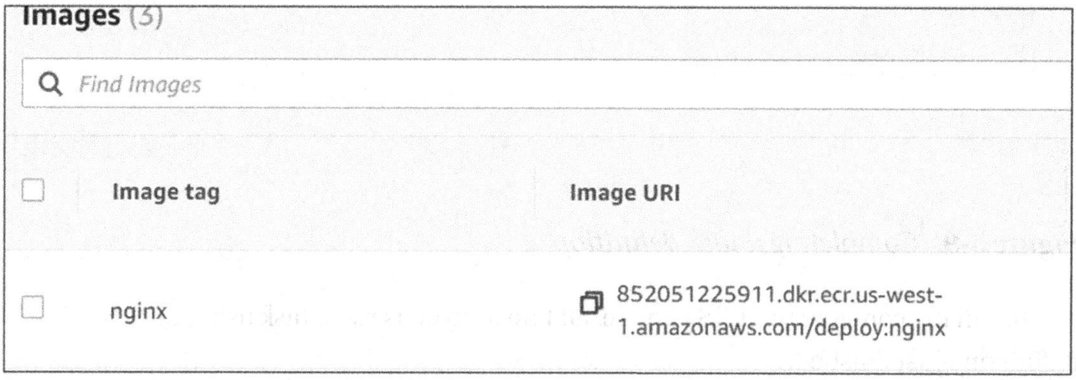

Figure 3-7. *Selecting an ECR image*

On the "Add container" page, I type the name of the image and image URI that I just copied from ECR, as shown in Figure 3-8.

At this stage, there is no need to add or select other configurations, which are considered advanced.

Figure 3-8. *Adding a container*

If you followed the previous steps, you would see the screen shown in Figure 3-9.

Figure 3-9. *Completing a task definition*

To run my container on ECS Fargate, all I need to do is run a task using the task definition I just finished.

To run a task, from the Task Definition page, click Actions and select Run Task, as shown in Figure 3-10. The wizard will guide you through the process of running your container.

Figure 3-10. *Running a task*

On the Run Task page, fill in the details, make sure you select Fargate as the launch type, and enter **1** for the number of tasks.

In the "VPC and security groups" section, select the VPC that was created by Fargate and follow the prompts, as shown in Figure 3-11 and Figure 3-12.

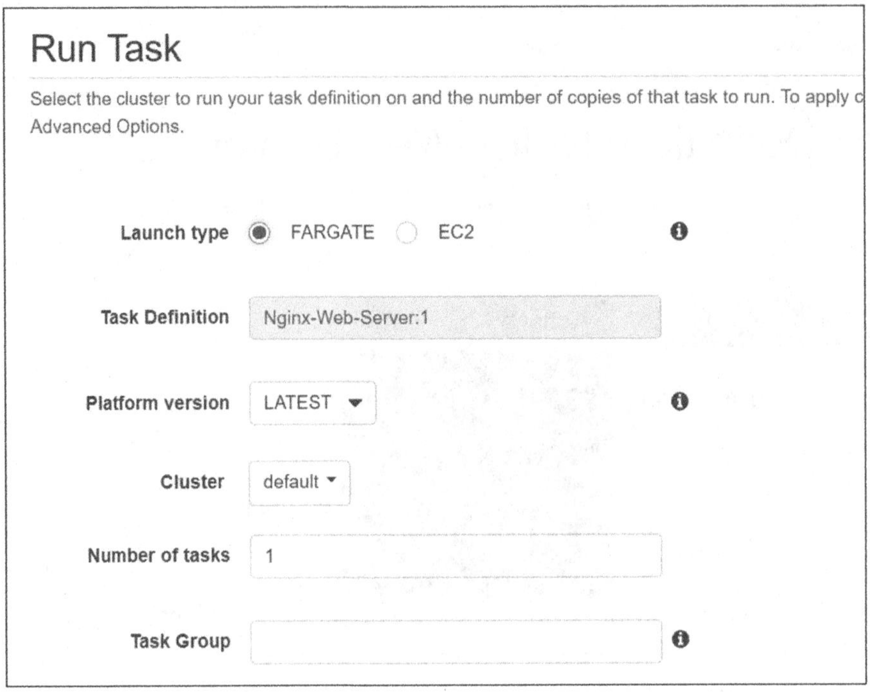

Run Task

Select the cluster to run your task definition on and the number of copies of that task to run. To apply c
Advanced Options.

Launch type	⦿ FARGATE ◯ EC2
Task Definition	Nginx-Web-Server:1
Platform version	LATEST ▾
Cluster	default ▾
Number of tasks	1
Task Group	

Figure 3-11. *Running the ECS Fargate task*

In Figure 3-12, select the VPC that was created by Fargate.

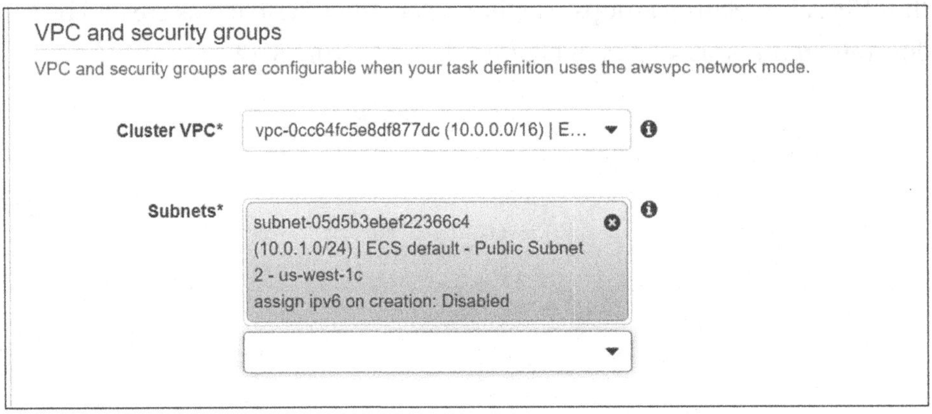

VPC and security groups

VPC and security groups are configurable when your task definition uses the awsvpc network mode.

Cluster VPC*	vpc-0cc64fc5e8df877dc (10.0.0.0/16)	E... ▾
Subnets*	subnet-05d5b3ebef22366c4 (10.0.1.0/24)	ECS default - Public Subnet 2 - us-west-1c assign ipv6 on creation: Disabled ✕

Figure 3-12. *Selecting the VPC and network*

Once the task is completed, you will see the status of it, starting with provisioning and running when it is ready.

To test and see whether it works, click the task listed on the Tasks tab, as shown in Figure 3-13.

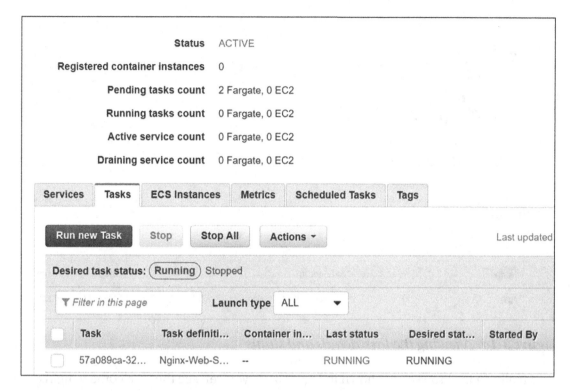

Figure 3-13. *Running the task*

On the Task page, copy the public IP address, as shown in Figure 3-14.

Figure 3-14. *Viewing the task details and status*

Finally, in my browser, as shown in Figure 3-15, you can see the "Welcome to nginx!" screen, which means my ECS task is working.

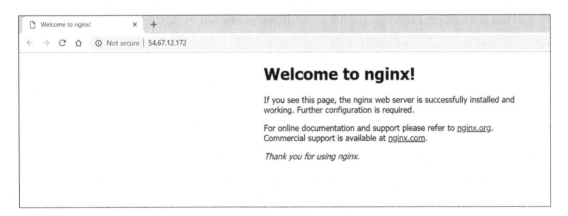

Figure 3-15. *"Welcome to nginx!" page*

If you followed the steps in this section, you saw that ECS is not complicated to get started with, and you can add more advanced features as you progress and deploy more complex solutions.

Figure 3-16 shows the workflow of ECS using Fargate; as you can see, it is straightforward. You create a task definition and then define your deployment with resources and a container image. To run your container, you run a task from the task definition, and you are done.

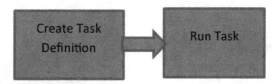

Figure 3-16. *Workflow of ECS using Fargate*

Modifying a Task Definition

If you need to modify your task definition, there is no need to delete it or create a new one. On the task definition page, click "Create new revision" and make the necessary changes to your task definition.

You can change the task size and add or remove memory and CPU power and change the container image. Once you are done, ECS will create a new revision, so you can always go back and track your changes or delete it by deregistering it.

Creating an ECS Service

What if you need to deploy many copies of your task definition with a network load balancer to balance the load between all the copies? For use cases like this, you need to create an ECS service. An ECS service can take a task definition and add advanced futures to it to prevent failure.

For example, if you define an X number of tasks that need to run all the time, the service will make sure they always run, and if one fails, it will start a new task, making sure the certain number is still maintained.

You can also use a load balancer in the service and put all the containers behind it.

Figure 3-17 shows the Create Service option available from the Actions button.

Figure 3-17. *Creating a service*

To create an ECS service, select the launch type as Fargate, give it a name, and use the Replica service type, which maintains a set number of tasks running all the time (defined in the "Number of tasks").

The Replica service type balances the tasks across Availability Zones by default, as shown in Figure 3-18.

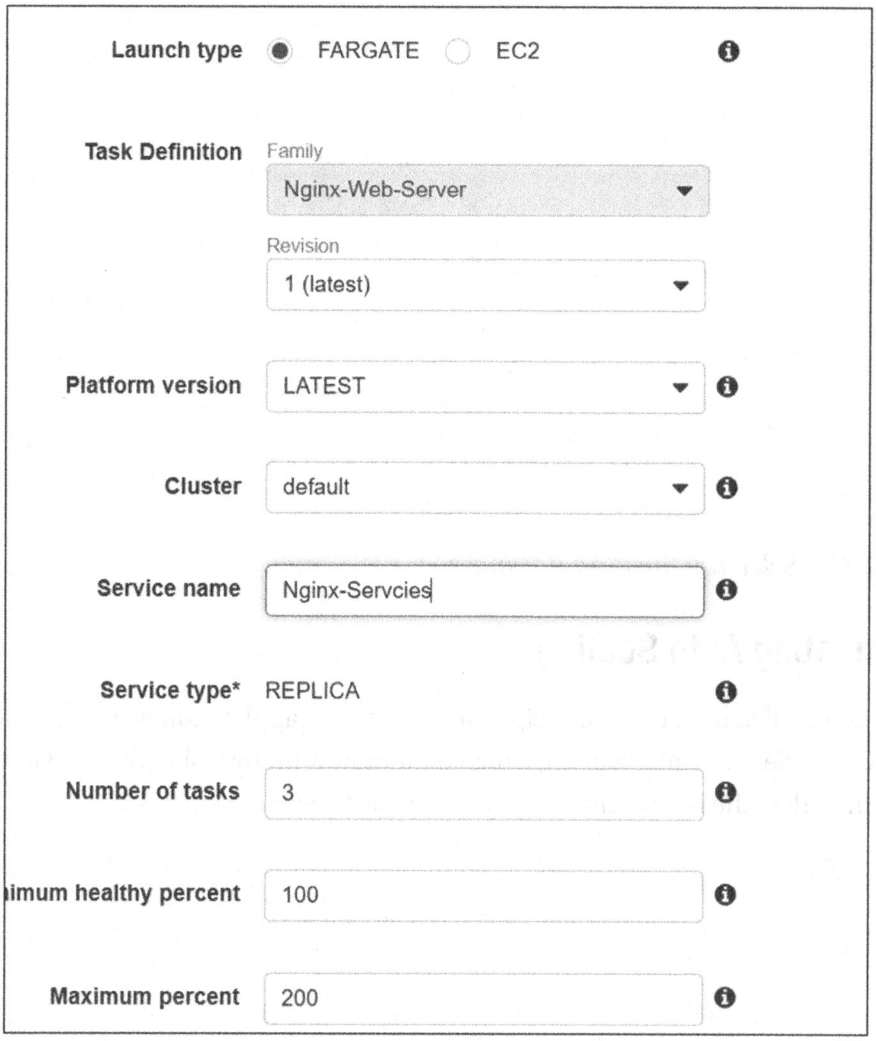

Figure 3-18. *Configuring the service*

On the next screen, you have the option to select my load balancer type or select not to use one, as shown in Figure 3-19. You can select one of the three options; however, in most cases, the second option is the most used method to load balance traffic.

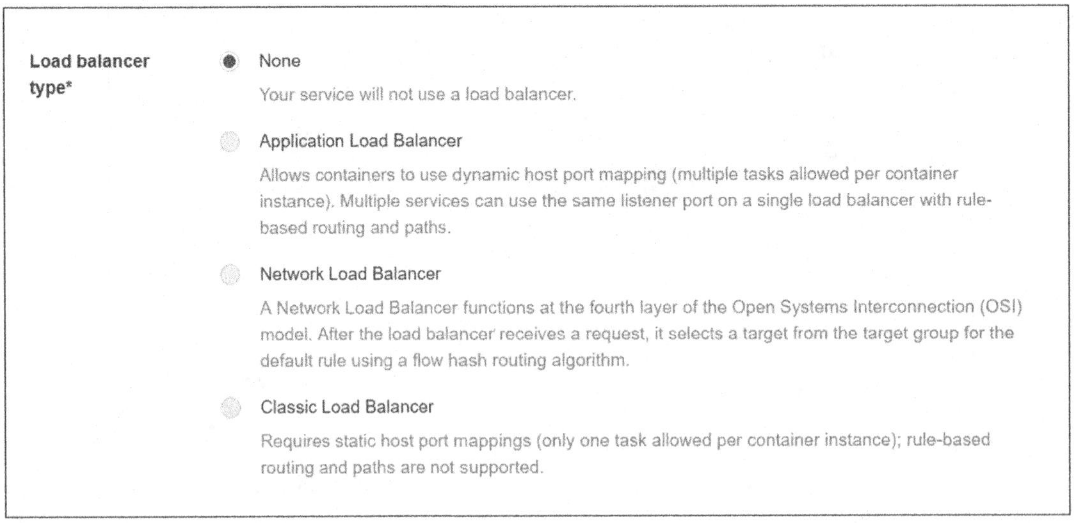

Load balancer type*

⦿ None
  Your service will not use a load balancer.

◯ Application Load Balancer
  Allows containers to use dynamic host port mapping (multiple tasks allowed per container instance). Multiple services can use the same listener port on a single load balancer with rule-based routing and paths.

◯ Network Load Balancer
  A Network Load Balancer functions at the fourth layer of the Open Systems Interconnection (OSI) model. After the load balancer receives a request, it selects a target from the target group for the default rule using a flow hash routing algorithm.

◯ Classic Load Balancer
  Requires static host port mappings (only one task allowed per container instance); rule-based routing and paths are not supported.

Figure 3-19. *Selecting the load balancer*

Implementing Auto Scaling

Another powerful feature that can help you protect your application is the Auto Scaling option and not Service Auto Scalling which defines how many tasks you need to run all the time including the minimum and maximum, as shown in Figure 3-20.

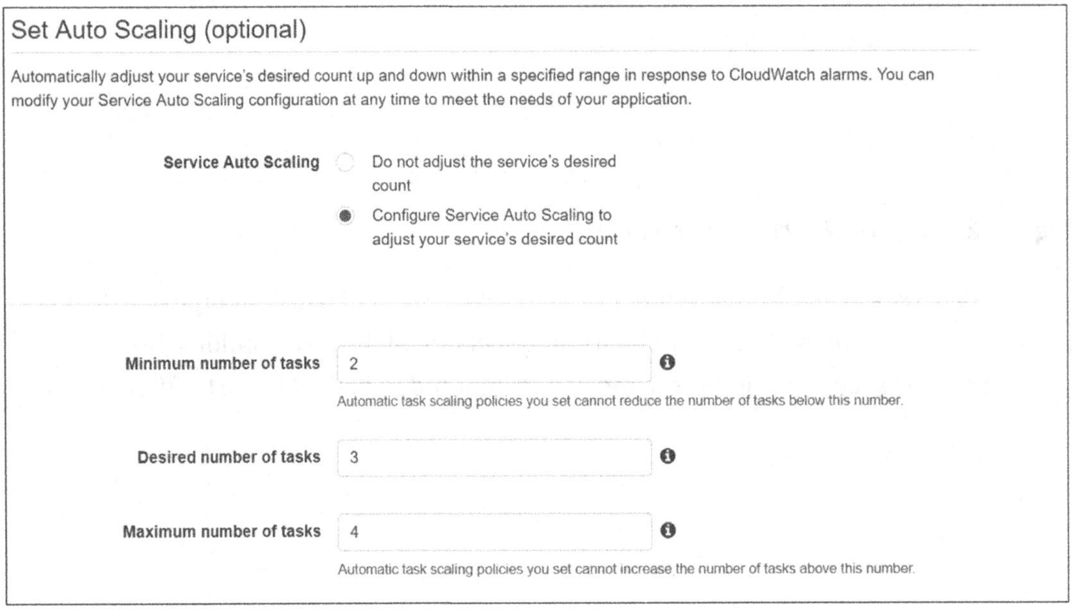

Set Auto Scaling (optional)

Automatically adjust your service's desired count up and down within a specified range in response to CloudWatch alarms. You can modify your Service Auto Scaling configuration at any time to meet the needs of your application.

Service Auto Scaling
◯ Do not adjust the service's desired count
⦿ Configure Service Auto Scaling to adjust your service's desired count

Minimum number of tasks   `2`   ℹ
Automatic task scaling policies you set cannot reduce the number of tasks below this number.

Desired number of tasks   `3`   ℹ

Maximum number of tasks   `4`   ℹ
Automatic task scaling policies you set cannot increase the number of tasks above this number.

Figure 3-20. *Setting autoscaling*

Once the service is deployed, you will see the number of the task on the Tasks tab in the Service page, as shown in Figure 3-21.

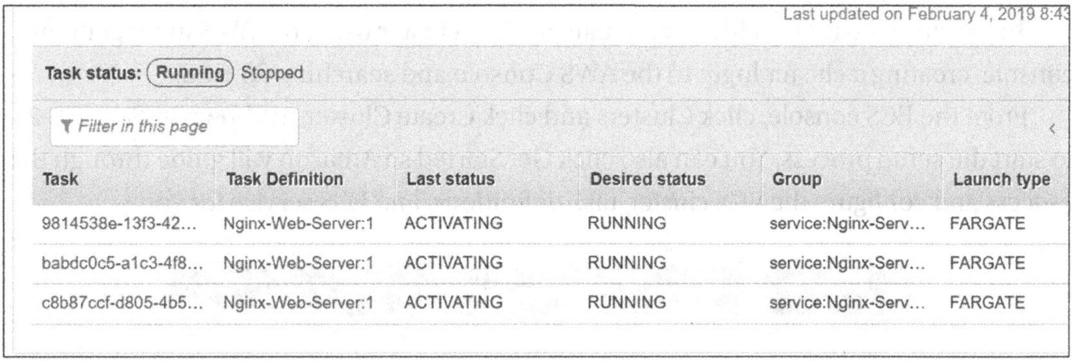

Task	Task Definition	Last status	Desired status	Group	Launch type
9814538e-13f3-42...	Nginx-Web-Server:1	ACTIVATING	RUNNING	service:Nginx-Serv...	FARGATE
babdc0c5-a1c3-4f8...	Nginx-Web-Server:1	ACTIVATING	RUNNING	service:Nginx-Serv...	FARGATE
c8b87ccf-d805-4b5...	Nginx-Web-Server:1	ACTIVATING	RUNNING	service:Nginx-Serv...	FARGATE

Last updated on February 4, 2019 8:43

Task status: (Running) Stopped

Filter in this page

Figure 3-21. *Running tasks view*

Updating an ECS Service

Once your service is up and running, you can update it while it is running without needing to delete the service and create a new one.

With an ECS service update, you can scale up or down the number of running tasks and even update the Docker image running the application.

The only thing that is *not* possible to add to an existing ECS service is load balancing. Once the service has been created with or without load balancing, it cannot be changed.

If needed, you can add or remove autoscaling and adjust the number of minimum and maximum tasks.

Creating, Managing, and Scaling an Amazon ECS Cluster

In this section, I will show you how to create and scale an ECS EC2 cluster for Linux containers.

Creating an ECS EC2 Cluster

I have shown you how to set up an ECS Fargate task and task definition and deploy an Nginx container in a matter of a few minutes. Now, I will show you the old way of running containers in AWS.

Using ECS with EC2 is far more complicated, is harder to configure, and costs more in the long term because you take on the role of managing the container host. As AWS promotes Fargate, many customers will move away from ECS EC2.

To get started with ECS EC2, you create an ECS cluster using the AWS management console, creating a cluster login to the AWS Console and searching for ECS.

From the ECS console, click Clusters and click Create Cluster, as shown in Figure 3-22, to start the setup process. You can also click Get Started so Amazon will guide through the process and configure the ECS cluster, task definitions, and ECS service for you.

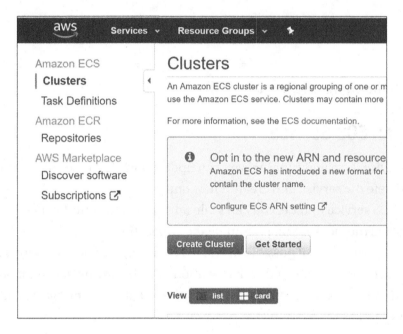

Figure 3-22. *Creating a cluster*

The Create Cluster page presents three options to choose from.

- **Networking Only**: Use this option to set up the cluster with networking only and without an EC2 instance.

- **EC2 Linux + Networking**: Use this option to set up a Linux containers ECS cluster.

- **EC2 Windows + Networking**: Use this option to set up a Windows containers cluster.

This time, I select EC2 Linux + Networking and click the Next Step button, as shown in Figure 3-23.

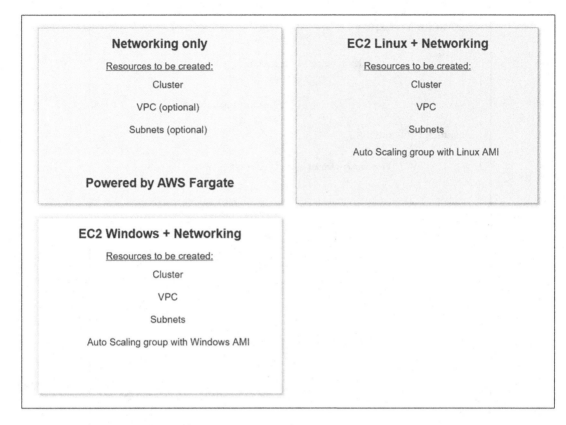

Figure 3-23. *ECS cluster options*

On the Configure Cluster page, give the cluster a name, and select the EC2 instance type. In my case, I am going to use a small instance type, but this can be changed later to a more notable instance.

In Figure 3-24 you can see the cluster configuration page and all the details that are needed for the configuration.

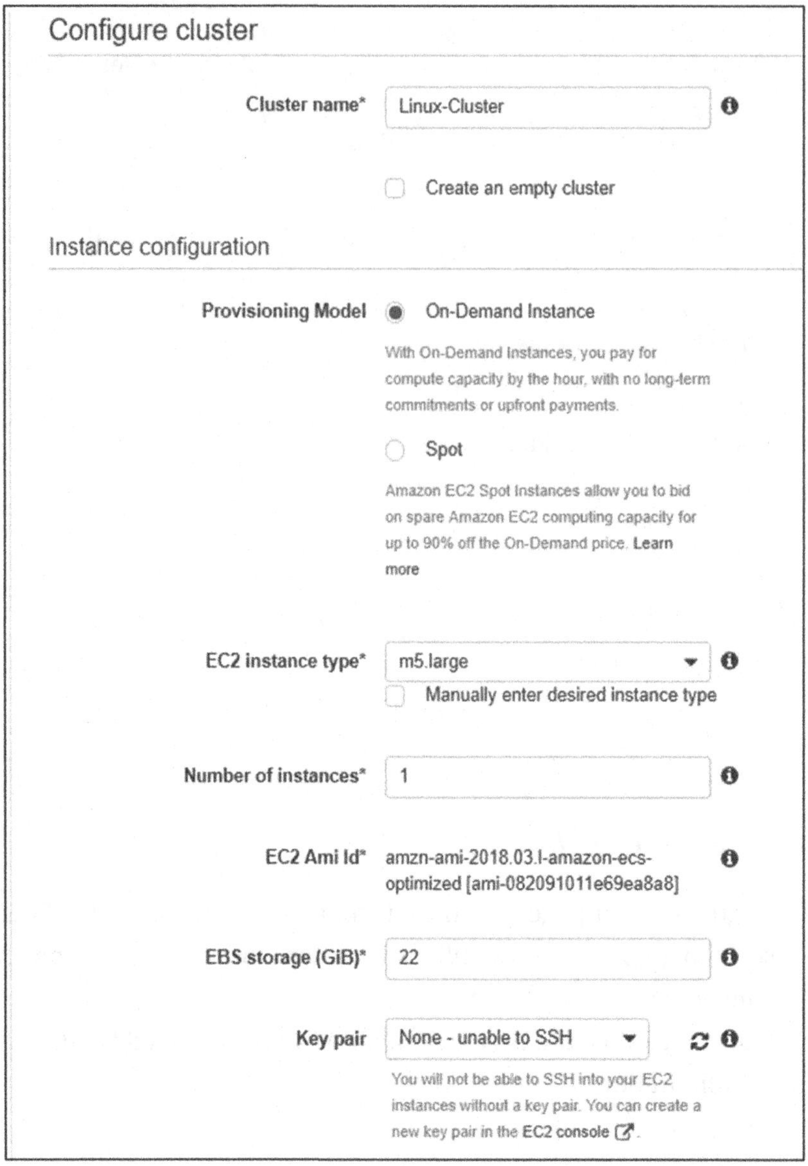

Figure 3-24. *Configuring a cluster*

In the networking section, you can create a new VPC or use an existing one.

The deployment process takes about four minutes, and when it's completed, you will see the ECS cluster deployment status page with the results, as shown in Figure 3-25.

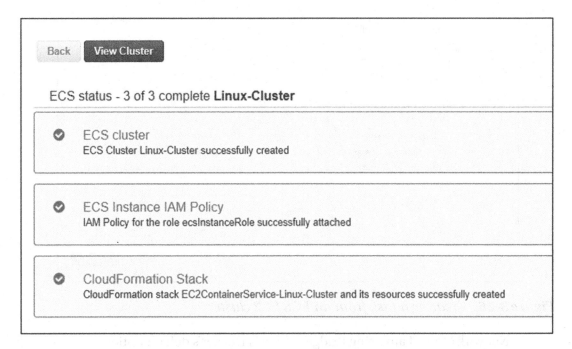

Figure 3-25. *ECS cluster successfully created page*

Creating a Task Definition for an ECS EC2 Cluster

To deploy containers to an ECS EC2 cluster, you need to create a task definition that is based on EC2, not Fargate.

To create a task definition for ECS EC2, click Task Definitions and click the Create new Task Definition button.

For the launch type, select EC2, and click "Next step" to complete the configuration, as shown in Figure 3-26.

Select launch type compatibility
Select which launch type you want your task definition to be compatible with based on where you want to launch your task.
FARGATE
Price based on task size
Requires network mode awsvpc
AWS-managed infrastructure, no Amazon EC2 instances to manage
EC2
Price based on resource usage
Multiple network modes available
Self-managed infrastructure using Amazon EC2 instances
*Required
Cancel
Next step

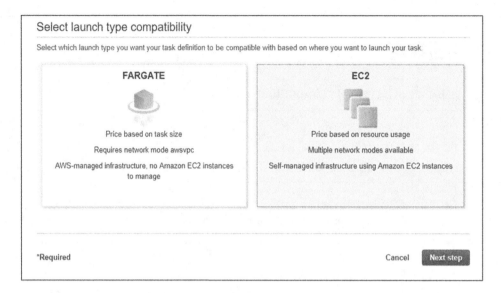

Figure 3-26. *Creating a task from an ECS EC2 cluster*

For Network Mode, I am using Bridge, which is Docker's default option. See Figure 3-27.

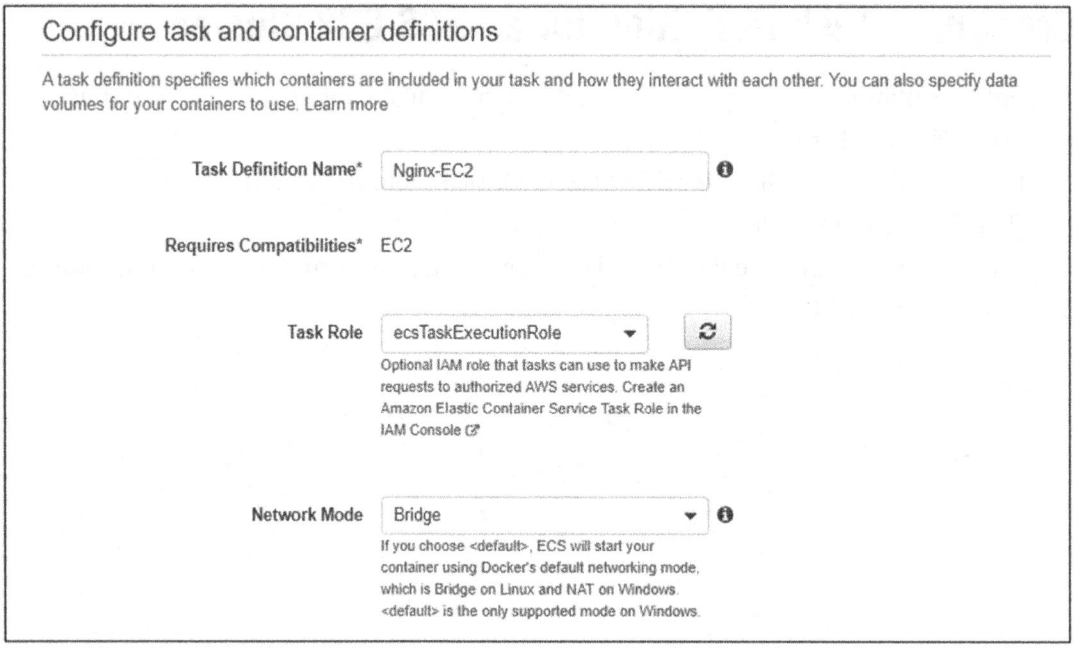

Configure task and container definitions
A task definition specifies which containers are included in your task and how they interact with each other. You can also specify data volumes for your containers to use. Learn more
Task Definition Name*
Nginx-EC2
Requires Compatibilities*
EC2
Task Role
ecsTaskExecutionRole
Optional IAM role that tasks can use to make API requests to authorized AWS services. Create an Amazon Elastic Container Service Task Role in the IAM Console
Network Mode
Bridge
If you choose <default>, ECS will start your container using Docker's default networking mode, which is Bridge on Linux and NAT on Windows. <default> is the only supported mode on Windows.

Figure 3-27. *Selecting the network mode (Bridge)*

In Figure 3-28, I am configuring the task size, which can be changed later.

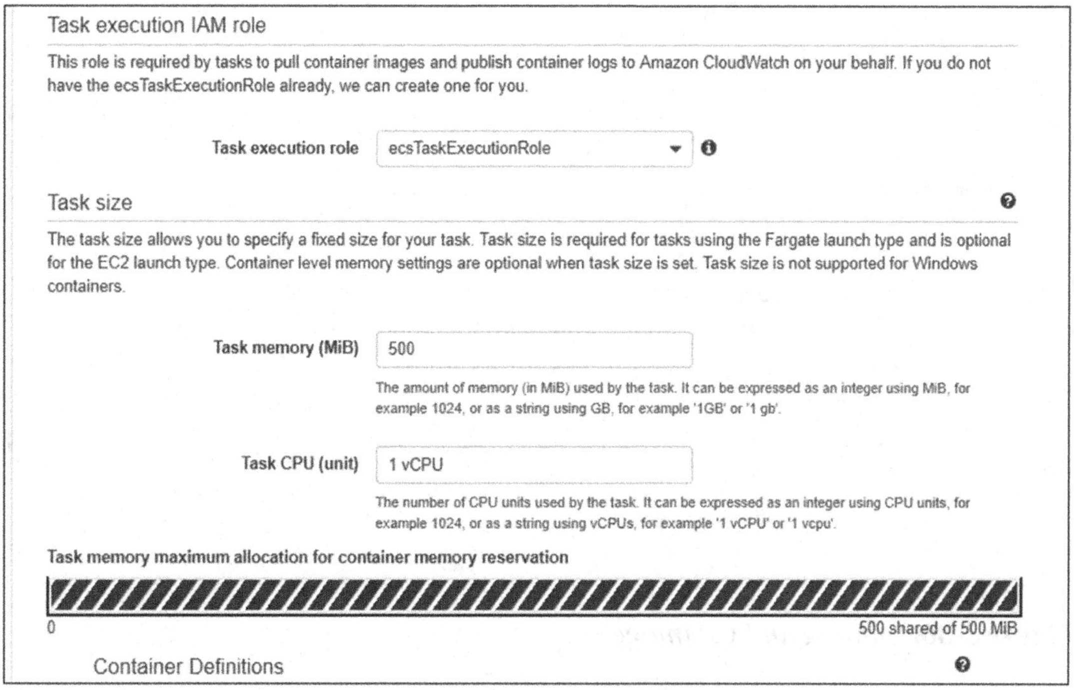

Figure 3-28.   *Configuring the task ECS EC2 task size*

To add your container image from ECR, click "Add container" in the Container Definitions section, as shown in Figure 3-29.

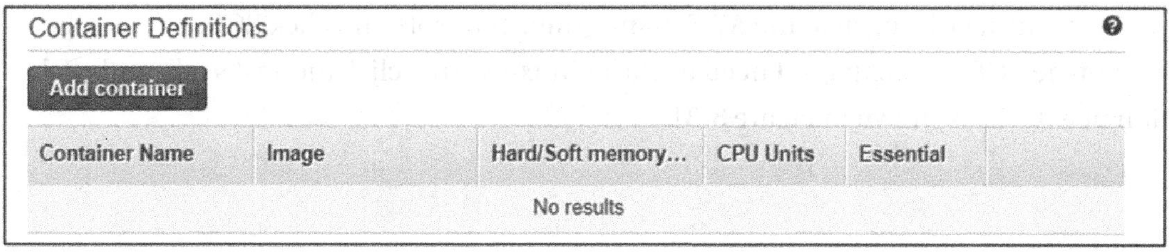

Figure 3-29.   *Adding a container*

In Figure 3-30, I am adding the ECR image URL that points to my Nginx container image.

In the "Port mappings" section, add port 80.

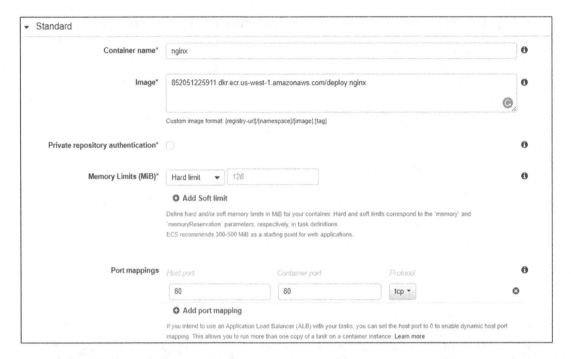

Figure 3-30. *Adding an ECR image*

Creating a Task

At this stage, you should have an ECS EC2 cluster configured and running and a task definition for it. The last step in the process is to create a task that will deploy the Nginx container image to the ECS EC2 cluster.

To create a task, log in to the AWS management console and click ECR.

On the ECR Cluster page, I need to click Linux-Cluster, click the Tasks tab, and click Run new Task, as shown in Figure 3-31.

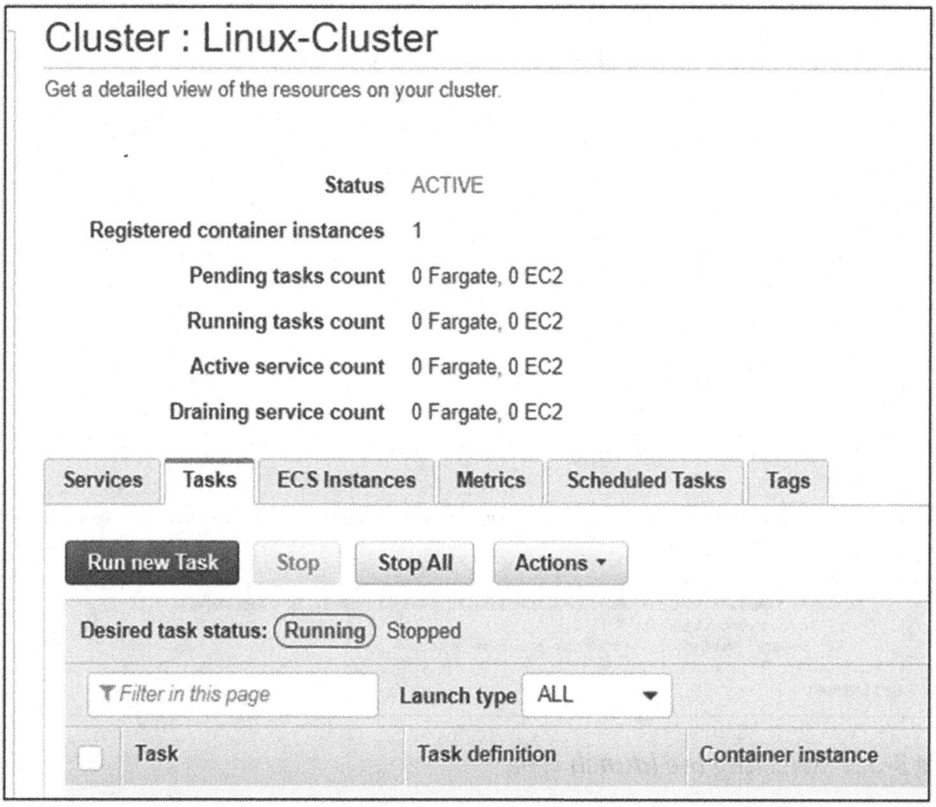

Cluster : Linux-Cluster

Get a detailed view of the resources on your cluster.

Status	ACTIVE
Registered container instances	1
Pending tasks count	0 Fargate, 0 EC2
Running tasks count	0 Fargate, 0 EC2
Active service count	0 Fargate, 0 EC2
Draining service count	0 Fargate, 0 EC2

Services	Tasks	ECS Instances	Metrics	Scheduled Tasks	Tags

Run new Task	Stop	Stop All	Actions ▾

Desired task status: (Running) Stopped

▼ *Filter in this page*   Launch type ALL ▼

☐	Task	Task definition	Container instance

Figure 3-31. *Running a new task*

From the new task window, I select EC2 as the launch type, choose the EC2 task definition, and select the number of tasks, which is the number of containers, as shown in Figure 3-32.

Figure 3-32. *Selecting the launch type*

To view my task and see whether my Nginx container is running, I need to click the running task on the Tasks tab, as shown in Figure 3-33.

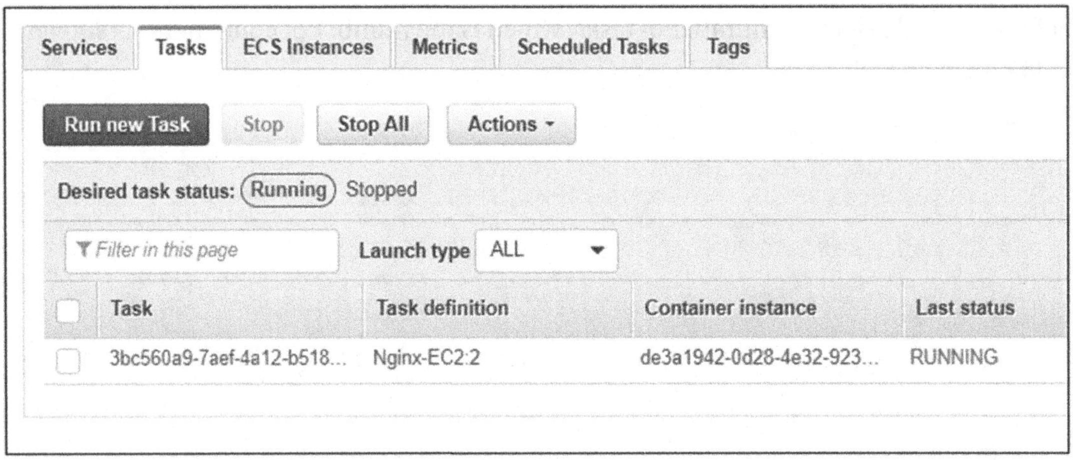

Figure 3-33. *Viewing the running tasks*

On the task page shown in Figure 3-34, click the external link IP address to test whether the container is running.

Name
Container Id
Status
nginx
977e5d7b-c2a7-4525-b788-218b53b1bb35
RUNNING
Details
Network bindings
Host Port
Container Port
Protocol
External Link
80
80
tcp
54.183.133.75:80
Environment Variables - not configured

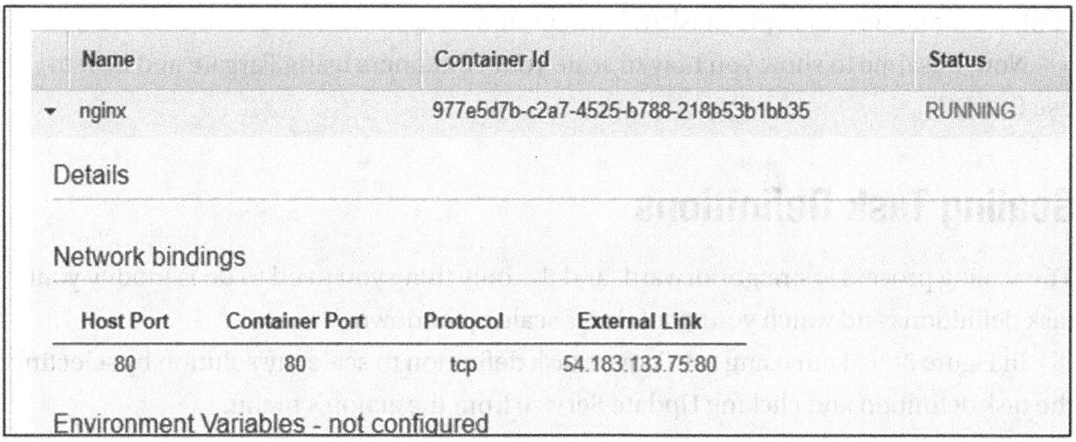

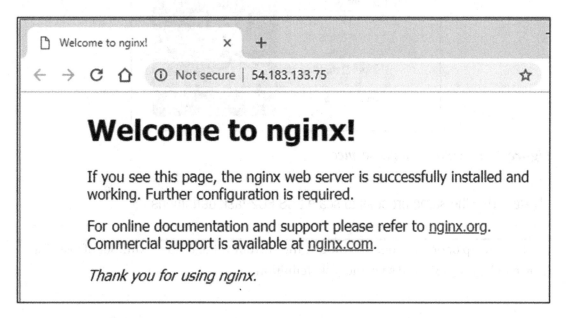

Figure 3-34. *Viewing an external link (IP)*

And as you can see in Figure 3-35, my container is running on my Linux ECS EC2 cluster without any issue.

Welcome to nginx!
Not secure | 54.183.133.75
Welcome to nginx!
If you see this page, the nginx web server is successfully installed and working. Further configuration is required.
For online documentation and support please refer to nginx.org.
Commercial support is available at nginx.com.
Thank you for using nginx.

Figure 3-35. *"Welcome to nginx!" page*

Scaling Tasks and Clusters

In the previous two sections, I showed you how to set up ECS Fargate and ECS EC2 containers and how to deploy task definitions and tasks.

Now, it is time to show you how to scale your containers using Fargate and how to use ECS EC2.

Scaling Task Definitions

The scaling process is straightforward, and the only thing you need to do is modify your task definitions and watch your containers scale up or down.

In Figure 3-36, I am using my Fargate task definition to scale my solution by selecting the task definition and clicking Update Service from the action's menu.

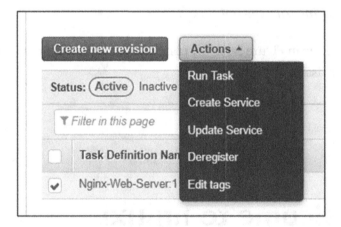

Figure 3-36. *Updating the service*

Note   Use the same process to scale ECS EC2 task definitions.

To scale up or down, I need to modify the current value under "Number of tasks," as shown in Figure 3-37, and save the task definition.

Cluster	default ▼	❶
Service name	Nginx-Service ▼	❶
Service type*	REPLICA	❶
Number of tasks	1	❶

Figure 3-37. *Scaling a service*

Scaling an ECS EC2 Cluster

Now, I will show you how to scale an ECS EC2 cluster instance. To scale an ECS EC2 instance, you can access ECS from the AWS management console and click your Linux cluster.

On the cluster page, click the ECS Instances tab to view your instances. In my case, I have one instance on an ECS EC2 server.

Note   When using ECS Fargate, the ECS Instances tab is not available.

To scale up an ECS instance, click Scale ECS Instances, as shown in Figure 3-38.

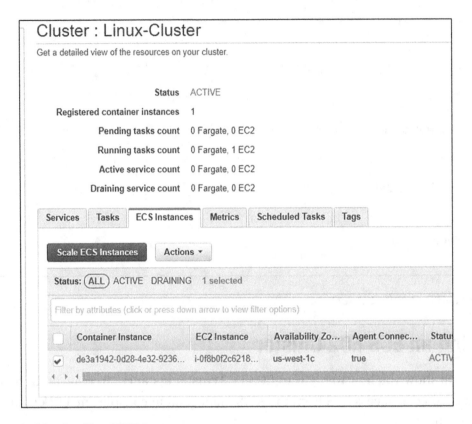

Figure 3-38. Scaling ECS instances

On the "Scale ECS instances in a cluster" page, you just need to type the number of instances you want to have and click the Scale button, as shown in Figure 3-39.

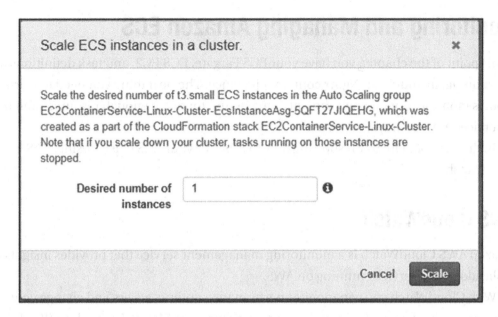

Figure 3-39. *Scaling the ECS instances number*

At the end of the process, I see two EC2 instances available for me, as shown in Figure 3-40.

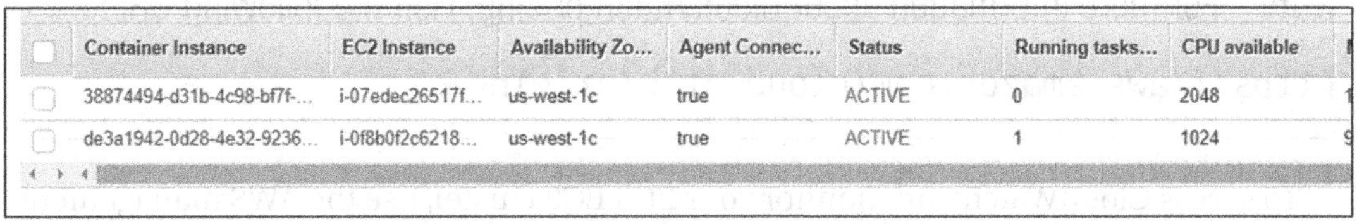

Container Instance	EC2 Instance	Availability Zo...	Agent Connec...	Status	Running tasks...	CPU available	
38874494-d31b-4c98-bf7f-...	i-07edec26517f...	us-west-1c	true	ACTIVE	0	2048	
de3a1942-0d28-4e32-9236...	i-0f8b0f2c6218...	us-west-1c	true	ACTIVE	1	1024	

Figure 3-40. *Viewing the running ECS instances*

To scale down, you can follow the same process and type a smaller number of instances.

Note   The scale-up or down process takes a few minutes.

Monitoring and Managing Amazon ECS

At this point of the chapter, you have your ECS Fargate, ECS EC2, and task definitions up and running, including an Nginx container instance. The next thing you need to learn about is monitoring your environment to make sure there are enough resources and that all services are running as expected.

In this section, I focus on showing how to monitor your ECS cluster using AWS CloudWatch.

AWS CloudWatch

Amazon AWS CloudWatch is a monitoring management service that provides insights to applications and services running on AWS.

With CloudWatch you can monitor performance uptime, access and change your environment, and make decisions based on insights from CloudWatch. CloudWatch offers a Free Tier plan to get started, with basic monitoring metrics, dashboards, alarms, logs, and event.

Note   For more information about CloudWatch pricing, visit the following URL:

`https://aws.amazon.com/cloudwatch/pricing/`

To access CloudWatch and monitor your ECS EC2 cluster, use the AWS management console and search for *CloudWatch* in the AWS Services search box.

In Figure 3-41 you can see the AWS CloudWatch home page with my main services listed under Services. To view your ECS Cluster EC2 host, you need to click EC2 in the Services section.

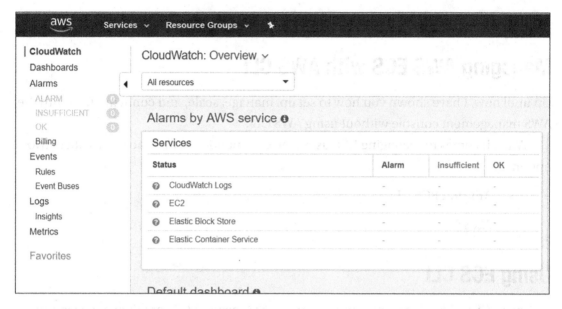

Figure 3-41.   CloudWatch home page

On the CloudWatch EC2 page, I can see the performance of my EC2 host running my EC2 cluster, as shown in Figure 3-42. The EC2 page shows performance metrics under CPU, Disks, Memory, and Networking, giving you full visibility into your EC2 cluster performance.

You can also view historical data using the time range menu at the top-right corner of the page.

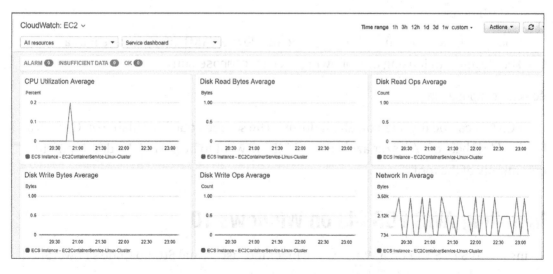

Figure 3-42.   CloudWatch EC2 dashboard view

In Chapter 8, I will talk more about monitoring AWS container services.

Managing AWS ECS with AWS CLI

Up until now, I have shown you how to set up, manage, scale, and configure ECS with the AWS management console without using AWS CLI.

When it comes to managing ECS using the command-line interface, AWS offers two options.

- Amazon ECS CLI
- AWS CLI

Using ECS CLI

Amazon ECS CLI is a command-line interface for Amazon ECS container services and supports Docker Compose files.

Docker Compose allows you to define and configure your deployment using a YAML file that specifies all the services that belong to the applications like the following:

- Front-end services
- Volumes
- Network ports
- Images

Once you have all the details configured inside the YAML file, you save it as a DockerFile and run it using the following `docker-compose` command:

```
docker-compose up
```

ECS CLI can be installed on all platforms. The source code is available on GitHub at `https://github.com/aws/amazon-ecs-cli` if you want to be part of the development community of the tool.

Installing AWS ECS CLI on Windows 10

To install AWS ECS CLI on a Windows 10 machine, use Visual Studio Code's PowerShell terminal and start VS as an administrator.

From VS Code's PowerShell terminal, you need the two commands in the following code and shown in Figure 3-43:

```
New-Item 'C:\Program Files\Amazon\ECSCLI' -type directory
Invoke-WebRequest -OutFile 'C:\Program Files\Amazon\ECSCLI\ecs-cli.exe'
https://s3.amazonaws.com/amazon-ecs-cli/ecs-cli-windows-amd64-latest.exe
```

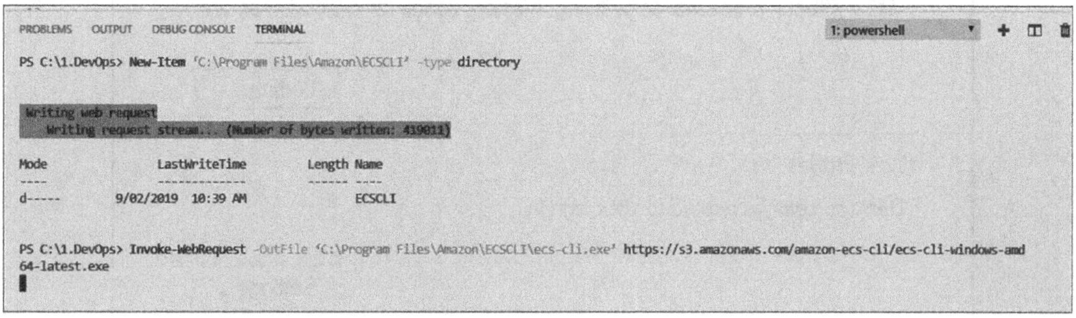

Figure 3-43. *Installing AWS ECS CLI*

The first line of the code creates a directory called ECSCLI under c:\program files, and the second line downloads the ECS CLI command-line tool from Amazon and installs it on the computer.

Now, let's add a permanent path to the ECS CLI tool by opening Windows Control Panel ➤ System. Click Change Settings next to "Computer name, domain, ..." and click the Advanced tab in the System Properties page, as shown in Figure 3-44.

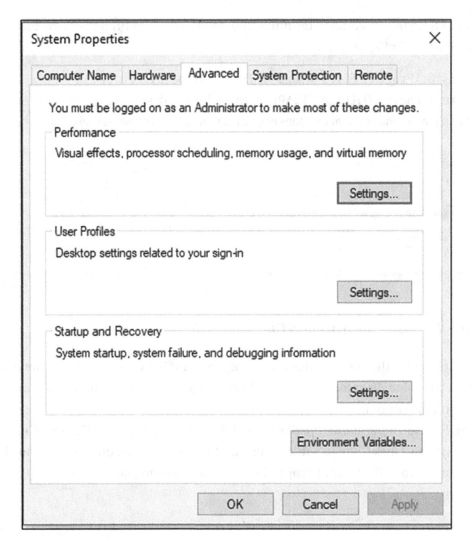

Figure 3-44. *System Properties page (Windows 10)*

On the System Properties page, select the path variable and click Edit, as shown in Figure 3-45.

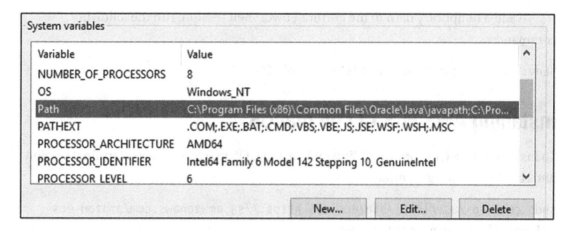

Figure 3-45. *System variables view*

Click New and type the path **C:\Program Files\Amazon\ECSCLI** to the ECS CLI tool, as shown in Figure 3-46.

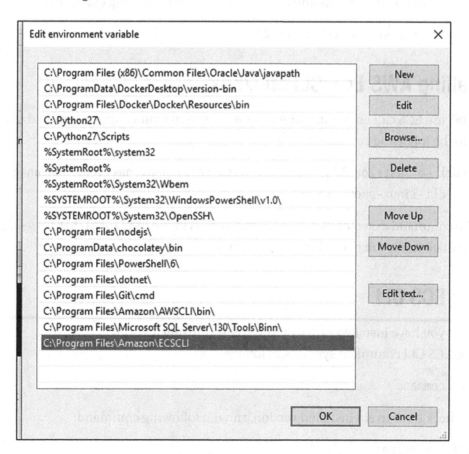

Figure 3-46. *Editing the environment variable*

To add a temporary path to the current PowerShell session, run the following command:

```
$Env:Path += ";C:\Program Files\Amazon\ECSCLI"
```

Installing AWS ECS CLI on macOS

To install the ECS CLI command-line tool on a macOS machine, open a terminal session and run the following command:

```
sudo curl -o /usr/local/bin/ecs-cli https://s3.amazonaws.com/amazon-ecs-cli/ecs-cli-darwin-amd64-latest
```

The command downloads AWS ECS and installs in the `usr/local/bin/ecs-cli` folder.

To apply to execute permissions to ECS CLI, run the following command:

```
sudo chmod +x /usr/local/bin/ecs-cli
```

Installing AWS ECS CLI on Linux

To install the ECS CLI command-line tool on a Linux machine, open a terminal session and run the following command:

```
sudo curl -o /usr/local/bin/ecs-cli https://s3.amazonaws.com/amazon-ecs-cli/ecs-cli-linux-amd64-latest
```

The command downloads AWS ECS and installs in the `usr/local/bin/ecs-cli` folder, which is like the macOS installation path.

Using ECS CLI

Now that you have installed ECS CLI, you can start using it.

The ECS CLI command syntax is as follows:

```
ecs-cli command
```

To check the current installed version, run the following command:

```
ecs-cli --version
```

Before you can start using ECS CLI, you need to configure it using the `ecs-cli` `configure` command, which will take your access key and secret key. (The access and secret key details can be found in the AWS CLI configuration steps in Chapter 1.)

To configure ECS CLI, you use the following command with your access and secret key:

```
ecs-cli configure profile --profile-name profile_name --access-key $AWS_
ACCESS_KEY_ID --secret-key $AWS_SECRET_ACCESS_KEY
```

My example looks like the following code:

```
ecs-cli configure profile --profile-name Shimon-ECS-Profile --access-key
Keydetails --secret-key Secretkey
```

The next line tells ECS CLI which launch type you are using in ECS:

```
ecs-cli configure --cluster cluster_name --default-launch-type launch_type
--region region_name --config-name configuration_name
```

In my example, the command looks like this:

```
ecs-cli configure --cluster default --default-launch-type FARGATE --region
us-west-1 --config-name Shimon-ECS
```

Now that the ECS CLI command tool is ready, you can run all the commands available in the ECS CLI. To view all the available commands, run the following command:

```
ecs-cli --help
```

To set up an ECS Fargate cluster, use the following ECS command:

```
ecs-cli up --launch-type FARGATE
```

As you can see in Figure 3-47, ECS CLI creates the cluster with two subnets for accessing the WAS portal.

```
PS C:\1.DevOps> ecs-cli up --launch-type FARGATE
?[36mINFO?[0m[0004] Created cluster                        ?[36mcluster?[0m=default ?[36mregion?[0m=us-west-1
?[36mINFO?[0m[0006] Waiting for your cluster resources to be created...
?[36mINFO?[0m[0007] Cloudformation stack status            ?[36mstackStatus?[0m=CREATE_IN_PROGRESS
VPC created: vpc-0f0569a0485f3d40a
Subnet created: subnet-0ed7306bfba83f6b5
Subnet created: subnet-08e7377d6d4584423
Cluster creation succeeded.
```

Figure 3-47. *Creating an ECS cluster using ECS CLI*

To view all the running containers on an ECS Fargate cluster, run the following command. As shown in Figure 3-48, I have one container running on the cluster.

```
ecs-cli ps
```

```
PS C:\1.DevOps> ecs-cli ps
Name                                        State    Ports  TaskDefinition        Health
b56ae1b2-dcc1-4a08-b504-2d7a7f48f7ac/nginx  RUNNING         Nginx-Web-Server:1    UNKNOWN
PS C:\1.DevOps>
```

Figure 3-48. Viewing running containers using CES CLI

Using AWS CLI

You can also manage AWS ACS using AWS CLI without needing to install extra tools and configuring your local environment.

If you have AWS CLI installed as shown in Chapter 1, you don't need to do anything. The AWS CLI ECS module offers more than 35 commands to manage ECS.

To get started with AWS CLI ECS, open the command line and type the following command to view all the available commands for ECS:

```
aws ecs help
```

Before you can run commands against AWS ECS, you must authenticate to AWS using the following command on Windows 10 PowerShell:

```
Invoke-Expression -Command (aws ecr get-login --no-include-email)
```

If you are on a macOS or Linux machine, use the following command to authenticate:

```
aws ecr get-login --region region --no-include-email
```

In the following command shown in Figure 3-49, I am listing all my ECS clusters using AWS CLI:

```
aws ecs list-clusters
```

```
PS C:\1.DevOps> aws ecs list-clusters
{
    "clusterArns": [
        "arn:aws:ecs:us-west-1:852051225911:cluster/default",
        "arn:aws:ecs:us-west-1:852051225911:cluster/Linux-Cluster"
    ]
}
```

Figure 3-49. *Listing ECS clusters using ECS CLI*

Running Windows Containers on an AWS ECS Cluster

Up until now I have shown you how to run ECS Fargate and ECS CE2 clusters for Linux only and not for Windows containers. The reason I did that is because running Windows containers on AWS is not as straightforward as running Linux containers.

To run Windows containers on AWS, you must first understand how to run ECS Fargate and EC2 first for Linux and understand the difference between the services. Running Windows containers is possible only with ECS EC2 and requires manual and separate configuration of the EC2 instance before running the first container.

In this section, I will also use a JSON file to create my task definition for Windows containers.

To get started, create an empty AWS ECS cluster using AWS CLI, as shown in the following code and in Figure 3-50:

```
aws ecs create-cluster --cluster-name windows
```

```
PS C:\1.DevOps> aws ecs create-cluster --cluster-name windows
{
    "cluster": {
        "clusterArn": "arn:aws:ecs:us-west-1:852051225911:cluster/windows",
        "clusterName": "windows",
        "status": "ACTIVE",
        "registeredContainerInstancesCount": 0,
        "runningTasksCount": 0,
        "pendingTasksCount": 0,
        "activeServicesCount": 0,
        "statistics": [],
        "tags": []
    }
}
```

Figure 3-50. *Creating an ECS Windows cluster using AWS ECS CLI*

Once the cluster has been created, create a Windows container host and join it to the cluster. In EC2 for Linux containers, the entire process is automated and requires zero configuration.

To create an EC2 container host, open the AWS management console and create an EC2 instance using the following image, as shown in Figure 3-51:

```
2016-English-Full-ECS_Optimized-2018.10.23
```

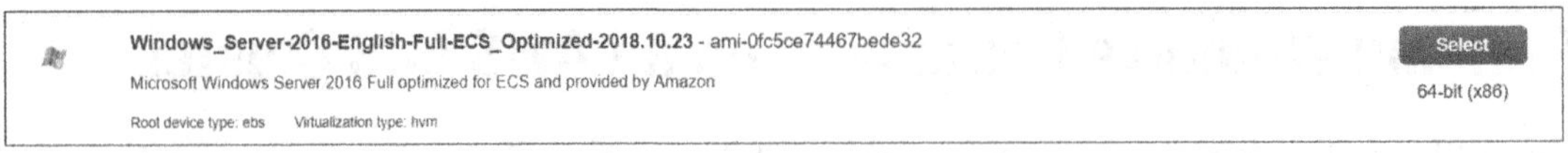

Figure 3-51. *Selecting the Windows Server AMI*

Once you've selected it, you need to use the settings shown in Figure 3-52; enable Auto-assign Public IP, set the IAM role to **ecsInstance**, and click Next to configure the Advanced Details section.

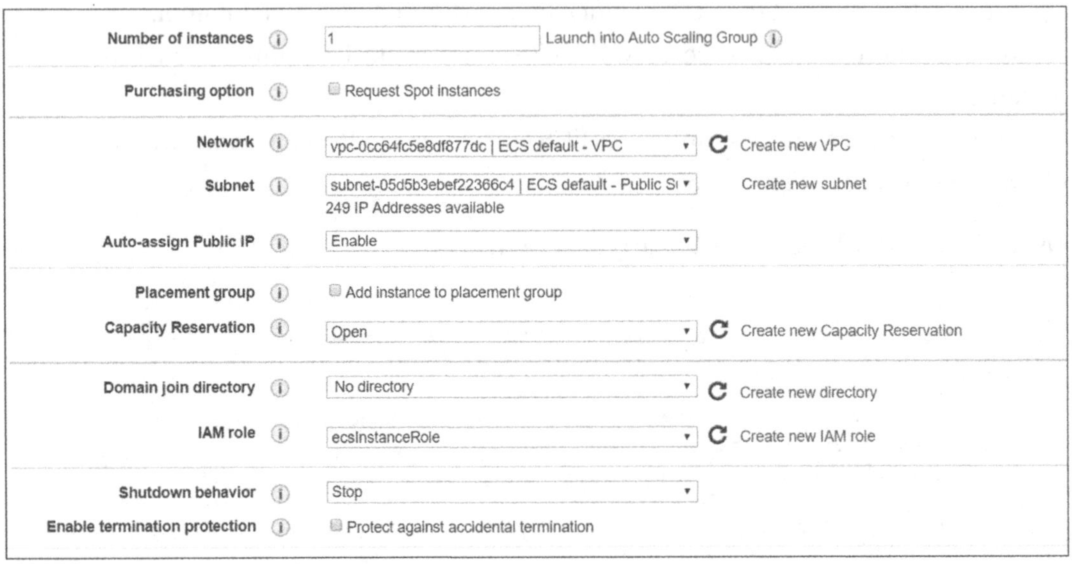

Figure 3-52. *Configuring the EC2 instance*

In the advanced section, copy the following code, as shown in Figure 3-53:

```
<powershell>
Import-Module ECSTools
Initialize-ECSAgent -Cluster 'windows' -EnableTaskIAMRole
</powershell>
```

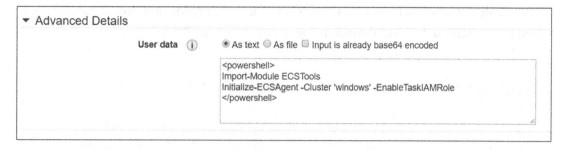

Figure 3-53. *EC2 Advanced Details page*

Click Next: Add Storage to change the default storage volume and click Review and Launch, as shown in Figure 3-54.

Volume Type ⓘ	Device ⓘ	Snapshot ⓘ	Size (GiB) ⓘ	Volume Type ⓘ	IOPS ⓘ	Throughput (MB/s) ⓘ	D
Root	/dev/sda1	snap-064c6931d1be21e67	50	General Purpose SSD (gp2) ▼	150 / 3000	N/A	☑
Add New Volume							

Figure 3-54. *Adding storage to an EC2 instance*

On the review page, go to the Configure Security Group section and click "Create a new security group."

Security groups in AWS are like a virtual firewall that control which protocols and networks are allowed to access EC2 instances. You can assign multiple EC2 instances to one security group, and in this example I am allowing ports 80, 8080, and 443 to access the instance from the Internet.

From the port Range column, I add the ports 80, 8080, and 443, as shown in Figure 3-55.

Step 6: Configure Security Group

A security group is a set of firewall rules that control the traffic for your instance. On this page, you can add rules to allow specific traffic to reach your instance. For example, if you want to set up a web server and allow Internet traffic to reach your instance, add rules that allow unrestricted access to the HTTP and HTTPS ports. You can create a new security group or select from an existing one below. Learn more about Amazon EC2 security groups.

Assign a security group: ⦿Create a **new** security group
　　　　　　　　　　　　　○Select an **existing** security group

Security group name:　launch-wizard-1

Description:　launch-wizard-1 created 2019-02-09T16:33:26.511+11:00

Type ⓘ	Protocol ⓘ	Port Range ⓘ	Source ⓘ		Description ⓘ
RDP ▼	TCP	3389	Anywhere ▼	0.0.0.0/0, ::/0	e.g. SSH for Admin Desktop
Custom TCP f ▼	TCP	80	Anywhere ▼	0.0.0.0/0, ::/0	e.g. SSH for Admin Desktop
Custom TCP f ▼	TCP	443	Anywhere ▼	0.0.0.0/0, ::/0	e.g. SSH for Admin Desktop
Custom TCP f ▼	TCP	8080	Anywhere ▼	0.0.0.0/0, ::/0	e.g. SSH for Admin Desktop
Add Rule					

Figure 3-55. *Configuring the security group*

To finish the process, I create a new key pair for the machine and download it in case I need to use RDP to the virtual machine, as shown in Figure 3-56.

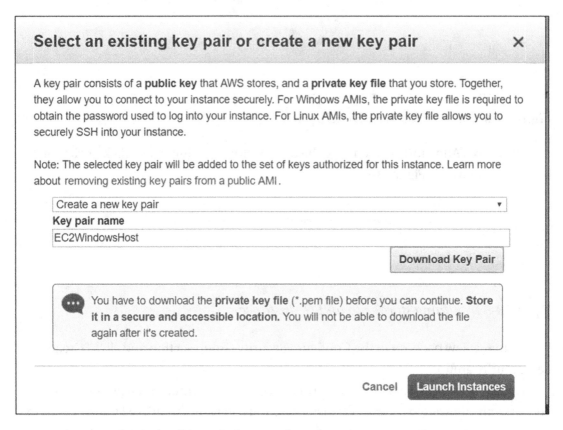

Figure 3-56. *Selecting a key pair for Windows hosts*

To run Windows containers, I need to create an EC2 task definition, as shown in Figure 3-57.

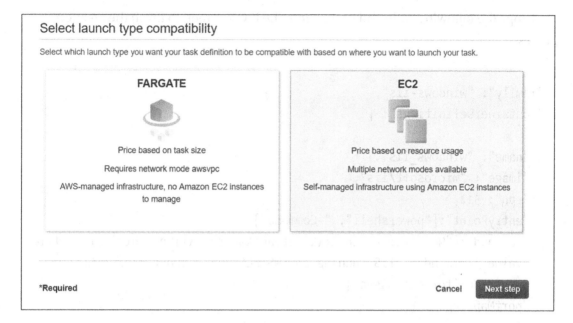

Figure 3-57. Selecting the ECS launch type

On the Task Definition page, I scroll down to the end of the page and click Configure via JSON, as shown in Figure 3-58.

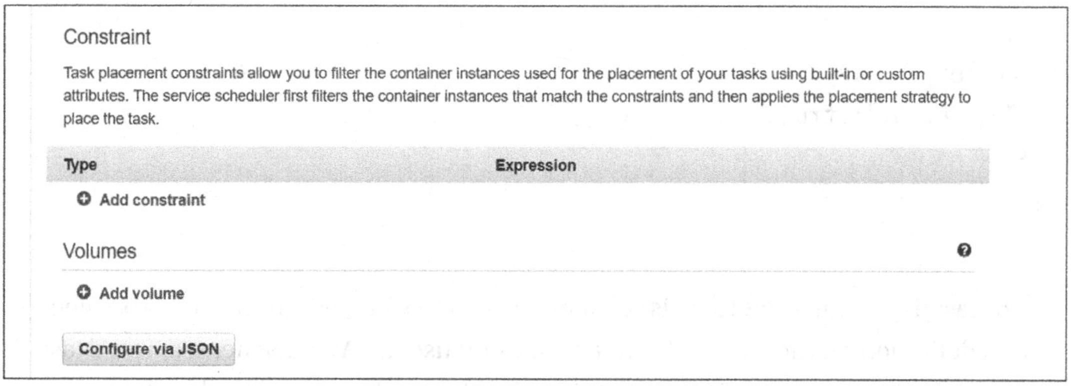

Figure 3-58. Configuring via JSON

I copy the following code and paste it into the JSON screen to finish the creation process:

```json
{
  "family": "windows-iis",
  "containerDefinitions": [
   {
    "name": "windows_iis",
    "image": "microsoft/iis",
    "cpu": 512,
    "entryPoint":["powershell", "-Command"],
    "command":["New-Item -Path C:\\inetpub\\wwwroot\\index.html -Type file
    -Value '<p>Windows IIS running on AWS ECS EC2</strong></p>'; C:\\
    ServiceMonitor.exe w3svc"],
    "portMappings": [
     {
      "protocol": "tcp",
      "containerPort": 80,
      "hostPort": 8080
     }
    ],
    "memory": 512,
    "essential": true
   }
  ]
}
```

The last thing that is left to do is run a task from the task definition. To do so, select the task definition on the Task Definitions page and use the Actions menu to run a task.

On the Task page, shown in Figure 3-59, select EC2, select "windows" as the cluster, and click Run.

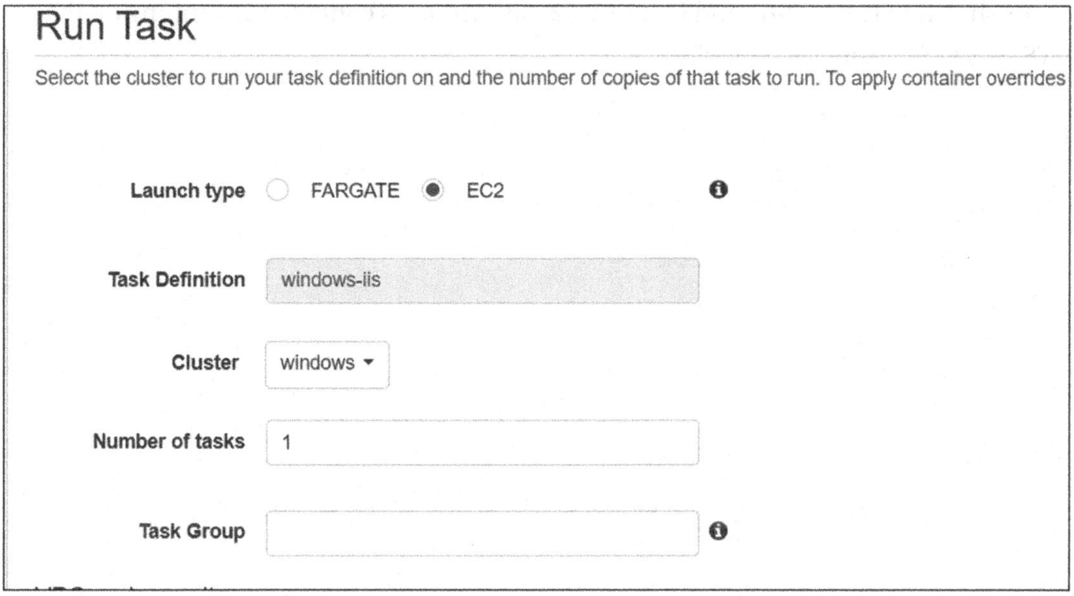

Figure 3-59. *Running a task*

On the Tasks tab, select the task and expand the Containers detail page to find the external IP address and test that the Windows container is running, as shown in Figure 3-60.

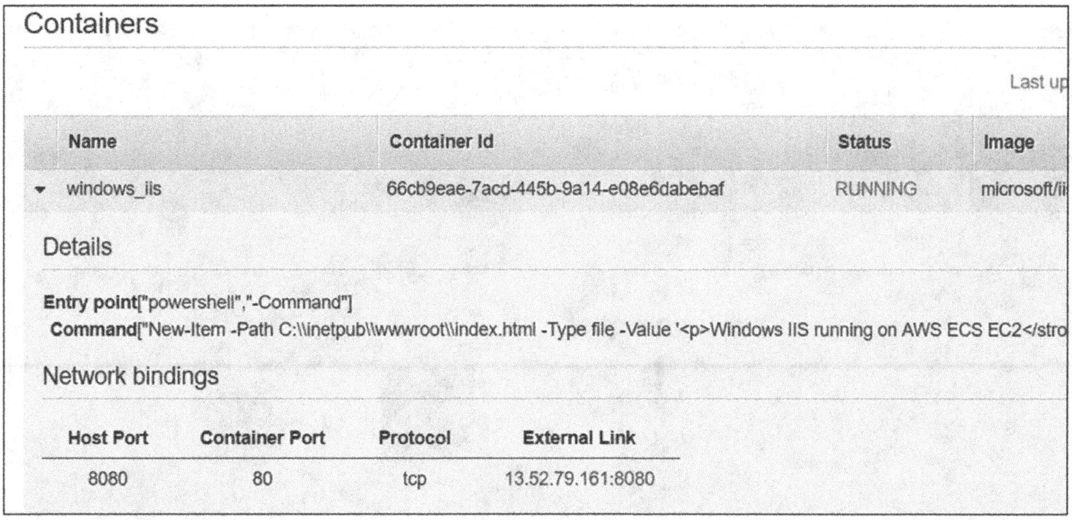

Figure 3-60. *External link (IP)*

As shown in Figure 3-61 and Figure 3-62, my Windows container is running on the AWS ECS EC2 cluster successfully.

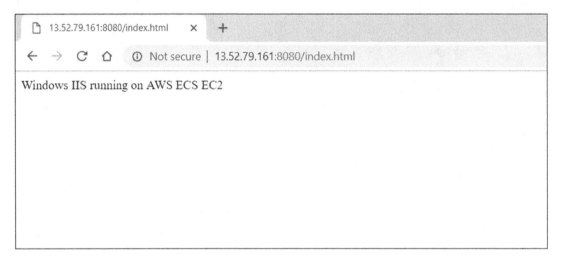

Figure 3-61. *IIS server page*

In Figure 3-62, you can see the Windows IIS Server home page when I use the default external address.

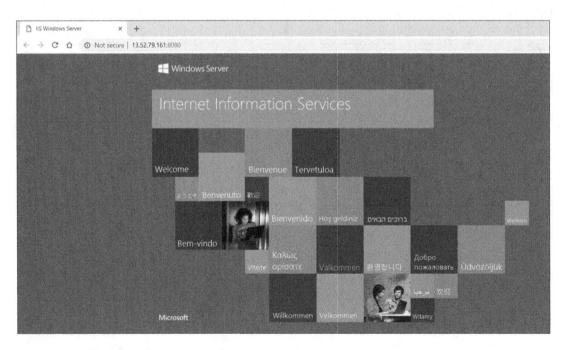

Figure 3-62. *IIS welcome page*

Summary

In this chapter, you learned how to deploy AWS ECS clusters for Linux and Windows deployments using ECS Fargate and ECS EC2. I covered support services such as CloudWatch and autoscaling that allow you to monitor and scale your deployments. In the last section, you deployed a Windows container running IIS web server and made it available over the Internet using port 8080.

CHAPTER 4

Deploy a Containerized Application with Amazon EKS

In Chapter 3, I covered AWS ECS and ECS Fargate and showed how to deploy both Linux and Windows containers.

In this chapter, I will introduce you to Amazon Elastic Container Service for Kubernetes (EKS) and cover the following topics:

- Kubernetes architecture overview

- How to set up and configure EKS tools on Windows, macOS, and Linux

- How to configure EKS networking (virtual private clouds and security groups) on AWS

- How to create an EKS cluster

- How to deploy the Kubernetes web UI (called the Dashboard)

- How to manage EKS on AWS

Kubernetes is an open source container orchestration system for automating containerized application deployment, scaling, and management.

EKS gives you the flexibility to run Kubernetes in AWS without needing to manage all the underlying infrastructure. The main difference between EKS and ECS is that EKS is highly scalable and provides more control over the deployment process of containers.

© Shimon Ifrah 2019
S. Ifrah, *Deploy Containers on AWS*, https://doi.org/10.1007/978-1-4842-5101-0_4

Getting Started with Amazon EKS

In Chapter 3 you learned about AWS ECS Fargate and ECS EC2 clusters and how to deploy containerized applications to a service, including Windows containers.

EKS is a cloud service managed by Amazon that allows you to use Kubernetes in AWS without needing to set up, maintain, and configure the Kubernetes infrastructure and the Kubernetes control plane.

Amazon AWS manages the Kubernetes control plane across multiple data centers, regions, and availability zones, giving you the best high availability configuration out of the box.

If you have an issue with EKS, AWS will automatically replace the unhealthy control plane servers and update them to the latest version. By default, many AWS services are integrated into EKS and don't need any extra configuration to work.

The following services work out of the box with EKS without extra configuration:

- Amazon ECR

- Load balancing

- IAM authentication

- VPC isolation

It is important to know that EKS runs the same version of Kubernetes on an on-premises deployment as on a Docker client with Kubernetes enabled.

In Figure 4-1, you can see what is under AWS control and what is under the tenant's control. AWS controls the master nodes and all the underlying infrastructure that supports them.

The AWS tenant, which in this case is you, can add worker nodes to the tenant and scale the EKS cluster. You can also control the version of the node, with limited control over the installed version. As the deployment grows, you can add or remove nodes from your EKS cluster without worrying about the master.

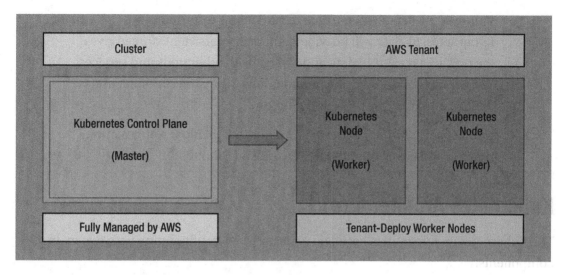

Figure 4-1. *AWS EKS management domain*

Before moving on to the EKS configuration steps and deployment, I will cover the basic structure of Kubernetes.

Kubernetes Building Blocks

Kubernetes is an open source container orchestration system for automating containerized application deployment, scaling, and management. It was designed by Google and is currently maintained by the Cloud Native Computing Foundation. In 2019, most deployments of Kubernetes are done in the cloud with cloud services like Amazon EKS and Azure AKS.

Kubernetes has the following building blocks:

- **Pods**: A *pod* is a logical group of containerized components that consist of one or more containers.

- **Services**: A *service* is a group of pods that work together to create a multitier application made of front-end and back-end components.

- **Volumes**: By default, every time a container is restarted in Kubernetes, its data will be wiped out. Using persistent storage gives the pod access to store data and share it with other pods and services. *Volumes* are mounted using mount points inside the container and defined as part of the pod configuration.

- **Namespaces**: *Namespaces* are partitions that divide resources into projects and environments such as test and production.

Kubernetes Architecture

The Kubernetes architecture is based on a master-slave configuration with two main components.

- **Kubernetes control plane (master)**: The *master* is the primary controlling unit in the cluster. It manages the workload and communication between all the components and processes.

- **Kubernetes node**: The *node* (slave) is the actual server or compute instance that runs and maintains containers (nodes) and other runtime environment components.

A Kubernetes cluster can have one or multiple masters to support a high availability configuration.

Control Panel (Master) Components

Kubernetes clusters have the following elements:

- **etcd**: This is the data store that stores the cluster configuration.

- **API server**: The API server processes all the requests between the worker nodes and the master using REST requests.

- **Scheduler**: The scheduler decides how to deploy new pods into the cluster based on the resource availability of each node.

- **Controller manager**: This load balances all pods across the cluster and makes sure the replication and scaling of nodes across the workers are even.

Worker Node (Slave) Components

The Kubernetes worker node is the server that Docker runs on, and it is responsible for running containers.

- **Kubelet**: The Kubelet process is responsible for the running state of each worker node, making sure all containers running on the host are healthy.

- **Kube-proxy**: This is the load balancer and network proxy component that runs the networking operation on the node and routes IP traffic to containers.

- **Container runtime**: This is the actual Docker container unit that resides inside a pod.

Other

Kubernetes also runs the following add-ons:

- **DNS**: This is the DNS server that serves DNS records to services and containers running in the cluster.

- **Web UI**: This is the GUI interface also known as Dashboard that allows you to manage and troubleshoot applications running on Kubernetes.

Setting Up AKS

Before you start configuring and deploying an AKS cluster, you need to do the following:

1. Install kubectl for AWS AKS.

2. Install aws-iam-authenticator for Amazon EKS.

3. Create an IAM role.

4. Create a virtual private cloud (VPC) and a security group.

Installing kubectl on Windows

kubectl is a command-line tool for running commands against Kubernetes clusters, nodes, and pods. In essence, it is the CLI management tool for Kubernetes.

To install the kubectl command-line tool on a Windows 10 machine, you can use the following curl command:

```
curl -o kubectl.exe https://amazon-eks.s3-us-west-2.amazonaws.
com/1.11.5/2018-12-06/bin/windows/amd64/kubectl.exe
```

As shown in Figure 4-2, the command downloads the tool to the location you ran the command from.

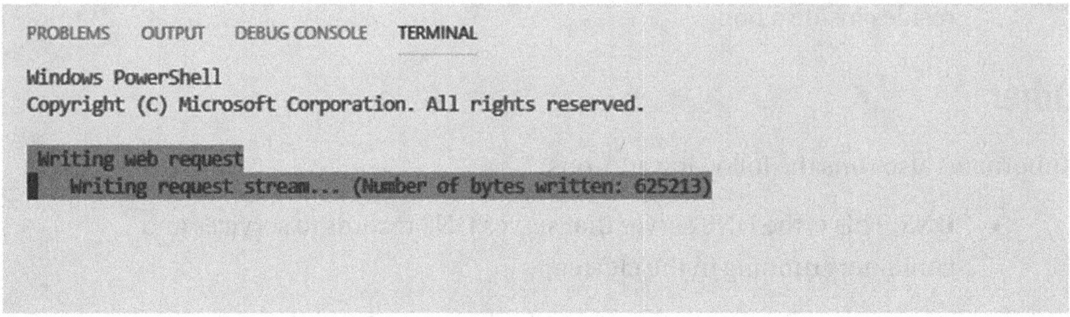

Figure 4-2.   Downloading kubectl.exe

Once the tool is downloaded, you can create a new directory called Bin on the C:\ drive and move the downloaded file to the directory using the following PowerShell cmdlets. (You can also use the GUI interface to create and move the file.)

```
New-Item Bin -Type Directory
cp C:\1.DevOps\kubectl.exe c:\bin
```

Next, you need to add the folder to the Windows 10 command path so you can run kubectl commands from any location using PowerShell or cmd.

To add it to the command path, type the following command in the Windows Start menu to open the advanced system properties, as shown in Figure 4-3:

```
sysdm.cpl
```

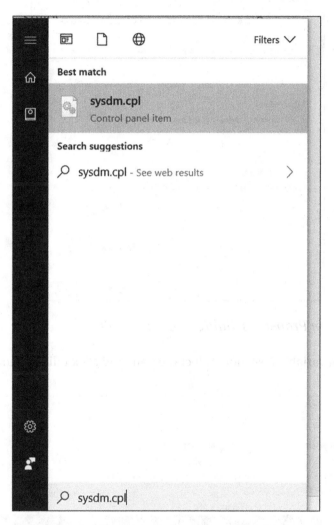

Figure 4-3. *Starting Windows 10 advanced system properties*

On the Advanced tab, click Environment Variables, as shown in Figure 4-4.

Figure 4-4. *System Properties dialog, Advanced tab*

In the "System variables" section, select the path and click Edit, as shown in Figure 4-5.

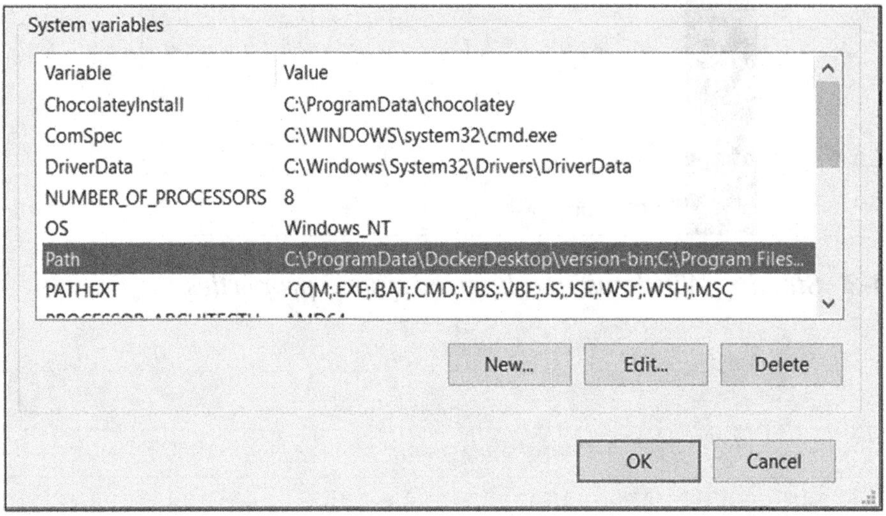

Figure 4-5. *System variables*

In the "Edit environment variable" dialog, click New and type **C:\bin** in the list of paths, as shown in Figure 4-6.

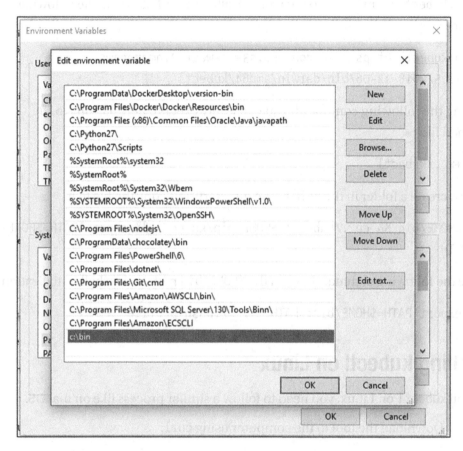

Figure 4-6. *Editing the environment variable*

To test that the installation and the path are working, open a new PowerShell screen from VS Code and type the following command, as shown in Figure 4-7:

```
kubectl version --short --client
```

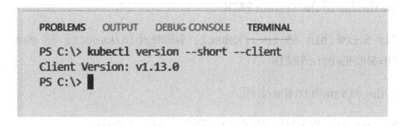

Figure 4-7. *Checking the kubectl version*

Installing kubectl on Mac

To install kubectl on macOS, first download kubectl for Mac using the following command:

```
curl -o kubectl https://amazon-eks.s3-us-west-2.amazonaws.
com/1.11.5/2018-12-06/bin/darwin/amd64/kubectl
```

Using the following command, you can apply execute permissions to the download file:

```
chmod +x ./kubectl
```

Next, create a folder in the PATH home directory and copy the file to it.

```
mkdir $HOME/bin && cp ./kubectl $HOME/bin/kubectl && export PATH=$HOME/
bin:$PATH
```

Use the following command to add the $HOME/bin path to the shell initialization file:

```
echo 'export PATH=$HOME/bin:$PATH' >> ~/.bash_profile
```

Installing kubectl on Linux

To install kubectl on Linux, you need to follow a similar process like on macOS.

1. Download the tool to the computer using curl.

   ```
   curl -o kubectl https://amazon-eks.s3-us-west-2.amazonaws.
   com/1.11.5/2018-12-06/bin/linux/amd64/kubectl
   ```

2. Apply execute permissions to the binary.

   ```
   chmod +x ./kubectl
   ```

3. Copy the file to the system PATH.

   ```
   mkdir $HOME/bin && cp ./kubectl $HOME/bin/kubectl && export
   PATH=$HOME/bin:$PATH
   ```

4. Add the BIN path to the shell.

   ```
   echo 'export PATH=$HOME/bin:$PATH' >> ~/.bashrc
   ```

Installing AWS IAM Authenticator for Kubernetes

The next tool you need to install is the AWS IAM Authenticator for Kubernetes, which EKS uses to authenticate access to the cluster. The tool is available on all platforms and works with the kubectl command-line tool by modifying the configuration file.

Installing AWS IAM Authenticator on Linux

To install the AWS IAM Authenticator on a Linux machine, you start with downloading the tool using the following command:

```
Curl -o aws-iam-authenticator https://amazon-eks.s3-us-west-2.amazonaws.com/1.11.5/2018-12-06/bin/linux/amd64/aws-iam-authenticator
```

After the download is completed, you add the permissions.

```
chmod +x ./aws-iam-authenticator
```

Finally, add the path to the $Home directory.

```
echo 'export PATH=$HOME/bin:$PATH' >> ~/.bashrc
```

Installing AWS IAM Authenticator on macOS

On macOS, you follow the same process by downloading the tool using the following command:

```
curl -o aws-iam-authenticator https://amazon-eks.s3-us-west-2.amazonaws.com/1.11.5/2018-12-O Add permissions
chmod +x ./aws-iam-authenticator
```

Add permissions, as shown here:

```
chmod +x ./aws-iam-authenticator
```

Add the tool to the $Home directory, as shown here:

```
echo 'export PATH=$HOME/bin:$PATH' >> ~/.bash_profile
```

Installing AWS IAM Authenticator on Windows

On a Windows machine, you need to create a directory inside `c:\bin` called `aws-iam-authenticator`.

From the command line, access the directory and download the file using the following `curl` command, as shown in Figure 4-8.

```
curl -o aws-iam-authenticator https://amazon-eks.s3-us-west-2.amazonaws.
com/1.11.5/2018-12-06/bin/windows/amd64/aws-iam-authenticator.exe
```

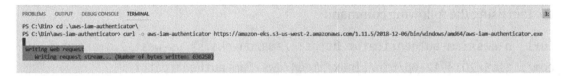

Figure 4-8. *Downloading the IAM Authenticator*

Finally, add the path to the environment variable path list, as shown in Figure 4-9.

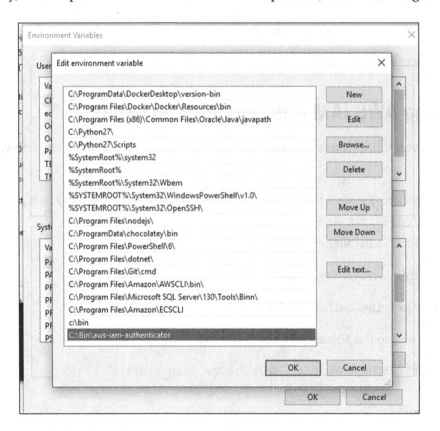

Figure 4-9. *Editing the environment variable*

146

Creating the EKS Service Role

The next step in the process is to create an IAM role that Kubernetes can assume to create AWS resources for EKS. To create an EKS service role, open the AWS management console and search for *IAM* in the services search box.

On the IAM console page, choose Roles and click the "Create role" button in the top-left corner, as shown in Figure 4-10.

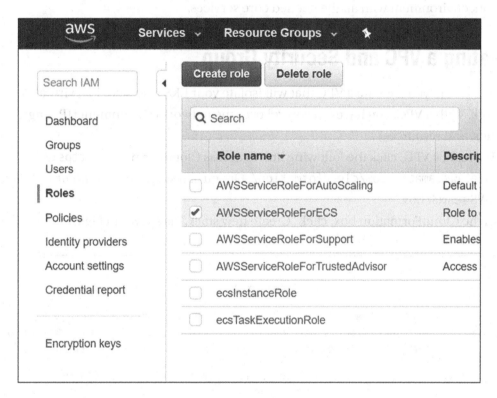

Figure 4-10. *Selecting an IAM role*

From the list of services, select EKS and click Next: Permissions to review the permissions and Next: Tags to add tags to the EKS group.

As the final step, name the EKS role and click the "Create role" button.

Setting Up and Configuring Amazon EKS Networking

Amazon AWS offers a vast array of networking services that outnumber most on-premises networking solutions. When it comes to EKS networking, AWS offers an impressive array of services that allow you to manage, secure, and expose to the Internet multiple containerized applications while maintaining high availability and redundancy.

The base configuration for EKS is a virtual private cloud, which creates a secure network environment with all the needed core services.

Creating a VPC and Security Group

In this section, you'll create a VPC that will isolate your EKS resources in a virtual network. With a VPC, you have full control over the network environment (IP range, subnets, and resources).

To create a VPC, click the following link to access CloudFormation: `https://console.aws.amazon.com/cloudformation/`. Or you can search for *CloudFormation* in the AWS search box.

In the CloudFormation box, click "Create new stack," as shown in Figure 4-11.

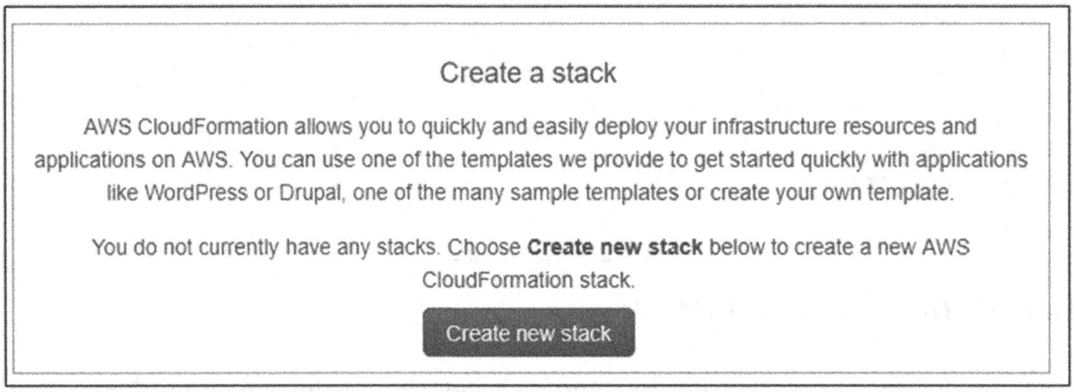

Create a stack

AWS CloudFormation allows you to quickly and easily deploy your infrastructure resources and applications on AWS. You can use one of the templates we provide to get started quickly with applications like WordPress or Drupal, one of the many sample templates or create your own template.

You do not currently have any stacks. Choose **Create new stack** below to create a new AWS CloudFormation stack.

Create new stack

Figure 4-11. *Creating a CloudFormation stack*

Note   EKS is not available in all AWS regions.

On the Select Template page, click "Specify an Amazon S3 template URL," as shown in Figure 4-12, and paste in the following URL. Then click Next.

```
https://amazon-eks.s3-us-west-2.amazonaws.com/cloudformation/2019-01-09/
amazon-eks-vpc-sample.yaml
```

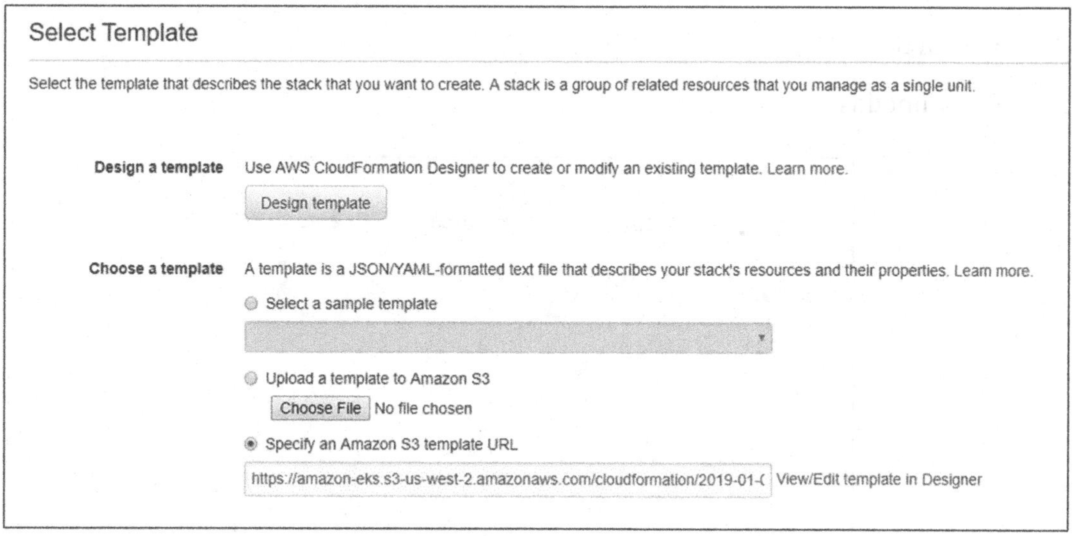

Figure 4-12. *The Select Template page*

On the Specify Details page, name the VPC and click Next, as shown in Figure 4-13.

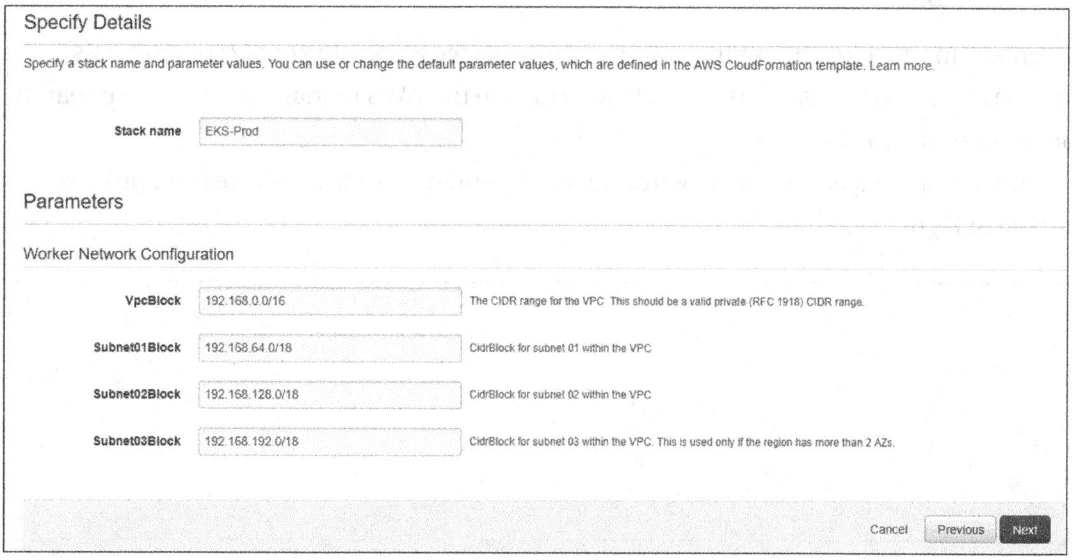

Figure 4-13. *Specifying the CloudFormation stack details*

On the Options page, click Next and Create to complete the process.

The VPC creation process can take a few minutes to complete.

Once the creation process is done, click the Outputs tab and note the values of the following items, as shown in Figure 4-14:

- SecurityGroups

- VpLd

- Subnetlds

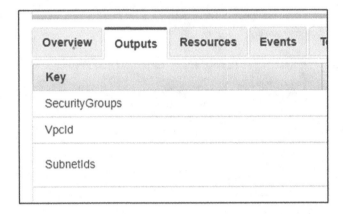

Figure 4-14. *Stack outputs*

Creating an EKS Cluster

To create an EKS cluster, use the following link to access EKS: `https://console.aws.amazon.com/eks/home#/clusters`. Or you can use the AWS management console search box to search for *EKS*.

On the EKS page, use the "Create cluster" button to start the EKS creation process, as shown in Figure 4-15.

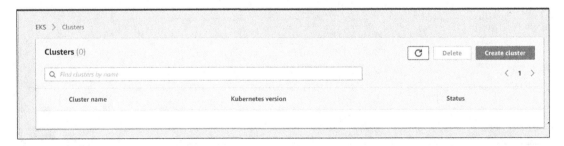

Figure 4-15. *Creating an EKS cluster*

On the "Create cluster" page, fill in the details for the VPC and "Security groups" sections using the values you noted earlier.

As shown in Figure 4-16, I have used the details I noted to complete the process and create my EKS cluster. The creation process can take 10 to 15 minutes to complete.

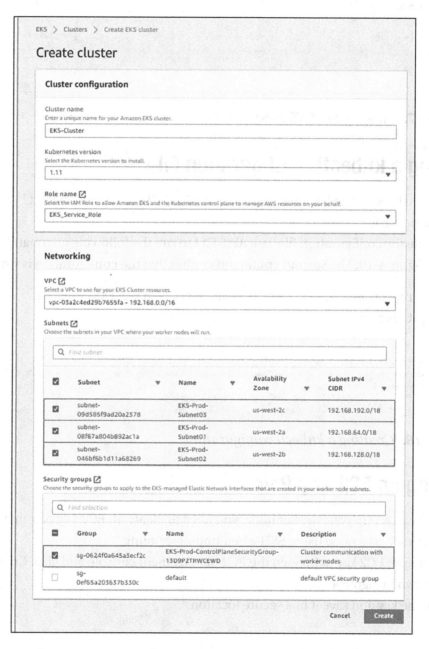

Figure 4-16. *Creating an EKS cluster*

Figure 4-17 shows that my EKS-Cluster is active.

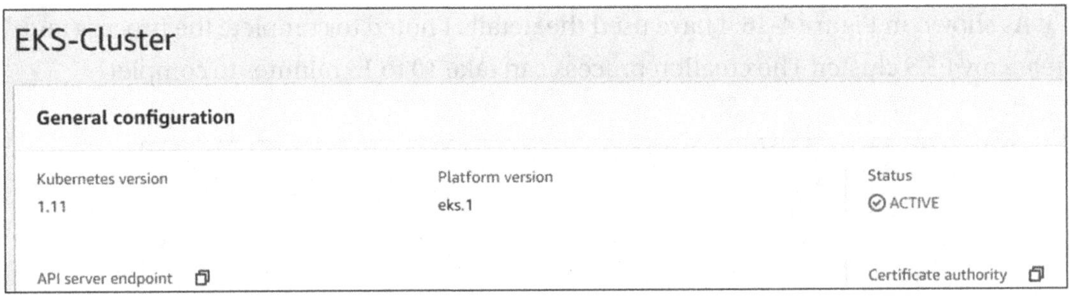

Figure 4-17. *Viewing the EKS cluster status*

Creating a kubectl Configuration File

Now that you have created a cluster, you can use AWS CLI to create a `kubectl` configuration file for Amazon EKS.

To create the configuration file, use AWS CLI to run the following command, as shown in Figure 4-18. The second command verifies that the configuration is working.

```
aws eks --region us-west-2 update-kubeconfig --name EKS-cluster
kubectl get svc
```

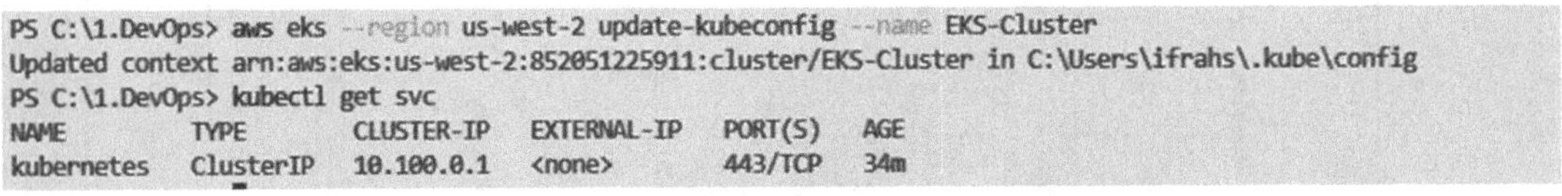

```
PS C:\1.DevOps> aws eks --region us-west-2 update-kubeconfig --name EKS-Cluster
Updated context arn:aws:eks:us-west-2:852051225911:cluster/EKS-Cluster in C:\Users\ifrahs\.kube\config
PS C:\1.DevOps> kubectl get svc
NAME         TYPE        CLUSTER-IP   EXTERNAL-IP   PORT(S)   AGE
kubernetes   ClusterIP   10.100.0.1   <none>        443/TCP   34m
```

Figure 4-18. *Creating a kubectl configuration*

Creating an EC2 Key Pair

Before you can set up your worker node, you need to create an EC2 key pair that will allow you to access a node using SSH when troubleshooting.

To create an EC2 key pair, open the EC2 management console and click Create Key Pair, as shown in Figure 4-19.

Name the key and save it in a secure location.

Figure 4-19. *Creating a key pair*

Creating a Worker Node

Now that the VPC and the cluster control plane have been created, you can configure a worker node.

Note   The Kubernetes worker node is the server that runs Docker and is responsible for running containers.

To create a worker node, open the AWS CloudFormation console using the following URL: `https://console.aws.amazon.com/cloudformation`. Or you can search for CloudFormation in the services search box.

On the CloudFormation page, click Create Stack, as shown in Figure 4-20.

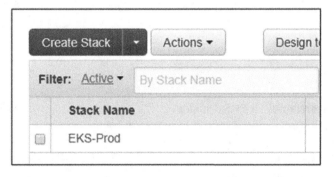

Figure 4-20. *Creating a stack*

On the Select Template page, click "Specify an Amazon S3 template URL" and paste in the following URL. Click the Next button.

```
https://amazon-eks.s3-us-west-2.amazonaws.com/cloudformation/2019-01-09/
amazon-eks-nodegroup.yaml
```

On the Create Stack page, you need to create the cluster and use the same details as in the "Creating an EKS Cluster" section.

For the stack name, you must use the cluster name, a hyphen, and then the node name, as shown in Figure 4-21. For "Stake name," you must enter the cluster name you used in the EKS cluster setup, as shown in Figure 4-21.

In the ClusterControlPlaneSecurityGroup field, select the security group you created in the setup section.

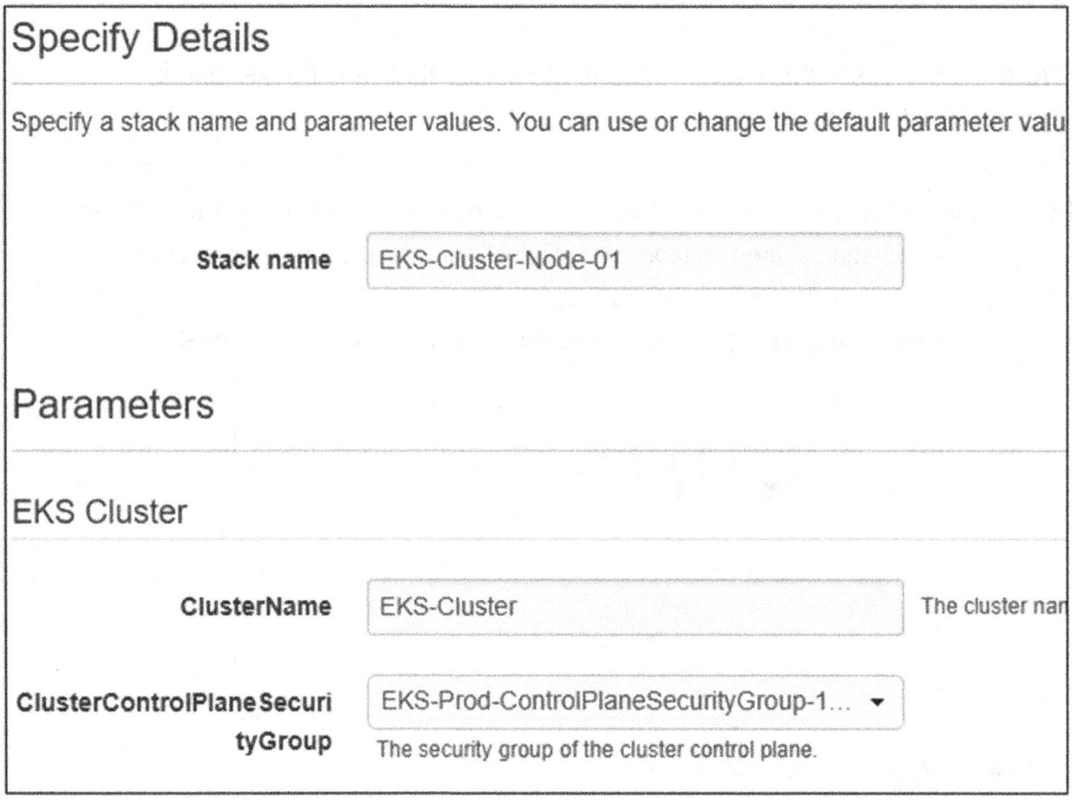

Figure 4-21. *Specifying the details*

On the Worker Node Configuration page, name the NodeGroupName and select an EC2 instance type under NodeInstanceType.

For NodeImageId, I am using the ami-081099ec932b99961 name and selecting the EC2 I created earlier, as shown in Figure 4-22.

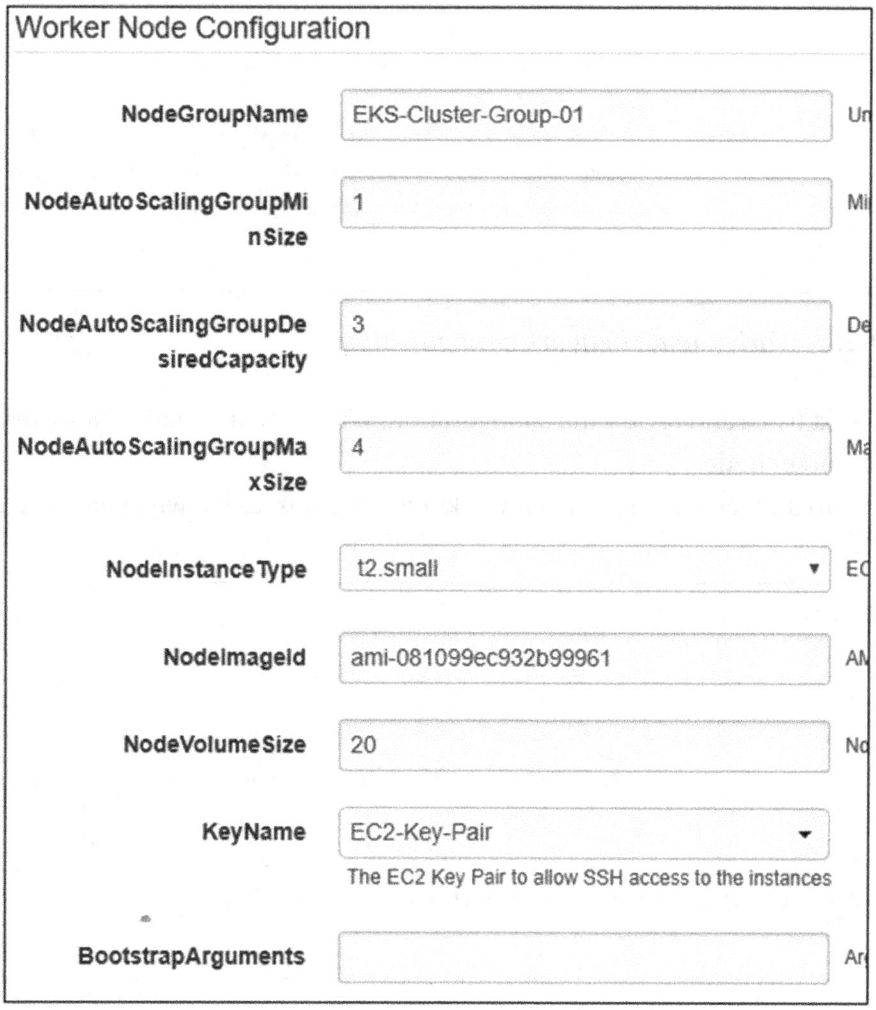

Figure 4-22. *Worker node configuration*

Next, I use the VpcId from the EKS setup section and the subnets I created in the setup section, as shown in Figure 4-23.

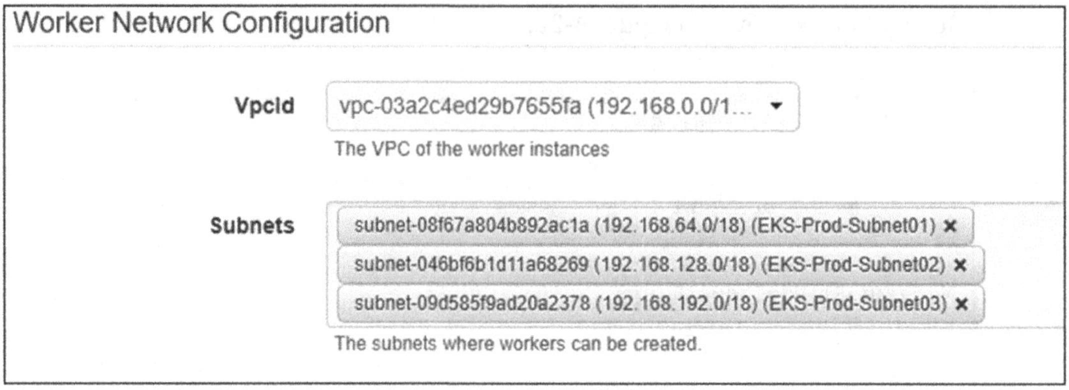

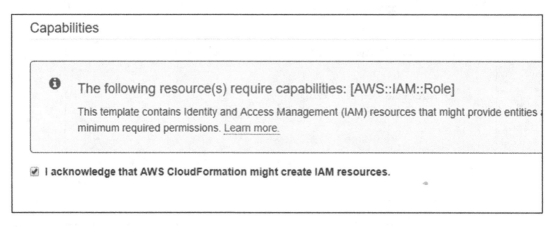

Figure 4-23. *Worker node network configuration*

Click Next twice and review the configuration. When you are ready, click Create to create the worker node.

In the Capabilities section, select the acknowledge box, as shown in Figure 4-24.

Figure 4-24. *Acknowledge check box*

Joining the Worker Node EKS Cluster

On the CloudFormation page, click the node name, as shown in Figure 4-25, and record the NodeInstanceRole value in the Outputs section.

The value looks like this:

```
arn:aws:iam::852051225911:role/EKS-Cluster-Node-02-NodeInstanceRole
-1K2TFC3CWGACT
```

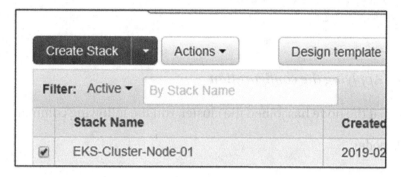

Figure 4-25. *Node details page*

After recording the instance role, you need to download the AWS Authenticator configuration map using the following `curl` command:

```
curl -O https://amazon-eks.s3-us-west-2.amazonaws.com/
cloudformation/2019-01-09/aws-auth-cm.yaml
```

After you download the file, replace the value in the `rolearn` field with the NodeInstanceRole value record in this section, as shown in Figure 4-26.

```
aws-auth-cm.yaml - Notepad
File  Edit  Format  View  Help
apiVersion: v1
kind: ConfigMap
metadata:
  name: aws-auth
  namespace: kube-system
data:
  mapRoles: |
    - rolearn: arn:aws:iam::852051225911:role/EKS-Cluster-Node-02-NodeInstanceRole-1K2TFC3CWGACT
      username: system:node:{{EC2PrivateDNSName}}
      groups:
        - system:bootstrappers
        - system:nodes
```

Figure 4-26. *aw2s-auth-cm.yaml file*

From the command line, run the following command, as shown in Figure 4-27:

```
kubectl apply -f aws-auth-cm.yaml
```

```
PS C:\Bin> kubectl apply -f aws-auth-cm.yaml
configmap/aws-auth created
PS C:\Bin>
```

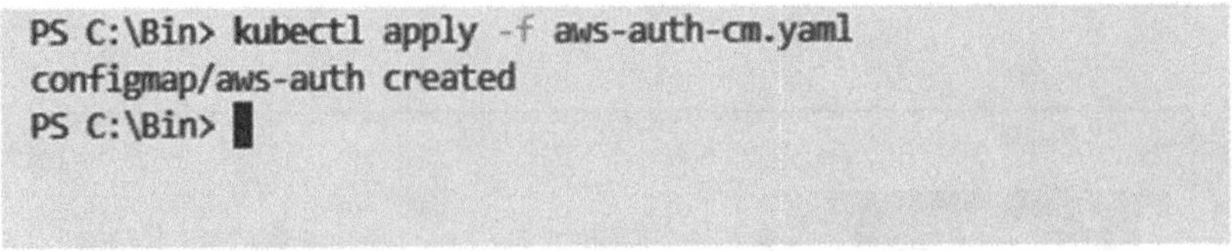

Figure 4-27. *Applying the configuration*

To check that the node has joined the cluster, run the following command:

```
kubectl get nodes
```

Deploying the Application

In the following code, I have an Nginx web server container that is configured using a YAML file. Using the kubectl command line, I am going to deploy it to AKS.

```
apiVersion: apps/v1 # for versions before 1.9.0 use apps/v1beta2
kind: Deployment
metadata:
 name: nginx-deployment
spec:
 selector:
  matchLabels:
   app: nginx
 replicas: 1
 template:
  metadata:
   labels:
    app: nginx
  spec:
   containers:
   - name: nginx
     image: nginx:1.7.9
     ports:
     - containerPort: 80
```

I have saved the file as `deploy.yaml` and run the following command:

```
kubectl apply -f .\deploy.yaml
```

Now, I am going to expose my container to the Internet using the following **expose** command:

```
kubectl expose deployment nginx-deployment --type=LoadBalancer
--name=nginx-web
```

To view the deployment and the external IP and hostname for the container, I run the following command, as shown in Figure 4-28:

```
get services -o wide
```

```
PS C:\Bin> kubectl get services -o wide
NAME        TYPE          CLUSTER-IP      EXTERNAL-IP                                                              PORT(S)       AGE   SELECTOR
kubernetes  ClusterIP     10.100.0.1      <none>                                                                   443/TCP       2d    <none>
nginx-web   LoadBalancer  10.100.195.52   a1635eff134b211e998920226e65592a-509243205.us-west-2.elb.amazonaws.com  80:31115/TCP  1m    app=nginx
PS C:\Bin>
```

Figure 4-28. *Checking the EKS services*

To delete the deployment, I use the following code:

```
kubectl delete deployment nginx-deployment
```

Deploying the Kubernetes Web UI

The Kubernetes web UI (also called the *dashboard*) is a web-based user interface where you can deploy a containerized application to a Kubernetes cluster. The web UI also allows you to troubleshoot containerized applications and manage resources in the cluster using a web interface. Monitoring and creating resources is also possible with web UI because you can run deployments and jobs, scale applications, and delete them.

By default, the web UI is not installed. To install the web UI, from the `kubectl` command line, run the following command, as shown in Figure 4-29:

```
kubectl apply -f https://raw.githubusercontent.com/kubernetes/dashboard/
v1.10.1/src/deploy/recommended/kubernetes-dashboard.yaml
```

```
PS C:\Bin> kubectl apply -f https://raw.githubusercontent.com/kubernetes/dashboard/v1.10.1/src/deploy/recommended/kubernetes-dashboard.yaml
secret/kubernetes-dashboard-certs created
serviceaccount/kubernetes-dashboard created
role.rbac.authorization.k8s.io/kubernetes-dashboard-minimal created
rolebinding.rbac.authorization.k8s.io/kubernetes-dashboard-minimal created
deployment.apps/kubernetes-dashboard created
service/kubernetes-dashboard created
PS C:\Bin> []
```

Figure 4-29. *Installing Dashboard*

The next three commands will install Heapster, a monitoring tool for Kubernetes:

```
kubectl apply -f https://raw.githubusercontent.com/kubernetes/heapster/
master/deploy/kube-config/influxdb/heapster.yaml
```

```
kubectl apply -f https://raw.githubusercontent.com/kubernetes/heapster/
master/deploy/kube-config/influxdb/influxdb.yaml
```

```
kubectl apply -f https://raw.githubusercontent.com/kubernetes/heapster/
master/deploy/kube-config/rbac/heapster-rbac.yaml
```

The following YAML file (shown in Figure 4-30) creates an admin service account that will be used to access the web UI. Save this file as eks-admin-service-account. yaml.

```
apiVersion: v1
kind: ServiceAccount
metadata:
 name: eks-admin
 namespace: kube-system
---
apiVersion: rbac.authorization.k8s.io/v1beta1
kind: ClusterRoleBinding
metadata:
 name: eks-admin
roleRef:
 apiGroup: rbac.authorization.k8s.io
 kind: ClusterRole
 name: cluster-admin
```

```
subjects:
- kind: ServiceAccount
 name: eks-admin
 namespace: kube-system
```

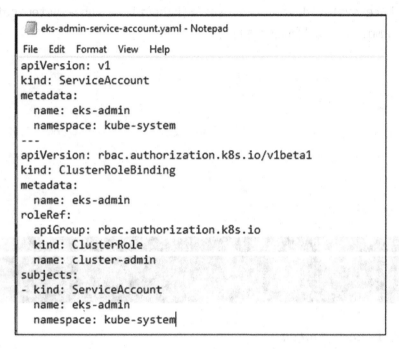

Figure 4-30. *eks-admin-service-account.yaml file*

As shown in Figure 4-31, you can run the following command to create the admin service account:

```
kubectl apply -f eks-admin-service-account.yaml
```

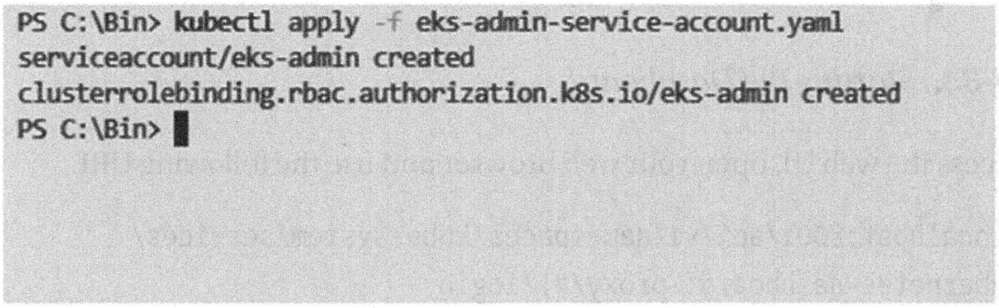

```
PS C:\Bin> kubectl apply -f eks-admin-service-account.yaml
serviceaccount/eks-admin created
clusterrolebinding.rbac.authorization.k8s.io/eks-admin created
PS C:\Bin>
```

Figure 4-31. *Applying the EKS admin account*

After creating the account, you need to copy the token for the service account. The token is used to access the web UI and act as a password.

To find the token, run the following command. The token is called eks-admin-token-X, as shown in Figure 4-32.

```
kubectl -n kube-system describe secret $(kubectl -n kube-system get secret
| grep eks-admin | awk '{print $1}')
```

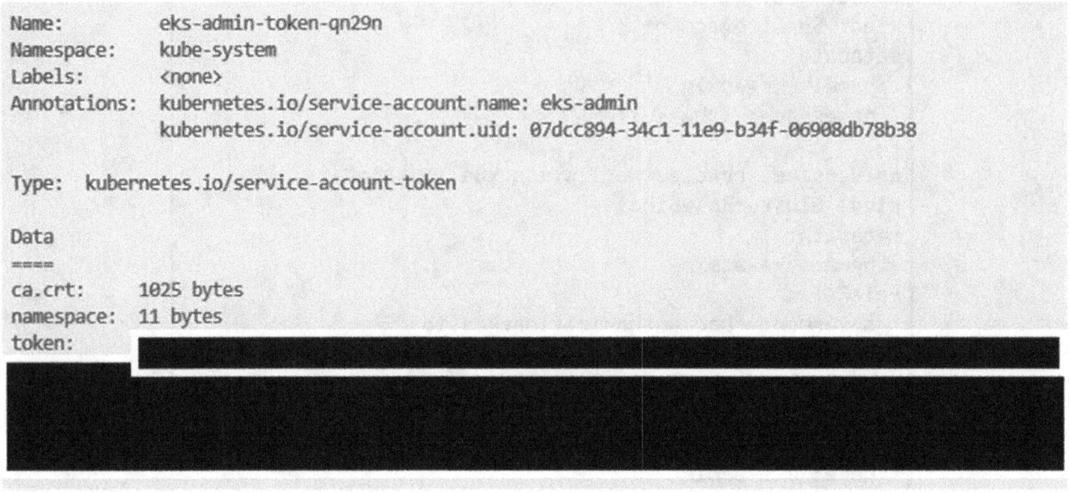

```
Name:           eks-admin-token-qn29n
Namespace:      kube-system
Labels:         <none>
Annotations:    kubernetes.io/service-account.name: eks-admin
                kubernetes.io/service-account.uid: 07dcc894-34c1-11e9-b34f-06908db78b38

Type:   kubernetes.io/service-account-token

Data
====
ca.crt:     1025 bytes
namespace:  11 bytes
token:
```

Figure 4-32. *Finding a token*

To start the web UI, run the following command (as shown in Figure 4-33):

```
kubectl proxy
```

```
PS C:\Bin> kubectl proxy
Starting to serve on 127.0.0.1:8001
```

Figure 4-33. *Starting the Dashboard*

To access the web UI, open your web browser and use the following URL:

```
http://localhost:8001/api/v1/namespaces/kube-system/services/
https:kubernetes-dashboard:/proxy/#!/login
```

In the Kubernetes Dashboard, paste the security token copied from the previous step into the Token field, and click Sign-In, as shown in Figure 4-34.

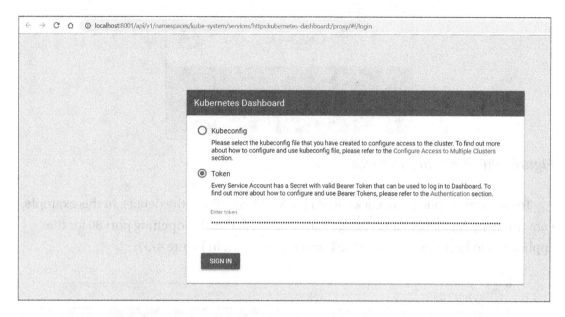

Figure 4-34. *Dashboard sign-in page*

Figure 4-35 shows my web UI. The web UI is easy to use, and it is very informative.

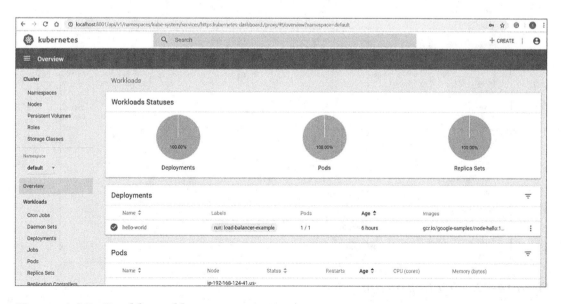

Figure 4-35. *Dashboard home page*

To deploy an application to EKS using the web UI, click the Create button in the top-right corner, as shown in Figure 4-36.

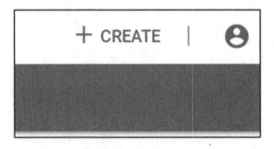

Figure 4-36. *Creating a service*

To create an application, click CREATE AN APP and fill in the details. In this example, I am using my Nginx container image stored on ECR. I'm also opening port 80 for the application to be accessible over the Internet, as shown in Figure 4-37.

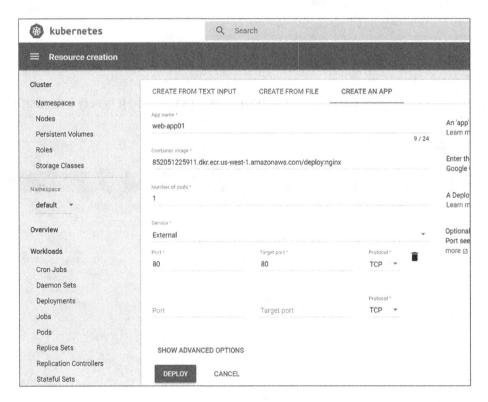

Figure 4-37. *Creating an app page*

To view the application and access it, click the Services menu in the web UI and click the link under "External endpoints," as shown in Figure 4-38.

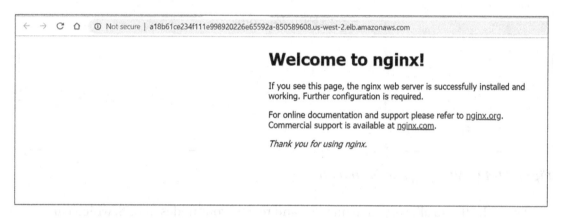

Figure 4-38. *Viewing services*

The result is shown in Figure 4-39.

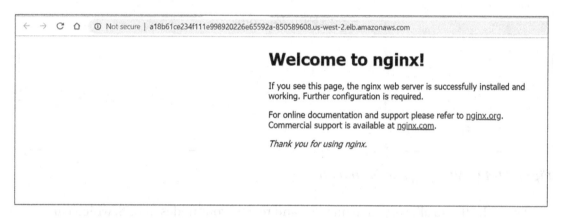

Figure 4-39. *"Welcome to nginx!" page*

Managing and Securing the EKS Cluster

In this section, I will show you how to manage your EKS cluster using the web UI and using the kubectl command-line tool.

The web UI offers great visibility into the EKS cluster and allows you to view all the available namespaces configured on EKS, as shown in Figure 4-40.

Cluster
Namespaces
Nodes
Persistent Volumes
Roles
Storage Classes
Namespace
default
Namespaces
Name
Labels
default
kube-public
kube-system

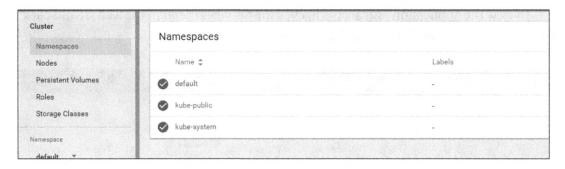

Figure 4-40. *Viewing namespaces*

If you have persistent volumes attached to your EKS cluster, you can manage them from the Persistent Volumes section, as shown in Figure 4-41.

Cluster
Namespaces
Nodes
Persistent Volumes
Roles
Storage Classes
Persistent Volumes

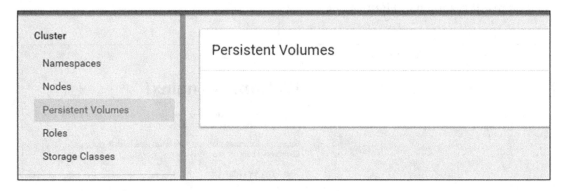

Figure 4-41. *Viewing persistent volumes*

The web UI also allows you to manage and review your nodes in EKS, which can be handy when managing multiple nodes, as shown in Figure 4-42.

In the Nodes section, you can view the resource utilization of each node in terms of CPU, memory, and uptime.

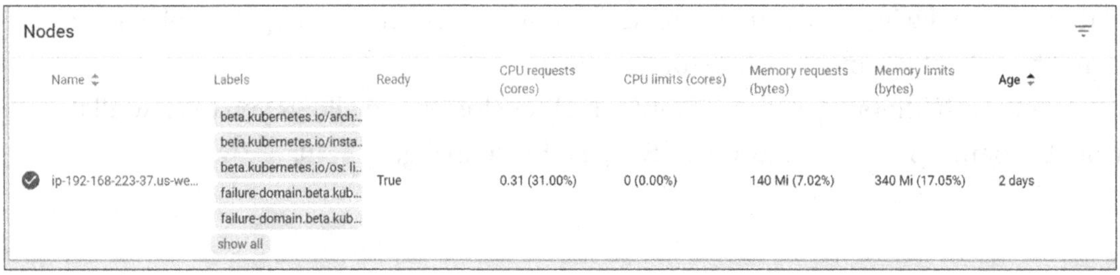

Nodes
Name
Labels
Ready
CPU requests (cores)
CPU limits (cores)
Memory requests (bytes)
Memory limits (bytes)
Age
ip-192-168-223-37.us-we...
beta.kubernetes.io/arch:..
beta.kubernetes.io/insta..
beta.kubernetes.io/os: li..
failure-domain.beta.kub...
failure-domain.beta.kub...
show all
True
0.31 (31.00%)
0 (0.00%)
140 Mi (7.02%)
340 Mi (17.05%)
2 days

Figure 4-42. *Viewing nodes*

If you click the node name, you can find all the information about the node such as the OS image, OS version, and installed Kubelet version, as shown in Figure 4-43.

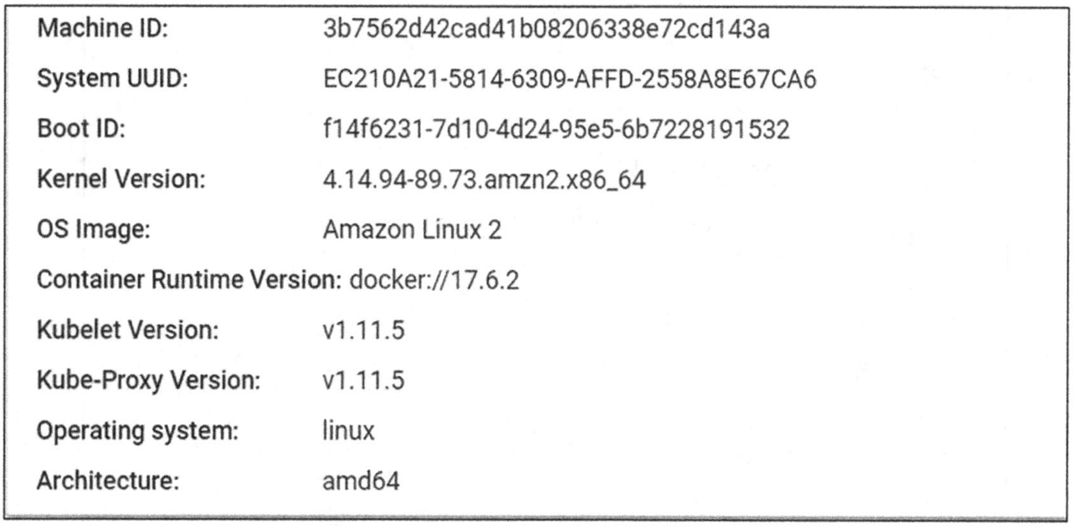

Machine ID:	3b7562d42cad41b08206338e72cd143a
System UUID:	EC210A21-5814-6309-AFFD-2558A8E67CA6
Boot ID:	f14f6231-7d10-4d24-95e5-6b7228191532
Kernel Version:	4.14.94-89.73.amzn2.x86_64
OS Image:	Amazon Linux 2
Container Runtime Version:	docker://17.6.2
Kubelet Version:	v1.11.5
Kube-Proxy Version:	v1.11.5
Operating system:	linux
Architecture:	amd64

Figure 4-43. Node details

You can also monitor your deployments and manage them from the Deployments section, as shown in Figure 4-44.

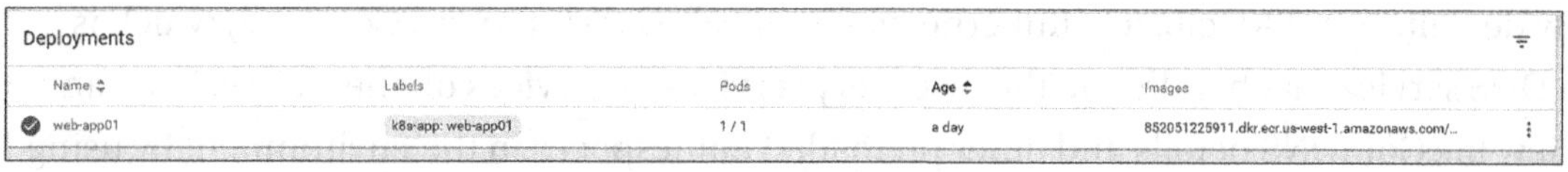

Figure 4-44. Monitoring deployments

Services can also be managed from the web UI, as shown in Figure 4-45. Using the Services section, you can find the external IP addresses of published applications and manage them.

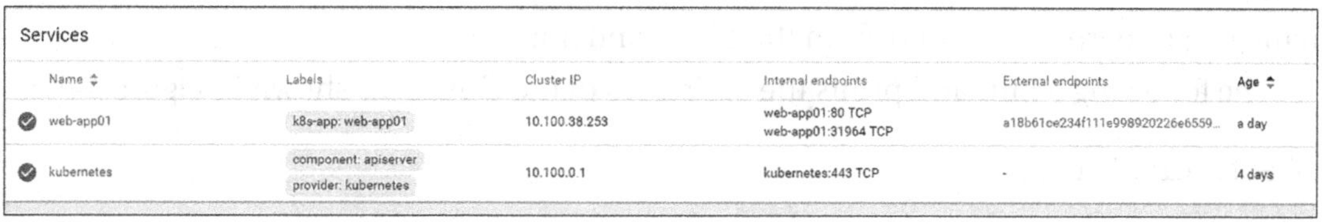

Figure 4-45. Viewing services

If you need to find out which version of Dashboard is installed, you can click the About section and write down the version number, as shown in Figure 4-46.

Figure 4-46. *Viewing the running Dashboard version*

Using CoreDNS

By default, your EKS cluster (Kubernetes 1.1 and above) ships with CoreDNS, which is a DNS service that handles all the discovery services of services on the cluster. You can view the CoreDNS details and other preloaded namespaces in the environment by using the following command:

```
kubectl get pods --all-namespaces
```

Using Useful Kubectl Commands

In this section, I will highlight many of the Kubectl commands I find handy when managing Kubernetes clusters from the command line.

The following command prints the addresses of the cluster, as shown in Figure 4-47:

```
kubectl cluster-info
```

```
PS C:\1.DevOps> kubectl cluster-info
Kubernetes master is running at https://291F9935413EE15906081DECC4237C0D.yl4.us-west-2.eks.amazonaws.com
Heapster is running at https://291F9935413EE15906081DECC4237C0D.yl4.us-west-2.eks.amazonaws.com/api/v1/namespaces/kube-system/services/heapster/
proxy
CoreDNS is running at https://291F9935413EE15906081DECC4237C0D.yl4.us-west-2.eks.amazonaws.com/api/v1/namespaces/kube-system/services/kube-dns:d
ns/proxy
monitoring-influxdb is running at https://291F9935413EE15906081DECC4237C0D.yl4.us-west-2.eks.amazonaws.com/api/v1/namespaces/kube-system/service
s/monitoring-influxdb/proxy
```

Figure 4-47. *Cluster info command*

If you need more information, you can use the following command, which prints the current state of the cluster:

```
kubectl cluster-info dump
```

To view all namespaces, run the following:

```
kubectl get pods --all-namespaces
```

To create a JSON file, use the following command:

```
kubectl create -f ./pod.json
```

To list all the posts in your EKS cluster, use the following command:

```
kubectl get pods
```

To list all the pods with advanced information, use the following command:

```
kubectl get pods -o wide
```

To deploy a single container from the command line, use the following command, which runs an Nginx container image from the public container registry. If you need to use an ECR image, simply type the image URI.

```
kubectl run nginx --image=nginx
```

To run the same image, but this time make it available on the Internet using port 80, run the following command:

```
kubectl run nginx --image= nginx --port=80
```

To add replicated instances of the deployment, use the following command:

```
kubectl run nginx --image=nginx --replicas=4
```

To create a service for an Nginx deployment, which runs on port 80 and connects to the container on port 8000, use the following command:

```
kubectl expose deployment nginx --port=80 --target-port=8000
```

To delete a deployed pod using a JSON file, use the following code:

```
kubectl delete -f ./pod.json
```

To delete all the deployed pods, run the following command:

```
kubectl delete pods --all
```

To delete a pod without any delay, run the following command:

```
kubectl delete pod Nginx --now
```

To print all the supported API resources on EKS, use the following command:

```
kubectl api-resources -o wide
```

Using AWS CLI

You can also use AWS CLI EKS commands to manage your EKS cluster from an AWS resource perspective.

The EKS command syntax is as follows:

```
aws eks command
```

Currently, AWS CLI offers the following commands for EKS cluster management:

- `create-cluster`
- `delete-cluster`
- `describe-cluster`
- `describe-update`
- `list-clusters`
- `list-updates`
- `update-cluster-version`
- `update-kubeconfig`
- `wait`

As you can see, there are only nine commands in AWS CLI for EKS management. This is because most EKS management tasks are done using the kubectl command-line tools and the web UI.

To view all the EKS clusters in AWS using AWS CLI, use the following command:

```
Aws eks list-clusters
```

Adding Worker Nodes

If you need to add or remove worker nodes from your EKS cluster, you can use the CloudFormation console.

To add worker nodes to my deployment, I use the CloudFormation console at the following link:

```
https://us-west-2.console.aws.amazon.com/cloudformation
```

From the CloudFormation console, click your node stack and use the Update Stack option to change the configuration, as shown in Figure 4-48.

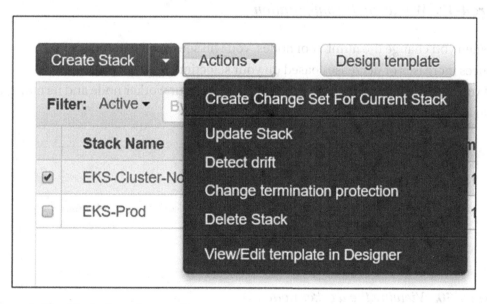

Figure 4-48. *Updating the stack*

On the Select Template page, select use the same template and click Next.

The Worker Node Configuration section allows you to modify the number of nodes used, the size of the instance, and the volume size on each node.

Figure 4-49 shows the configuration.

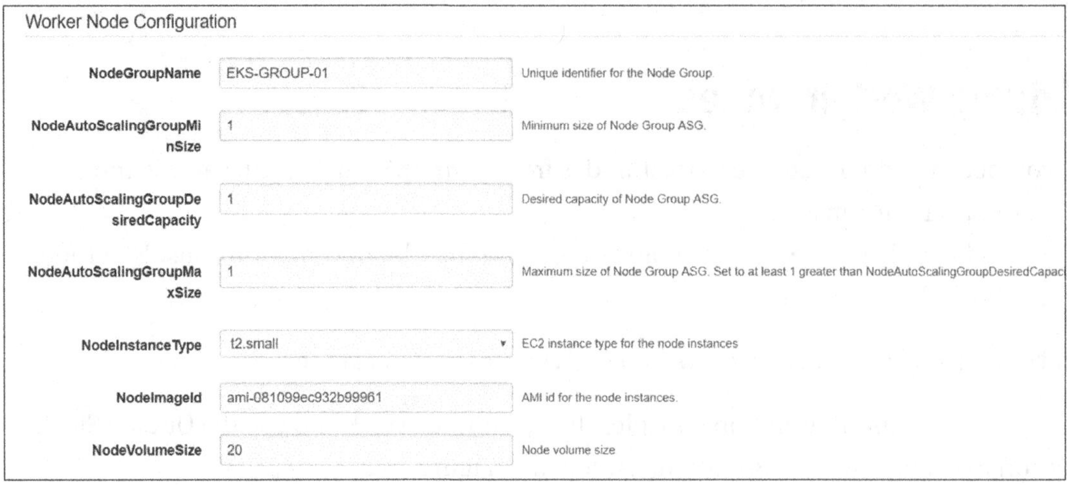

Figure 4-49. *Worker node configuration*

When you change the number of nodes, you will see that the number of EC2 instances increases or decreases based on your selection.

If you access your EC2 console page, you can see your worker node and its name, as shown in Figure 4-50.

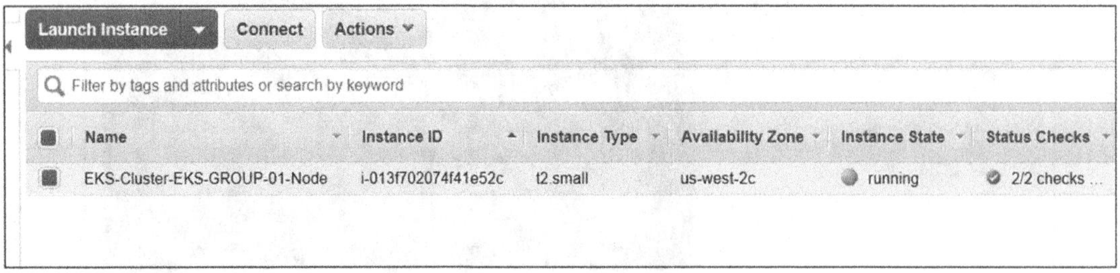

Figure 4-50. *Viewing the worker node*

Understanding the EKS Service Limits

If you are going to scale your EKS environment, you need to be aware of the following limits. On AWS, you can have a maximum number of 50 EKS clusters and five control plane security groups per cluster.

Summary

In this chapter, you used the most advanced container service in AWS that probably takes the longest time to configure. EKS is an enterprise-ready solution that might not be suitable for everyone; however, if you need an advanced solution for multiple and large-scale deployments, EKS is the right product.

Keep in mind that AKS cannot run Windows containers or Windows applications; however, if your applications run on .NET Core, you can deploy them on Linux containers and use EKS. In this chapter, I used one node in my EKS deployment. If you have many services and need high availability, you will need to use more than one worker node.

In the next chapter, you'll learn how to set up and deploy Windows and Linux containers on an AWS EC2 instance (Windows and Linux). The next chapter will also help you understand the complexity and time-consuming task of running containers without using AWS container services like ECS and EKS.

CHAPTER 5

Installing a Docker Host on an Amazon EC2 Instance

In this chapter, I will show you how to install Docker on an Amazon Elastic Compute Cloud (EC2) instance. Amazon EC2 provides a computing infrastructure that is scalable and allows you to run all kinds of workloads including Docker containers.

Up until now, you have used Amazon container services to run containers without setting up container hosts, storage, and networking because it was all done by AWS. This time, you are going to deploy Docker without using AWS container services.

In this chapter, you will go back to the basics and learn how to deploy Docker on a virtual machine running on EC2. I have chosen to show this because you might need a development environment to run your containers without using AWS ECS or EKS. Or you might need to test your application directly on an actual host. Regardless of the reason, knowing how to deploy Docker directly on a Linux or Windows server will allow you to understand AWS better because behind the scenes when you are implementing ECS or EKS, AWS sets up a container host and attaches it to your container service.

In this chapter, I will cover the following topics:

- How to install a Docker container host on an EC2 Linux virtual machine

- How to connect to an EC2 instance using SSL with a private key

- How to install Docker and run Linux containers inside an EC2 instance

- How to install a Windows Server EC2 Docker container host

- How to install Docker and run Windows containers

© Shimon Ifrah 2019
S. Ifrah, *Deploy Containers on AWS*, https://doi.org/10.1007/978-1-4842-5101-0_5

Installing a Docker Host on a Linux EC2 Virtual Machine

In this section, I'll show how to set up a Linux EC2 virtual machine to run a container host. I will also show how to install Docker on a Windows Server EC2 instance and run Windows containers.

Setting Up a Linux Instance as a Docker Container Host

To set up a Docker container on a Linux EC2 machine, log in to the AWS management console and click EC2. On the EC2 page, click New Instance and search for the following AMI image, as shown in Figure 5-1:

Amazon Linux AMI 2018.03.0 (HVM), SSD Volume Type

Figure 5-1. *Amazon Linux AMI*

Follow the prompts to configure the virtual machine. In the Storage section, make sure you set the volume size to a minimum of 20 GB, because all container images will be stored on the local drive.

After you click Create, AWS will ask you to create or use an existing key pair so you can SSH into the machine and configure it.

Next, you need to connect to your EC2 Linux host using SSH, which I'll cover next.

But before connecting, you need to copy the public DNS hostname of your virtual machine. You can find the public DNS address of the virtual machine by clicking the virtual machine at the bottom of the AWS management console.

In Figure 5-2, you can see the public DNS name of my instance.

Public DNS (IPv4)	ec2-34-220-194-142.us-west-2.compute.amazonaws.com
IPv4 Public IP	34.220.194.142
IPv6 IPs	-
Private DNS	ip-172-31-12-121.us-west-2.compute.internal

Figure 5-2. *Public DNS (IPv4)*

SSHing to a Linux Host from Windows 10

At this stage, you should have an EC2 Linux container host up and running and know its public DNS address. Now you need to connect to it from your Windows 10 machine.

Before you can connect to a Linux host, you need to install Putty and PuTTYgen. To install PuTTY and PuTTYgen, browse to the following URL and download the latest releases:

`https://www.chiark.greenend.org.uk/~sgtatham/putty/latest.html`

After you start the installation, make sure all features are selected to be installed, as shown in Figure 5-3.

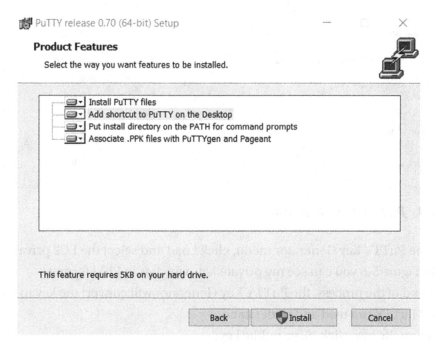

Figure 5-3. *Installing PuTTY*

Importing a Private Key to PuTTY

After the installation is completed, you need to convert your private key to a format that PuTTY can read, and to do that, you need to use PuTTYgen.

From the Windows 10 Start menu, locate the PuTTY Key Generator and click it.

In Figure 5-4 you can see the PuTTY Key Generator application.

Figure 5-4. *PuTTY Key Generator*

From the PuTTY Key Generator menu, click Load and select the EC2 private key you created. In Figure 5-5 you can see my private key, which is in PEM format.

At the end of the process, the PuTTY Key Generator will convert the key to a PPK format that PuTTY can read and understand.

To convert the key, click "Save public key."

Figure 5-5. *Private key*

In Figure 5-6 you can see the successfully imported message.

Figure 5-6. *PuTTYgen notice*

When the conversion process is complete, save the key in PPK format, as shown in Figure 5-7.

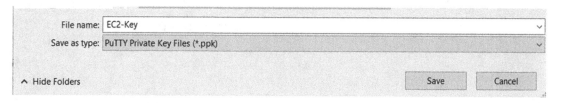

Figure 5-7. *Saving the EC2 key*

Configuring Putty to Connect to a Container Host

To configure PuTTY to connect to the virtual machine, you use the following format as the address:

```
ec2-user@ec2-34-212-231-52.us-west-2.compute.amazonaws.com
```

On the main PuTTY configuration screen, paste the address into the Host Name field to set the connection type to SSH, as shown in Figure 5-8.

I recommend you save the connection now.

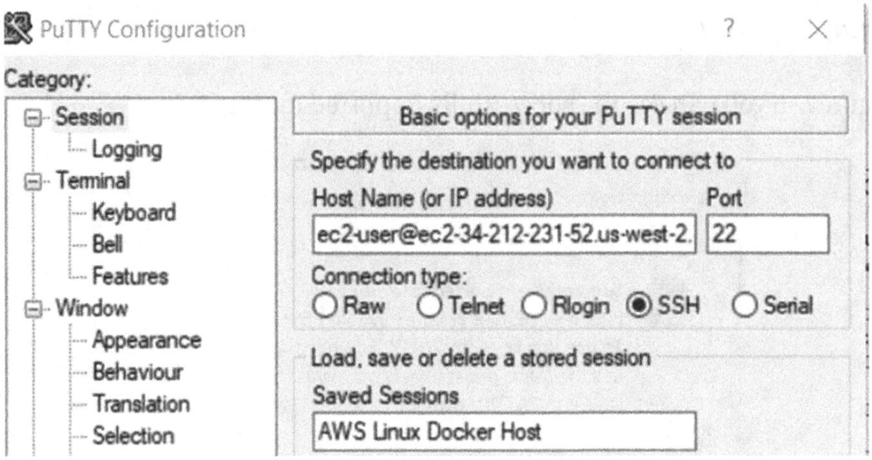

Figure 5-8.   *Configuring PuTTY*

Next, you need to add the private key to PuTTY. To do so, on the PuTTY configuration screen, expand the SSH menu on the left and click Auth, as shown in Figure 5-9.

To load the PPK private key you converted earlier, click Browse and select it.

To connect to the virtual machine, click Open.

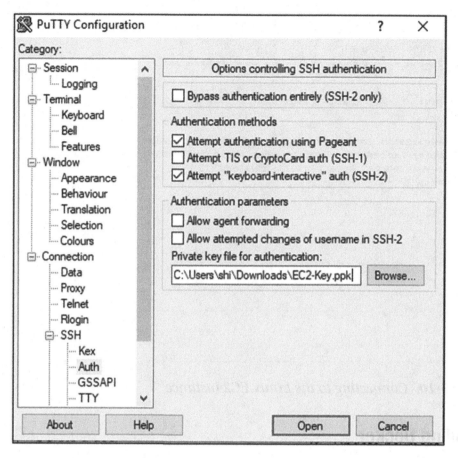

Figure 5-9. *Selecting the private key*

After you click Open, PuTTY will connect to the virtual machine using the private key without asking for a username or password.

In Figure 5-10, you can see that my PuTTY screen is connecting to the virtual machine without asking me to provide a credential.

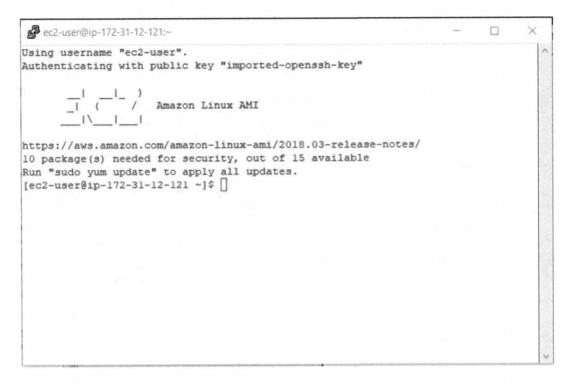

Figure 5-10. *Connecting to the Linux EC2 instance*

Installing Docker

When you are connected to a virtual machine, the only thing left to do is to install Docker and test the installation by deploying a container.

To install Docker on the EC2 virtual machine, you need to run a few commands that will update the yum software repository, install the latest Docker version, restart the Docker service after installation, and assign permissions to the EC2-User instance.

```
sudo yum update -y
sudo yum install docker
sudo service docker start
sudo usermod -a -G docker ec2-user
```

After completing the installation process, you can run the following command to make sure you have installed the latest Docker version, as shown in Figure 5-11:

```
sudo docker version
```

```
[ec2-user@ip-172-31-12-121 ~]$ sudo docker version
Client:
 Version:           18.06.1-ce
 API version:       1.38
 Go version:        go1.10.3
 Git commit:        e68fc7a215d7133c34aa18e3b72b4a21fd0c6136
 Built:             Mon Jan 28 20:25:39 2019
 OS/Arch:           linux/amd64
 Experimental:      false

Server:
 Engine:
  Version:          18.06.1-ce
  API version:      1.38 (minimum version 1.12)
  Go version:       go1.10.3
  Git commit:       e68fc7a/18.06.1-ce
  Built:            Mon Jan 28 20:27:05 2019
  OS/Arch:          linux/amd64
  Experimental:     false
```

Figure 5-11. *Checking the Docker version*

The final test is deploying a container on a Linux host. You can do so using the
following command, which runs the `hello-world` container, as shown in Figure 5-12:

```
sudo docker run hello-world
```

```
[ec2-user@ip-172-31-12-121 ~]$ sudo docker run hello-world
Unable to find image 'hello-world:latest' locally
latest: Pulling from library/hello-world
1b930d010525: Pull complete
Digest: sha256:2557e3c07ed1e38f26e389462d03ed943586f744621577a99efb77324b0fe535
Status: Downloaded newer image for hello-world:latest

Hello from Docker!
This message shows that your installation appears to be working correctly.

To generate this message, Docker took the following steps:
 1. The Docker client contacted the Docker daemon.
 2. The Docker daemon pulled the "hello-world" image from the Docker Hub.
    (amd64)
 3. The Docker daemon created a new container from that image which runs the
    executable that produces the output you are currently reading.
 4. The Docker daemon streamed that output to the Docker client, which sent it
    to your terminal.

To try something more ambitious, you can run an Ubuntu container with:
 $ docker run -it ubuntu bash

Share images, automate workflows, and more with a free Docker ID:
 https://hub.docker.com/

For more examples and ideas, visit:
```

Figure 5-12. *Running the hello-world container*

Connecting from a Linux Machine to an EC2 Container Host

This section will show you how to connect to a Docker container host from a Linux machine. The first thing you need to do is copy the security key to your Linux machine; however, you need to convert it to a PPK file first.

The Linux SSH client understands and reads the key in its native file type of PEM.

Once the file has been copied to your Linux machine, run the following `ssh` command to connect an EC2 Docker container host:

```
ssh -i EC2-Key-Pair.pem ec2-user@ec2-34-212-231-52.us-west-2.compute.
amazonaws.com
```

As shown in Figure 5-13, after running the SSH command, the SSH client asks you if you want to connect and then connects you to the host.

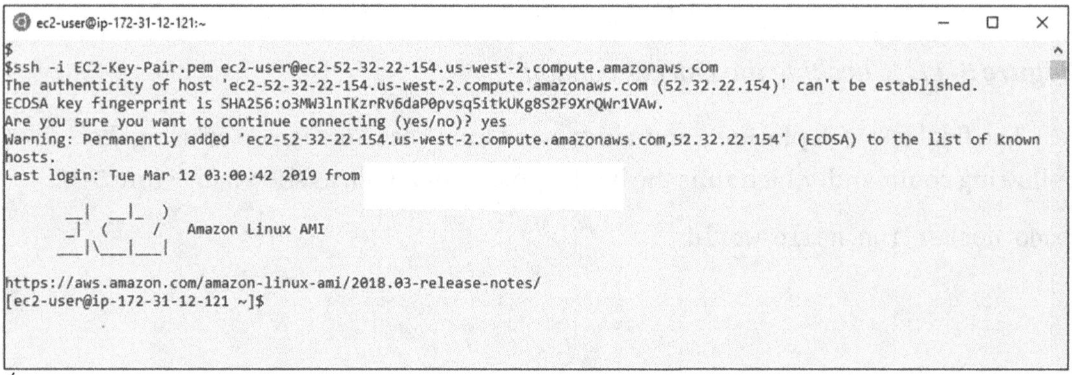

Figure 5-13. *Connecting to an EC2 container host*

After connecting, you can run all the commands shown earlier in the Windows 10 section. If your EC2 machine is used for development, I recommend you turn it off every day after you finish working on it. Because EC2 billing is based on usage, you don't want the machine to run while you are not using it.

Installing a Docker Host on a Windows Server Virtual Machine

After I showed you how to install a Docker container host on a Linux EC2 virtual machine, it is time to show you how I install Docker on a Windows server. In this section, I will how to install Docker on a Windows container host and how to run Windows containers.

The process of spinning up a Windows container host on a Windows virtual machine is like with Linux; however, on a Windows machine, you will use a Remote Desktop client to connect to the machine.

The first step is to create a Windows Server virtual machine that supports Docker. Currently, AWS offers the ECS-optimized Windows Server 2016 image that can run Windows containers on Docker.

To create the virtual machine, access EC2 from the AWS management console and search for *ECS-optimized Windows Server*, as shown in Figure 5-14.

Figure 5-14. Amazon Windows ECS AMI

You can also use the new Windows Server 2019 With Containers image; in my case, I selected the 2016 model because it is more optimized; however, both images can run Docker and Windows containers.

After selecting the ECS-optimized Windows Server 2016 container image, choose the instance type in the step 2 section.

Selecting the right instance is important because the performance of the container will depend on the size of the instance. If you are spinning up a development machine, it is not critical; however, for a production environment, make sure you size your deployment correctly by selecting the correct instance size for your workloads.

Step 2: Choose an Instance Type

Amazon EC2 provides a wide selection of instance types optimized to fit different use cases. Instances are virtual s
resources for your applications. Learn more about instance types and how they can meet your computing needs.

Filter by: [All instance types ⌄]   [All generations ⌄]   Show/Hide Columns

Currently selected: t2.medium (Variable ECUs, 2 vCPUs, 2.3 GHz, Intel Broadwell E5-2686v4, 4 GiB memory, E

Note: The vendor recommends using a **m3.large** instance (or larger) for the best experience with this product.

	Family ⌄	Type ⌄	vCPUs ⓘ ⌄
⊘	Micro instances	t1.micro Free tier eligible	1
⊘	General purpose	t2.nano	1
☐	General purpose	t2.micro Free tier eligible	1
☐	General purpose	t2.small	1
☑	General purpose	t2.medium	2

Figure 5-15. *Choosing the EC2 instance size*

In my case, I am selecting the t2.medium size instance. After selecting the instance size, you need to configure the instance's public IP address.

On the Configure Instance Details page, select the Enable option for the "Auto-assign Public IP" address, which will allow the containers to be accessible over the Internet, as shown in Figure 5-16.

Step 3: Configure Instance Details

Configure the instance to suit your requirements. You can launch multiple instances from the same AMI, request Spot instances to take advantage c

Number of instances ⓘ	[1]	Launch into Auto Scaling Group ⓘ
Purchasing option ⓘ	☐ Request Spot instances	
Network ⓘ	[vpc-39d10941 (default) ▾]	⟳ Create new VPC
Subnet ⓘ	[No preference (default subnet in any Availability Zon ▾]	Create new subnet
Auto-assign Public IP ⓘ	[Enable ▾]	

Figure 5-16. *Configuring the instance details*

In step 4, you need to configure the storage of the virtual machine, and because the Windows container images are larger than Linux containers, I am setting the storage volume to 70GB, which will allow me to store a few large images and not worry about the VM running out of disk space.

In Figure 5-17, you can see the volume size configuration screen.

Step 4: Add Storage

Your instance will be launched with the following storage device settings. You can attach additional EBS volumes and instance store volumes to your instance, or edit the settings of the root volume. You can also attach additional EBS volumes after launching an instance, but not instance store volumes. Learn more about storage options in Amazon EC2.

Volume Type ⓘ	Device ⓘ	Snapshot ⓘ	Size (GiB) ⓘ	Volume Type ⓘ	IOPS ⓘ	Throughp (MB/s) ⓘ
Root	/dev/sda1	snap-07c5588ca85a01452	70	General Purpose SSD (gp2) ▾	210 / 3000	N/A

Add New Volume

Figure 5-17. *Adding storage*

The next step in the configuration is to configure the security group. Security groups in AWS control traffic to one or more virtual machine and act as a firewall using rules you define. By default, AWS configures basic firewall rules to the VM that permit management access to it.

On Linux EC2 instances, AWS preconfigures SSH access using port 22, and on a Windows server with EC2 instances, it allows RDP access on port 3389.

Security groups can be modified any time, and you can add, remove, or modify rules between AWS networks, the Internet, and specific instances in AWS.

As shown in Figure 5-18, AWS created a new security group for my EC2 Windows Server instance with port 22 for SSH access and port 3389 for RDP access.

To open port 80 or 443, I can use the Add Rule button now or later if needed.

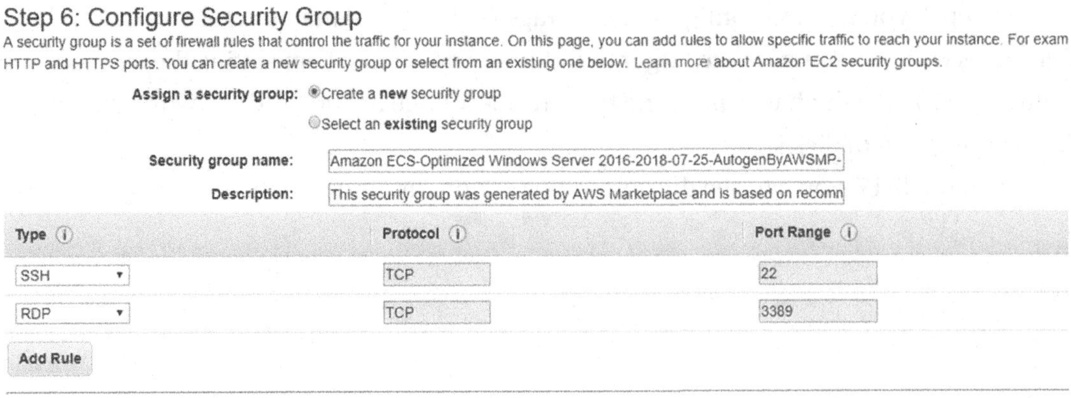

Step 6: Configure Security Group

A security group is a set of firewall rules that control the traffic for your instance. On this page, you can add rules to allow specific traffic to reach your instance. For exam
HTTP and HTTPS ports. You can create a new security group or select from an existing one below. Learn more about Amazon EC2 security groups.

Assign a security group: ⦿ Create a **new** security group

◯ Select an **existing** security group

Security group name: | Amazon ECS-Optimized Windows Server 2016-2018-07-25-AutogenByAWSMP-

Description: | This security group was generated by AWS Marketplace and is based on recomm

Type ⓘ	Protocol ⓘ	Port Range ⓘ
SSH ▾	TCP	22
RDP ▾	TCP	3389

[Add Rule]

Figure 5-18. *Configuring the security group*

To access Windows Server EC2 instances on AWS, you also need to use a security key the same way you did this for a Linux instance. Because you have already created a security key, AWS asks you to confirm which key you want to use and if you need to create a new one. Select the option "Choose an existing key pair."

In Figure 5-19, you can see the screen to select a key pair. Notice that without the key pair you can't start a new instance.

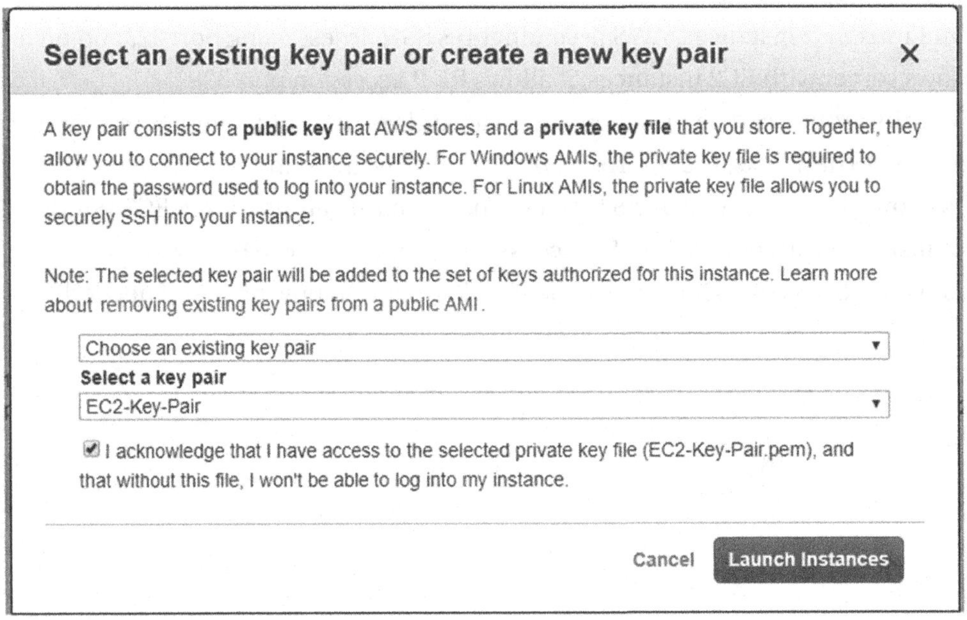

Select an existing key pair or create a new key pair   ✕

A key pair consists of a **public key** that AWS stores, and a **private key file** that you store. Together, they allow you to connect to your instance securely. For Windows AMIs, the private key file is required to obtain the password used to log into your instance. For Linux AMIs, the private key file allows you to securely SSH into your instance.

Note: The selected key pair will be added to the set of keys authorized for this instance. Learn more about removing existing key pairs from a public AMI .

| Choose an existing key pair | ▾ |

Select a key pair

| EC2-Key-Pair | ▾ |

☑ I acknowledge that I have access to the selected private key file (EC2-Key-Pair.pem), and that without this file, I won't be able to log into my instance.

Cancel   [**Launch Instances**]

Figure 5-19. *Selecting an existing key pair*

After launching the instance, you need to connect to it using Remote Desktop.

AWS offers a straightforward method to connect to a Windows EC2 instance. However, you also need to decrypt the password to the instance using the security key. To connect and decrypt the password, select the VM on the EC2 page and click Connect.

On the Connect To Your Instance screen, as shown in Figure 5-20, you need to do two things.

- Download the Remote Desktop file

- Decrypt the password

First download the Remote Desktop file to your Windows 10 machine. After downloading the Remote Desktop file, click the Get Password button, as shown in Figure 5-20.

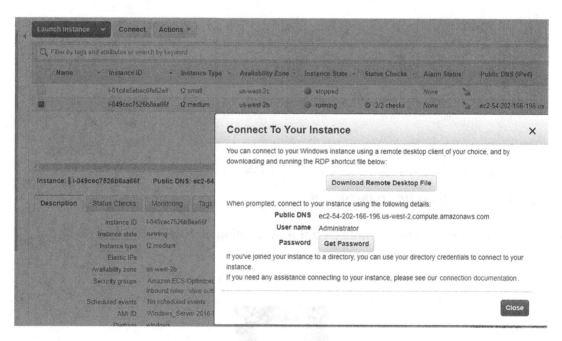

Figure 5-20. *Connecting to an EC2 instance*

On the Connect To Your Instance ➤ Get Password screen (shown in Figure 5-21), click Choose File and browse to the location of the EC2 key pair you created.

After selecting the file, the security key will be populated in the blank space in the middle of the screen.

To get the password to log in to the instance, click Decrypt Password. The password and username to log in to the machine will show up, and all you need to do is copy and paste them and keep them in a secure location.

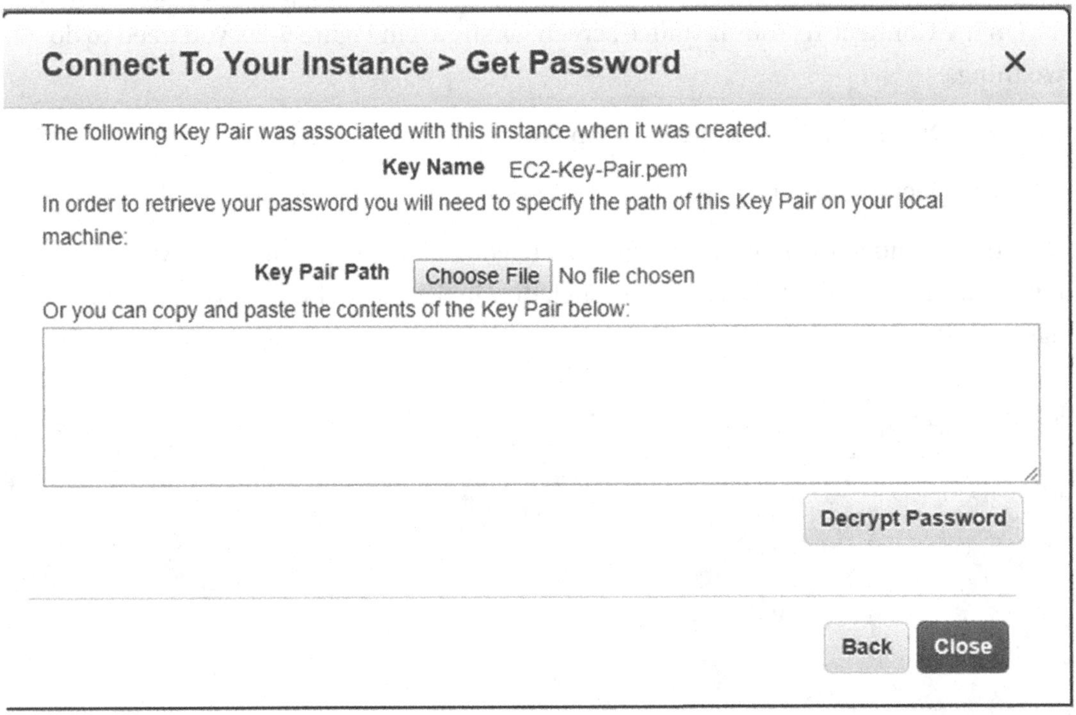

Connect To Your Instance > Get Password   ✕

The following Key Pair was associated with this instance when it was created.

Key Name   EC2-Key-Pair.pem

In order to retrieve your password you will need to specify the path of this Key Pair on your local machine:

Key Pair Path   [Choose File] No file chosen

Or you can copy and paste the contents of the Key Pair below:

Decrypt Password

[Back]   [Close]

Figure 5-21. *Decrypting a password*

Now that you have the Remote Desktop connection file, username, and password, all you need to do is connect to your EC2 instance.

Click the Remote Desktop file, as shown in Figure 5-22.

ec2-54-202...

Figure 5-22. *Remote Desktop file*

After double-clicking the Remote Desktop file, Windows will prompt you for the username and password. On the "Enter your credentials" screen, as shown in Figure 5-23, use the username and password that you copied on the Connect To Your Instance screen.

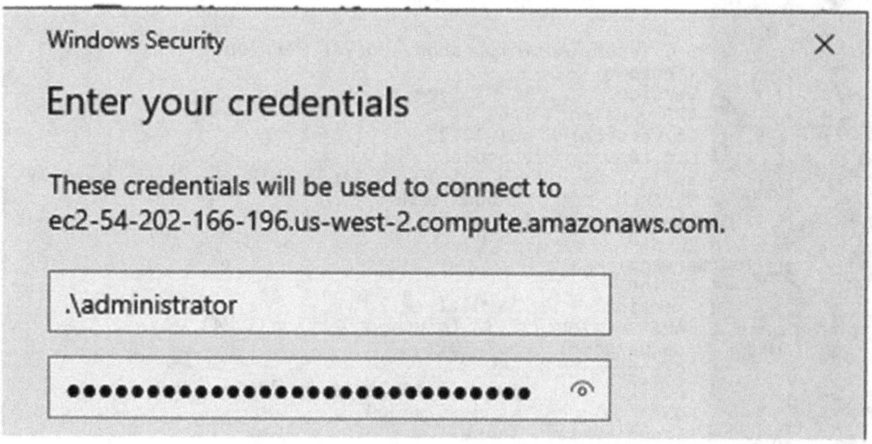

Figure 5-23. Enter credentials window

After providing the correct username and password, you can connect to the EC2 instance. In Figure 5-24, you can see the Windows Server EC2 instance screen.

If you run the docker version command, you can see that Docker is installed; however, the installed version is not the latest Docker engine version.

In the next section, I will show you how to update Docker to the latest version on Windows Server 2016. The process is like with Linux; however, the commands are different and based on PowerShell.

Before you update to the latest version, first deploy a test container to make sure all the components are working. For this test, use the hello-world container image, which is available on Docker Hub, and use it to verify whether Docker is working.

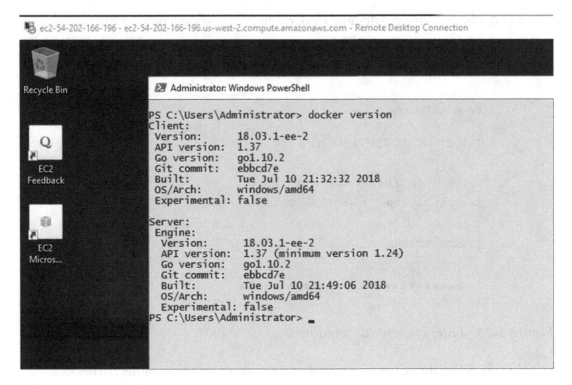

Figure 5-24. *Docker version*

To run the `hello-world` container image on your Windows Server EC2 instance, type the following command:

```
docker run hello-world
```

In Figure 5-25 you can see `hello-world` container image output that confirms that the installation of Docker on Windows Server appears to be working correctly.

You can also see the steps Docker used to verify that Docker is installed correctly.

The steps include connecting to the Docker daemon, pulling an image from the Docker Hub container registry, creating a new container from the downloaded image, and finally outputting information to the terminal.

```
PS C:\Users\Administrator> docker run hello-world
Unable to find image 'hello-world:latest' locally
latest: Pulling from library/hello-world
bce2fbc256ea: Already exists
6f2071dcd729: Pull complete
909cdbafc9e1: Pull complete
a43e426cc5c9: Pull complete
Digest: sha256:2557e3c07ed1e38f26e389462d03ed943586f744621577a99efb77324b0fe535
Status: Downloaded newer image for hello-world:latest

Hello from Docker!
This message shows that your installation appears to be working correctly.

To generate this message, Docker took the following steps:
 1. The Docker client contacted the Docker daemon.
 2. The Docker daemon pulled the "hello-world" image from the Docker Hub.
    (windows-amd64, nanoserver-sac2016)
 3. The Docker daemon created a new container from that image which runs the
    executable that produces the output you are currently reading.
 4. The Docker daemon streamed that output to the Docker client, which sent it
    to your terminal.

To try something more ambitious, you can run a Windows Server container with:
 PS C:\> docker run -it mcr.microsoft.com/windows/servercore powershell

Share images, automate workflows, and more with a free Docker ID:
 https://hub.docker.com/

For more examples and ideas, visit:
 https://docs.docker.com/get-started/
```

Figure 5-25. *Running hello-world on the Windows container host*

Microsoft also offers its own Windows .NET sample image to test Windows containers and Docker. To run the Windows .NET sample container image, use the following command:

```
docker run microsoft/dotnet-samples
```

Deploying, Managing, and Running Containers on an Amazon EC2 VM

In this section, I will show you how to manage Docker and your Docker container host on Amazon AWS. Managing Docker containers involves updating your container host's underlying operating system, managing containers on the host, managing Docker volumes, and doing housekeeping on virtual machines.

Updating Docker on Windows Server

To update Docker on my Windows Server 2016 EC2 instance, I will use the Microsoft PowerShell console.

Because Docker on Windows is installed as a PowerShell package, you also need to update or uninstall Docker using PowerShell.

To check the currently installed version of Docker for Windows on your machine, use the following PowerShell cmdlet, as shown in Figure 5-26:

```
get-Package -Name Docker -ProviderName DockerMSFTProvider
```

```
PS C:\Users\Administrator> get-Package -Name Docker -ProviderName DockerMSFTProvider

Name                          Version            Source                         ProviderName
----                          -------            ------                         ------------
docker                        18.03.1-ee-2       DockerDefault                  DockerMsftProvider
```

Figure 5-26. *Checking the installed version*

To update Docker to the latest version, first check the latest version number using the following command:

```
Find-Package -Name Docker -ProviderName DockerMSFTProvider
```

To install the latest Docker version on a Windows Server EC2 instance, run the following command from a PowerShell console.

```
Install-Package -Name Docker -ProviderName DockerMSFTProvider -Update -Force
```

If you have running containers on the host, the containers will be turned off during the update process until the Docker Windows service is restarted.

Note   In a production environment, you will have a limited window of time to reboot. You would have to set up Docker in a cluster configuration using Docker Swarm, and your containers will be moved or load balanced between two or more hosts; otherwise, your application will experience downtime during reboots.

```
Install-Package -Name Docker -ProviderName DockerMSFTProvider
-Update -Force
```

After the installation process is complete, all you need to do is restart the Docker service on your machine using the following command:

```
Restart-service docker
```

To check that the latest version is installed, use the following command, as shown in Figure 5-27:

```
docker version
```

```
PS C:\Users\Administrator> docker version
Client:
 Version:           18.09.3
 API version:       1.39
 Go version:        go1.10.8
 Git commit:        142dfcedca
 Built:             02/28/2019 06:33:17
 OS/Arch:           windows/amd64
 Experimental:      false

Server:
 Engine:
  Version:          18.09.3
  API version:      1.39 (minimum version 1.24)
  Go version:       go1.10.8
  Git commit:       142dfcedca
  Built:            02/28/2019 06:31:15
  OS/Arch:          windows/amd64
  Experimental:     false
PS C:\Users\Administrator> _
```

Figure 5-27. *Docker version output*

Downloading Images

Before you can start deploying Linux or Windows containers, you need to download, or *pull*, a container image that is compatible with the container host. Docker Hub is a great source to find images and currently is the only reliable and trustworthy source for container images. To access Docker Hub and explore public images from vendors such as Microsoft, AWS, Ubuntu, WordPress, and more, visit the following URL:

```
https://hub.docker.com/
```

Using the search box on the Docker Hub web site, you can search images for your deployment, as shown in Figure 5-28.

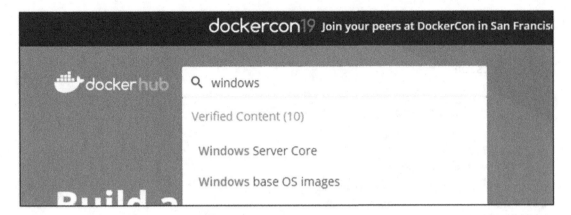

Figure 5-28. *Searching for Windows Server Core images*

To download an image, select the image from the search results and use the Docker pull URL on the right side of the image page, as shown in Figure 5-29.

Figure 5-29. *Pulling a URL for Windows Server Core*

Once you have the image pull address, you can use the docker pull command in your command-line tool (PowerShell, cmd, Bash, or VS Code) and download the image.

The following command will download the latest Windows Server Core image to your Windows container host, as shown in Figure 5-30:

```
docker pull mcr.microsoft.com/windows/servercore
```

```
Administrator: Windows PowerShell

Windows PowerShell
Copyright (C) 2016 Microsoft Corporation. All rights reserved.

PS C:\Users\Administrator> docker pull mcr.microsoft.com/windows/servercore
Using default tag: latest
latest: Pulling from windows/servercore
3889bb8d808b: Already exists
d0c71fc8924e: Downloading [==>                                              ]    87MB/1.566GB
```

Figure 5-30. *Docker pull request*

Depending on the size of the image, the download process will take a few minutes.

You can also use the tag option to download a specific image release. To download the long-time service channel release of Windows Server 2019 image, for instance, you can use the following command:

```
docker pull mcr.microsoft.com/windows/servercore:ltsc2019
```

You can also download the semi-channel release image using the following command:

```
docker pull mcr.microsoft.com/windows/servercore:1809
```

If needed, you can download an image based on the knowledge-based ID as part of the Windows Server update schedule.

```
docker pull mcr.microsoft.com/windows/servercore:1809-KB{Knowledge Base ID}
```

Once an image has been downloaded, Docker will extract it and expand it, so in most cases, the download size is not the same as the size on disk after extracting the image.

To view all downloaded images, use the following command, as shown in Figure 5-31:

```
docker images
```

```
PS C:\Users\Administrator> docker images
REPOSITORY                              TAG       IMAGE ID        CREATED         SIZE
microsoft/dotnet-samples                latest    afca1083bf22    4 weeks ago     1.27GB
mcr.microsoft.com/windows/servercore    latest    ea9f7aa13d03    2 months ago    11GB
hello-world                             latest    2c911f8d79db    2 months ago    1.17GB
microsoft/windowsservercore             latest    7d89a4baf66c    8 months ago    10.7GB
microsoft/nanoserver                    latest    e2c314f76df6    8 months ago    1.13GB
PS C:\Users\Administrator>
```

Figure 5-31. *Docker images*

In Figure 5-31, you can see all the images I have downloaded to my machine with all the relevant information such as image size on disk and image ID.

To delete an image, use the following command, as shown in Figure 5-32. Keep in mind that you can't remove an image if a deployed container is using it.

```
docker image rm microsoft/dotnet-samples
```

```
PS C:\Users\Administrator> docker image rm  microsoft/dotnet-samples
Untagged: microsoft/dotnet-samples:latest
Untagged: microsoft/dotnet-samples@sha256:06df3478be0269ceea4005c582780dc68fb9e3488462b193a7b9a2640c3563b3
Deleted: sha256:afca1083bf22e059e473bbdc90ea4ff1f61adae8901700f92ed6f53ff5582712
Deleted: sha256:4457b42770589b8ec7d61926b5597264c56795f1294f09624a65d4da421eb118
Deleted: sha256:3b70679aec9b4373ae4c5b83ec4595ec9cd9bc5663aba1e95b4a60e64799a93e
Deleted: sha256:e1cc2ffdcc6d0376d2f0a0b3d1e828ff13e4057ee0c00682427cecf963a87f1b
Deleted: sha256:1d184d8d2f853c658d7886eb8eb5dacd1b65f5ecc36b34e49b38084b426e6a60
```

Figure 5-32. *Deleting a Docker image*

Deploying Containers

After deploying your Windows or Linux EC2 Docker container host, you are ready to deploy Linux or Windows containers. The best thing about Docker is that once you have it installed, it doesn't matter what containers you are running because the Docker commands are the same regardless of the host operating system.

Deploying containers with Docker is a two-step process; first, you need to download the container image, and then, you need to deploy a container that will use the image.

The most basic form of deploying a Docker container is using the command shown earlier in Figure 5-25. The command deploys a Windows Server Core 2016 container and enters a terminal session with PowerShell.

In Figure 5-33, I typed hostname after running the command to show the hostname that is the name of the container, not the host, that I am running it from.

```
docker run -it microsoft/windowsservercore powershell
```

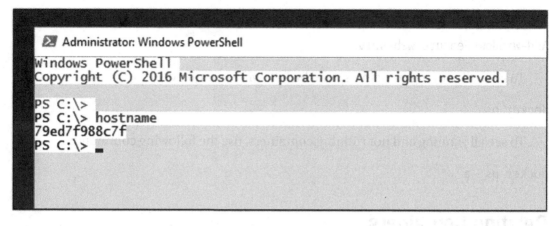

Figure 5-33. Docker run command for Windows Server Core

From here I can use any PowerShell command or Linux Bash commands to manage the container or install roles, applications, or services.

To view all the available Windows Server features on a Windows container image, run the following command, as shown in Figure 5-34:

```
Get-WindowsFeature
```

```
PS C:\> Get-WindowsFeature

Display Name                                           Name                        Install State
------------                                           ----                        -------------
[ ] Active Directory Certificate Services              AD-Certificate              Available
    [ ] Certification Authority                        ADCS-Cert-Authority         Available
    [ ] Certificate Enrollment Policy Web Service      ADCS-Enroll-Web-Pol         Available
    [ ] Certificate Enrollment Web Service             ADCS-Enroll-Web-Svc         Available
    [ ] Certification Authority Web Enrollment         ADCS-Web-Enrollment         Available
    [ ] Network Device Enrollment Service              ADCS-Device-Enrollment      Available
    [ ] Online Responder                               ADCS-Online-Cert            Available
[ ] Active Directory Domain Services                   AD-Domain-Services          Available
[ ] Active Directory Federation Services               ADFS-Federation             Available
[ ] Active Directory Lightweight Directory Services    ADLDS                       Available
[ ] Active Directory Rights Management Services        ADRMS                       Available
    [ ] Active Directory Rights Management Server      ADRMS-Server                Available
    [ ] Identity Federation Support                    ADRMS-Identity              Available
[ ] Device Health Attestation                          DeviceHealthAttestat...     Available
[ ] DHCP Server                                        DHCP                        Available
[ ] DNS Server                                         DNS                         Available
[X] File and Storage Services                          FileAndStorage-Services     Installed
    [ ] File and iSCSI Services                        File-Services               Available
        [ ] File Server                                FS-FileServer               Available
        [ ] BranchCache for Network Files              FS-BranchCache              Available
        [ ] Data Deduplication                         FS-Data-Deduplication       Available
        [ ] DFS Namespaces                             FS-DFS-Namespace            Available
        [ ] DFS Replication                            FS-DFS-Replication          Available
        [ ] File Server Resource Manager               FS-Resource-Manager         Available
        [ ] File Server VSS Agent Service              FS-VSS-Agent                Available
        [ ] iSCSI Target Server                        FS-iSCSITarget-Server       Available
        [ ] iSCSI Target Storage Provider (VDS and V...  iSCSITarget-VSS-VDS       Available
        [ ] Server for NFS                             FS-NFS-Service              Available
        [ ] Work Folders                               FS-SyncShareService         Available
    [X] Storage Services                               Storage-Services            Installed
```

Figure 5-34. Windows features

To install Windows Server IIS server, run the following command:

```
Add-WindowsFeature web-server
```

To view all running containers, use the following command:

```
docker ps
```

To see all running and not running containers, use the following command:

```
docker ps -a
```

Deleting Containers

To delete a specific container, the first step is to check all the running containers and their IDs using the following command, as shown in Figure 5-35:

```
Docker ps -a
```

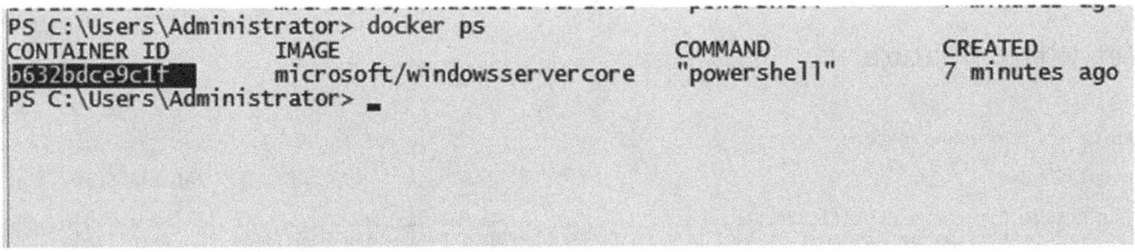

Figure 5-35. *The docker ps command*

Once you have the container ID, you can use the rm command to delete it as follows:

```
Docker rm b632bdce9c1f
```

If you get an error message saying that the container is running, use the following command to stop the container first and then delete it, as shown in Figure 5-36:

```
docker stop b632bdce9c1f
```

Figure 5-36. *The docker stop command*

If you are testing things with your Docker deployment, I suggest you use the -rm switch, which will delete the container on exit.

The following command will deploy a Windows container running an IIS image, and when you press Ctrl+C or type exit, the container will be deleted automatically by Docker:

```
docker run --rm -it -p 80:80 mcr.microsoft.com/windows/servercore/iis
```

Deleting Multiple Containers

If you need to refresh your development environment because of all the deployed containers, you can use the following command, which will first stop all the containers without specifying individual containers:

```
docker stop $(docker ps -a -q)
```

After all the containers are stopped, run the following command and delete all the containers on your host:

```
docker rm $(docker ps -a -q)
```

Figure 5-37 shows the complete process of creating, stopping, and deleting all the containers on a Docker container host.

```
PS C:\Users\Administrator> docker run microsoft/windowsservercore
Microsoft Windows [Version 10.0.14393]
(c) 2016 Microsoft Corporation. All rights reserved.

C:\>
PS C:\Users\Administrator> docker stop $(docker ps -a -q)
572a74754a5b
PS C:\Users\Administrator> docker rm $(docker ps -a -q)
572a74754a5b
PS C:\Users\Administrator> _
```

Figure 5-37. *Deleting multiple containers*

Note   I recommend you establish a habit of cleaning up your Docker environment every few weeks by removing unused containers and images from the system. This will keep your Docker environment running faster and smoother and keep it tidy.

Modifying a Security Group on an EC2 Host

Managing a Docker container host on EC2 involves making sure the host is secure and that only the required ports on the host are open. I strongly recommend you open only the specific ports that are needed for development and management on the host, and when you complete your work or project for the port, remove them from the security group.

In this section, I will show you how to manage the security groups on an EC2 instance. To get started, log into the AWS management portal and open the EC2 page with your running instance.

As shown in Figure 5-38, under the Security Groups header, you will see the name of the security group that is attached to each instance.

IPv6 IPs	⌄	Key Name	⌄	Monitoring	⌄	Launch Time	Security Groups	⌄	Owner	⌄
-		EC2-Key-Pair		disabled		March 16, 2019 at 6:46:26 P...	launch-wizard-1		852051225911	
-		EC2-Key-Pair		▉ disabled		March 19, 2019 at 2:29:17 P...	Amazon ECS-Opt...		852051225911	

Figure 5-38. *Security groups*

If you click a security group's hyperlink, you will see the security group's details page, as shown in Figure 5-39.

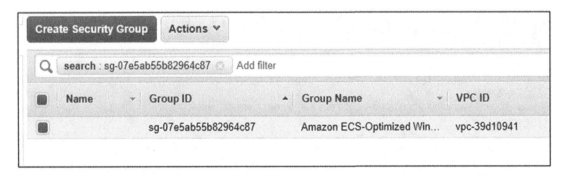

Figure 5-39. *Security group's details page*

To add, remove, or modify a rule, select the security group, and from the Actions menu, select the action you need to take from the list.

Figure 5-40 shows the Actions menu.

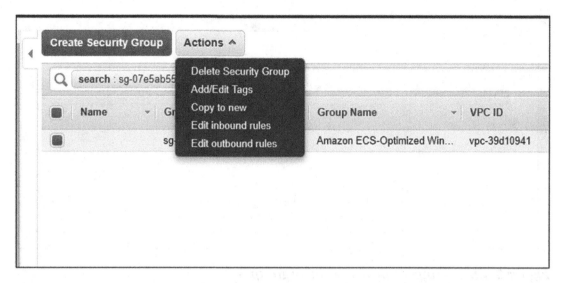

Figure 5-40. *Security group's Actions menu*

To edit and allow inbound rules, click "Edit inbound rules" and access the rules menu, as shown in Figure 5-41.

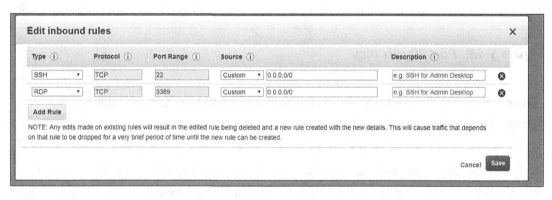

Figure 5-41. *Editing the inbound rules*

From the Edit menu, you can add rules by clicking Add and selecting the port or protocol to allow access.

Figure 5-42 shows that I am adding a rule for port 80 (HTTP) and allowing access from anywhere to it using the Source field.

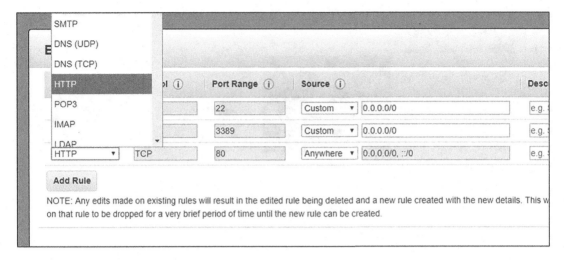

Figure 5-42. *Adding a rule to a security group*

You can also lock down the access to the host to a specific IP address using a custom address, as shown in Figure 5-43.

Figure 5-43. *Port 80 rule view*

Note   It is recommended when possible to lock down the source address to particular IP addresses and subnets.

Using the Edit menu, you can also delete or change existing rules without needing to remove them. Once a rule has been added, traffic will flow immediately without any delays.

Another cool feature that I like in security groups is the ability to copy a security group and use it on another EC2 instance. In large deployments, your security group can contain many rules that have been put in place over a long period.

If you need to create another deployment with similar rules, you can copy an existing security group, apply it to the new implementation, and modify it if needed. To copy a security group, select it from the Security Groups column and use the Actions menu's "Copy to new" item, as shown in Figure 5-44.

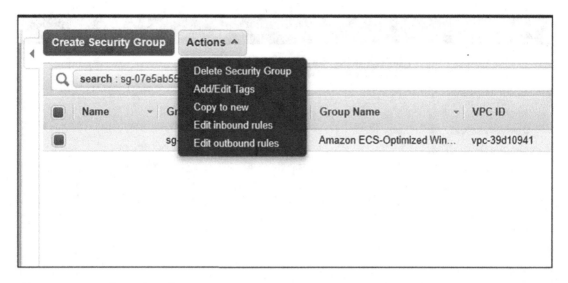

Figure 5-44.   *Copying the security group*

After you click "Copy to new," you will see the Create Security Group window with all
the rules from the existing group, as shown in Figure 5-45.

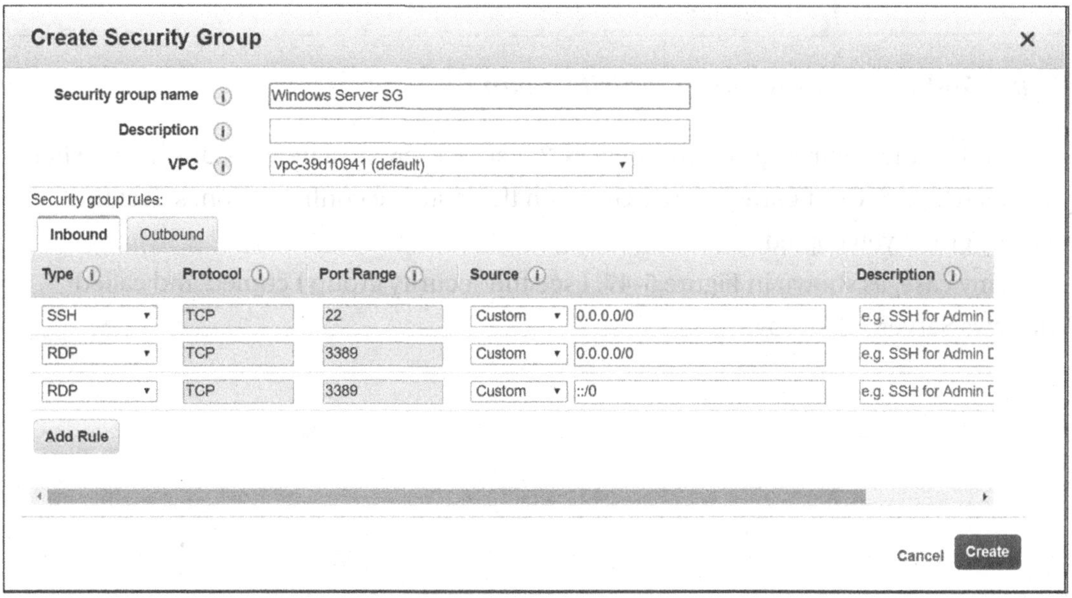

Figure 5-45.   *Creating a security group*

After the copy process is complete, you can view the new security group by clicking
Security Groups in the left menu under Network & Security, as shown in Figure 5-46.

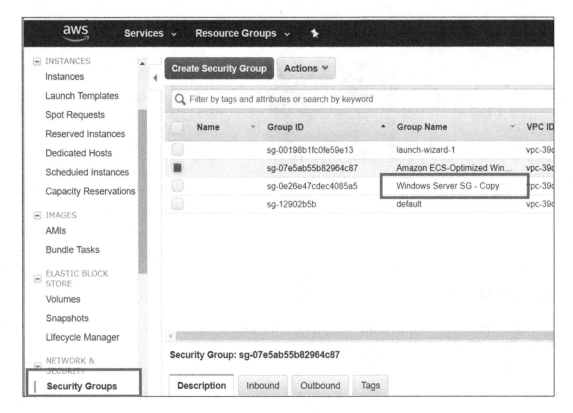

Figure 5-46. *Viewing a copied security group*

To apply the security group to a new EC2 instance, create a new instance, and when you reach Step 6: Configure Security Group in the instance configuration, select the security group you copied.

In my case, as shown in Figure 5-47, I see the security group I copied and called Windows Server SG - Copy.

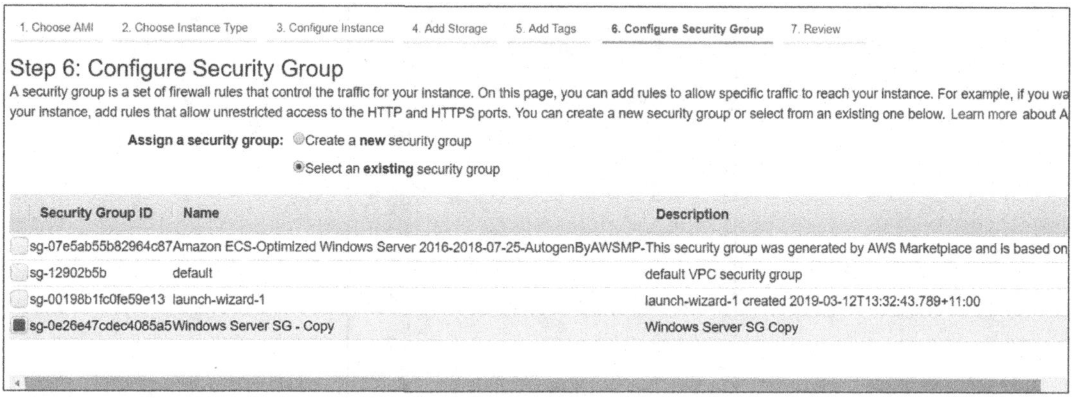

Figure 5-47. *Configuring the security group*

The copy feature is also useful in environments where the security team controls and manages the security infrastructure, and in cases like this they can design and configure the security groups and point the deployment engineer to the security group needed for the deployment.

Managing Storage Volumes

The last point I would like to touch on in this chapter involves storage volumes and how to manage them when your EC2 instance is acting as your Docker container host.

At the beginning of this chapter when I created my hosts, I used basic volume sizes, 20GB for my Linux host and 70GB for my Windows host. After a few months of usage and updates, the volume size can fill up.

With AWS, you can quickly scale up storage quickly and for low cost.

To access your storage volume, use the left menu on the EC2 page and click Volumes under Elastic Block Storage, as shown in Figure 5-48.

The Elastic Block Storage page offers three main options that allow you to manage storage volumes. To manage currently attached volumes on your virtual machines, click Volumes.

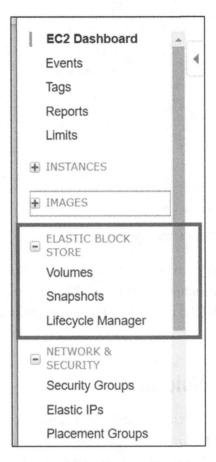

Figure 5-48. *Elastic Block Store menu*

In the volume page shown in Figure 5-49, you can see all my volumes; in this case, I have two—one for the Linux host and one for the Windows host.

	Name		Volume ID		Size		Volume Type	IOPS		Snapshot		Created		Availability Zon
			vol-0b0d687f...		70 GiB		gp2	210		snap-07c5588...		March 14, 2019 at 3...		us-west-2b
			vol-033162c...		17 GiB		gp2	100		snap-0af9c0b1...		March 12, 2019 at 1...		us-west-2c

Figure 5-49. *Viewing volumes*

To increase the volume size, select the volume and click Modify Volume in the Actions menu, as shown in Figure 5-50.

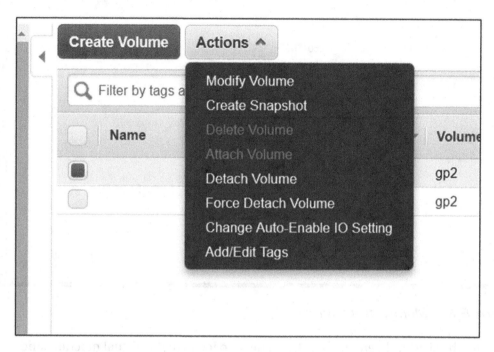

Figure 5-50. *Increasing the volume size*

On the Modify Volume page, select the new volume size needed for the virtual machine, as shown in Figure 5-51.

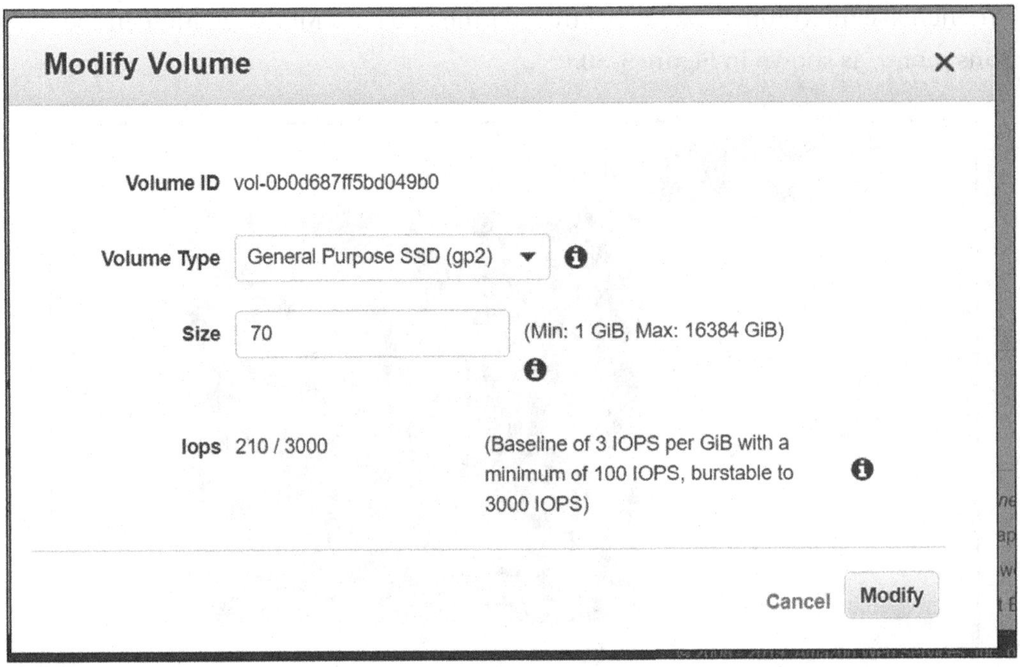

Figure 5-51. *Modifying a volume*

After the size has been increased, you need to log in to the virtual machine and expand the disk using the native tools.

To create a snapshot of the disk in the case of a significant change where you need to test something or deploy a patch, use the Actions menu, but this time click "Create snapshot," as shown in Figure 5-52.

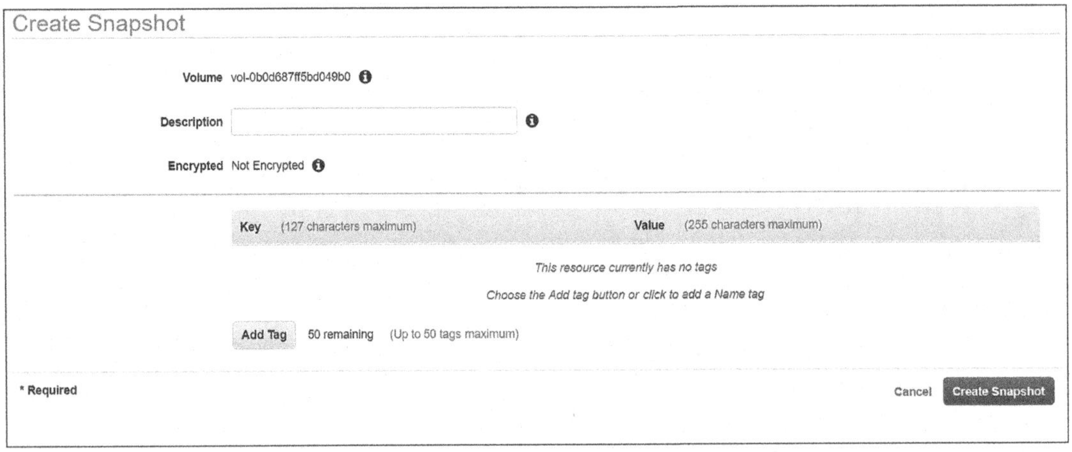

Figure 5-52. *Creating a snapshot*

The last feature in the EC2 Storage section is the Data Lifecycle Manager for storage, as shown in Figure 5-53.

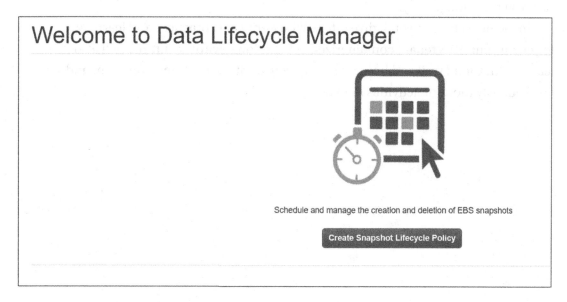

Figure 5-53. *Data Lifecycle Manager*

With data lifecycle policies, you can fully automate the creation and deletion of snapshots based on tags and a schedule and not worry about cleaning up snapshots.

This process can also reduce the storage cost of your AWS subscription and keep it tidy.

If you are using snapshots of EC2 volumes, I recommend you use this feature and reduce your manual maintenance work.

Summary

In this chapter, you learned how to deploy a Docker container host on AWS using Linux and Windows. You also learned how to connect to your container host using SSH and a Remote Desktop session. To connect to the Docker container host, you used the security key you created at the beginning of the book. After connecting to the host, you installed Docker, restarted the service, and ran the hello-world container to test that Docker was running. You also updated Docker to the latest version and ran a few handy Docker commands to help you keep Docker tidy and optimized.

Then, you learned how to manage security groups, and I showed you how to copy and redeploy a security group to a new instance. On the storage volume front, I showed you how to manage volumes by increasing an existing volume's size and creating snapshots. In the final section, I spoke about data lifecycle policies and how they can save you time and money.

In the next chapter, you'll dive into AWS security best practices and learn how to secure your AWS tenant containerized application environment. You will also learn about CloudTrail and how it can help you audit your AWS environment and continuously monitor activities in AWS.

CHAPTER 6

Securing Your Containerized Environment

In Chapter 5, you learned how to configure an EC2 instance as a Docker container host and learned how to deploy Windows and Linux containers directly on the host. In this chapter, I will cover AWS security and how to protect your user accounts, container hosts (EC2 instances), applications, and containers.

Security is an essential part of AWS simply because AWS is a public cloud where all servers and services can be accessed from anywhere anytime. Therefore, it is essential to protect your applications, data, and public cloud resources from unauthorized access. A security breach can damage the reputation of the organization and cause huge financial and brand value loss.

With the right best practices in place, your AWS environment can be as secure as any private cloud environment. Luckily, AWS offers many services and features that can give you the right tools to protect any aspect of your environment and make sure you have the right features and tools at your disposal to protect and safeguard your AWS cloud.

Preventive maintenance is important in any public and private cloud environment. When you have the right plan and routines to protect your AWS cloud, the overall security level of your tenant increases. Active management and using AWS best practices can go a long way in helping you to control and maintain a protected and more secure tenant.

In this chapter, I will introduce you to many AWS best practices and show you how to access them from the AWS Portal and AWS CLI. If you adopt and integrate some of these techniques into your cloud management routines, you will be in a better position because these practices have a proven record of securing tenants.

For example, not many AWS engineers and developers realize that enabling multifactor authentication on a user account can reduce the chances of the account being compromised by 70 percent.

© Shimon Ifrah 2019
S. Ifrah, *Deploy Containers on AWS*, https://doi.org/10.1007/978-1-4842-5101-0_6

These are the topics covered in this chapter:

- How to use AWS Identity and Access Management (IAM) groups to manage users

- How to set up permissions

- How to set up password policies

- How to use IAM roles

- How to use security keys

- How to set up billing alerts

- How to turn on AWS Web Application Firewall

Protecting Your Service Accounts on Amazon AWS Container Services

In this section, I will talk about AWS Identity and Access Management and how it can help you secure and control access to your AWS tenant by controlling who is authenticated and authorized to access resources hosted on AWS.

By default, the first account you use to create your AWS account is the root user account with full admin permissions to everything in your AWS tenant.

Note   It is strongly recommended that you don't use this root account for everyday tasks and routines; you should use this account only to create your first IAM user and to perform a few administrative functions such as ordering services and dealing with billing matters.

With AWS IAM you can create users, groups, and custom permissions and apply fine-grained policies and granular permissions to control them.

Multifactor authentication is also part of the IAM feature set and highly recommended.

IAM is accessible from both from the AWS management console and from AWS CLI.

Using IAM Groups

Using groups to assign permissions is an AWS best practice and an efficient way of managing users. When using IAM groups, it is recommended that you create groups that match job roles, such as Administrators, Developers, Marketing, and so on, and then configure the permissions for each group, rather than individually.

This way, permissions are assigned only to groups based on user roles and not per individual user, which leads to inconsistency and is not sustainable in the long run.

To access IAM groups, open the AWS management console and click IAM under Services. You can also use the following direct link:

```
https://console.aws.amazon.com/iam/home
```

Figure 6-1 shows the IAM Groups menu.

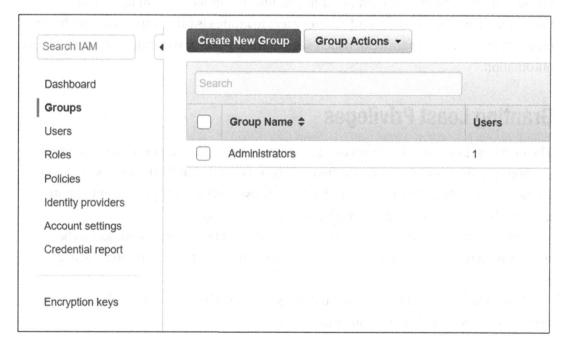

Figure 6-1. *Viewing the IAM Groups menu*

As shown in Figure 6-1, I have one group called Administrators that I created in Chapter 1. To add more administrators to my group, all I need to do is click Add Users to Group at the top-right corner of the group's details page, as shown in Figure 6-2.

Group ARN:	arn:aws:iam::852051225911:group/Administrators ☐
Users (in this group):	1
Path:	/
Creation Time:	2019-01-19 14:24 UTC+1100

Users   Permissions   Access Advisor

This view shows all users in this group: **1 User**

Remove Users from Group   Add Users to Group

User	Actions
👤 Administrator	Remove User from Group

Figure 6-2. *Viewing the IAM users*

When using the Administrators group, you can easily add and remove AWS admins from the group when someone leaves your organization or moves to a new role. Without groups, this process can be cumbersome and difficult to manage. In fact, in large organizations, the process of adding users to groups is fully automated and based on user job title and department, which saves administrative work hours through automation.

Granting Least Privileges

The next best practice is to always assign the least privileges and permissions to users.

Start by giving a user the minimum permissions needed to do their work, and when a new task is assigned to the user, adjust the permissions by adding the user to another group or by creating a new group with the needed permissions.

I have seen many times where developers are given tenant root permissions because there was an urgent need to do something quickly but then the permissions were never removed.

AWS IAM has a great feature called Access Adviser, which you can find in the user account details, as shown in Figure 6-3.

Figure 6-3. *Access Advisor view*

Access Advisor offers the opportunity to review the kind of resources any AWS user is using to see if they are necessary. For example, if a developer is accessing billing resources that do not apply to their account or role, you take action and adjust the groups the user is a member of or the individual permissions the user is using.

AWS also allows you to investigate account activities and events for those activities using CloudTrail logs, which record events based on accounts and applications.

Using Policies

Creating AWS groups can take time and knowledge, and if you are new to AWS, you might not understand the importance of creating groups. For that reason, AWS offers *managed policies*, which are ready-made groups configured by AWS for every role you could think of. Using managed policies, you can configure your users with preconfigured groups.

To access managed policies, click Policies in the AWS IAM console, as shown in Figure 6-4.

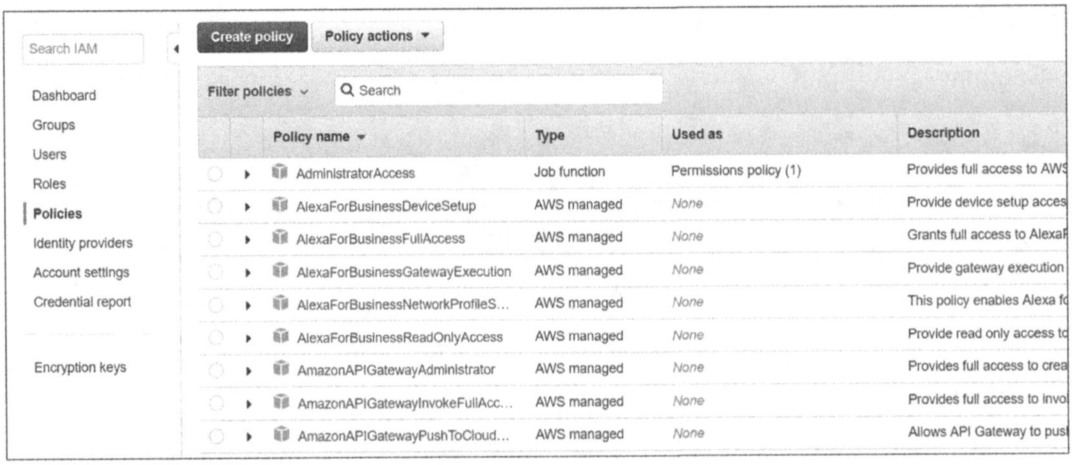

Figure 6-4. IAM policies

As shown in Figure 6-4, I am already using a managed policy, and if you followed the instructions in earlier chapters of this book, you are also using one.

Before I show you how to use a managed policy, I will go ahead and create a new IAM user and group from the user's menu, as shown in Figure 6-5.

In my case, I am creating a user that will manage all S3 storage-related tasks. For the username, I typed **S3Administrator** and set the access to the AWS management console at this stage because I am following the best practice of least privileges, as shown in Figure 6-5.

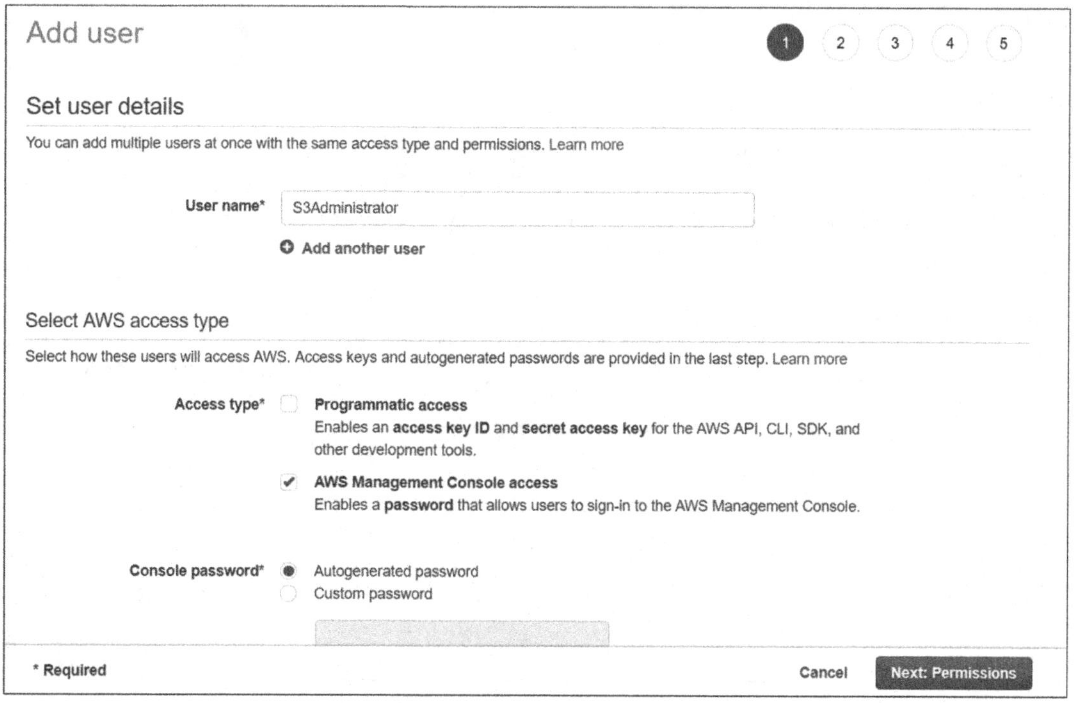

Figure 6-5. *Adding an IAM user*

As you can see, I am also setting the password to be autogenerated.

On the next screen, I will configure the permissions, and as you can see in Figure 6-6, I have the option to add the user to an existing group or to use a managed policy. In this case, I won't use any of these options, so I click Next.

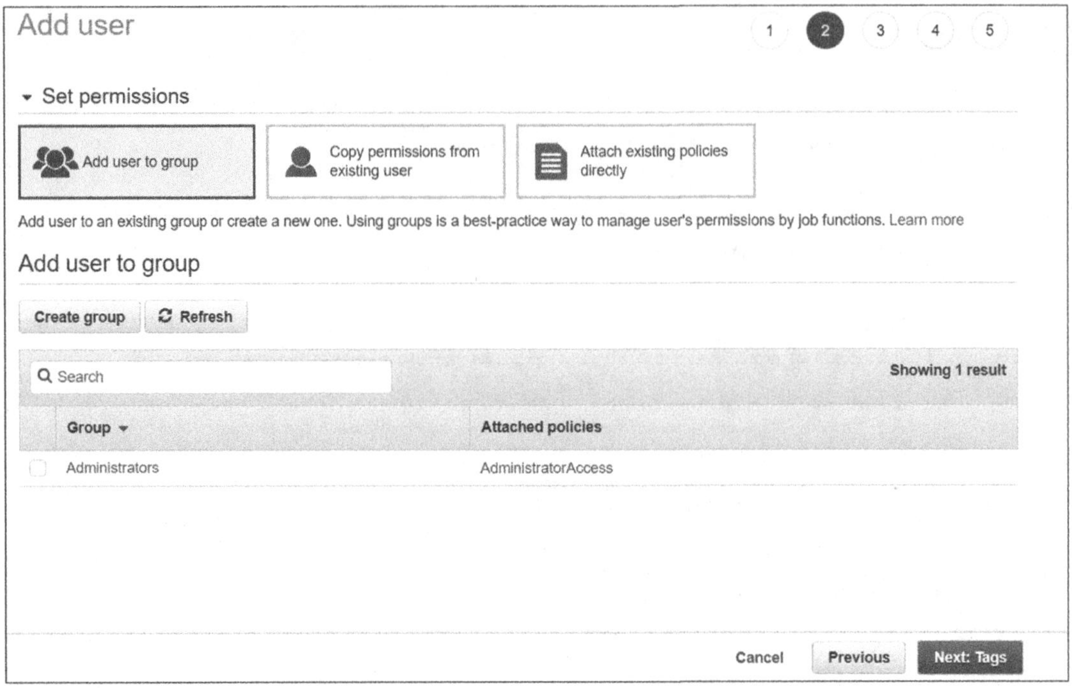

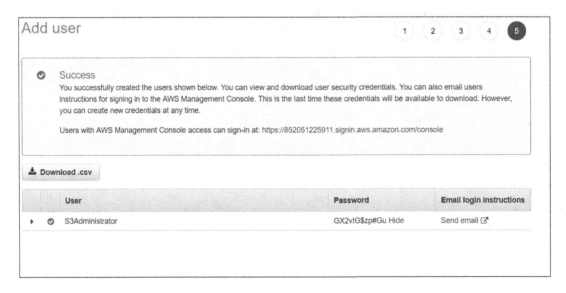

Figure 6-6. *Adding a user*

After the user has been created successfully, as shown in Figure 6-7, go to the
Groups page.

Figure 6-7. *User created successfully*

After creating the user, I will create a group called S3Administrators from the Groups menu, as shown in Figure 6-8.

Figure 6-8. *Creating a new group*

After creating the group, I will add my S3 admin user to it by clicking the group in the Groups menu, as shown in Figure 6-9.

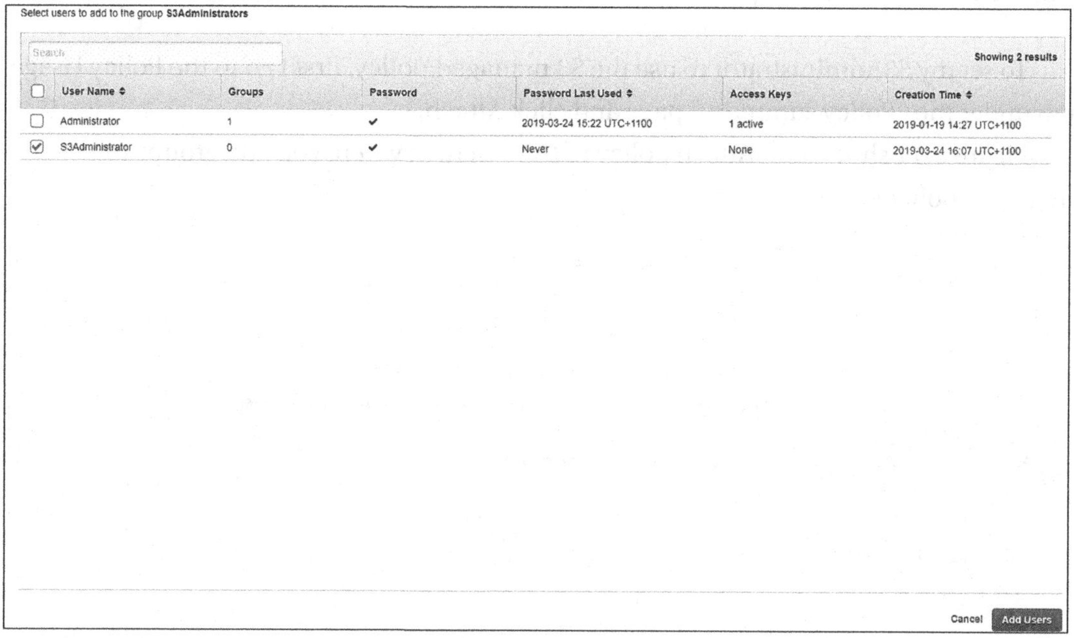

Select users to add to the group **S3Administrators**

	User Name ⇕	Groups	Password	Password Last Used ⇕	Access Keys	Creation Time ⇕
☐	Administrator	1	✓	2019-03-24 15:22 UTC+1100	1 active	2019-01-19 14:27 UTC+1100
☑	S3Administrator	0	✓	Never	None	2019-03-24 16:07 UTC+1100

Cancel   Add Users

Figure 6-9. *Adding the S3Administrator user*

The objective now is to add my S3Administrator user to a managed policy group where the S3 admin role is predefined for me. Therefore, I don't need to worry about or deal with permissions configuration.

On the Policies page, use the search box to search for *S3* and select the AmazonS3FullAccess managed policy.

Figure 6-10 shows the Policies page and the S3 managed policy I am using.

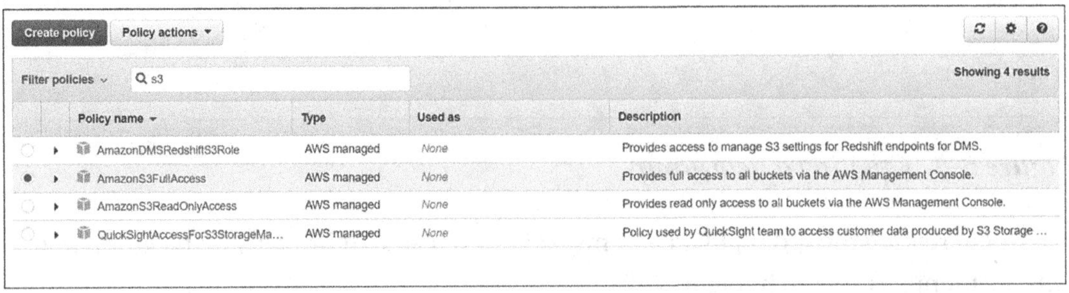

Figure 6-10. *S3 Policies page*

To set my S3Administrator to use the S3 managed policy, first I go to the Policy Usage tab under the "Policy summary" page and click Attach.

Figure 6-11 shows the "Attach policy to IAM" screen where you add groups to managed policies.

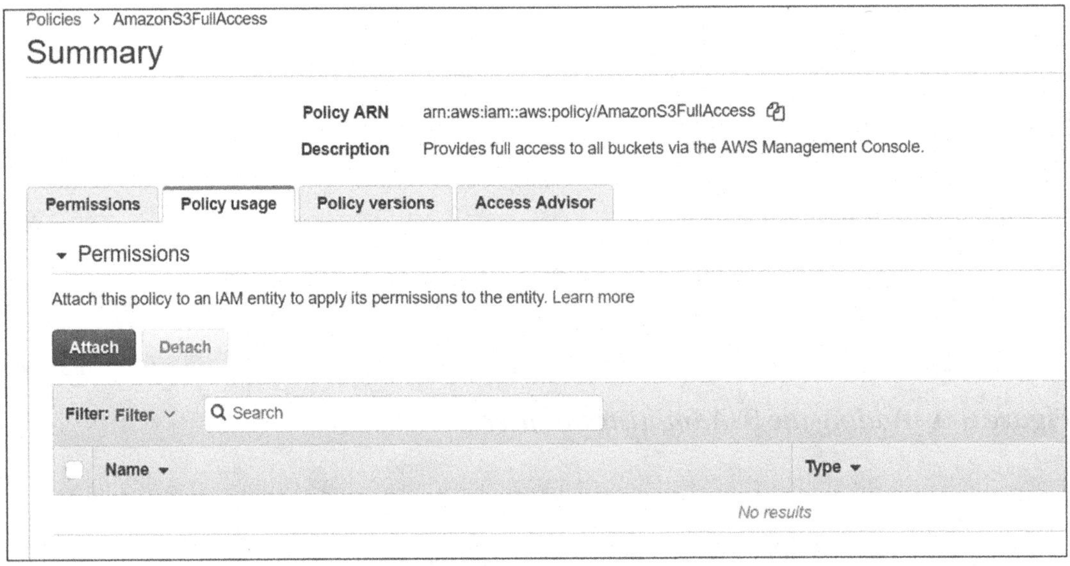

Figure 6-11. *Policy usage view*

On the "Attach policy" page, as shown in Figure 6-12, I select my S3Administrators group.

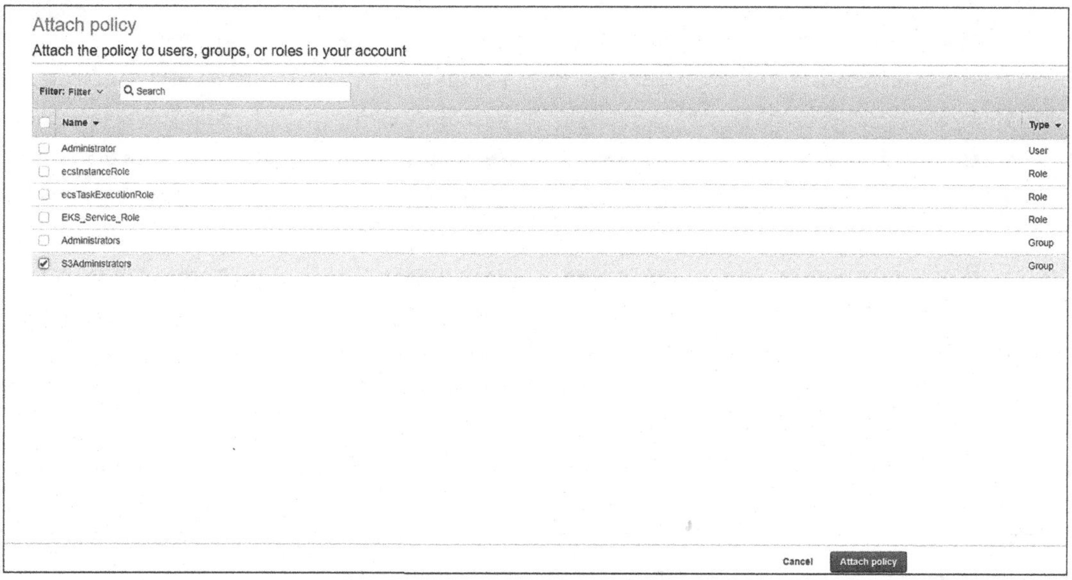

Figure 6-12. *Attaching a policy*

At this stage, the process is complete, and my new S3administrator user has full access permissions to all the S3 administrative tasks in my tenant. Performing this task took a few minutes, and adding new admins or removing them will take even less time.

Using managed policies takes the hard work of configuring groups from you and lets AWS do it. Managed policies also prevent people from making mistakes by using the wrong permissions when configuring a new policy.

Figure 6-13 shows all the managed policies groups in use by using the "Filter policies" option next to the search bar on the Policies page.

	Policy name ▼	Type	Used as	Description
○ ▸	AdministratorAccess	Job function	Permissions policy (1)	Provides full access to AWS ser
○ ▸	AmazonEC2ContainerServiceforEC...	AWS managed	Permissions policy (1)	Default policy for the Amazon EC
○ ▸	AmazonECSServiceRolePolicy	AWS managed	Permissions policy (1)	Policy to enable Amazon ECS to
○ ▸	AmazonECSTaskExecutionRolePolicy	AWS managed	Permissions policy (1)	Provides access to other AWS se
○ ▸	AmazonEKSClusterPolicy	AWS managed	Permissions policy (1)	This policy provides Kubernetes
○ ▸	AmazonEKSServicePolicy	AWS managed	Permissions policy (1)	This policy allows Amazon Elasti
● ▸	AmazonS3FullAccess	AWS managed	Permissions policy (1)	Provides full access to all bucket
○ ▸	AutoScalingServiceRolePolicy	AWS managed	Permissions policy (1)	Enables access to AWS Services
○ ▸	AWSElasticLoadBalancingServiceR...	AWS managed	Permissions policy (1)	Service Linked Role Policy for A\
○ ▸	AWSSupportServiceRolePolicy	AWS managed	Permissions policy (1)	
○ ▸	AWSTrustedAdvisorServiceRolePolicy	AWS managed	Permissions policy (1)	Access for the AWS Trusted Adv

Figure 6-13. *Viewing managed policies*

Reviewing Policies and Policy Usage

AWS recommends that you review your policies every few weeks or months depending on the size of your environment. If you don't have time to review all the policies in use, I recommend you review monthly the ones that have full access permissions and the users who are assigned to these policies.

Checking policy usage is simple and effective when done regularly because it makes sure the right people have the proper access to the right resources.

To check your organization's policy usage, click a policy on the Policies page and then click the "Policy usage" tab, as shown in Figure 6-14.

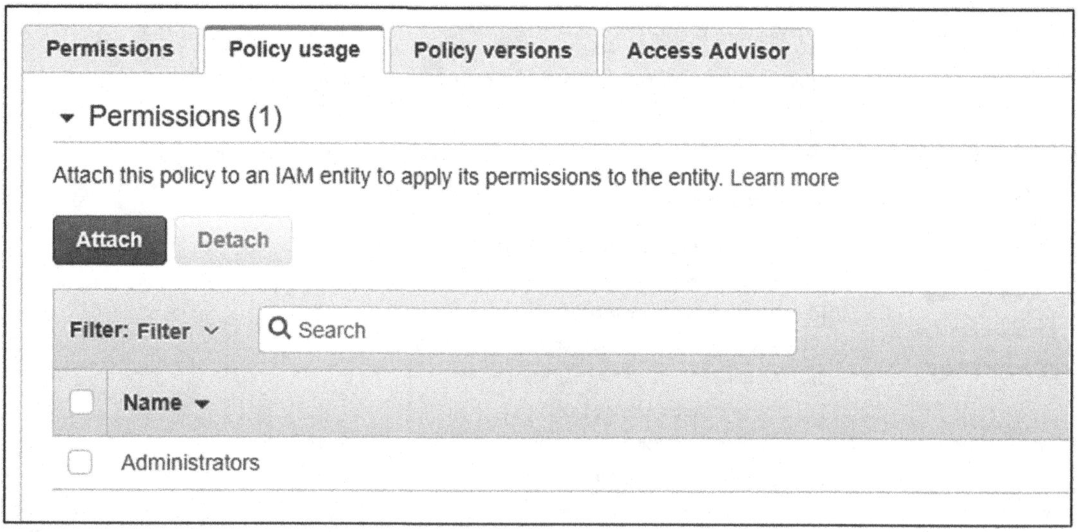

Figure 6-14. *Checking the policy usage*

As you can see, only the Administrators group has access to the Administrator access policy, which gives access to almost all the resources in AWS.

Using a Password Policy

At the heart of IAM user management sits the AWS password policies and their configuration. Every year millions of accounts are compromised because of weak passwords or mismanagement of passwords.

A good IAM policy needs to include a password policy that provides the proper protection from weak password usage.

AWS password policies offer admins the opportunity to control the usage of passwords in AWS by setting policies and applying them to users. To access your password policy, on the IAM page click "Account settings," and you will see the Password Policy page, as shown in Figure 6-15.

Figure 6-15. *Password Policy page*

Note   Password policies do not apply to the root account.

By default, AWS sets the password policy to require six characters and gives users the option to change their passwords.

I recommend you use the following items in your policy:

- Minimum password length = 8

- Prevent password reuse = 2

- Require at least one uppercase letter

- Require at least one lowercase letter

- Require at least one number

These settings will give you a good starting point when it comes to password management.

Setting Up Multifactor Authentication for Root Accounts

It has been proven that using multifactor authentication (MFA) reduces the risk and number of security incidents by 70 percent.

AWS best practices recommend that you enable MFA for your root account and other privileged accounts that have root access to many AWS services. Amazon MFA can work with many MFA devices, including SMS verification, and other advanced two-factor authentication (2FA) hardware.

To enable MFA on your root account, use the My Security Credentials menu item at the top-right corner, as shown in Figure 6-16.

Figure 6-16. *User menu*

On the Your Security Credentials page, click Activate MFA and follow the prompts, as shown in Figure 6-17.

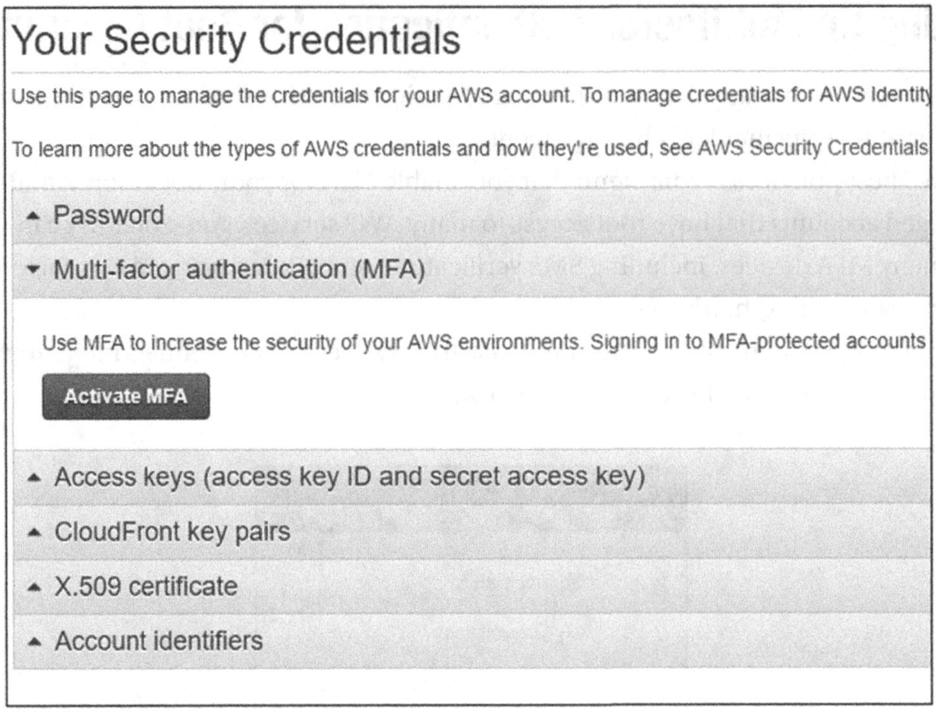

Your Security Credentials

Use this page to manage the credentials for your AWS account. To manage credentials for AWS Identity

To learn more about the types of AWS credentials and how they're used, see AWS Security Credentials

▲ Password

▼ Multi-factor authentication (MFA)

Use MFA to increase the security of your AWS environments. Signing in to MFA-protected accounts

Activate MFA

▲ Access keys (access key ID and secret access key)

▲ CloudFront key pairs

▲ X.509 certificate

▲ Account identifiers

Figure 6-17.   Security credentials screen

Setting Up IAM Roles

IAM roles are used to manage temporary access to or from applications to AWS resources without using credentials or access key.

When you use IAM roles, the role supplies the permissions to the application without the need to provide a username and password. You can create IAM roles from the IAM management console using the Roles menu, as shown in Figure 6-18.

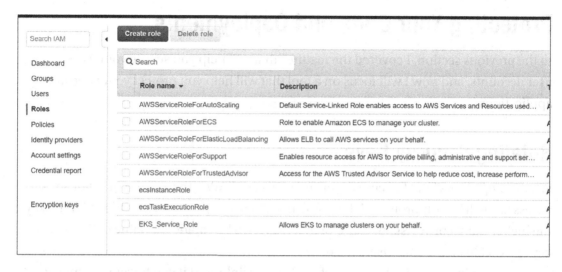

Figure 6-18. *Creating an IAM role*

As you can see in Figure 6-18, I have created a few roles in the previous chapters for my EKS and ECS services. If I click the EKS_Service_Role item and review the Permissions tab, I will see that inside the role there are AWS managed policies and a JSON file that describes the permissions, as shown in Figure 6-19.

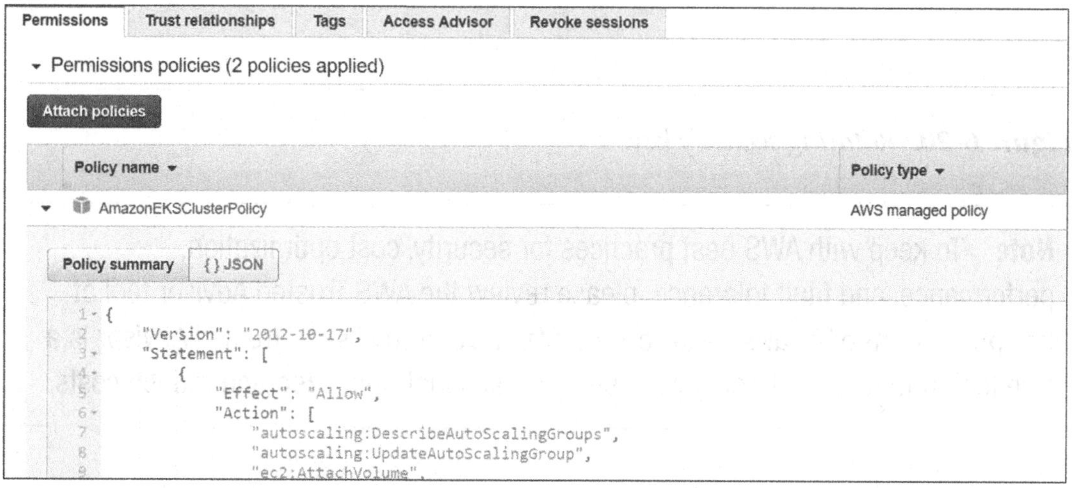

Figure 6-19. *Attaching policies*

Protecting Your Code and Deployments

In the previous section, I covered the features that will help you secure your AWS user accounts, and now I will focus on a tool that will help you protect your code and applications.

Rotating Security Keys

When using access keys to access data and services in AWS, there is the risk that an access key will be compromised. It is known in AWS best practices that the older the key, the higher the security risk. Because of that risk, AWS has made the value of the access key age visible on the IAM Users page.

As shown in Figure 6-20, the age of the key is visible, and if you hover your mouse over it, you can see the age rotation recommendation, as shown in Figure 6-21.

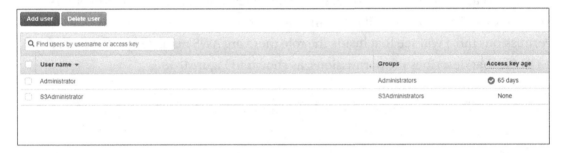

Figure 6-20. *Rotating security keys*

Note   To keep with AWS best practices for security, cost optimization, performance, and fault tolerance, please review the AWS Trusted Advisor tool at `https://console.aws.amazon.com/trustedadvisor`. Trusted Advisor is a free tool from AWS that helps you keep your account optimized and reduce costs.

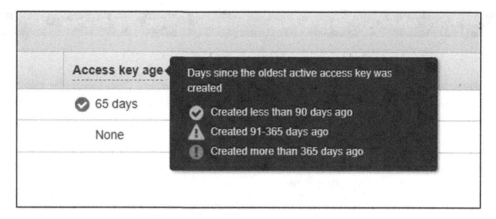

Figure 6-21. *Accessing the key age*

The next feature that I recommend you use and get familiar with is CloudTrail. CloudTrail is a user event logging system that logs the login events of users to AWS. With CloudTrail you can view and search users and their API, AWS CLI, and SDK access activities.

By default, CloudTrail is enabled on every AWS account.

To create a permanent event login strategy, it is recommended you create a trail and direct the logs to an S3 storage bucket. A single trail will log data from all AWS regions regardless of the location of the S3 storage. To view events in CloudTrail, search for *CloudTrail* in the services search bar.

In the CloudTrail console, you will see all the activities from the last 90 days, as shown in Figure 6-22. If you click an event, you will see detailed information about the request such as the following:

- Username

- Event time

- AWS region the request was made to

- Source IP address

- User agent (browser version and device)

- Login status (success or failure)

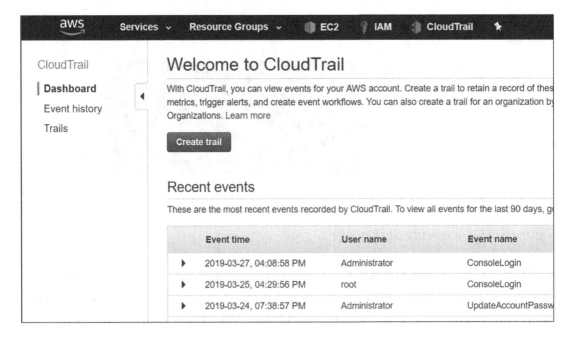

Figure 6-22.   *Welcome to CloudTrail screen*

Creating a Trail

If you need to extend the life of your event login beyond 90 days, you can create a trail and send the logs to an S3 storage bucket. With a trail you can automatically monitor incoming requests and act on them using Amazon CloudWatch.

To create a trail, click the "Create trail" button, as shown in Figure 6-23.

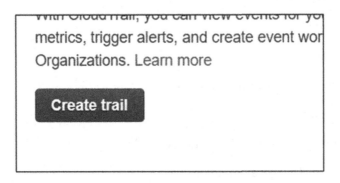

Figure 6-23.   *Creating a trail*

On the Create Trail page, you have the option to configure the trail to capture read-only, write-only, or all events.

You can also opt to create a new S3 bucket or use an existing one, as shown in Figure 6-24.

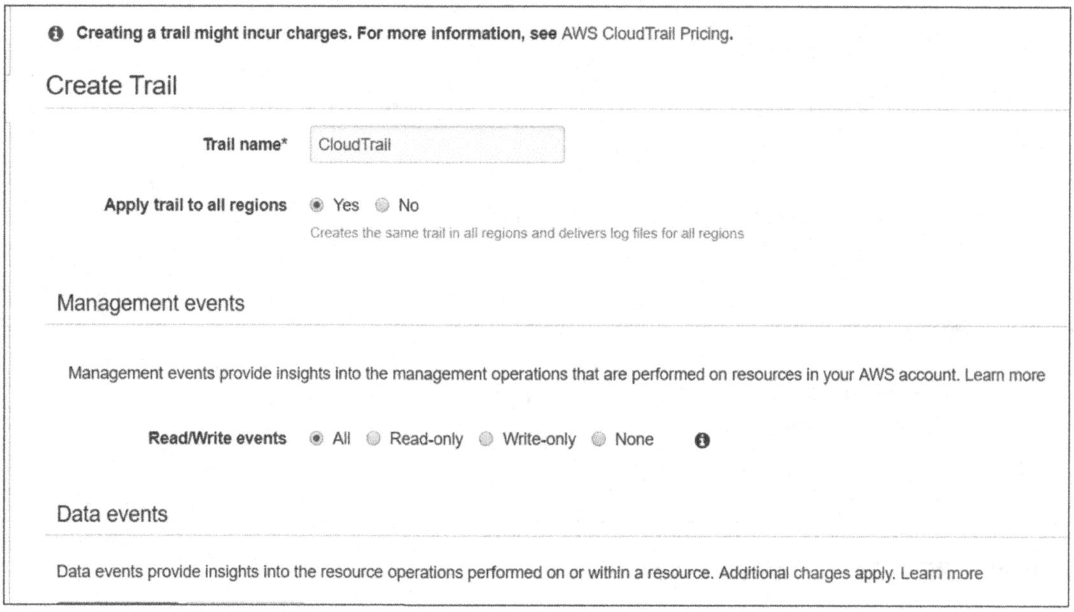

ⓘ Creating a trail might incur charges. For more information, see AWS CloudTrail Pricing.

Create Trail

Trail name*   CloudTrail

Apply trail to all regions   ⦿ Yes ○ No
Creates the same trail in all regions and delivers log files for all regions

Management events

Management events provide insights into the management operations that are performed on resources in your AWS account. Learn more

Read/Write events   ⦿ All ○ Read-only ○ Write-only ○ None   ⓘ

Data events

Data events provide insights into the resource operations performed on or within a resource. Additional charges apply. Learn more

Figure 6-24. *Trail name screen*

The storage option gives you the opportunity to select the log file prefix, encrypt logs, and send an SNS notification for every log file delivery.

Figure 6-25 shows the storage options.

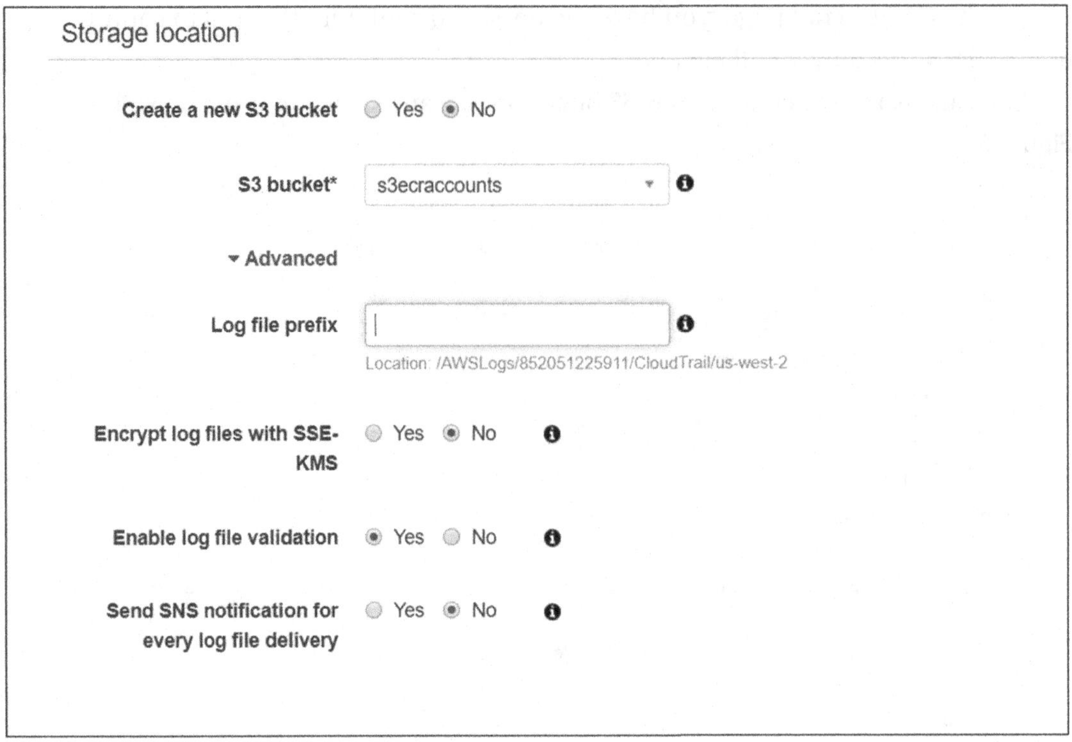

Figure 6-25. *CloudTrail storage location*

After a trail has been created, it is easy to delete the trail and create a new one. You can also turn on or off the logging of a trail without deleting it using the On/Off button at the top-right corner of the trail, as shown in Figure 6-26.

Note   CloudTrail is free for the first 150,000 events and then $2 per the next 150,000 events.

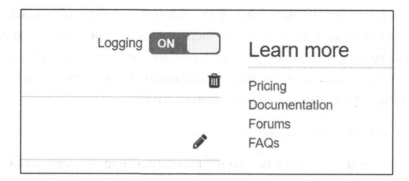

Figure 6-26. *Enabling Cloud Trail logging*

Protecting Your Containers and Container Host on Amazon EC2

In this section, I will cover some tools that will help you protect your containers and Docker hosts on AWS.

Using AWS CloudWatch

Protecting your servers and services on AWS is something that needs to be done on two fronts. The first is security, by controlling and managing users and permissions. By following AWS best practices, you can prevent unauthorized users from accessing your AWS resources.

The second type of protection is to make sure your servers are not being misused from external and internal resources. If you have a front-end application that is exposed to the Internet via a public IP address, you need to have the right tools in place and know if you are under a denial-of-service (DOS) attack.

To monitor AWS resources, AWS provides CloudWatch as a service, and using CloudWatch you can monitor your resources on AWS. CloudWatch is a multilayer application monitoring service that helps AWS customers get insights into their resource availability and performance. With CloudWatch, developers, systems operators, and engineers can review and understand if an application is being overloaded or is under a security attack.

Once you understand CloudWatch, you can automate responses as and when the application state changes. With one-second metrics data and retention of all data, you can see whether there is a growth in usage and can plan for the future by scaling up or down.

CloudWatch offers free and paid tier options with different features and usage. For more information about pricing, visit the following URL:

`https://aws.amazon.com/cloudwatch/pricing/`

To get started with CloudWatch, search for *CloudWatch* in the applications search bar. You can use the navigation menu for easy access, as explained in the next section.

Customizing the Navigation Menu

For quick access, I suggest you add CloudWatch to the navigation shortcut menu in the AWS Portal, as shown in Figure 6-27.

Figure 6-27. *AWS navigation menu*

To add a shortcut, click the pin icon in the Navigation menu and drag it to the top list, as shown in Figure 6-28.

Figure 6-28. *Adding an item to the navigation menu*

You can also customize the look and feel of the navigation menu using the Settings menu located on the right side of the customization page.

Figure 6-29 shows the Settings menu options for the navigation menu.

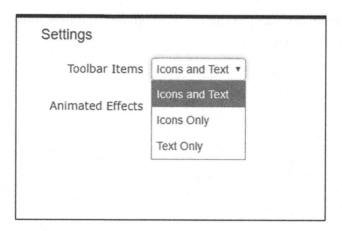

Figure 6-29. *Toolbar items display settings*

In Figure 6-30 you can see the navigation menu's icons-only view.

Figure 6-30. *Icons-only view*

In Figure 6-31, you can see the text-only navigation menu view.

Figure 6-31. *Text-only view*

Getting Started with CloudWatch

After customizing your navigation menu, we can continue with the CloudWatch overview.

In Figure 6-32 you can see how the main CloudWatch console looks. By default, the option "All resources" is selected.

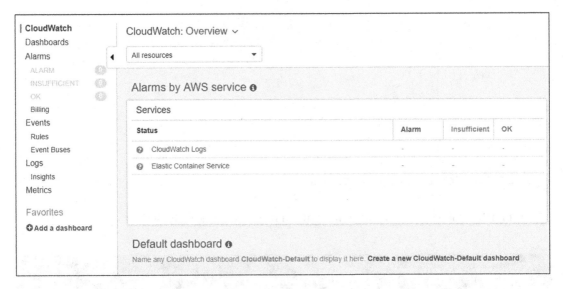

Figure 6-32. *CloudWatch overview screen*

You can also view the logs by clicking the Logs menu, as shown in Figure 6-33.

Figure 6-33. *Logs view*

As you can see in Figure 6-33, the logs have a name prefix that allows you to know from which service the logs have originated.

In my case, the logs come from my ECS container service.

Using CloudWatch Dashboards

Using Dashboards, you can customize the views of the resources you are monitoring and get up-to-date statistics of your AWS resources.

The CloudWatch Free Tier plan offers three free dashboards and 50 metrics per month without any charges. The paid tier will cost you $3 per month for an additional dashboard and $0.30 per month for the first 10,000 metrics.

You can review the pricing plans at the following URL:

```
https://aws.amazon.com/cloudwatch/pricing/
```

To create a dashboard, click the CloudWatch console icon or use the following URL to access CloudWatch:

```
https://console.aws.amazon.com/cloudwatch/
```

In the left menu, click Dashboards and click the "Create dashboard" button on the main page, as shown in Figure 6-34.

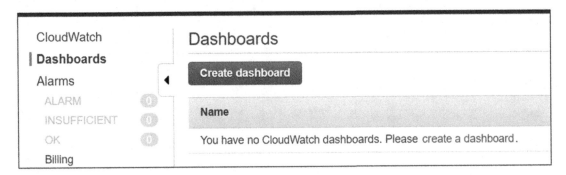

Figure 6-34. *CloudWatch dashboards*

Name the dashboard, as shown in Figure 6-35.

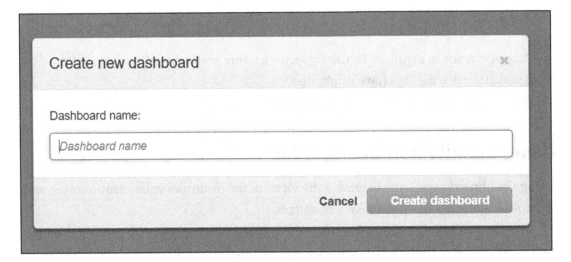

Figure 6-35. *Creating a new dashboard*

In my case, I will call the dashboard S3.

On the "Add to this dashboard" page, select the widget type and click Configure, as shown in Figure 6-36.

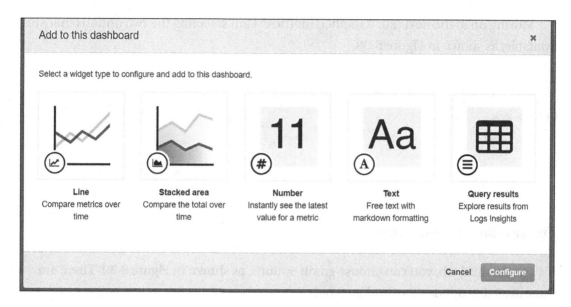

Figure 6-36. *Selecting a widget type*

On the "All metrics" tab, you can select the metrics you want to see on your page, as shown in Figure 6-37.

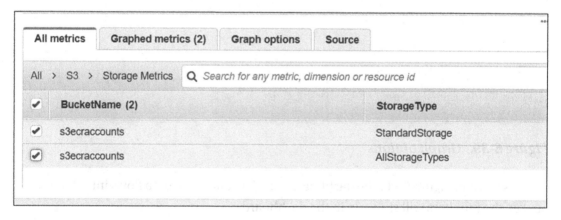

Figure 6-37. *Adding metrics*

To get information from a storage account, select the storage account on the "All metrics" tab.

Moving on to the next tab, "Graphed metrics," I am selecting the two options that are available, as shown in Figure 6-38.

Figure 6-38. *"Graphed metrics" tab*

On the third tab, you can choose graph options, as shown in Figure 6-39. There are three available options for "Widget type."

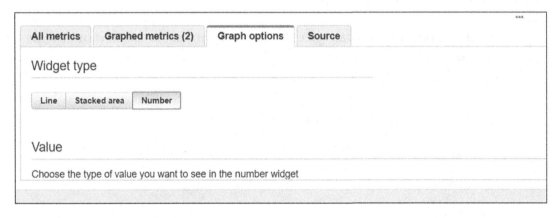

Figure 6-39. *Graph options*

As shown in Figure 6-40, the dashboard is active, and once data flows into the bucket, the numbers will show up in the dashboard.

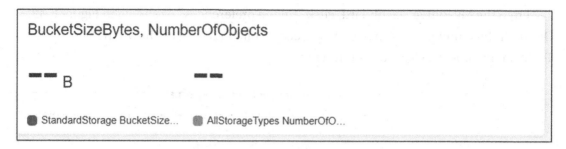

Figure 6-40. *Bucket size in bytes metric*

Configuring Billing Alerts

CloudWatch offers a great feature that can help you control your AWS costs by setting up billing alerts. To configure billing alerts with CloudWatch, you need to first log in with the AWS root admin account and enable billing alerts.

To do so, log in to the AWS management console with the root account and click My Billing Dashboard, as shown in Figure 6-41.

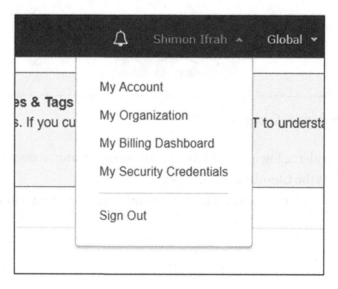

Figure 6-41. *My Billing Dashboard menu item*

From the My Billing Dashboard, click "Billing preferences," as shown in Figure 6-42. On the "Billing preferences" page, select Receive Billing Alerts, as shown in Figure 6-42. To finish the process, click Save Preferences.

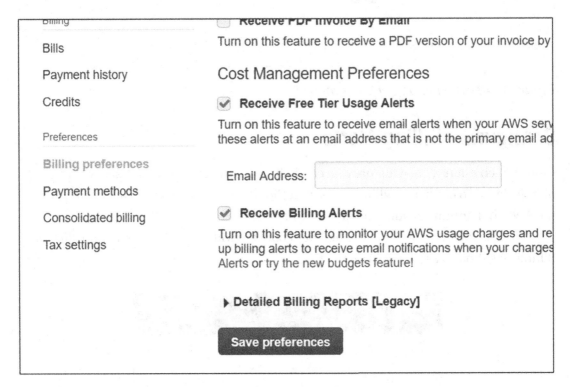

Figure 6-42. *Saving preferences*

After setting up alerts, log in to AWS with your administrator account (not your root account) and access the CloudWatch console.

I the CloudWatch console, click Billing in the left menu, as shown in Figure 6-43.

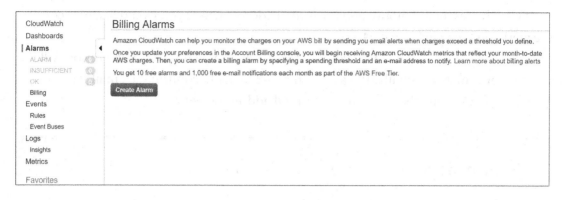

Figure 6-43. *Creating an alarm*

To create a billing alert, click Create Alarm and fill in the details under "Billing alarm," as shown in Figure 6-44.

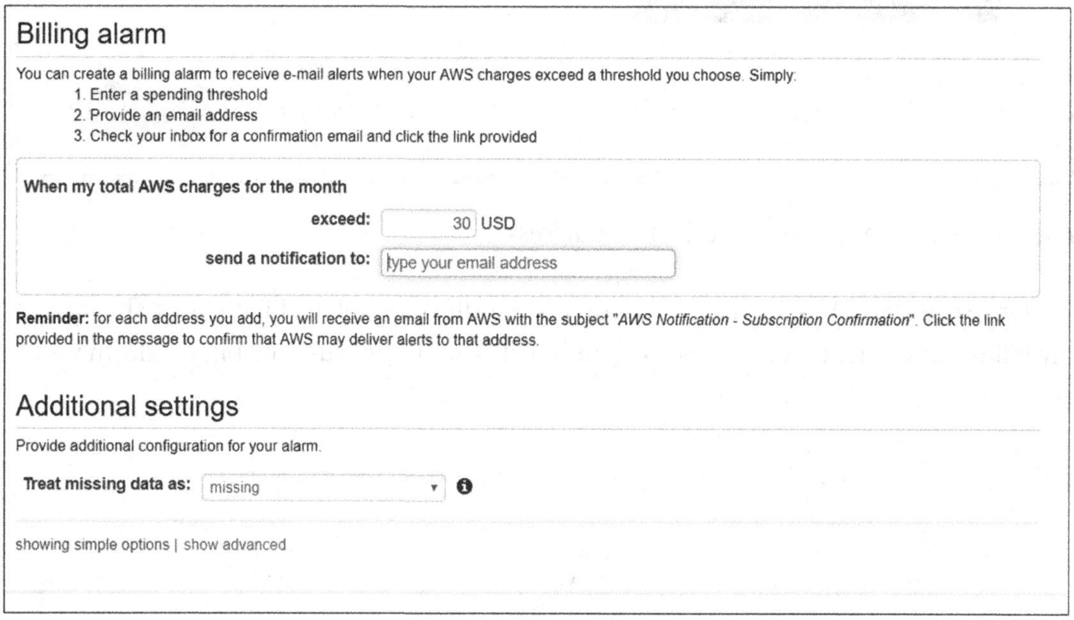

Billing alarm

You can create a billing alarm to receive e-mail alerts when your AWS charges exceed a threshold you choose. Simply:
1. Enter a spending threshold
2. Provide an email address
3. Check your inbox for a confirmation email and click the link provided

---

When my total AWS charges for the month

exceed: `30` USD

send a notification to: `type your email address`

Reminder: for each address you add, you will receive an email from AWS with the subject "*AWS Notification - Subscription Confirmation*". Click the link provided in the message to confirm that AWS may deliver alerts to that address.

Additional settings

Provide additional configuration for your alarm.

Treat missing data as: `missing` ▾ ⓘ

---

showing simple options | show advanced

Figure 6-44. *Exceeding the limit*

Enter the "exceed" amount and the e-mail address where you would like to receive the alert and then click Create Alarm.

Once you generate the alarm, you will receive an e-mail from AWS where you will need to confirm your e-mail address. You have 72 hours to confirm the email.

Figure 6-45 shows the confirmation e-mail address screen.

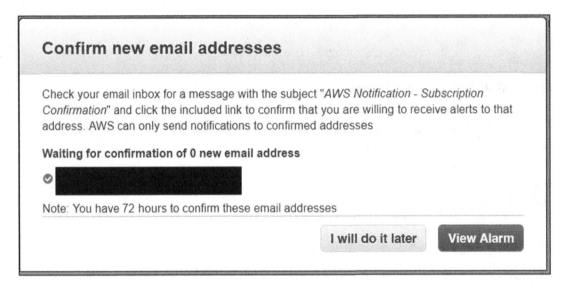

Figure 6-45. *Confirming the e-mail address*

Once the alarm has been created, you can modify it or delete. Figure 6-46 shows my billing alarm in action, and as you can see, it is active because my billing alarm was activated.

Figure 6-46. *Viewing alarms*

Using AWS Config

In this section, you will learn about AWS Config and how it can help you better manage your resources in AWS. AWS Config provides you with an inventory of your AWS resources and a configuration history for resources in AWS.

To get started with AWS Config, search for *Config* in the services search bar from the AWS management console. On the AWS Config page, click "Get started," as shown in Figure 6-47.

Figure 6-47. *AWS Config getting started screen*

On the configuration page, select the check box for the type of resource you want to track. To store your AWS Config data, you need to create or use an existing S3 storage bucket.

In my case, I am using the existing S3 bucket that I created earlier, as shown in Figure 6-48.

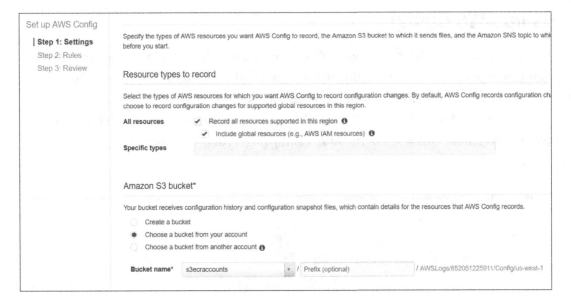

Figure 6-48. *Selecting resources*

AWS will also create an AWS Config role, as shown in Figure 6-49, to manage the permissions between all the services and AWS Config.

Figure 6-49. *AWS Config role*

In the Rules menu, you can select the services you want to track changes for, or you can select all of them.

In Figure 6-50, I have selected all the rules and clicked All.

AWS Config rules

AWS Config can check the configuration of your resources against rules that you define. Choose one or more of the following rules to get started. After setting up AWS Con rules, set up other rules provided by AWS Config, or create your own rules.

Learn more about AWS Config rules and pricing details.

Filter by rule name, label or description

« ‹ Viewing 1 - 9 of 52 AWS managed rules › »

Select all 52 | Clear all

acm-certificate-expiration-check	autoscaling-group-elb-healthcheck-re...	cloud-trail-cloud-watch-logs-enabled
Checks whether ACM Certificates in your account are marked for expiration within the specified number of days. Certificates provided by ACM are automatically renewed.	Checks whether your Auto Scaling groups that are associated with a load balancer are using Elastic Load Balancing health checks.	Checks whether AWS CloudTrail trails are configured to send logs to Amazon CloudWatch logs. The trail is non-compliant if the CloudWatchLogsLogGroupArn property of
ACM	AutoScaling	CloudTrail . Periodic

Figure 6-50. *AWS config rules*

Using AWS Web Application Firewall

In this chapter, I will cover AWS Web Application Firewall (AWS WAF). AWS WAF is a web application firewall service that you place in front of your EC2 hosts or applications and route traffic to them.

WAF protects your application from threats like distributed denial-of-service (DDoS) attacks and SQL injections using predefined rules and access control lists. With WAF, your applications are not the first touchpoint of external traffic. WAF will drop all traffic that is not defined on the access list without passing it to your servers by rejecting the connection. By filtering the requests, your servers are responding and processing only valid requests from real clients and users. WAF is fully integrated with CloudWatch and CloudTrail and allows visibility into your systems and servers.

The main benefits of WAF are as follows:

- Allows all requests except specified requests

- Blocks all requests except specified requests

- Counts requests that match your rules

Exploring WAF Pricing

WAF pricing is based on the number of web access control lists (web ACLs) you have, at $5 per ACL per month. Each rule costs $1 per ACL per month, and for every 1 million requests you will pay $0.60.

The AWS Marketplace also offers managed rules that are predefined and tested by third-party providers.

Configuring WAF

To configure WAF in the AWS console, search for *WAF* and click "Configure web ACL," as shown in Figure 6-51.

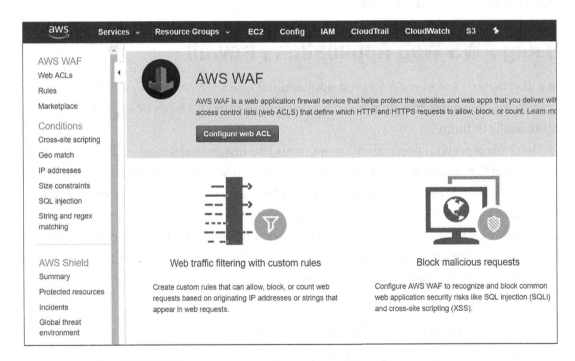

Figure 6-51. *AWS WAF getting started page*

On the "Set up a web access control list (web ACL)" page, as shown in Figure 6-52, you can see all the available concepts in WAF.

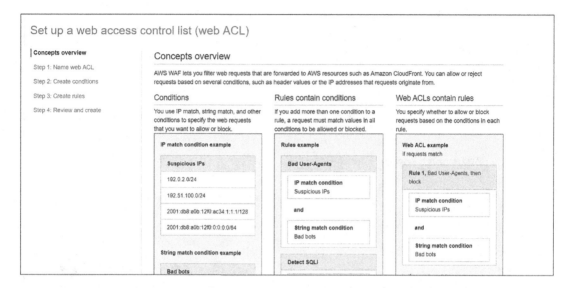

Figure 6-52. *AWS WAF concepts overview*

On the "Name web ACL" page (shown in Figure 6-53), you can give your web ACL a name that will show up in CloudWatch.

You can also select a specific region, or you can use the global AWS region if you are planning to use AWS CloudFront.

Note   AWS CloudFront is a content delivery network (CDN) that uses the AWS global network to deliver, secure, and distribute applications.

In many cases, WAF and CloudFront are used together to mitigate DDOS attacks. To read more about CloudWatch, visit the following URL:

```
https://aws.amazon.com/cloudfront/
```

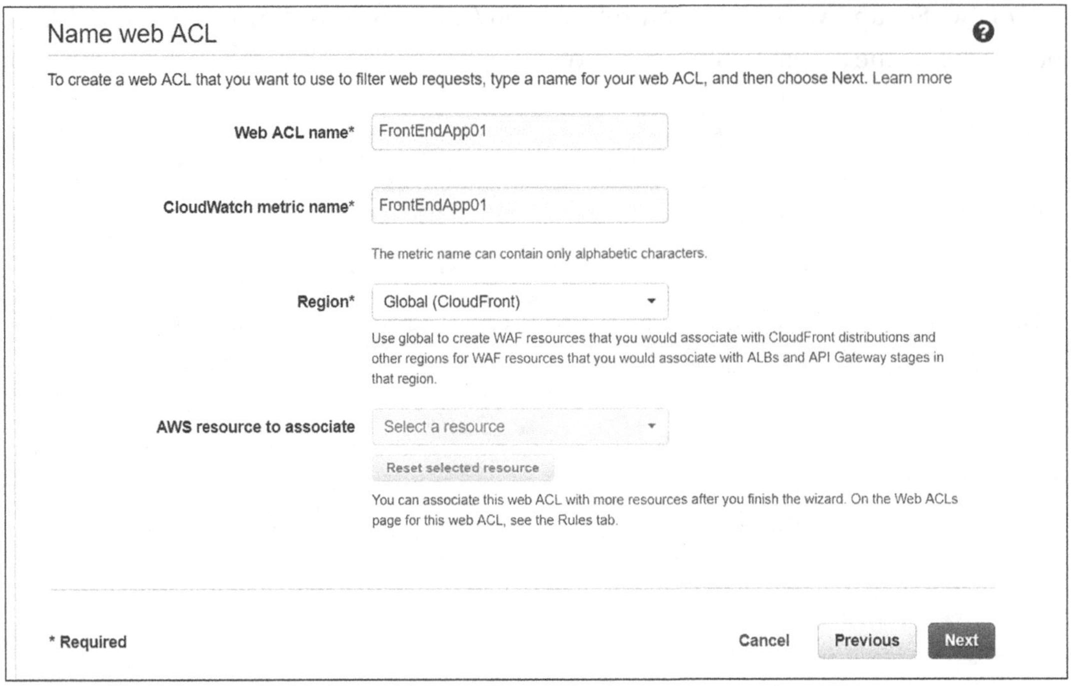

Figure 6-53. *The "Name web ACL" page*

On the Create Condition page, you can define the following conditions:

- **Cross-site scripting match conditions**: These requests allow WAF to review conditions that are part of the web request such as headers and scripts.

- **Geo match conditions**: This allows you to block or allow requests based on countries and locations.

- **IP match conditions**: This allows you to block or allow an IP range of addresses that are coming from dangerous networks.

- **Size constraint conditions**: This allows you to block user agent headers based on size.

- **SQL injection match conditions**: This lets WAF inspect all SQL queries and block them.

- **String and regex match conditions**: This allows you to match regex conditions and block or allow requests.

Figure 6-54 shows the "Create conditions" page with all the conditions you can configure.

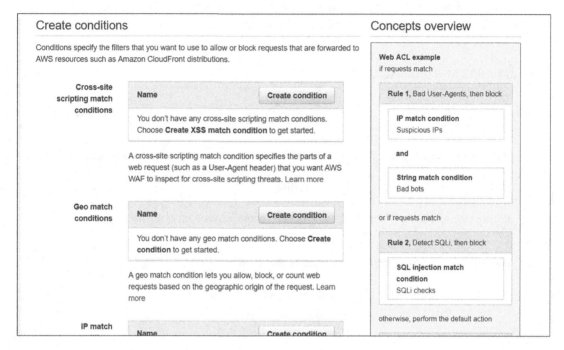

Figure 6-54. *The "Create conditions" page*

In the last configuration step, you create a rule and set the default action that will be taken, as shown in Figure 6-55.

When you configure the default action of the rule, it is essential you test all the possible scenarios and devices that will use your application.

From my experience, it is better to use the "Block all requests that don't match any rules." Using the block rule will prevent attackers from somehow finding a rule or condition that you have not thought about and gaining access to your front-end servers.

It is also recommended that you review your WAF conditions and rules every quarter and update them if needed.

Make sure you use CloudWatch data to see whether all malicious traffic is being blocked and try to reduce it.

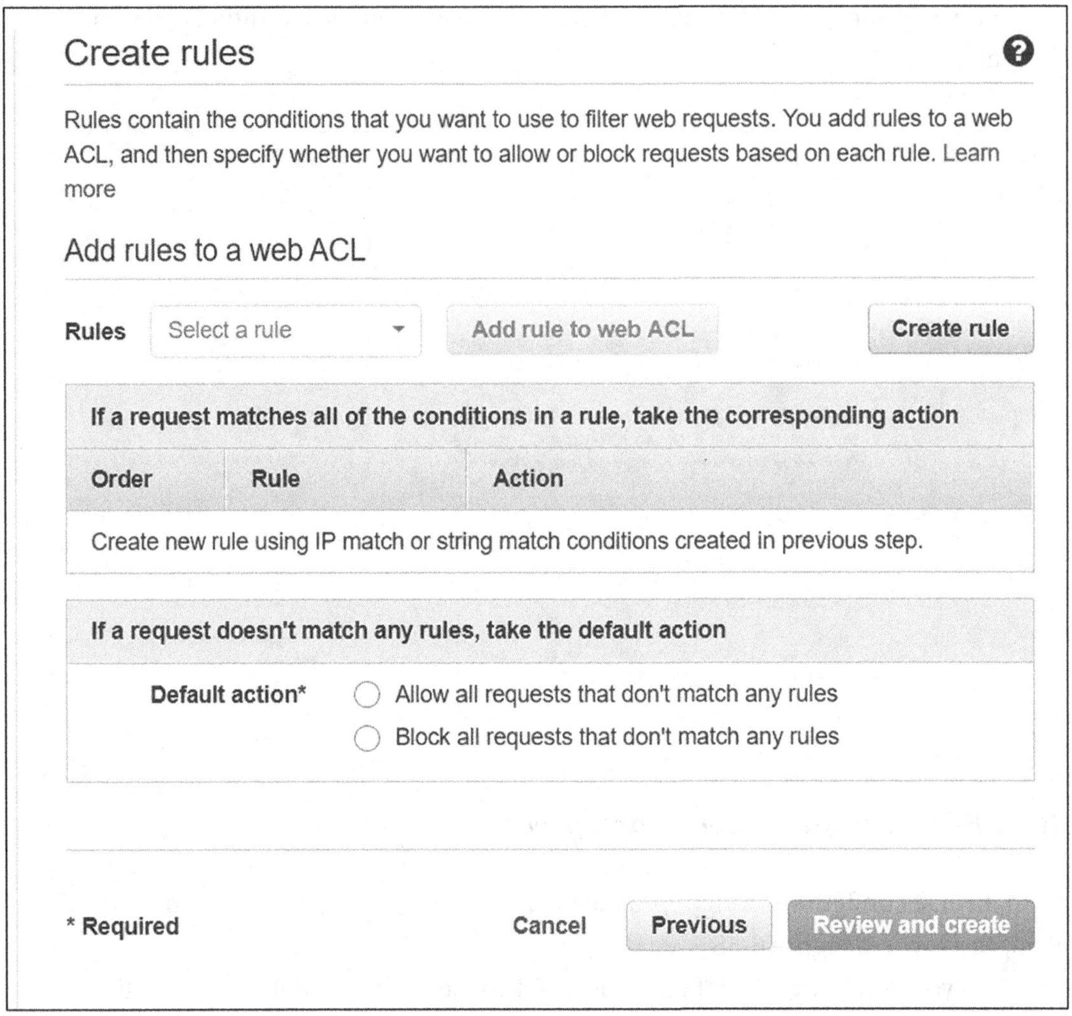

Create rules   ❓

Rules contain the conditions that you want to use to filter web requests. You add rules to a web ACL, and then specify whether you want to allow or block requests based on each rule. Learn more

Add rules to a web ACL

Rules   Select a rule   ▼   Add rule to web ACL   Create rule

If a request matches all of the conditions in a rule, take the corresponding action

Order	Rule	Action

Create new rule using IP match or string match conditions created in previous step.

If a request doesn't match any rules, take the default action

Default action*   ◯   Allow all requests that don't match any rules
                        ◯   Block all requests that don't match any rules

* Required   Cancel   Previous   Review and create

Figure 6-55. *Creating rules*

Summary

In this chapter, you learned how to secure your AWS tenant using AWS best practices. Following these guidelines will ensure your tenant is secure, optimized, and scalable in the long run.

I also recommend you review the AWS Trusted Advisor tool, which will help you maintain your AWS account, keep it optimized, and reduce costs.

CHAPTER 7

Scaling the AWS EKS, ECS, and ECR Containerized Environments

In the previous chapter, I showed you how to secure your AWS tenant using AWS best practices. In this chapter, you will dive into the world of scaling containers on AWS. Amazon AWS allows you to scale the AWS container services in several ways.

Scaling container services in AWS is essential because of the following reasons:

- **Cost**: When running services on AWS, you might have times where the activity and usage are low, and therefore there is no need to run a service on a costly instance or tier.

- **Demand**: When the demand increases, you need a way to increase the capacity quickly with minimum disruption.

In this chapter, I will cover the following topics:

- How to scale an AWS EKS cluster

- How to scale the AWS ECS Fargate services and an ECS EC2 cluster

- How to scale and monitor AWS ECR

- How to update an EKS cluster with the latest software release

© Shimon Ifrah 2019
S. Ifrah, *Deploy Containers on AWS*, https://doi.org/10.1007/978-1-4842-5101-0_7

Creating an EKS Cluster

Before I show you how to scale EKS, I will show you how to create an EKS cluster; however, because you saw the detailed steps in Chapter 4, these setup instructions will be shorter and used as a refresher. For more details, please review Chapter 4.

These are the overall steps for setting up an EKS cluster:

1. Create an EKS IAM role.

2. Create a VPC.

3. Create an EKS cluster.

4. Create a local kubectl configuration file.

5. Create a worker node.

Creating an EKS IAM Role

The first step when creating an EKS cluster is to create an IAM role for the EKS cluster service.

To create an EKS role, open the IAM console, click Roles, and click "Create role," as shown in Figure 7-1.

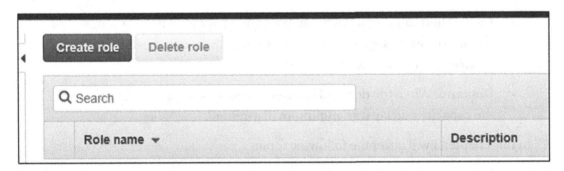

Figure 7-1. *Creating an EKS IAM role*

On the "Choose the service..." page, select EKS, as shown in Figure 7-2.

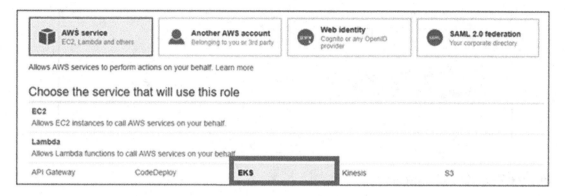

Figure 7-2. *Choosing an EKS service role*

Click Next, and review the policies listed. Then click and follow the prompts to finish the creation process.

Figure 7-3 shows the EKS cluster policies that will be used in the examples in this chapter.

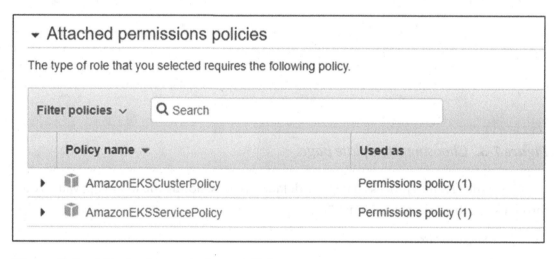

Figure 7-3. *Attached permissions policies*

Now that you have created a role, you need to create a VPC.

Creating a VPC

To create a VPC, open the CloudFormation console and click Create Stack, as shown in Figure 7-4.

Figure 7-4. *Creating a stack*

On the "Choose a template" screen, select "Specify an Amazon S3 template URL" and paste the following into the text box, as shown in Figure 7-5:

```
https://amazon-eks.s3-us-west-2.amazonaws.com/cloudformation/2019-01-09/
amazon-eks-vpc-sample.yaml
```

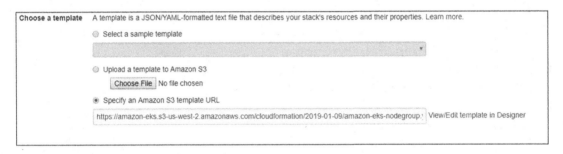

Figure 7-5. *Choosing a template page*

Finish the creation process using the default options, noting the following values on the Outputs tab, as shown in Figure 7-6:

- SecurityGroups
- Vpcid
- Subnetlds

Overview	Outputs	Resources	Events	Template	Parameters	Tags	Stack Policy	Change Sets	Rollback Trigger

Key	Value
SecurityGroups	sg-04084c7132e38f585
VpcId	vpc-0207a37adedf986ef
SubnetIds	subnet-01a6547d5b7bafdf1,subnet-0ee13d81a44a68c15,subnet-06e4a9a04c103710b

Figure 7-6. *Outputs tab*

You will use these values to link the EKS cluster to the VPC.

Creating the Cluster

Now that you have your VPC configured, you need to create the EKS cluster. In the AWS management console, open the EKS management console. Please review Chapter 4 for detailed information about EKS.

On the EKS console page, click Clusters and then click "Create cluster," as shown in Figure 7-7 and Figure 7-8.

Figure 7-7. *EKS menu*

Note   Please review the AWS EKS pricing details for the latest EKS information.

Figure 7-8. *Clicking to create an EKS cluster*

On the "Create cluster" page, I am naming my cluster **EKS-Cluster** and selecting version 1.11 for the Kubernetes version. For the role name, I am selecting EKS_Service_ Role from the drop-down list, as shown in Figure 7-9.

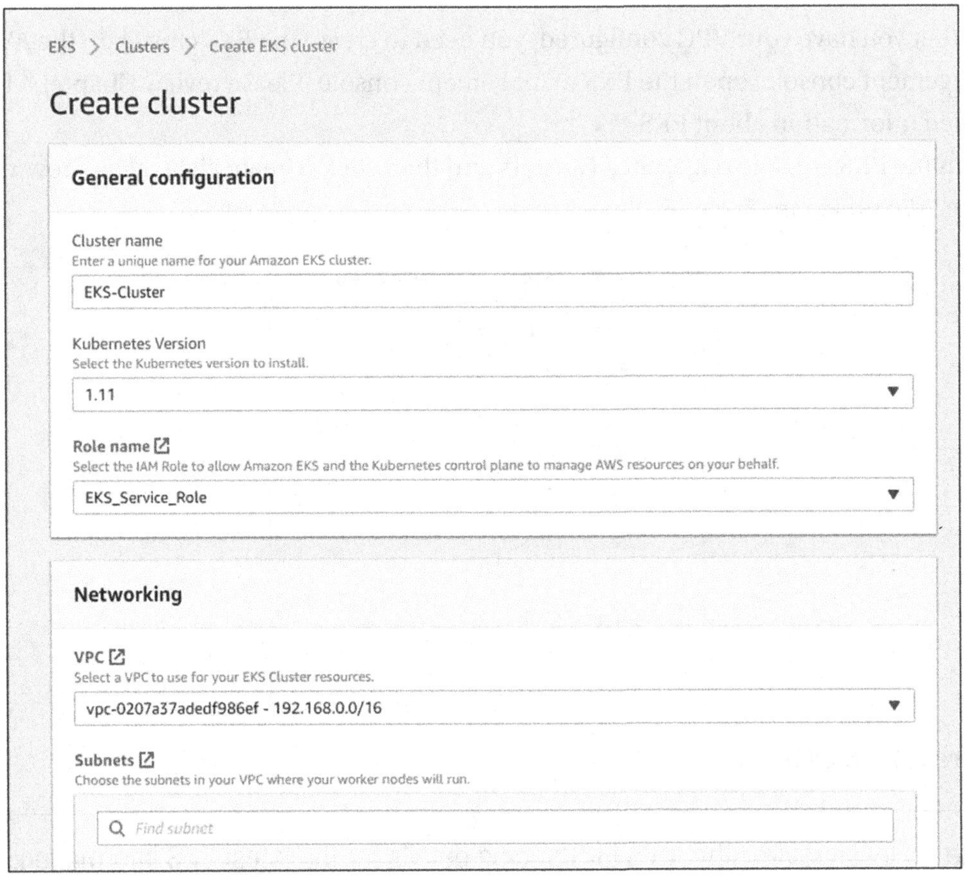

EKS > Clusters > Create EKS cluster

Create cluster

General configuration

Cluster name
Enter a unique name for your Amazon EKS cluster.

EKS-Cluster

Kubernetes Version
Select the Kubernetes version to install.

1.11

Role name ☑
Select the IAM Role to allow Amazon EKS and the Kubernetes control plane to manage AWS resources on your behalf.

EKS_Service_Role

Networking

VPC ☑
Select a VPC to use for your EKS Cluster resources.

vpc-0207a37adedf986ef - 192.168.0.0/16

Subnets ☑
Choose the subnets in your VPC where your worker nodes will run.

Q Find subnet

Figure 7-9. *"Create cluster" page*

In the Networking section, you need to select the VPC that you have created for the EKS cluster and the subnets. Figure 7-10 shows the VPC drop-down list and subnets.

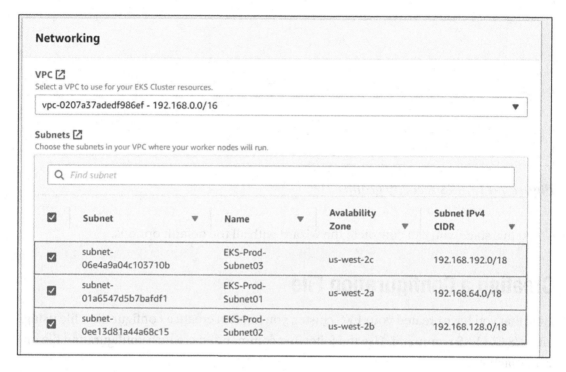

Figure 7-10. *EKS networking*

In the "Security groups" section, select the security groups that you noted from the VPC creation process. Figure 7-11 shows the "Security groups" section with the security group I am using.

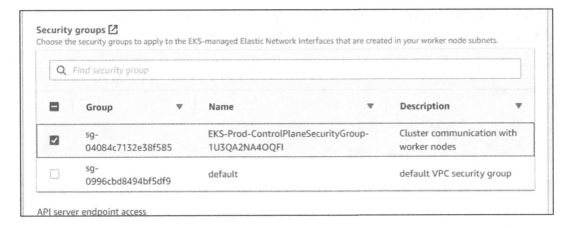

Figure 7-11. *EKS security groups*

At this stage, you can complete the wizard with all the default options.

Creating a Configuration File

Now that you have created your EKS cluster, you need to create a configuration file using an AWS CLI EKS command. Use the following command to create a configuration file on your machine:

```
aws eks --region us-west-2 update-kubeconfig --name EKS-Cluster
```

To check whether the command worked, you can use the following `kubectl` command.

```
.\kubectl.exe get svc
```

As shown in Figure 7-12, I can see my cluster, which tells me that the configuration is OK.

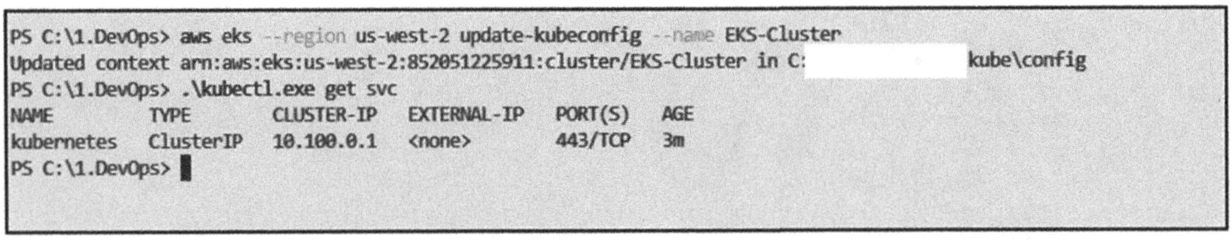

```
PS C:\1.DevOps> aws eks --region us-west-2 update-kubeconfig --name EKS-Cluster
Updated context arn:aws:eks:us-west-2:852051225911:cluster/EKS-Cluster in C:              kube\config
PS C:\1.DevOps> .\kubectl.exe get svc
NAME         TYPE         CLUSTER-IP      EXTERNAL-IP    PORT(S)      AGE
kubernetes   ClusterIP    10.100.0.1      <none>         443/TCP      3m
PS C:\1.DevOps>
```

Figure 7-12. *Getting the EKS service*

Before continuing to the next step of creating a worker node, you need to make sure the cluster is ready. Specifically, in the EKS management console, you need to verify that the status is set to Active.

Figure 7-13 shows my EKS-Cluster status set to Active, which gives me the green light to create a worker node.

Figure 7-13. *EKS cluster status*

Creating a Worker Node

In this section, you'll learn how to create a worker node, which is an EC2 instance running Docker and the Kubernetes agent client.

To create a worker node, you can use the CloudFormation console again to create a stack with a custom configuration file. In the CloudFormation console, click Create Stack, as shown in Figure 7-14.

Figure 7-14. *Creating a stack for the worker node*

You can use the following YAML template file to create the node:

```
https://amazon-eks.s3-us-west-2.amazonaws.com/cloudformation/2019-01-09/
amazon-eks-nodegroup.yaml
```

Copy the path and paste it into the "Choose a template" page, specifically in the "Specify an Amazon S3 template URL" text box, as shown in Figure 7-15.

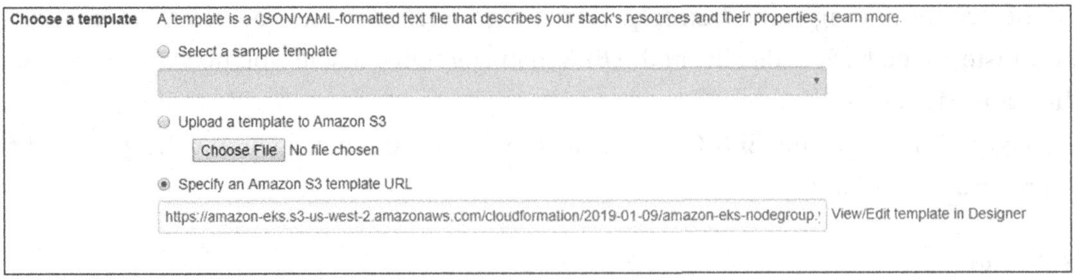

Figure 7-15. *Selecting a template*

In your configuration menu, you need to review the details of your cluster because misconfiguration can lead to a worker node not being able to connect to the cluster.

As shown in Figure 7-16, I have the following details:

- **Stack Name**: This is the name of the worker node.

- **Node Group Name**: This is the name of the worker node group.

- **NodeAutoScalingGroupMinSize**: Select the minimum number of nodes you need the group to have; the default is 1.

- **NodeAutoScalingGroupDesiredCapacity**: This is how many nodes you want the node to have at a standard operating capacity.

- **NodeAutoScalingGroupMaxSize**: This the maximum number of nodes you want the node to have at maximum capacity.

- **NodeInstanceType**: This is where you specify the node instance type.

- **NodeImageId**: This is the AMI image used for the EC2 instance. In my case, I am using ami-081099ec932b99961.

As you can see in Figure 7-16, AWS has filled in the autoscaling values, which you can change. Just remember that by default your cluster node group will have three EC2 instances.

If you are running a development environment, I suggest you reduce this number; later in this chapter, I will show you how to do it.

Specify Details

Specify a stack name and parameter values. You can use or change the default parameter values, which are defined in the AWS CloudFormation template. Learn more.

Stack name	EKS-Cluster-Node-01

Parameters

EKS Cluster

ClusterName	EKS-Cluster	The cluster name provided when the cluster was created. If it is incorrect, nodes will not be able to join the cluster.
ClusterControlPlaneSecuri tyGroup	EKS-Prod-ControlPlaneSecurityGroup-1... ▼ The security group of the cluster control plane.	

Worker Node Configuration

NodeGroupName	EKS-Cluster-Group-01	Unique identifier for the Node Group.
NodeAutoScalingGroupMi nSize	1	Minimum size of Node Group ASG.
NodeAutoScalingGroupDe siredCapacity	3	Desired capacity of Node Group ASG.
NodeAutoScalingGroupMa xSize	4	Maximum size of Node Group ASG. Set to at least 1 greater than NodeAutoScalingGroupDesiredCapacity.
NodeInstanceType	t2.small ▼	EC2 instance type for the node instances

Figure 7-16. *Specifying worker node details*

The other setting you need to configure is the KeyName setting, which I have already covered in Chapter 4. I'm also selecting the VPC ID and subnets based on the VPC that I created earlier.

Figure 7-17 shows these values.

Worker Node Configuration		
NodeGroupName	EKS-Cluster-Group-01	Unique identifier for the Node Group.
NodeAutoScalingGroupMinSize	1	Minimum size of Node Group ASG.
NodeAutoScalingGroupDesiredCapacity	3	Desired capacity of Node Group ASG.
NodeAutoScalingGroupMaxSize	4	Maximum size of Node Group ASG. Set to at least 1
NodeInstanceType	t2.small ▼	EC2 instance type for the node instances
NodeImageId	ami-081099ec932b99961	AMI id for the node instances.
NodeVolumeSize	20	Node volume size
KeyName	EC2-Key-Pair ▼	
	The EC2 Key Pair to allow SSH access to the instances	
BootstrapArguments		Arguments to pass to the bootstrap script. See files/

Worker Network Configuration

VpcId	vpc-0207a37adedf986ef (192.168.0.0/1... ▼	
	The VPC of the worker instances	
Subnets	subnet-01a6547d5b7bafdf1 (192.168.64.0/18) (EKS-Prod-Subnet01) ✖	
	subnet-06e4a9a04c103710b (192.168.192.0/18) (EKS-Prod-Subnet03) ✖	
	subnet-0ee13d81a44a68c15 (192.168.128.0/18) (EKS-Prod-Subnet02) ✖	
	The subnets where workers can be created.	

Figure 7-17. *Worker node configuration*

After the worker node setup is complete, note the value used for the NodeInstanceRole field. Figure 7-18 shows my NodeInstanceRole value.

Outputs		
Key	**Value**	**Description**
NodeInstanceRole	arn:aws:iam::852051225911:role/EKS-Cluster-Node-01-NodeInstance Role-1UZWR3G9YT27H	The node instance role
NodeSecurityGroup	sg-07e6d90627f8fc0c4	The security group for the node group

Figure 7-18. *Worker node outputs*

In the last step of the configuration, register the node using the following configuration file, which I am downloading with the `curl` command:

```
curl -O https://amazon-eks.s3-us-west-2.amazonaws.com/cloudformation/
2019-01-09/aws-auth-cm.yaml
```

The following is the NodeInstanceRole value I copied. You should copy yours into the configuration file, as shown in Figure 7-19, next to `rolearn`.

```
arn:aws:iam::852051225911:role/EKS-Cluster-Node-01-NodeInstanceRole-
1UZWR3G9YT27H
```

```
aws-auth-cm.yaml - Notepad
File  Edit  Format  View  Help
apiVersion: v1
kind: ConfigMap
metadata:
  name: aws-auth
  namespace: kube-system
data:
  mapRoles: |
    - rolearn: arn:aws:iam::852051225911:role/EKS-Cluster-Node-01-NodeInstanceRole-1UZWR3G9YT27H
      username: system:node:{{EC2PrivateDNSName}}
      groups:
        - system:bootstrappers
        - system:nodes
```

Figure 7-19. *aws-auth-cm.yaml content*

To run the command from your local machine, use the following `kubecl` command with the configuration file, as shown in Figure 7-20:

```
kubectl apply -f aws-auth-cm.yaml
```

```
PS C:\1.DevOps> cd C:\Bin\
PS C:\Bin> kubectl apply -f aws-auth-cm.yaml
configmap/aws-auth created
PS C:\Bin>
```

Figure 7-20. *Applying aws-auth-cm.yaml*

To confirm that everything is working well, run the following Kubectl command to see all your worker nodes, as shown in Figure 7-21:

Kubectl get nodes

```
PS C:\Bin> kubectl get nodes
NAME                                            STATUS   ROLES    AGE   · VERSION
ip-192-168-126-156.us-west-2.compute.internal   Ready    <none>   2m      v1.11.5
ip-192-168-157-139.us-west-2.compute.internal   Ready    <none>   2m      v1.11.5
ip-192-168-228-136.us-west-2.compute.internal   Ready    <none>   2m      v1.11.5
PS C:\Bin>
```

Figure 7-21. *The get nodes command*

Figure 7-21 shows that all my worker nodes are ready and that I have completed the cluster configuration successfully.

Scaling Amazon EKS

Now that you have an EKS cluster up and running, you will learn how to scale it up and how to scale it down. In this section, I will show you how I scale my EKS cluster from 0 to 1 nodes.

It is important to note that the scaling operation of EKS is done from the CloudFormation console in the AWS management console.

To scale your cluster, select it from the CloudFormation screen, and from the Actions menu, click Update Stack, as shown in Figure 7-22.

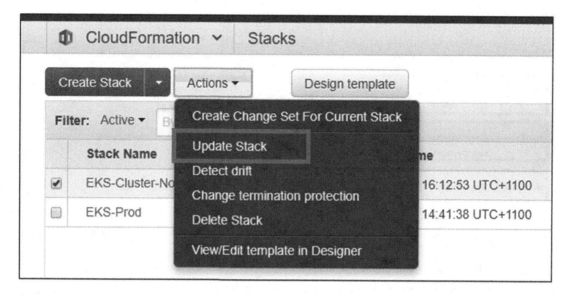

Figure 7-22. *Updating the stack*

On the Select Template page, select "Use current template" and click Next, as shown in Figure 7-23.

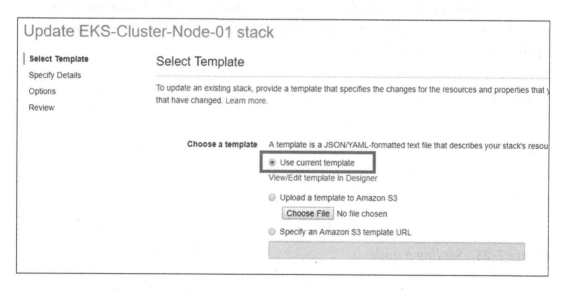

Figure 7-23. *Using the current template*

In the Worker Node Configuration section, change the NodeAutoScaling values, as shown in Figure 7-24. Also notice that I don't have any nodes in my cluster and all the values are set to 0.

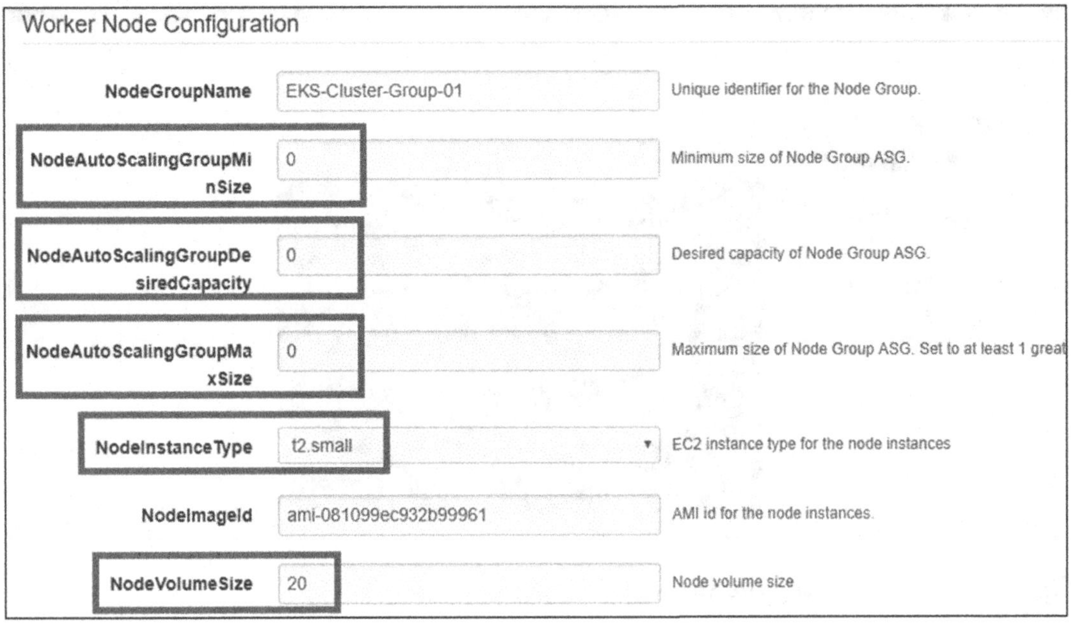

Figure 7-24. *Worker node configuration*

To scale your cluster, modify the values in the Worker Node Configuration section to the desired states. As mentioned, I'm going to scale my cluster to only one node. Figure 7-25 shows the configuration.

Figure 7-25. *Scaling a node*

After updating the values, click Next and Next again on the Options page.

On the Review page, select the acknowledge box and review the changes in the preview section, as shown in Figure 7-26.

To start the scaling process, click Update.

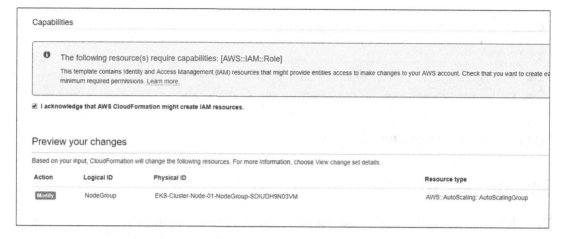

Figure 7-26. *Acknowledging*

To verify that the scaling process has completed, run the following command from your local machine:

```
kubectl get nodes
```

In Figure 7-27, you can see that my EKS cluster has one worker node running after I updated the worker node configuration.

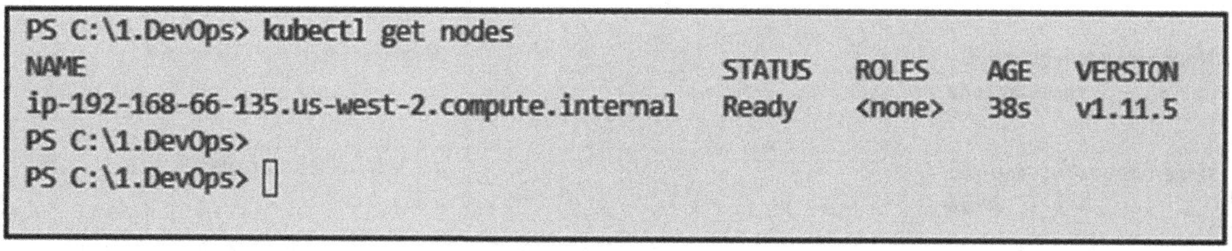

```
PS C:\1.DevOps> kubectl get nodes
NAME                                         STATUS   ROLES    AGE   VERSION
ip-192-168-66-135.us-west-2.compute.internal Ready    <none>   38s   v1.11.5
PS C:\1.DevOps>
PS C:\1.DevOps> []
```

Figure 7-27. *The get nodes command*

If you open the EC2 console, you will see the same worker node you just created.

Figure 7-28 shows the node, which highlights the seamless integration between all the AWS services.

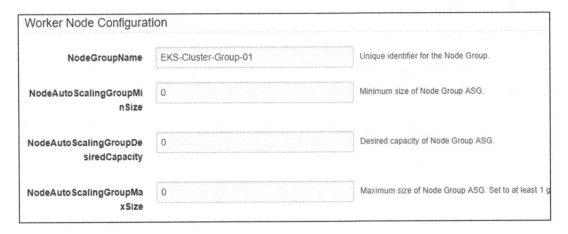

Figure 7-28. *EC2 running instances*

Scaling Down

To scale your EKS cluster back to zero nodes, you can use the same process you used to scale up but this time use 0 in the NodeAutoScaling options.

Figure 7-29 shows the values I am using to scale down the cluster to zero nodes. You can use the same process to scale to one node, for example.

Worker Node Configuration		
NodeGroupName	EKS-Cluster-Group-01	Unique identifier for the Node Group.
NodeAutoScalingGroupMinSize	0	Minimum size of Node Group ASG.
NodeAutoScalingGroupDesiredCapacity	0	Desired capacity of Node Group ASG.
NodeAutoScalingGroupMaxSize	0	Maximum size of Node Group ASG. Set to at least 1 g

Figure 7-29. *Scaling a worker node*

If you check your EC2 console, you will see that the worker node's EC2 instance has been terminated, as shown in Figure 7-30.

Figure 7-30. *Terminated EC2 instance after scaling down*

Scaling Amazon ECS

I have shown you how to scale EKS clusters and worker node groups, so it is time to move on and learn how to scale ECS instances. If you remember, in Chapter 3 I showed you how to use Amazon ECS to deploy containers in an AWS shared containerized environment. ECS offers the perfect environment for an infrastructure-free, low-cost platform to run your containers.

Scaling the ECS Fargate Service

In this section, I will show you how to scale your ECS Fargate container instances. In ECS, containers are grouped under services, where you define what to run and how. On the Service page, you can specify the image, compute, and memory that each container will run.

When you are ready to run your containers, you merely run a task from the service. Remember, you create a task definition with your service.

In Figure 7-31, you can see my Task Definitions page with my AmazonLinux02 service.

Amazon ECS
  Clusters
  Task Definitions
Amazon ECR
  Repositories
AWS Marketplace
  Discover software
  Subscriptions ⬀

Task Definitions

Task definitions specify the container information for your application, such as how many containers are part of your task, what and which host ports they will use. Learn more

Create new Task Definition   Create new revision   Actions ▾   Last upd

Status: (ACTIVE) INACTIVE

▼ Filter in this page

	Task Definition	Latest revision status
☐	amazonlinux2	ACTIVE
☐	first-run-task-definition	ACTIVE

Figure 7-31. *Task definitions*

You can scale your service using the following steps.

Select the task definition, click the Actions menu and choose Update Service.

Figure 7-32 shows the Update Service menu item.

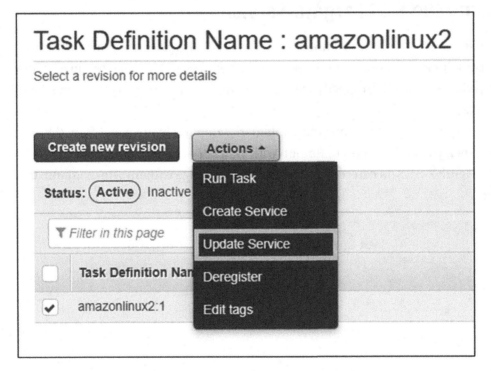

Task Definition Name : amazonlinux2

Select a revision for more details

Create new revision   Actions ▲

Status: (Active) Inactive

▼ Filter in this page

	Task Definition Nan
☑	amazonlinux2:1

Run Task

Create Service

Update Service

Deregister

Edit tags

Figure 7-32. *Updating the service*

In ECS, containers are called *tasks*, so to scale your service, you need to increase the number of tasks.

Figure 7-33 shows the Task Page and which values you need to change.

To scale up and run more containers, increase the number. Decrease the number to scale down. To have zero tasks and make the service offline, type **0** (zero).

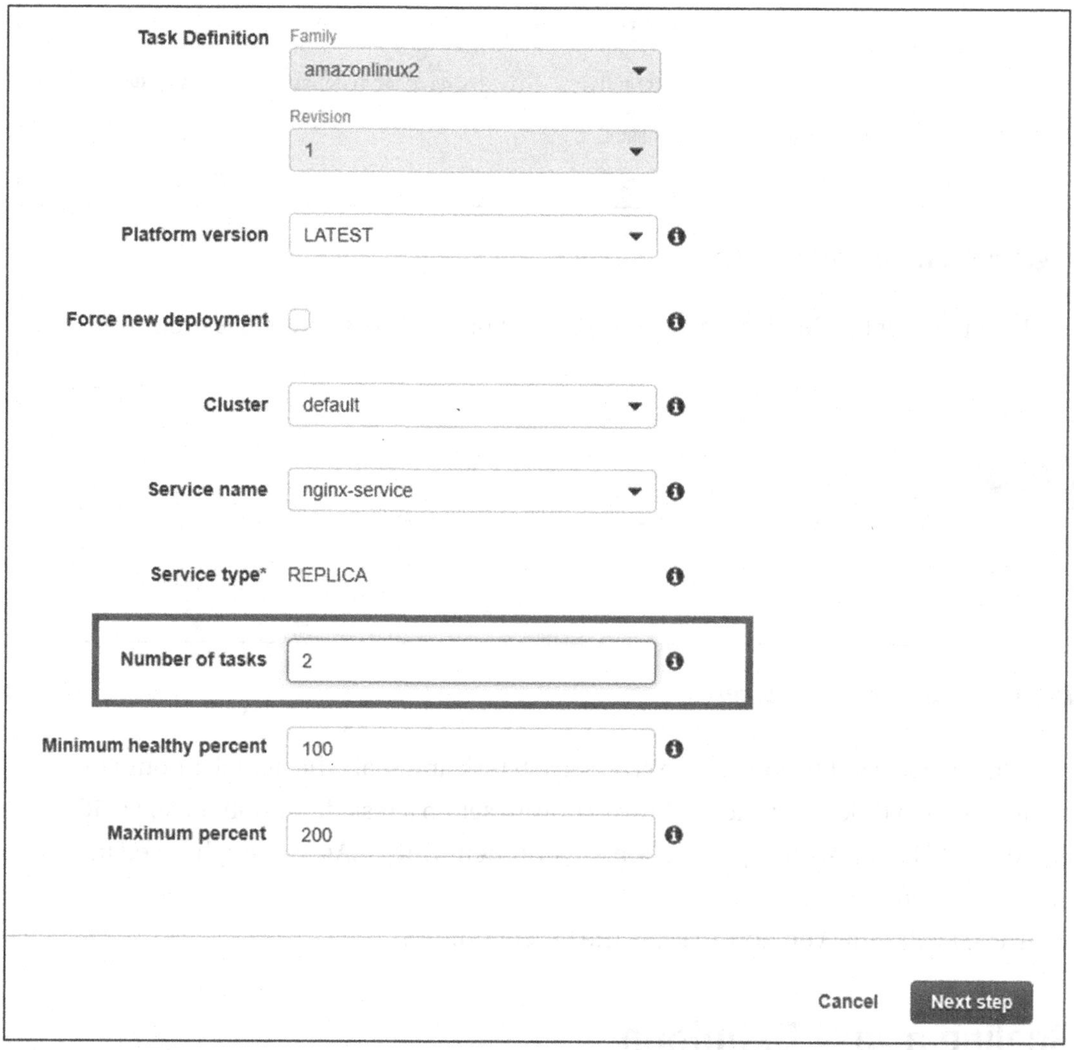

Figure 7-33. Number of tasks

Figure 7-34 shows the Tasks tab after I run a new task and after scaling the task to two tasks (containers).

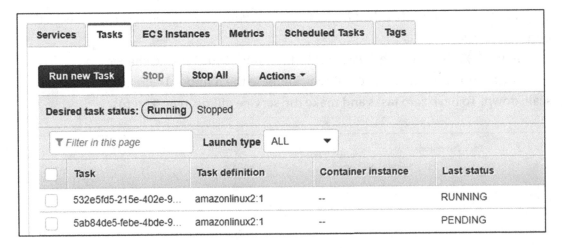

Figure 7-34. *Running tasks*

If you look at the Services tab (Figure 7-35), you will see 2 under "Desired tasks."

Figure 7-35. *Active services*

What if you want to change the size of each task and scale the actual amount of resources each task has? When I showed how to set up a task definition, I used 0.5GB and 0.25 CPU per task. In a production environment with SLAs, you might need more power for each task.

Next, I will show you how to scale the task definition.

Scaling a Task Definition

To scale a task definition (also known as a *service*), you can use the following steps.

Select the task from the Task Definitions menu and click "Create new revision."

Figure 7-36 shows the task definition revision menu.

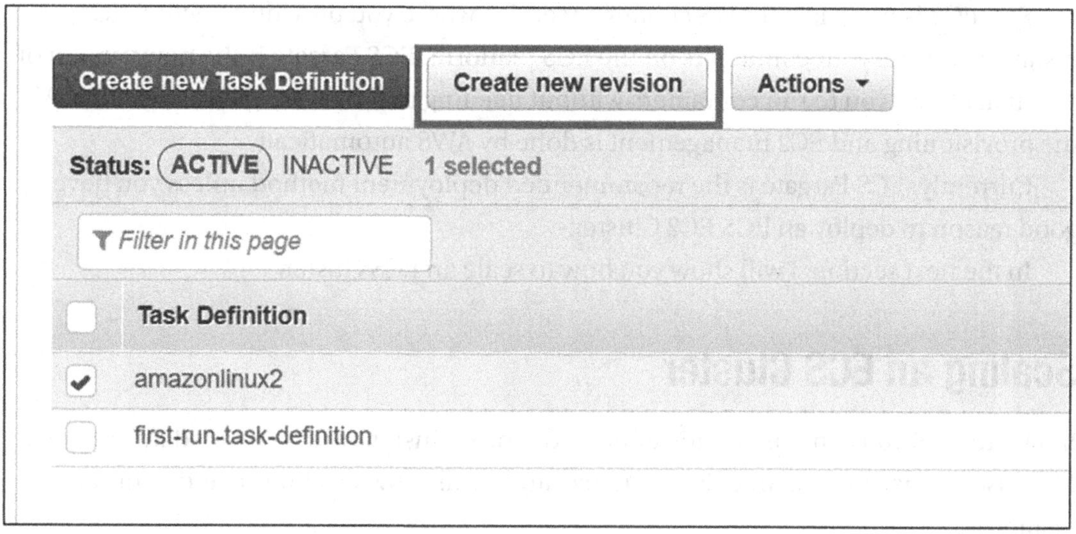

Figure 7-36. *Creating a new revision*

In Figure 7-37 you can see task size configuration I have used for my task. You will notice that it is very low. To change it, you use the drop-down list to update the task size. Once it's changed, click the Create button to save the new configuration.

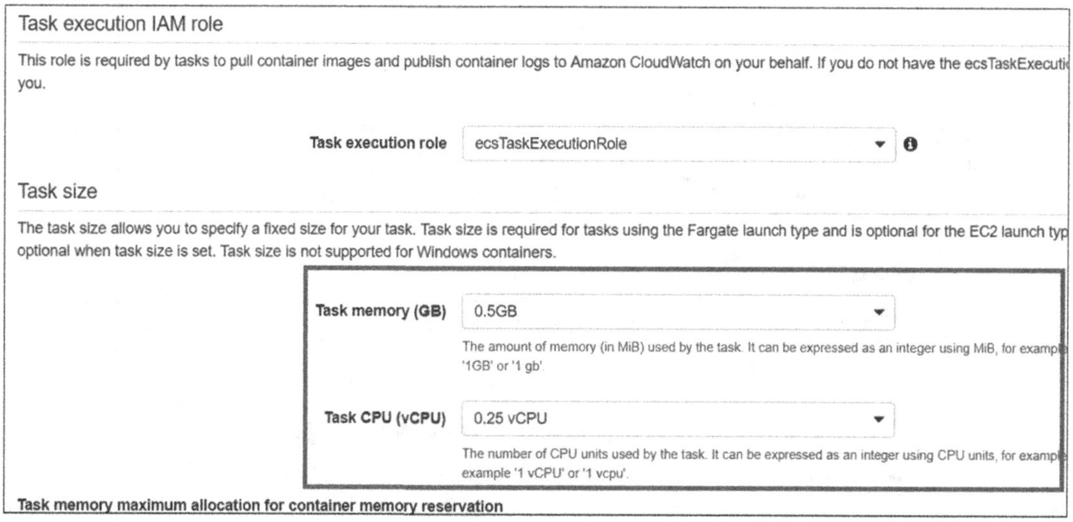

Figure 7-37. *Task size configuration*

The next scaling operation you need to do is to scale a standard ECS cluster. If you remember from Chapter 3, ECS has two deployment methods, an ECS EC2 and ECS Fargate.

ECS EC2 is the original AWS container service where you provide an actual EC2 instance and run your containers on the ECS platform. ECS Fargate is the new version of ECS that allows you to run containers without needing to provision an EC2 instance. All the provisioning and EC2 management is done by AWS automatically.

Currently, ECS Fargate is the recommended deployment method unless you have a good reason to deploy an ECS EC2 Cluster.

In the next section, I will show you how to scale an ECS cluster.

Scaling an ECS Cluster

In Figure 7-38 you can see my cluster named Linux-Cluster, which I created in Chapter 3. My cluster runs one M5.large EC2 instance, and I will show you how to add another instance.

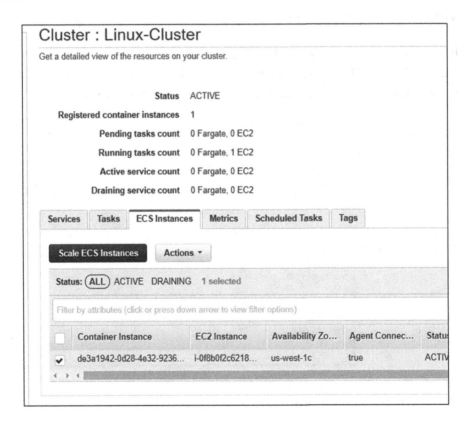

Figure 7-38. *Viewing ECS instances*

To scale a cluster and another EC2 instance, you need to select your cluster from the list and click Scale, as shown in Figure 7-39. On the "Scale ECS instances in a cluster" page, modify the number of ECS instances you want to add or remove.

You can scale up or down and set it to zero. Just remember that if you scale down, the running tasks will stop, so make sure you plan your change to happen during nonbusiness hours.

Figure 7-39 shows the scaling menu.

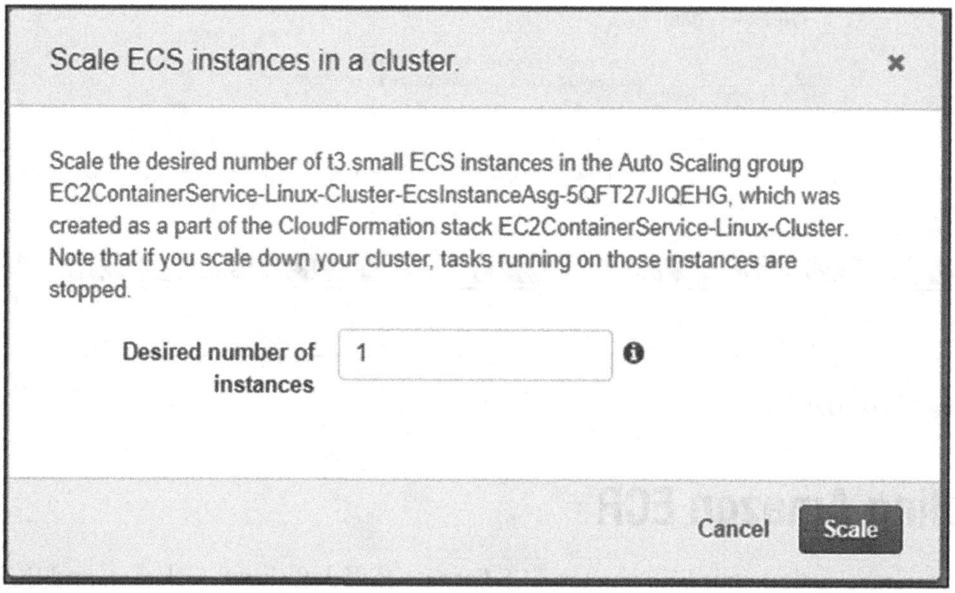

Figure 7-39. *Scaling ECS instances*

Scaling a Task Definition with an ECS Cluster

With an ECS cluster, you can also change the task definition, specifically, the task size, in the same way as with ECS Fargate.

To scale a task definition, you need to select the task and click the "Create new revision" button. Figure 7-40 shows the task size options. To scale the size, modify the values and click Create.

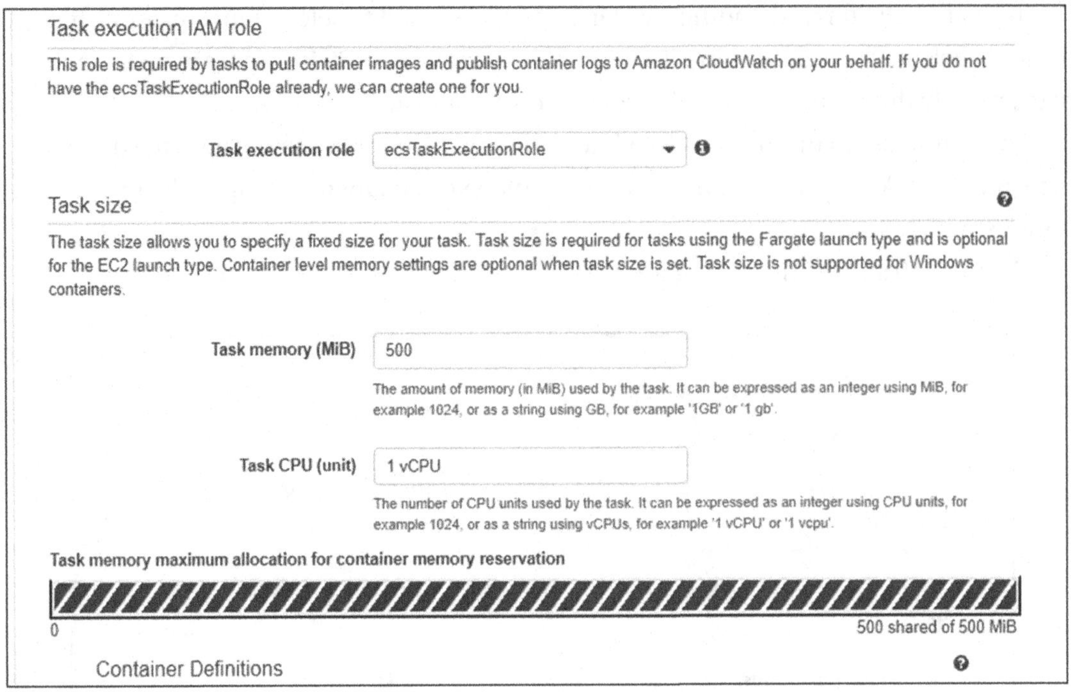

Figure 7-40. Task size

Scaling Amazon ECR

After you have scaled your EKS cluster, ECS Fargate task definition, task size, and ECS cluster, it is time to move on to ECR.

Amazon Elastic Container Registry (ECR) is a storage service that allows you to store container images in a secure location. Because ECR is a storage service, there is no option to scale the underlying resources because they are not relevant to the process. However, ECR has some limitations that you might want to consider if you have a large environment. If your development team is located in multiple locations around the world, for example, you might want to consider creating various ECR repositories.

For example, if you have a development team in the United States and another team in Australia, it is better to create two repositories, one for the U.S.-based team and another for the Australian team.

Placing the ECR repository in the same region as your team can save time when uploading and downloading images.

Table 7-1 lists the ECR registry limitations per region and per repository.

Table 7-1. *ECR Registry Limitations*

Resource	Default Limit
Maximum number of repositories per region	1,000
Maximum number of images per repository	1,000
Number of Docker pull transactions to a repository per second, per region, per account	200
Number of Docker pull layer transactions to a repository per second, per region, per account	200 sustained
Number of Docker push transactions to a repository per second, per region, per account	10 sustained

As shown in Table 7-1, you can have only 1,000 images per repository, which sounds like a lot, but in a large environment, you can easily reach this number.

You might want to consider creating multiple repositories for production, test, and development and place them in regions that are close to the teams that will use them the most.

Using lifecycle policies, you can control and scale the repositories down to keep them under control.

Please read Chapter 2 for detailed information about ECR.

Creating an ECR Repository in a Different Region

To create an ECR repository in a different region, from the AWS Console change the region to the region you are planning to build the repository in, as shown in Figure 7-41.

Figure 7-41. *Selecting a region*

By reviewing the current repository address, you can tell in which region it is located.

Figure 7-42 shows my US-West-1 registry address, and if you review the address, you will see that as part of the URL.

Figure 7-42. *Repository region*

Continuing with the new repository setup, from the AWS Console in the newly selected region, open the ECR console.

Click the Create Repository link and enter the name of the new repository, as shown in Figure 7-43.

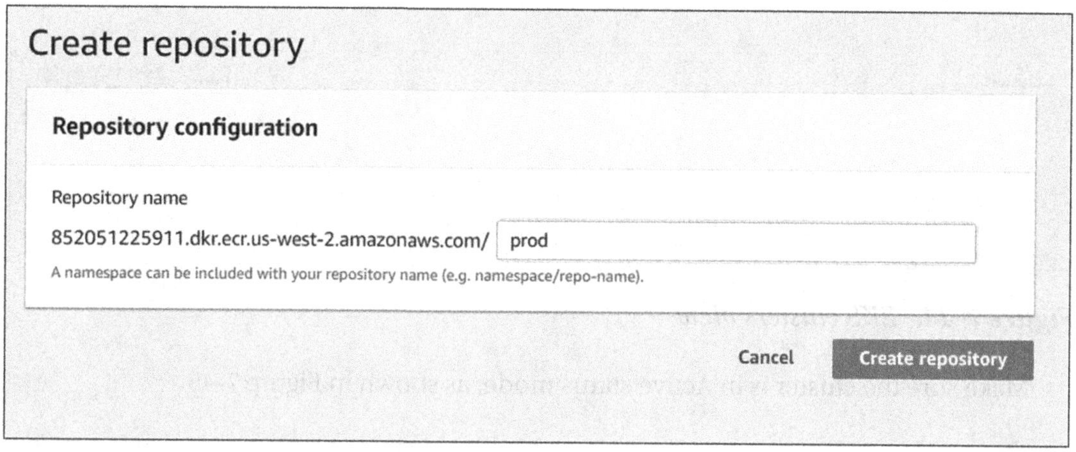

Create repository

Repository configuration

Repository name

852051225911.dkr.ecr.us-west-2.amazonaws.com/ | prod

A namespace can be included with your repository name (e.g. namespace/repo-name).

Cancel   **Create repository**

Figure 7-43. *Creating a repository*

It is a good idea to use names like PROD for production images and Dev for development to avoid confusion.

Regardless of the size of your organization, it is a good idea to have one repository for production and one for development. I have seen many instances where production images were deleted by mistake because they were considered to be in development.

Updating the EKS Cluster Version

In some cases, as part of scaling your EKS cluster, you might need to update the EKS Kubernetes version to the latest version.

When I created my cluster named EKS-Cluster in Chapter 4, I chose version 1.1, which is not the latest version. The reason I did that was to show you the process of updating an EKS cluster.

In some busy environments with a short downtime window, you might need to scale and update the cluster at the same time or one after another.

To update my EKS-Cluster cluster, I need to note my current version, which is 1.11, as shown in Figure 7-44 and Figure 7-45.

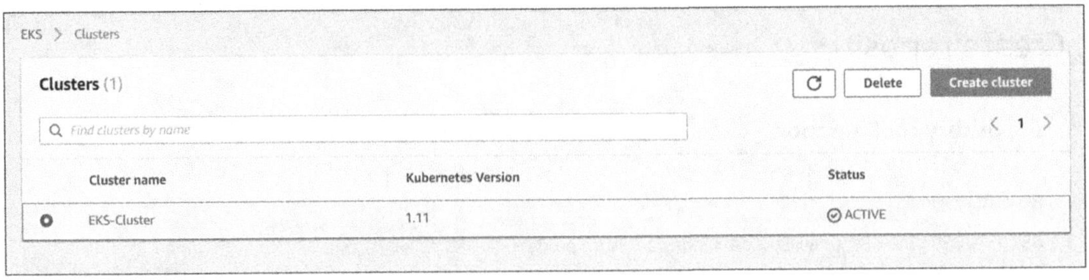

EKS > Clusters

Clusters (1)   ⟳   Delete   **Create cluster**

🔍 Find clusters by name   ⟨ 1 ⟩

Cluster name	Kubernetes Version	Status
○ EKS-Cluster	1.11	⊘ ACTIVE

Figure 7-44. EKS clusters view

Make sure the cluster is in Active status mode, as shown in Figure 7-45.

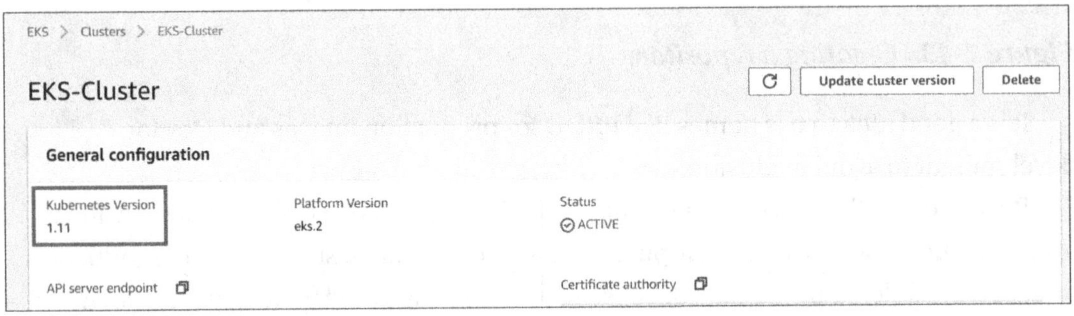

EKS > Clusters > EKS-Cluster

EKS-Cluster   ⟳   Update cluster version   Delete

General configuration

Kubernetes Version	Platform Version	Status
1.11	eks.2	⊘ ACTIVE

API server endpoint ⧉   Certificate authority ⧉

Figure 7-45. Kubernetes version

To update the cluster, use the "Update cluster version" button at the top-right corner, as shown in Figure 7-46.

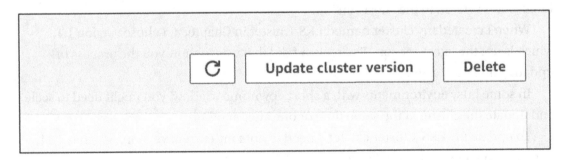

Figure 7-46. Updating a cluster version

On the "Update cluster version" page, select the latest version from the drop-down list. Note that you can't downgrade the cluster version after you update it.

Figure 7-47 shows the update page. To start the update process, click Update.

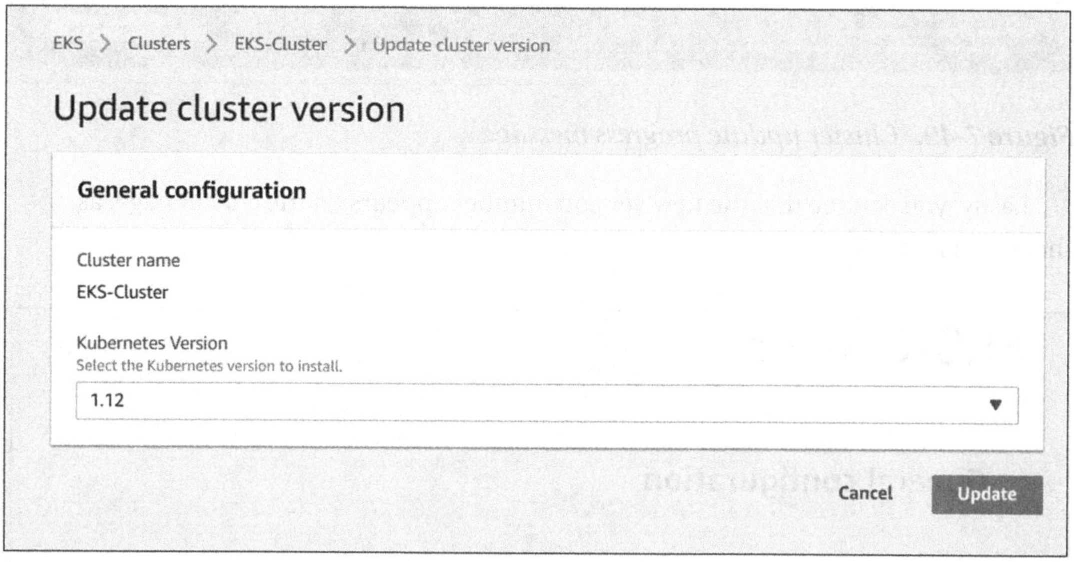

EKS > Clusters > EKS-Cluster > Update cluster version

Update cluster version

General configuration

Cluster name
EKS-Cluster

Kubernetes Version
Select the Kubernetes version to install.

1.12   ▼

Cancel   **Update**

Figure 7-47. *Updating the cluster version*

On the next screen, type the cluster name and click Confirm, as shown in Figure 7-48.

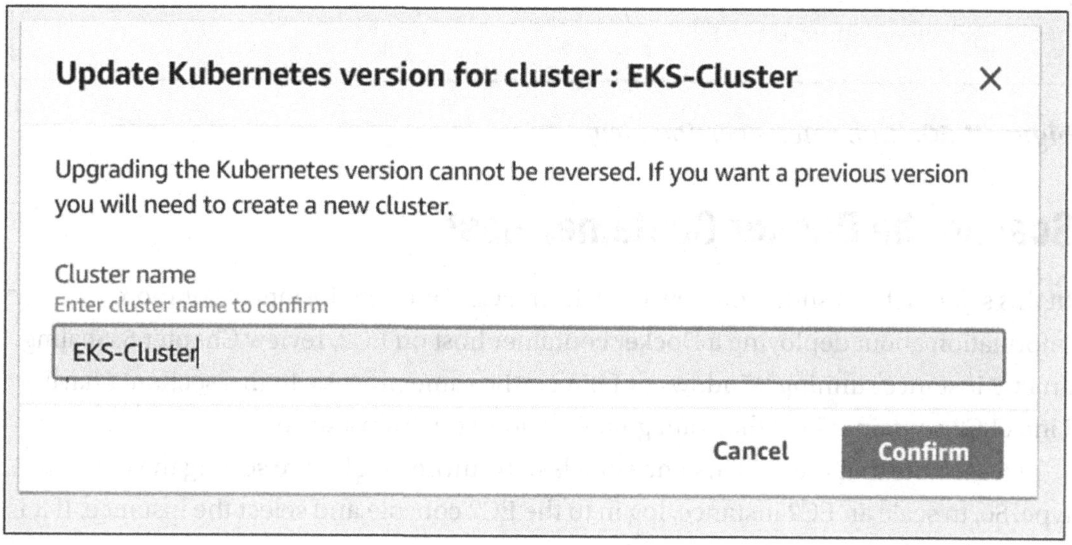

Update Kubernetes version for cluster : EKS-Cluster   ✕

Upgrading the Kubernetes version cannot be reversed. If you want a previous version
you will need to create a new cluster.

Cluster name
Enter cluster name to confirm

EKS-Cluster

Cancel   **Confirm**

Figure 7-48. *Confirming the cluster update*

On the EKS cluster page, the cluster update message will appear until the process is completed, as shown in Figure 7-49.

Figure 7-49. *Cluster update progress message*

Lastly, you can see that the new version number appears on the cluster page, as shown in Figure 7-50.

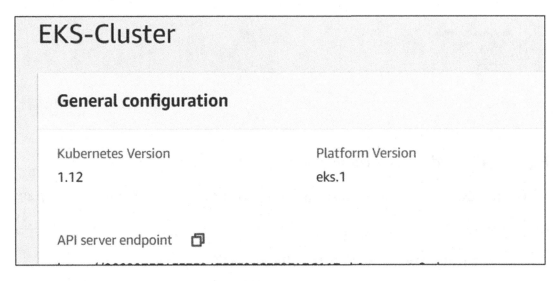

Figure 7-50. *Kubernetes version view*

Scaling the Docker Container Host

In this section, I will show you how to scale an EC2 container instance. For more information about deploying a Docker container host on EC2, review Chapter 5. Scaling an EC2 instance running Windows or Linux is the same process. In this section, I have a Linux EC2 container host that I am going to show you how to scale.

Please note that the EC2 instance needs to be turned off before scaling the instance type. So, to scale an EC2 instance, log in to the EC2 console and select the instance. If it is on, turn it to the Off state before continuing.

Select the instance, and from the Actions menu, click Change Instance Type under Instance Settings, as shown in Figure 7-51.

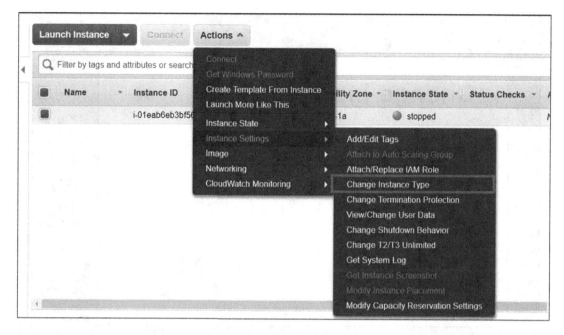

Figure 7-51. *Changing the instance type*

On the Change Instance Type screen, select the new instance type and click Apply to complete the process, as shown in Figure 7-52.

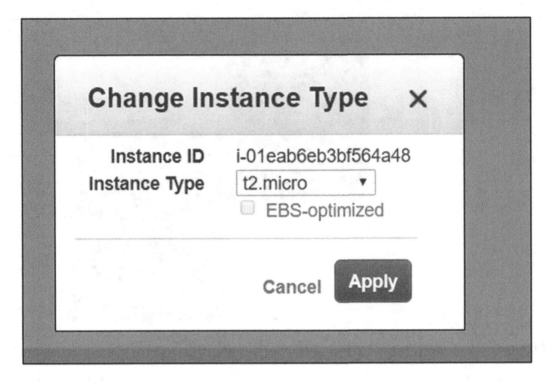

Figure 7-52. *Applying the instance type change*

Summary

In this chapter, I covered all the available methods that allow you to scale your AWS container services. Scaling is a great way to optimize containerized applications and also control costs during off-peak periods.

In the next chapter, you'll learn how to monitor AWS container services.

CHAPTER 8

Monitoring Your Containerized Environment

In this chapter, I will cover the ins and out of monitoring your AWS container services.

AWS offers monitoring tools and features that help you keep an eye on the performance of these services. Monitoring your services is an essential part of the lifecycle management of applications and services.

At the center of monitoring, AWS offers CloudWatch, which gives you real-time monitoring data and insights that help you make better decisions.

In this chapter, I will cover the following topics:

- How to install and configure the Kubernetes web UI (Dashboard)

- How to monitor EKS pods and nodes

- How to monitor ECS

- How to monitor ECR

- How to monitor EC2

© Shimon Ifrah 2019
S. Ifrah, *Deploy Containers on AWS*, https://doi.org/10.1007/978-1-4842-5101-0_8

Monitoring an Amazon EKS Cluster

The first service I will cover is the Amazon Elastic Container Service for Kubernetes, also known as EKS. EKS is the most advanced container management system in the world and is considered as the industry standard. It is being used by most Fortune 500 companies worldwide.

When it comes to monitoring, Kubernetes offers advanced monitoring capabilities using the Kubernetes web UI (Dashboard). The Kubernetes web UI can help you monitor hosts, pods, tasks, and utilization.

Installing the Kubernetes Web UI (Dashboard)

Before I show you the web UI monitoring capabilities and how to access them, I will start with a short step-by-step guide on how to install the web UI. For a detailed overview and installation guide, please review Chapter 4.

To install the web UI, you need to download the web UI code using the following kbectl command, shown in Figure 8-1:

```
kubectl apply -f https://raw.githubusercontent.com/kubernetes/dashboard/
v1.10.1/src/deploy/recommended/kubernetes-dashboard.yaml
```

```
PS C:\1.DevOps> kubectl apply -f https://raw.githubusercontent.com/kubernetes/dashboard/v1.10.1/src/deploy/recommended/kubernetes-dashboard.yaml
secret/kubernetes-dashboard-certs created
serviceaccount/kubernetes-dashboard created
role.rbac.authorization.k8s.io/kubernetes-dashboard-minimal created
rolebinding.rbac.authorization.k8s.io/kubernetes-dashboard-minimal created
deployment.apps/kubernetes-dashboard created
service/kubernetes-dashboard created
```

Figure 8-1. *Installing the web UI (Dashboard)*

Installing Heapster

To monitor your EKS cluster, you will use a monitoring tool called Heapster. Heapster, which has been deprecated, is the only supported metric provider for EKS and works well. Using Heapster, you will be able to collect and monitor the performance for your EKS cluster.

You can read more about Heapster at the following link:

```
https://github.com/kubernetes-retired/heapster
```

Figure 8-2 shows the Heapster GitHub project page.

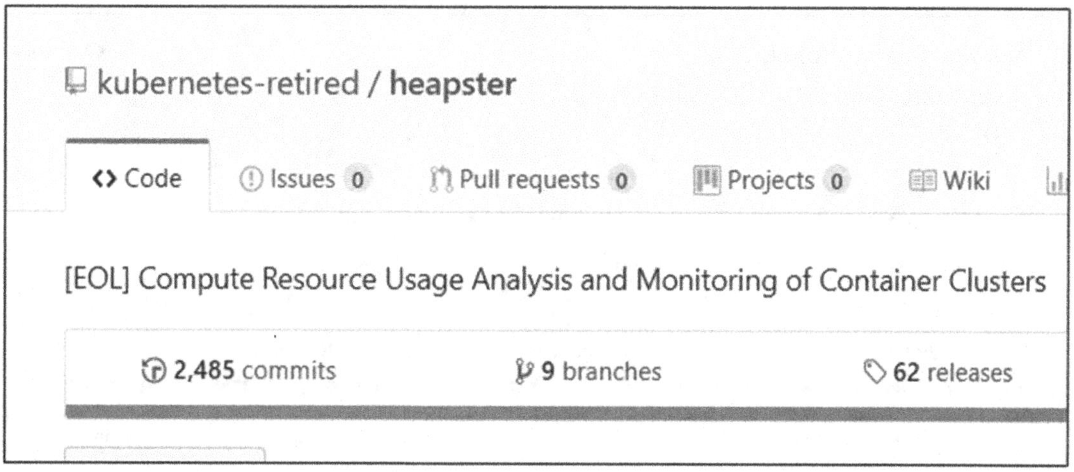

Figure 8-2. *Heapster on GitHub*

To install Heapster, run the following command, as shown in Figure 8-3:

```
kubectl apply -f https://raw.githubusercontent.com/kubernetes/heapster/
master/deploy/kube-config/influxdb/heapster.yaml
```

Figure 8-3. *Installing Heapster*

To capture and store all your monitoring data coming from Heapster, you need a database.

So, next you will install a database to keep all the data.

Installing influxdb

influxdb is an open source time-series platform that uses APIs to store data and processing in the background.

If you want to read more about influxd, please visit the following link:

```
https://github.com/influxdata/influxdb
```

Figure 8-4 shows the GitHub project page.

Figure 8-4. *influxdb GitHub*

To install influx, run the following command:

```
kubectl apply -f https://raw.githubusercontent.com/kubernetes/heapster/
master/deploy/kube-config/influxdb/influxdb.yaml
```

Figure 8-5 shows the installation command and the message you get after the deployment has been completed.

```
PS C:\1.DevOps> kubectl apply -f https://raw.githubusercontent.com/kubernetes/heapster/master/deploy/kube-config/influxdb/influxdb.yaml
deployment.extensions/monitoring-influxdb created
service/monitoring-influxdb created
```

Figure 8-5. *Installing influxdb*

The next few commands will connect Heapster to influxdb.

Creating a Heapster Cluster Role

Using the following command, create a cluster role for Heapster and give it access to the web UI. Figure 8-6 shows the command output.

```
kubectl apply -f https://raw.githubusercontent.com/kubernetes/heapster/
master/deploy/kube-config/rbac/heapster-rbac.yaml
```

```
PS C:\1.DevOps> kubectl apply -f https://raw.githubusercontent.com/kubernetes/heapster/master/deploy/kube-config/rbac/heapster-rbac.yaml
clusterrolebinding.rbac.authorization.k8s.io/heapster created
```

Figure 8-6. *Creating a Heapster cluster role*

Creating an EKS-Admin Service Account

In this section, you will create a service account for the EKS-Admin user. The service account will connect to the Dashboard with admin rights and help you manage it. Copy the following text and save it as eks-admin-service-account.yaml:

```
apiVersion: v1
kind: ServiceAccount
metadata:
  name: eks-admin
  namespace: kube-system
---
apiVersion: rbac.authorization.k8s.io/v1beta1
kind: ClusterRoleBinding
metadata:
  name: eks-admin
roleRef:
  apiGroup: rbac.authorization.k8s.io
  kind: ClusterRole
  name: cluster-admin
subjects:
- kind: ServiceAccount
  name: eks-admin
  namespace: kube-system
```

Figure 8-7 shows the eks-admin-service-account.yaml file.

```
eks-admin-service-account.yaml - Notepad

File  Edit  Format  View  Help
apiVersion: v1
kind: ServiceAccount
metadata:
  name: eks-admin
  namespace: kube-system
---
apiVersion: rbac.authorization.k8s.io/v1beta1
kind: ClusterRoleBinding
metadata:
  name: eks-admin
roleRef:
  apiGroup: rbac.authorization.k8s.io
  kind: ClusterRole
  name: cluster-admin
subjects:
- kind: ServiceAccount
  name: eks-admin
  namespace: kube-system
```

Figure 8-7. *eks-admin-service-account.yaml content*

From the kubectl command line, run the following code, as shown in Figure 8-8:

```
kubectl apply -f eks-admin-service-account.yaml
```

```
PS C:\bin> kubectl apply -f eks-admin-service-account.yaml
serviceaccount/eks-admin created
clusterrolebinding.rbac.authorization.k8s.io/eks-admin created
```

Figure 8-8. *Applying eks-admin-service-account.yaml*

The last step in the process is to retrieve the authentication token for the EKS-Admin user. The authentication token acts as a password to log in to the Dashboard UI and monitor the environment.

Retrieving an Authentication Token

To retrieve the token, you can run the following command, as shown in Figure 8-9. Then, from the command output, copy the token that appears.

```
eks-admin-token
```

```
kubectl -n kube-system describe secret $(kubectl -n kube-system get secret
| grep eks-admin | awk '{print $1}')
```

```
eks-admin-token
```

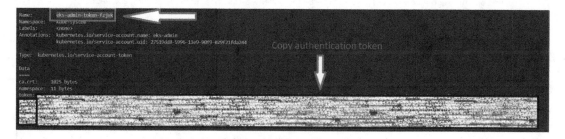

Figure 8-9. *Copying the authentication token*

Make sure you copy the correct token. Otherwise, you will receive an error message and won't be able to view anything in EKS.

Opening a Dashboard

Once the code has been copied, open the command prompt and run the following command to start the Dashboard:

```
kubectl proxy
```

To open the Dashboard web UI, click the following link:

```
http://localhost:8001/api/v1/namespaces/kube-system/services/
https:kubernetes-dashboard:/proxy/#!/login
```

In the Token field, paste the copied authentication code from the earlier "Retrieving an Authentication Token" section.

Figure 8-10 shows the token login screen.

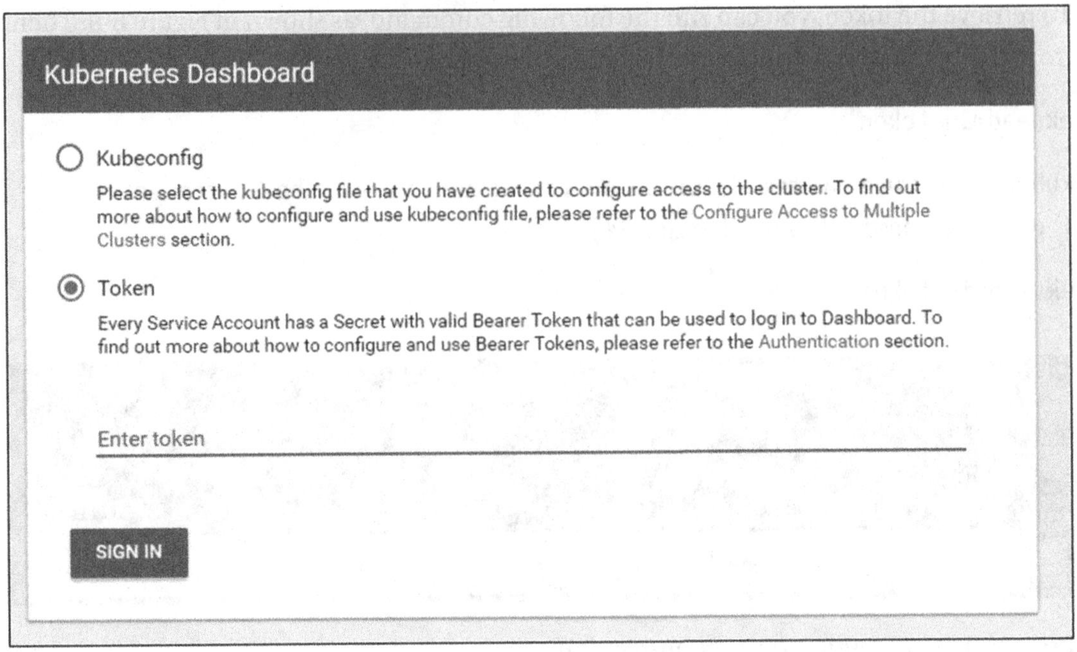

Kubernetes Dashboard

○ Kubeconfig
Please select the kubeconfig file that you have created to configure access to the cluster. To find out more about how to configure and use kubeconfig file, please refer to the Configure Access to Multiple Clusters section.

◉ Token
Every Service Account has a Secret with valid Bearer Token that can be used to log in to Dashboard. To find out more about how to configure and use Bearer Tokens, please refer to the Authentication section.

Enter token

SIGN IN

Figure 8-10. *Entering the authentication token*

Monitoring EKS

Now that the Dashboard web UI is installed and running with Heapster, you can start reviewing the performance and capacity of your cluster.

As you can see in Figure 8-11, the main Dashboard window shows you the status of all the workloads, with the following:

- Daemon sets

- Deployments

- Pods

- Replica sets

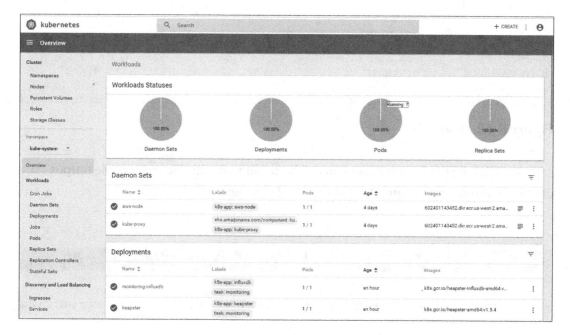

Figure 8-11. *Web UI (Dashboard)*

The main window gives a good indication of the overall performance and state of the EKS cluster and whether you need to add more resources.

Each section can provide information about the status of each workload. For example, for deployments, it shows you how many are running and when they were deployed.

Each workload can give you insight into performance, and I suggest you review the Dashboard every week.

Monitoring Pods

In Kubernetes, pods are the smallest deployment unit, representing a container. For that reason, it is imperative you review the Pods section and understand how many pods (containers) are running on EKS. You can find the Pods monitoring menu on the left side of the Dashboard.

In Figure 8-12, you can see the running pods on my EKS cluster. Using the menu button on the right side, you can access the container console, as shown in Figure 8-12.

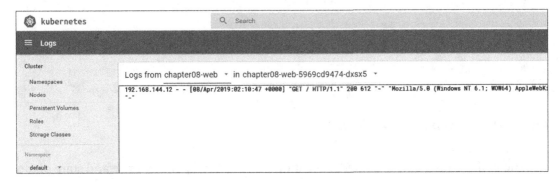

Figure 8-12. *Pods view*

After clicking the Logs button, you will be presented with the log console output directly in the console. Figure 8-13 shows the Logs view.

![Logs view screenshot]

Figure 8-13. *Viewing the logs*

Monitoring Nodes

Nodes are the driving force that allows you to deploy pods (containers) and run your applications. Using the Nodes menu, you can get insight into each node's performance and state.

Figure 8-14 shows the Nodes menu.

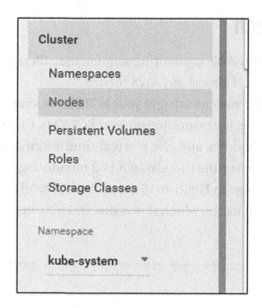

Figure 8-14. *Nodes menu item*

Once in the Nodes menu, you can see each node's performance data.

The "Allocated resources" section shows the following for nodes in the cluster:

- CPU allocation

- Memory allocation

- Pods allocation

You can review the performance of each resource and scale the host if needed. For scaling, please review Chapter 7.

Figure 8-15 shows the "Allocated resources" screen.

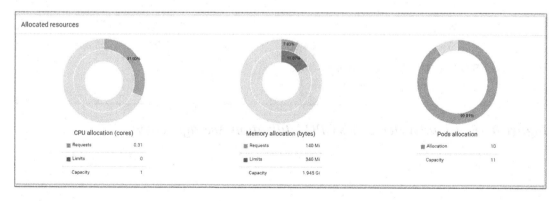

Figure 8-15. *"Allocated resources" section*

299

Using CloudWatch

CloudWatch is the primary AWS monitoring solution that offers you the opportunity to monitor the performance of almost any AWS service.

By using CloudWatch, you can tap into your EC2 EKS worker nodes, your ECS EC2 instances, and your Docker hosts running on your EC2 VMs. CloudWatch can monitor any VM type, Linux or Windows, and give you real-time information about it.

In Figure 8-16 you can see the CloudWatch EC2 monitoring screen for CPU utilization. The CPU average in Figure 8-16 shows the EC2 worker node for EKS, and it is standing at 5.57 percent usage, which shows that you have enough capacity to deploy more pods.

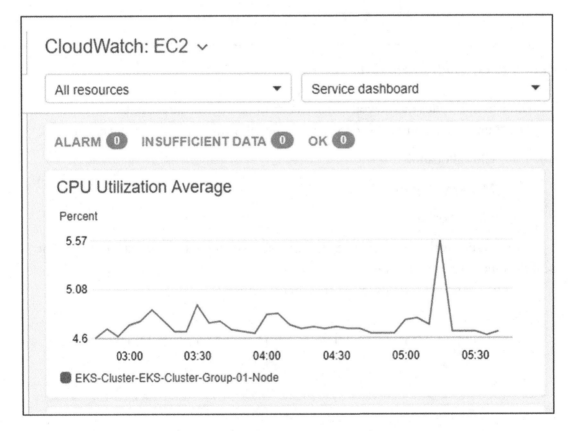

Figure 8-16. *CloudWatch EC2's CPU Utilization Average screen*

You can also check the network usage by looking at the Networking screen.

Figure 8-17 shows the network usage and utilization for the entire EKS cluster; you can also change the date range to view the performance over time.

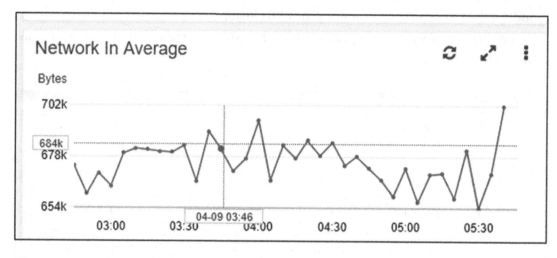

Figure 8-17. *Network In Average screen*

Figure 8-18 shows the number of network packets in and out of the EKS worker node.

You can see the name of the EKS cluster group, and if you have a few of them, you can compare the usage of each group.

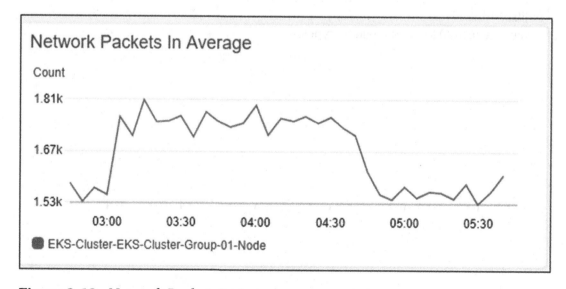

Figure 8-18. *Network Packets In Average screen*

Creating a New CloudWatch Dashboard

Using CloudWatch, you can also create a customized Dashboard and monitor specific services such as EKS, S3, and EC2. In this section, I will show you how to create a CloudWatch Dashboard and monitor your EKS cluster.

From the CloudWatch main page, click Dashboards and click "Create dashboard," as shown in Figure 8-19.

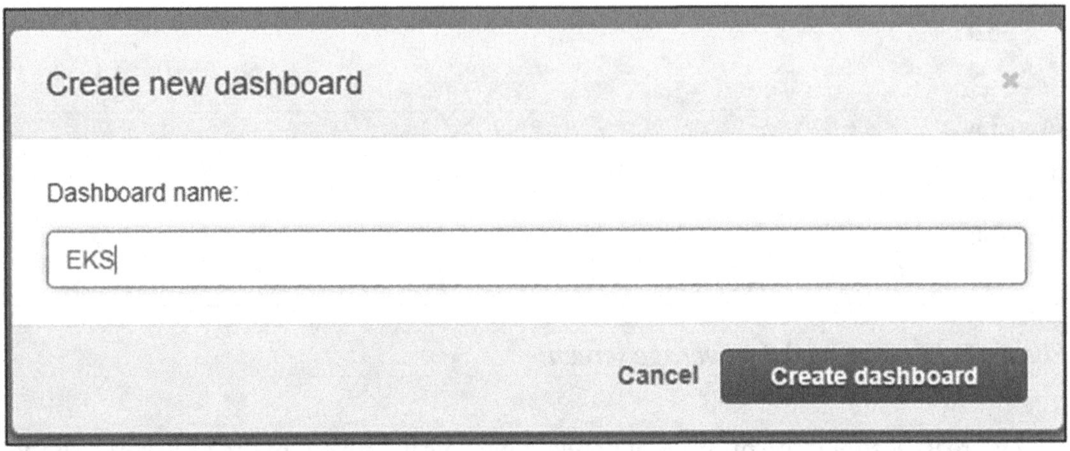

Create new dashboard   ✖

Dashboard name:

EKS|

                                              Cancel   Create dashboard

Figure 8-19.   Creating a new dashboard

On the "Add to this dashboard" page, select the widget type you want to use and display your data.

See Figure 8-20 for all the widget types.

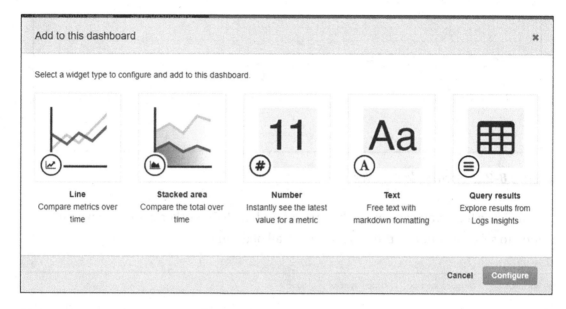

Figure 8-20. *Selecting a widget type*

On the "Add metric" graph page, select which metrics you want to use and display on your EKS Dashboard.

Figure 8-21 shows three options that are available for EKS, as follows:

- EBS—Elastic Block Storage

- EC2—The worker nodes of your EKS cluster

- ELB—Elastic Load Balancer

In my case, I will select EC2, as shown in Figure 8-21.

Figure 8-21. *Selecting metrics*

Monitoring EC2 will allow you to see whether your worker nodes are having any performance and capacity issues.

In the EC2 metric menu, select Per-Instance Metrics, as shown in Figure 8-22. As you can see, I have 128 metrics to choose from.

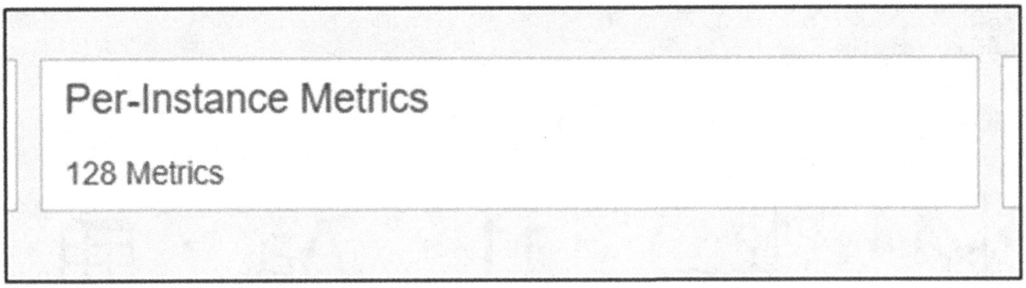

> **Per-Instance Metrics**
>
> 128 Metrics

Figure 8-22. *Available metrics*

In Figure 8-23, you can see all the metrics and my EKS worker nodes; I have the option to select any one of the 128 metrics or all of them.

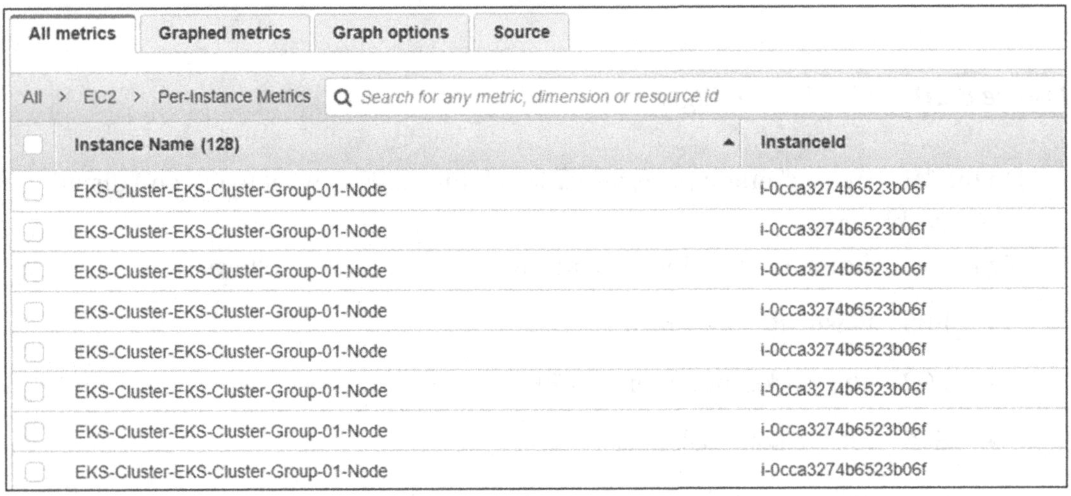

All metrics	Graphed metrics	Graph options	Source

All > EC2 > Per-Instance Metrics   🔍 *Search for any metric, dimension or resource id*

Instance Name (128)	▲	InstanceId
☐ EKS-Cluster-EKS-Cluster-Group-01-Node		i-0cca3274b6523b06f
☐ EKS-Cluster-EKS-Cluster-Group-01-Node		i-0cca3274b6523b06f
☐ EKS-Cluster-EKS-Cluster-Group-01-Node		i-0cca3274b6523b06f
☐ EKS-Cluster-EKS-Cluster-Group-01-Node		i-0cca3274b6523b06f
☐ EKS-Cluster-EKS-Cluster-Group-01-Node		i-0cca3274b6523b06f
☐ EKS-Cluster-EKS-Cluster-Group-01-Node		i-0cca3274b6523b06f
☐ EKS-Cluster-EKS-Cluster-Group-01-Node		i-0cca3274b6523b06f
☐ EKS-Cluster-EKS-Cluster-Group-01-Node		i-0cca3274b6523b06f

Figure 8-23. *All metrics*

Figure 8-24 shows the Metric Name column with the metrics you can monitor. For example, you can use the CPUUtilization metric, the DiskWriteOps metric, and more.

InstanceId	Metric Name
i-0075339811ec8d316	CPUUtilization
i-0075339811ec8d316	DiskWriteOps
i-0075339811ec8d316	NetworkIn
i-0075339811ec8d316	NetworkPacketsOut
i-0075339811ec8d316	NetworkOut
i-0075339811ec8d316	DiskReadBytes
i-0075339811ec8d316	DiskWriteBytes
i-0075339811ec8d316	DiskReadOps
i-0075339811ec8d316	NetworkPacketsIn

Figure 8-24. *Available metrics*

After adding a metric, you can see the data that is presented in almost real time. Figure 8-25 shows the CPU metric widget.

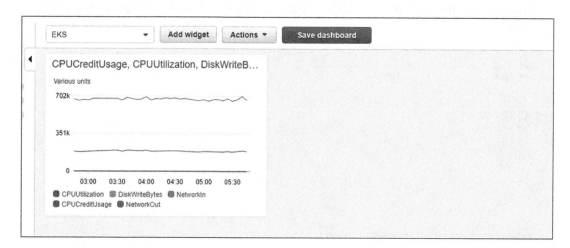

Figure 8-25. *CPU metric widget*

Now, I will show how to add another widget, but this time I will select a widget number on the "Add to this dashboard" screen (shown in Figure 8-26).

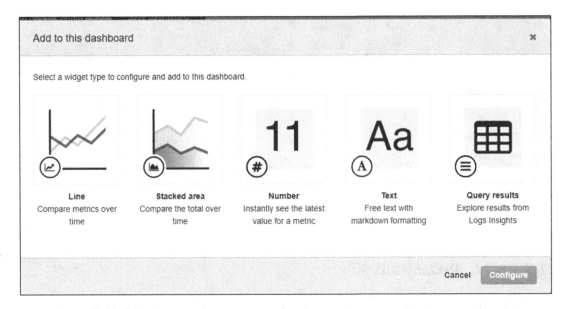

Figure 8-26. *Selecting another widget type*

Using the same process, I will choose metrics to appear on the widget, as shown in Figure 8-27.

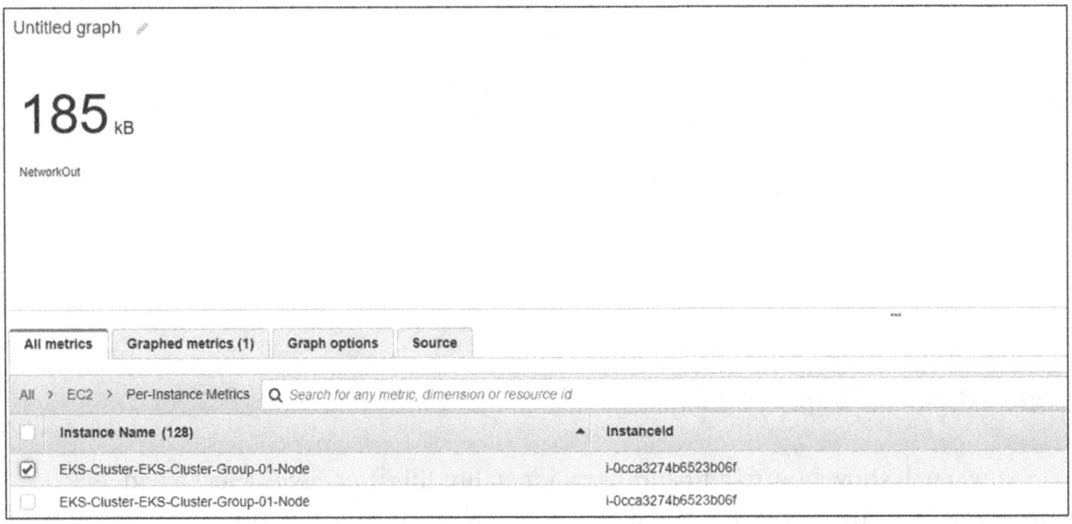

Figure 8-27. *Untitled graph*

After adding more metrics, you can see the result of my Dashboard in Figure 8-28. As you can see, I also added information about my disks.

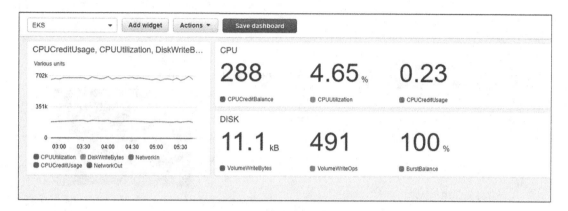

Figure 8-28. *CPU widget view, with disk information*

When you are happy with the results, click the "Save dashboard" button, as shown in Figure 8-29.

Figure 8-29. *Saving the dashboard*

Monitoring Container Instances on Amazon ECS

In this section, I will show you how to monitor AWS containers running in ECS Fargate. If you remember, in Chapter 3, I covered ECS EC2 and ECS Fargate and the fact that Fargate is the new offering for ECS.

To get started, I will show how to spin up a new task from ECS Fargate using the Run Task option, as shown in Figure 8-30.

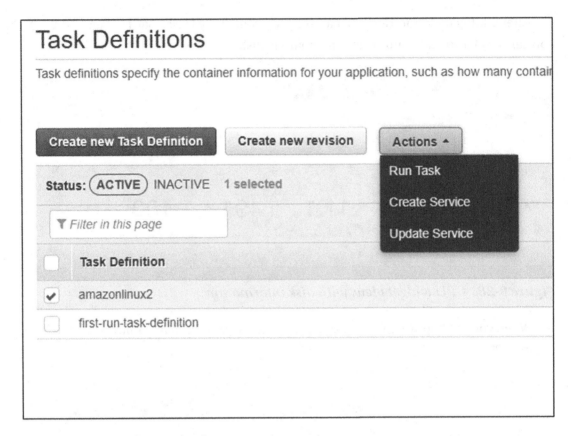

Figure 8-30. *Running a task*

On the Run Task page, select Fargate as the launch type followed by all the other needed details.

Figure 8-31 shows the Run Task page.

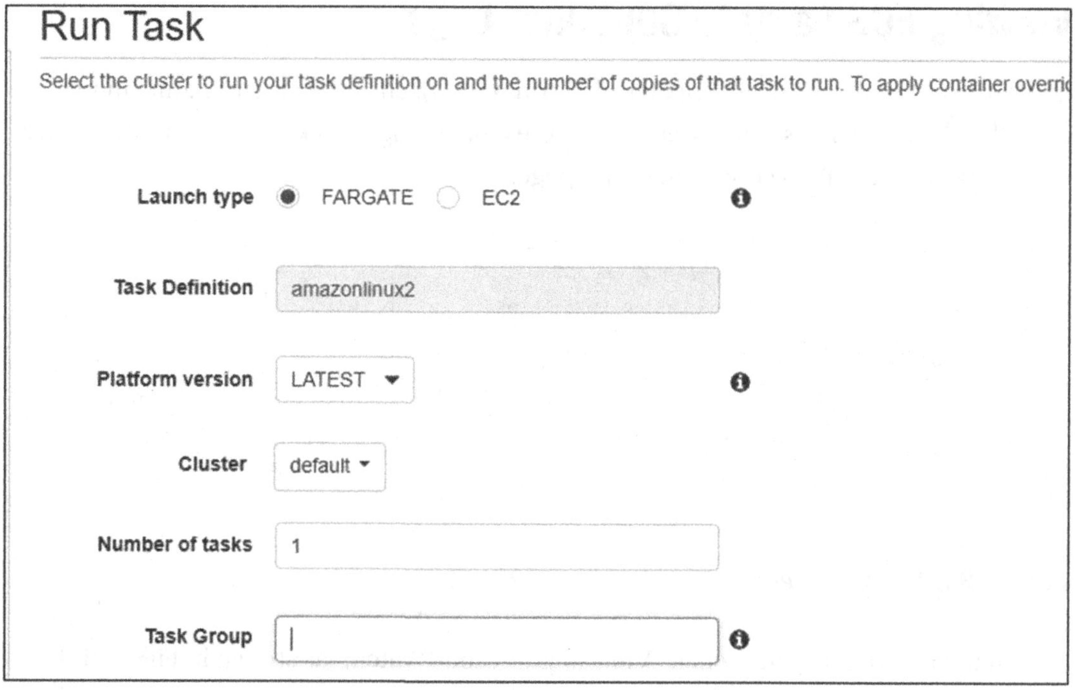

Figure 8-31. *Running the Fargate task*

The first screen that can provide you with some essential monitoring is the ECS main page.

As you can see in Figure 8-32, under the default cluster I have two services configured and two tasks running. In my case, each task is one container.

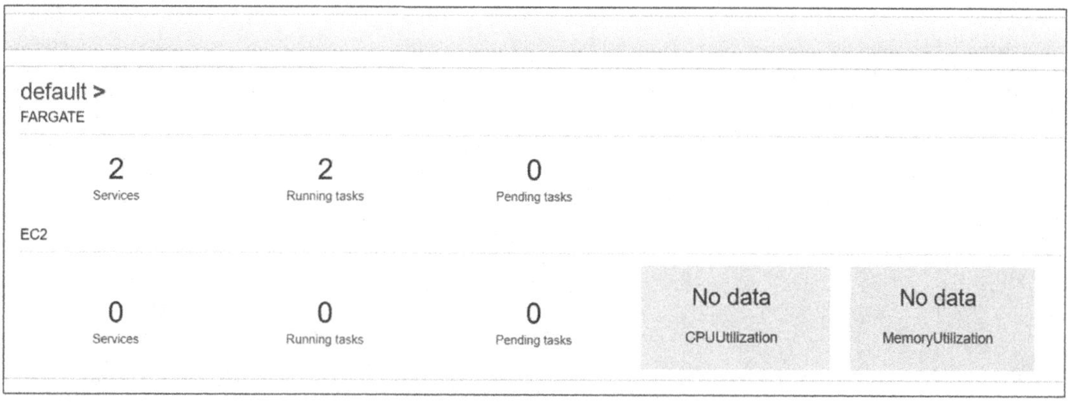

Figure 8-32. *Default Fargate cluster view*

Viewing ECS Fargate Container Logs

To view the logs of your ECS Fargate tasks (containers), click the cluster name; in my case, the cluster name is called default. On the cluster page, click the Tasks tab and click the first task. Figure 8-33 shows the Tasks page.

Figure 8-33. *Tasks view*

On the task details page, click "View logs in CloudWatch," as shown in Figure 8-34. You can also see the status of the task.

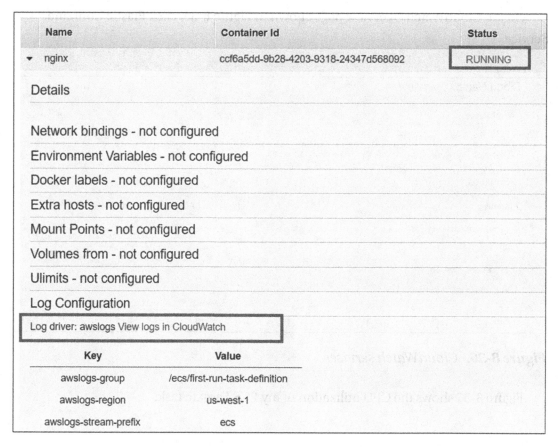

Figure 8-34. *Viewing the logs in CloudWatch*

As shown in Figure 8-35, the logs of the container appear in the CloudWatch window.

CloudWatch > Log Groups > /ecs/first-run-task-definition > ecs/nginx/268eddac-9d3b-4904-a33d-ef0dc96e3051

Filter events	
Time (UTC +00:00)	**Message**
2019-04-15	
▸ 01:53:29	2019/04/15 01:53:29 [error] 6#6: *383 open() "/usr/share/nginx/html/wp-content/plugins/portable-phpmyadmin/w
▸ 01:53:29	106.12.92.31 - - [15/Apr/2019:01:53:29 +0000] "GET /manager/html HTTP/1.1" 404 556 "-" "Mozilla/5.0 (X11; Lir
▸ 01:53:29	2019/04/15 01:53:29 [error] 6#6: *383 open() "/usr/share/nginx/html/manager/html" failed (2: No such file or direc
▸ 02:08:24	192.241.204.70 - - [15/Apr/2019:02:08:24 +0000] "GET / HTTP/1.1" 200 612 "-" "Mozilla/5.0 zgrab/0.x" "-"
▸ 02:29:33	187.56.236.69 - - [15/Apr/2019:02:29:33 +0000] "GET / HTTP/1.1" 200 612 "-" "Mozilla/5.0 (Windows NT 6.1; W

Figure 8-35. *Logs*

On the CloudWatch Overview page shown in Figure 8-36, click Elastic Container Service.

Figure 8-36. *CloudWatch services*

Figure 8-37 shows the CPU utilization of my ECS Fargate task.

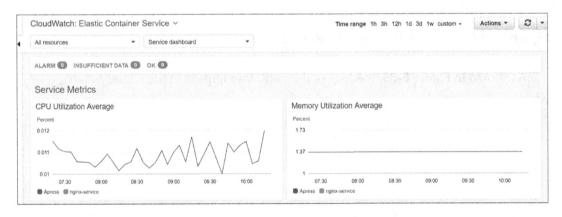

Figure 8-37. *Service metrics*

Using CloudWatch, you can tap into ECS and monitor your tasks.

Monitoring Amazon ECR Performance

In this section, I will show you a few ways you can keep an eye on your ECR container registry. Because ECR is a storage service under the hood, there are not a lot of things you can monitor.

However, ECR has a few limitations you need to remember, as follows:

- 1,000 repositories per region

- 1,000 images per repository

- 200 Docker pull requests per second per repository and region

If you are planning on deploying a large ECR environment, make sure you aware of these limits. To check how much space your ECR repository is using, click the ECR repository, as shown in Figure 8-38.

Figure 8-38. *ECR repositories view*

Figure 8-39 shows the image name and the size of my image.

Figure 8-39. *ECR image tag*

To keep the number of images low and save space on your ECR, I recommend you use lifecycle policies.

To learn more about lifecycle policies, review Chapter 2.

Using ECR Commands

To list all images stored and information about your ECR configuration, you can use the following ECR commands:

```
aws ecr list-images --repository-name deploy
aws ecr describe-repositories --repository-name deploy
aws ecr describe-images --repository-name deploy
```

Monitoring the Docker Container Host

To monitor the Docker container hosts running on EC2 instances, you can use the same methods you use to monitor EKS worker nodes. After all, the worker nodes are EC2 instances that CloudWatch can easily monitor and track.

One of my favorite methods of monitoring EC2 instances is directly from the EC2 VM page. As you can see in Figure 8-40, you can use the Monitoring tab to monitor EC2 machines.

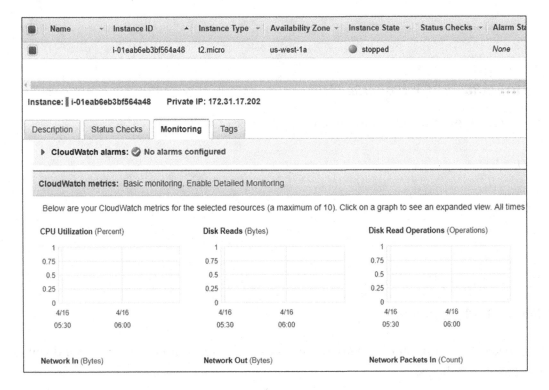

Figure 8-40. *EC2 monitoring view*

If you look closely, you can see many metrics that are available for monitoring directly on the EC2 screen.

Figure 8-41 shows all the metrics.

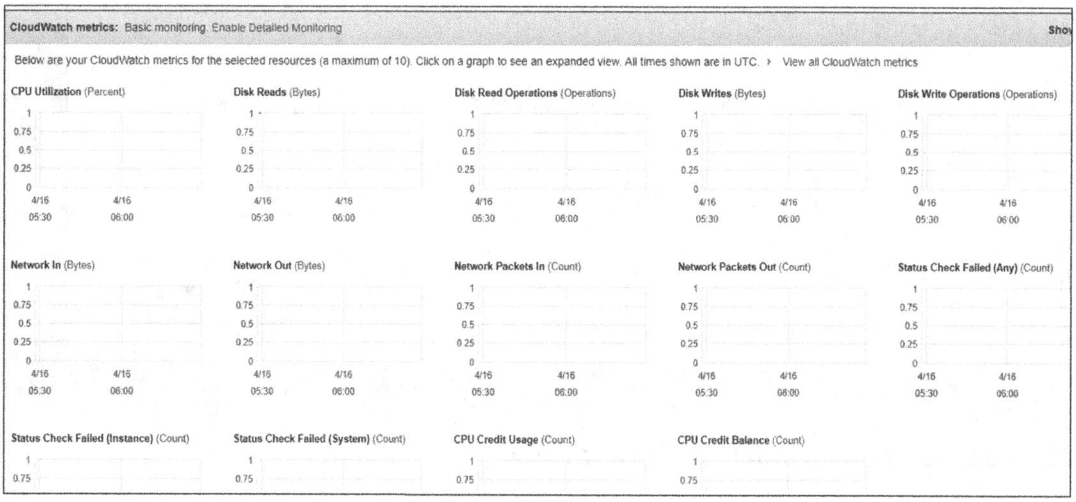

Figure 8-41. CloudWatch metrics

You can also click the "View all CloudWatch metrics" link, which will take you to the CloudWatch Dashboard.

If you click the Enable Detailed Monitoring page, you will have the option to use CloudWatch's advanced monitoring; note that this costs extra.

Figure 8-42 shows the Enable Detailed Monitoring screen.

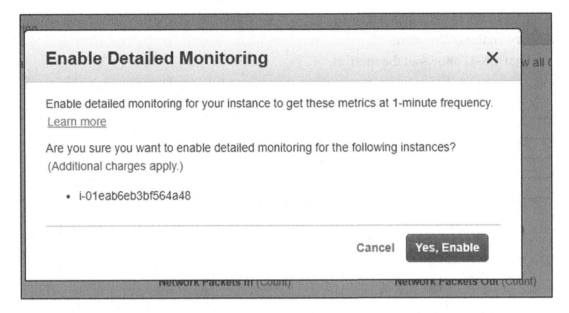

Figure 8-42. *Enabling detailed monitoring*

Note   Basic CloudWatch monitoring has a five-minute frequency compared to one minute on the paid tier.

Creating an Alarm

Using CloudWatch integration with EC2, you can create a monitoring alarm that will send you an e-mail if something happens to your VM. To create an alarm, you can use the Monitoring tab shown in Figure 8-43.

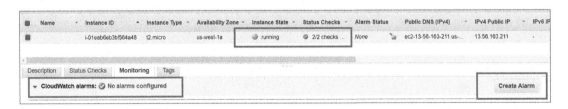

Figure 8-43. *Create Alarm button*

On the Monitoring tab, click the Create Alarm button on the right side.

On the Create Alarm screen, shown in Figure 8-44, click the "Create a topic" link and type a message and an e-mail address. On the configuration section, you can select what you want to be alerted on and click Create Alarm.

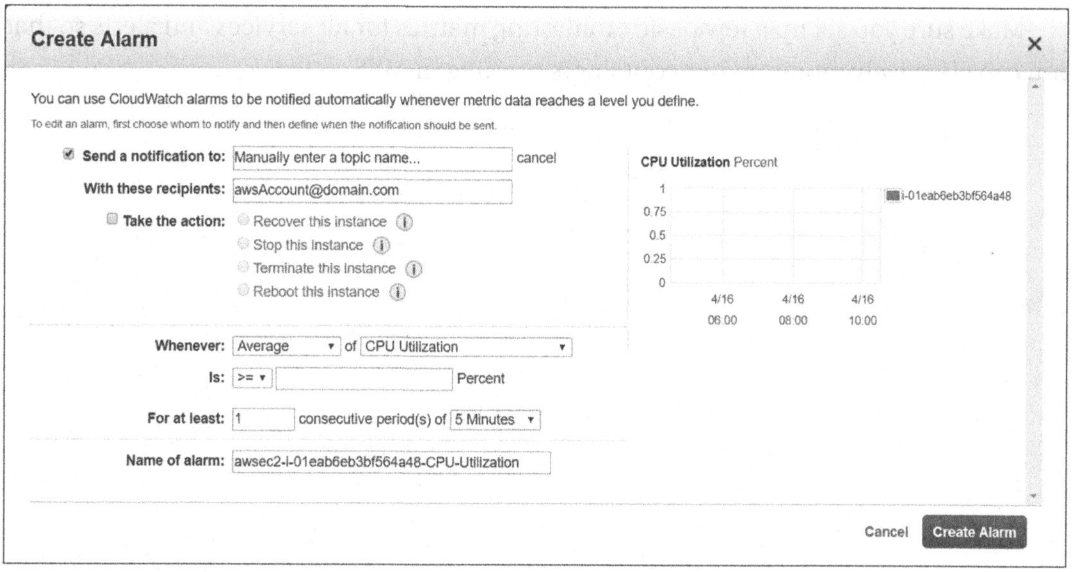

Figure 8-44. *Creating an alarm*

To create an alarm that will notify you every time the EC2 instance is above 90 percent, you can use the configuration shown in Figure 8-45.

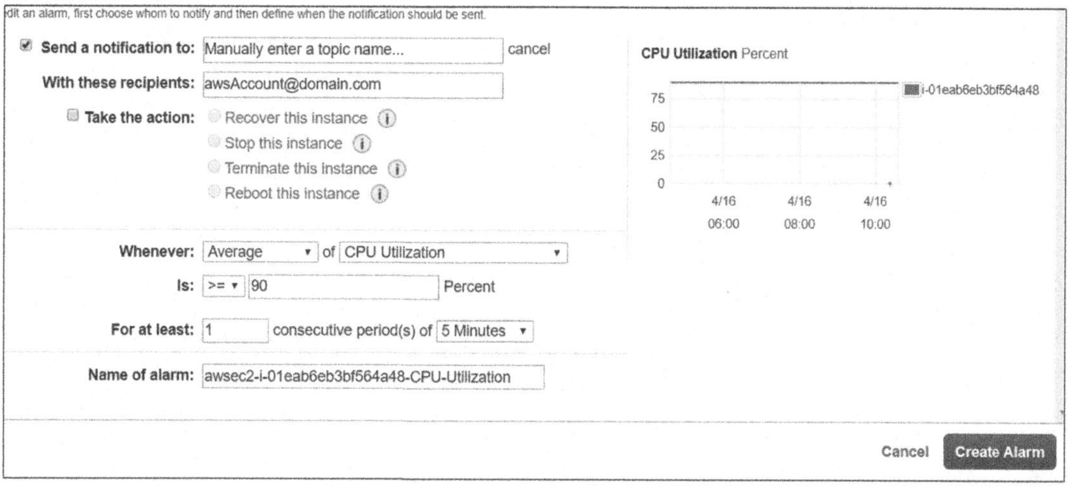

Figure 8-45. *Configuring an alarm notification*

Summary

In this chapter, I showed you how to monitor all the container services available on AWS. With the tools and information you have seen in this chapter, you will be able to keep an eye on your containers and hosts.

Make sure you set up a few basic monitoring metrics for all services and alerts so that you can effectively monitor your containers running in AWS.

CHAPTER 9

Backing Up and Restoring Your Containers and Hosts on Amazon AWS

In this chapter, you will focus on backing up and restoring your Docker container hosts and containers. Backing up your data and making sure the backup is working is a critical part of maintaining your environment. Neglecting this part of deployment can result in failing to restore services when needed and thus directly impact the applications and the business.

The best rule I have developed over the years is to configure a backup on any production system before it is moved to production. Ignoring this rule can lead to delays in enabling backups because sometimes once the application is moved to production, no one wants to risk downtime.

For this reason, I will explore all the possible backup options for your containerized environment.

You might find that some services offer limited backup and restore methods because of the nature of the service. Regardless of the limitation, you should always have a backup strategy in place to overcome an unexpected disaster.

In this chapter, I will cover the following topics:

- How to use EC2 EBS snapshots to back up EC2 instances

- How to restore EC2 instances using snapshots

- How to back up and restore ECS containers

- How to back up your EKS configuration

- How to use AWS Backup to back up instances

© Shimon Ifrah 2019
S. Ifrah, *Deploy Containers on AWS*, https://doi.org/10.1007/978-1-4842-5101-0_9

Backing Up and Restoring Amazon EC2 Container Hosts

In this section, I will show you how to back up and restore EC2 container instances. The reason I am starting with EC2 is because EC2 gives you the most control over the backup and restore process compared to the other services, as you will see in the following sections.

Understanding EBS Snapshots

All AWS EC2 instances have a storage volume on which the OS is installed and a data volume is added. The way you back up your EC2 virtual machines is by backing up the EBS volumes to an S3 storage account. With an EBS snapshot backup, you are taking a point-in-time snapshot of the volumes of the instance.

AWS also uses incremental backups to back up volumes, which means that only the changes on the volume since the last full backup are being backed up. Incremental backups allow you to reduce the time it takes to back up an instance and minimize the load on the server if it under a heavy load. Another upside to incremental backups is the reduced cost because of less storage being used.

Taking an EBS Snapshot (Backup)

In this section, I will show you how to back up an EC2 Docker container host running on a Windows server. The first step in this process is to open the EC2 console and access the EC2 Dashboard. You can use the following direct URL:

```
https://console.aws.amazon.com/ec2/
```

In my case, I am using the menu I have created, as shown in Figure 9-1.

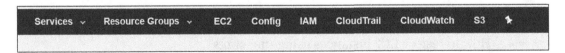

Figure 9-1. *Menu*

On the EC2 Dashboard, you need to locate the EBS volume ID that your EC2 instance is using. To find the EBS volume ID, you can click the EC2 instance and review the block device settings.

Figure 9-2 shows the EC2 instance's Description tab where you will find the EBS ID.

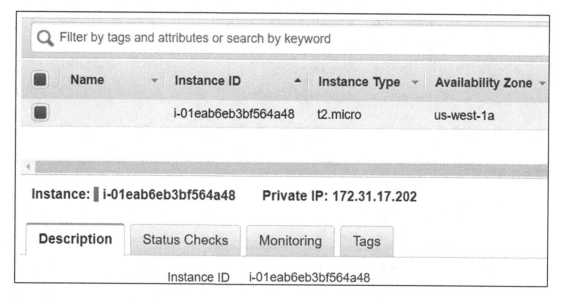

Figure 9-2. *EBS instance*

In the Description tab's details, click the "Block devices" hyperlink, as shown in Figure 9-3.

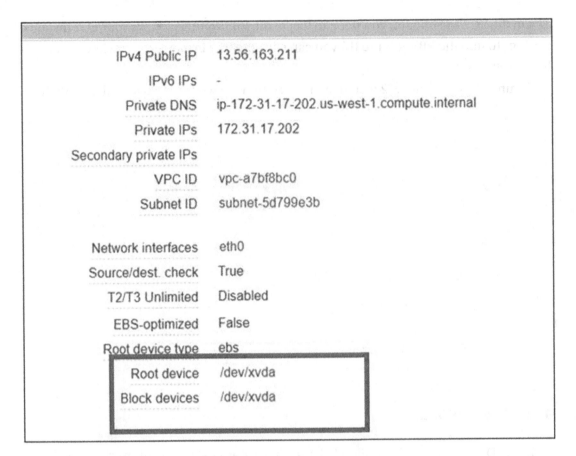

Figure 9-3. *"Block devices" hyperlink*

In the Block Device details menu, note the EBS volume ID.
Figure 9-4 shows my EBS ID.

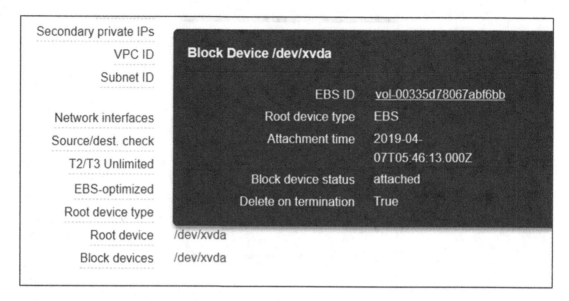

Figure 9-4. *EBS volume ID*

Now that you have the EBS volume ID, you can start the backup process for the EBS storage volume.

Taking an EC2 Snapshot

To take a snapshot of an EC2 instance volume, you can use the Elastic Block Storage menu located in the EC2 Dashboard menu.

Figure 9-5 shows the Snapshots option that you can click to start the backup process.

Figure 9-5. *EBS menu*

The Snapshots page lists all the available snapshots if there are any and gives you the option to restore or delete them.

In my case, I don't have any snapshots, so I am going to create a new one by clicking the Create Snapshot button, as shown in Figure 9-6.

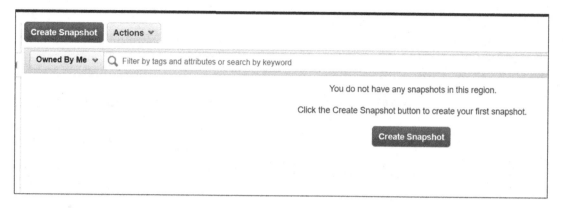

Figure 9-6. *Creating a snapshot*

On the "Create snapshot" page, you can select the volume of the EC2 instance in the Volume menu, as shown in Figure 9-7. Here you can see that it has the same volume ID as the volume I noted in Figure 9-4.

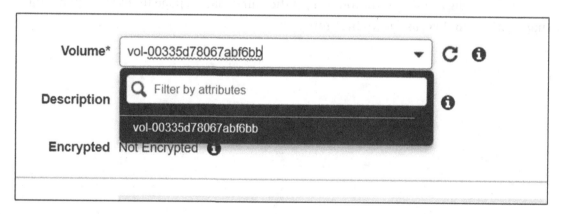

Figure 9-7. *Selecting a volume*

The next step is to give the snapshot a description.

Make sure you use a good description that will make it clear to which EC2 instance the snapshot belongs.

Figure 9-8 shows the description and volume I am using.

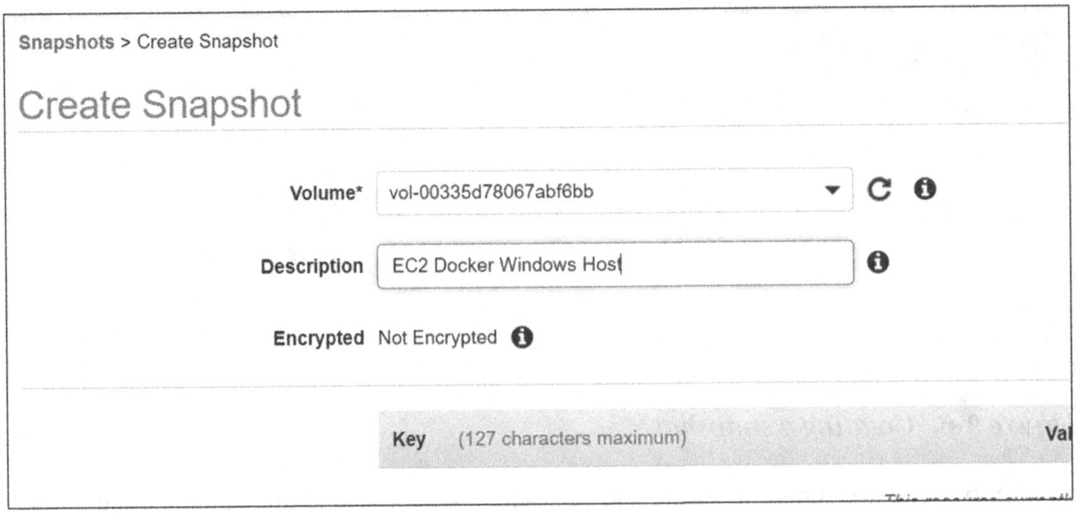

Figure 9-8. *Adding a description*

After creating the snapshot, you will get the confirmation page that tells you that the snapshot is complete, as shown in Figure 9-9.

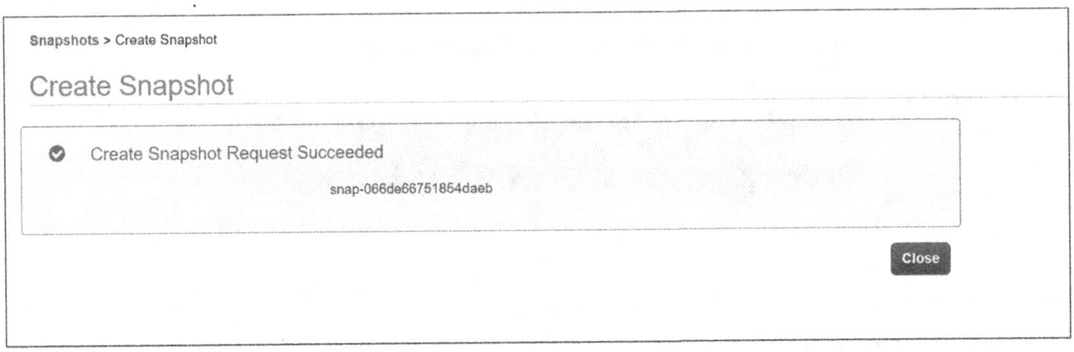

Figure 9-9. *Confirmation page*

You can monitor the progress of the snapshot on the Snapshot page.
Figure 9-10 shows that the backup was completed.

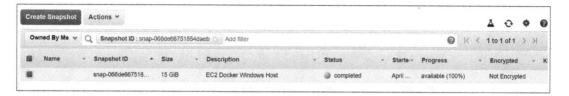

Figure 9-10. *Monitoring a snapshot's progress*

Restoring an EC2 Instance

The most important part of the backup and restore process is restoring or knowing how to restore your EC2 instance.

The process of restoring an EC2 instance is very structured, and because volumes can be attached and detached, the changes made can be reverted by restoring from the snapshot taken at a point in time.

Creating a Volume from a Snapshot

To restore a snapshot to your EC2 instance, you need to start by creating a volume from the snapshot you have taken. To create a volume from the snapshot, click the snapshot on the Snapshot page, and in the Actions menu click Create Volume.

Figure 9-11 shows the Create Volume item.

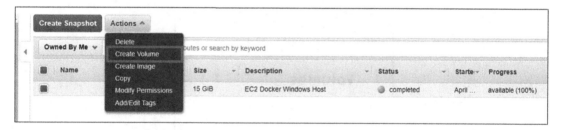

Figure 9-11. *Create Volume item*

When creating the volume from the snapshot, the volume size needs to be the same size as the source disk or larger.

Figure 9-12 shows the Create Volume screen.

Create Volume

Snapshot ID	snap-066de66751854daeb
Volume Type	General Purpose SSD (gp2) ▾ ⓘ
Size (GiB)	15 (Min: 1 GiB, Max: 16384 GiB) ⓘ
IOPS	100 / 3000 (Baseline of 3 IOPS per GiB with a minimum of 100 IOPS, burstable to 3000 IOPS) ⓘ
Availability Zone*	us-west-1a ▾ ⓘ
Throughput (MB/s)	Not applicable ⓘ

Figure 9-12. *Create Volume screen*

Attaching a Volume to an EC2 Instance

At this stage, you need to find the current volume that is attached to your EC2 instance and detach it. After detaching it, you can attach the new volume to the EC2 instance.

To start the process, click Volumes in the Elastic Block Store menu.

Figure 9-13 shows the menu.

Figure 9-13. *EBS volumes*

On the Volumes page, note the volume ID of the attached volume and the ID of the new volume. This will make the process easy, and if you need to revert the change, you can use the values for reference.

In Figure 9-14, you can see the current volume that is in use in my environment.

Name	Volume ID	Size	Volume Type	IOPS	Snapshot	Created	Availability Zone	State
	vol-0c0f9a390e3758ca4	15 GiB	gp2	100	snap-066de66...	April 24, 2019 at 9:5...	us-west-1a	● available
	vol-00335d78067abf6bb	15 GiB	gp2	100	snap-0608a06...	April 7, 2019 at 3:46...	us-west-1a	● in-use

Figure 9-14. *Current EBS volume in use*

Detaching an Old Volume

Before starting this process, you need to turn off the EC2 instance by right-clicking the EC2 instance, selecting Instance State, and clicking Stop, as shown in Figure 9-15. You can also use the following AWS CLI command to stop the instance:

```
aws ec2 stop-instances --instance-ids idnumber
```

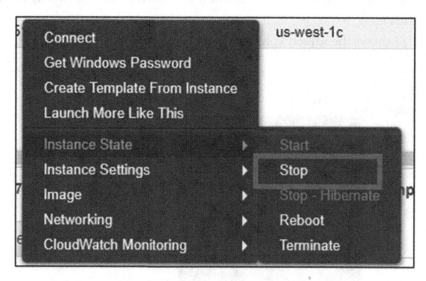

Figure 9-15. *Stopping an EC2 instance*

To detach the attached volume, you can select it from the list and use the Actions menu to detach it using the Detach Volume menu item.

Figure 9-16 shows the Detach Volume menu item.

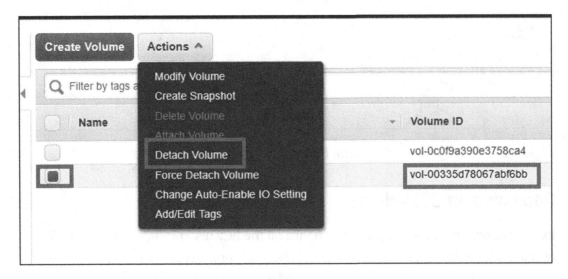

Figure 9-16. *Detaching an EBS volume*

After the volume is detached, select the new volume and use the Attach Volume option to attach it.

Figure 9-17 shows the Attach Volume option.

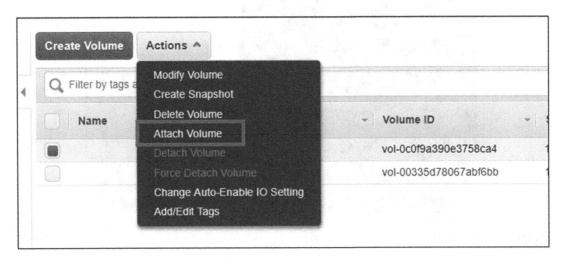

Figure 9-17. *Attach Volume menu item*

On the Attach Volume screen, you need to select the instance ID and set the device you will attach the volume to.

In my case, because it is a Windows Server machine, I am using the following value:

/dev/xvda

For a Linux machine, you would use this:

```
/dev/sdp
```

Figure 9-18 shows the Attach Volume screen.

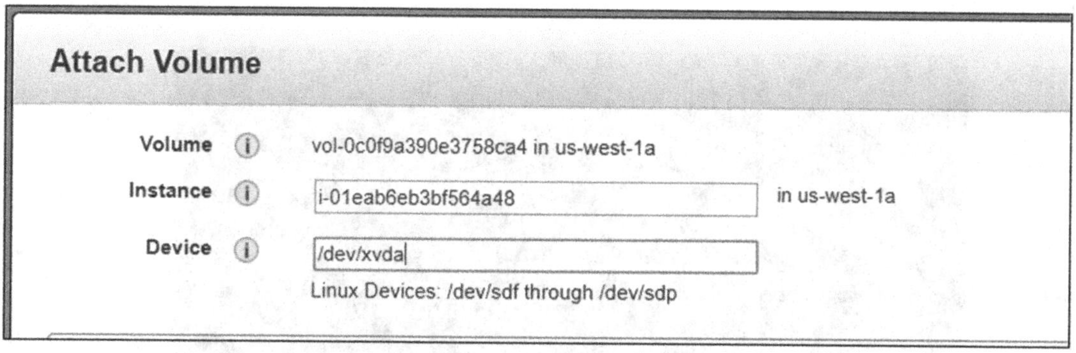

Attach Volume

Volume ⓘ	vol-0c0f9a390e3758ca4 in us-west-1a
Instance ⓘ	i-01eab6eb3bf564a48 in us-west-1a
Device ⓘ	/dev/xvda

Linux Devices: /dev/sdf through /dev/sdp

Figure 9-18. *Attaching an EBS volume*

Note Please review the following links to understand the AWS device naming configuration for EC2:

https://docs.aws.amazon.com/AWSEC2/latest/UserGuide/device_naming.html

https://docs.aws.amazon.com/AWSEC2/latest/WindowsGuide/device_naming.html

---

Once the volume has attached to the EC2 instance, it will show up as "In-use" in the State Column.

Figure 9-19 shows the attached volume after the attached operation.

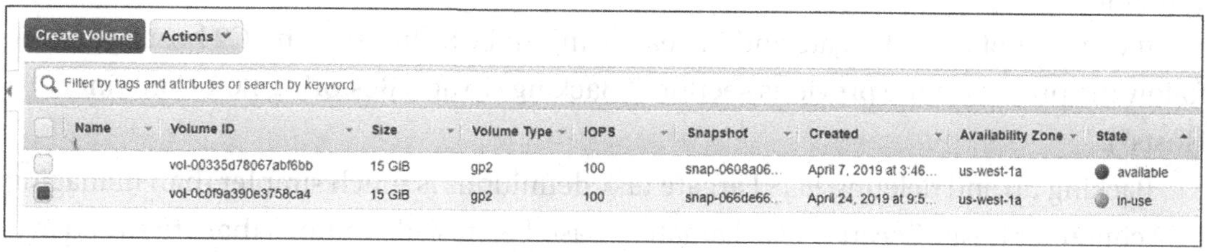

	Name	Volume ID	Size	Volume Type	IOPS	Snapshot	Created	Availability Zone	State
☐		vol-00335d78067abf6bb	15 GiB	gp2	100	snap-0608a06...	April 7, 2019 at 3:46...	us-west-1a	● available
■		vol-0c0f9a390e3758ca4	15 GiB	gp2	100	snap-066de66...	April 24, 2019 at 9:5...	us-west-1a	● in-use

Figure 9-19. *EBS volume's status view*

To confirm that the volume has been attached, you can start the EC2 instance and review the block device status and ID.

Figure 9-20 shows my attached device.

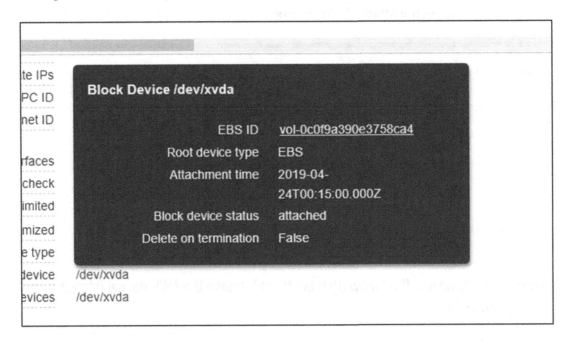

Figure 9-20. *Block device status*

My recommendation is to try this process with your Docker container host. Once you complete the process successfully, document the process so that you can repeat it in the case of a disaster.

Backing Up and Restoring ECS Fargate Containers

In this section, you will explore the backup and restore process for AWS ECS Fargate containers.

If you are not using Fargate and instead using an ECS cluster with EC2 hosts, you can follow the process in the previous section ("Backing Up and Restoring EC2 Container Hosts").

Backing up and deleting ECS Fargate task definitions is much simpler than managing EC2 container hosts. Because ECS Fargate is based on task definitions that are stored in JSON files, you can always restore them on the Inactive screen.

To restore a deleted task definition, click the Inactive link on the Task Definitions page, as shown in Figure 9-21.

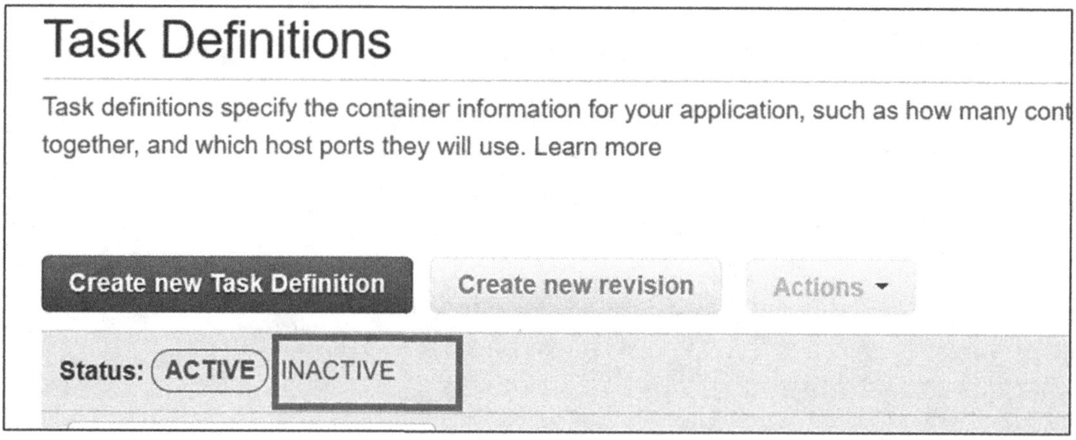

Figure 9-21. *Inactive task definitions*

On the Inactive page, you can see all the task definitions I have previously deleted. Figure 9-22 shows the Inactive page. To restore my ASP01 task definition, I select it and click the "Create new revision" button.

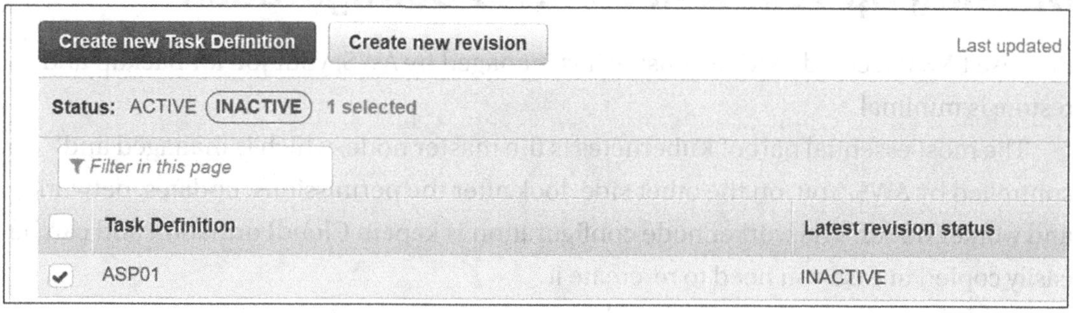

Figure 9-22. *ASP01 task definition*

Once you click the button, all you need to do is follow the wizard to create the task definition. AWS will use the same details of the task definition before it is deleted.

Figure 9-23 shows the prepopulated values.

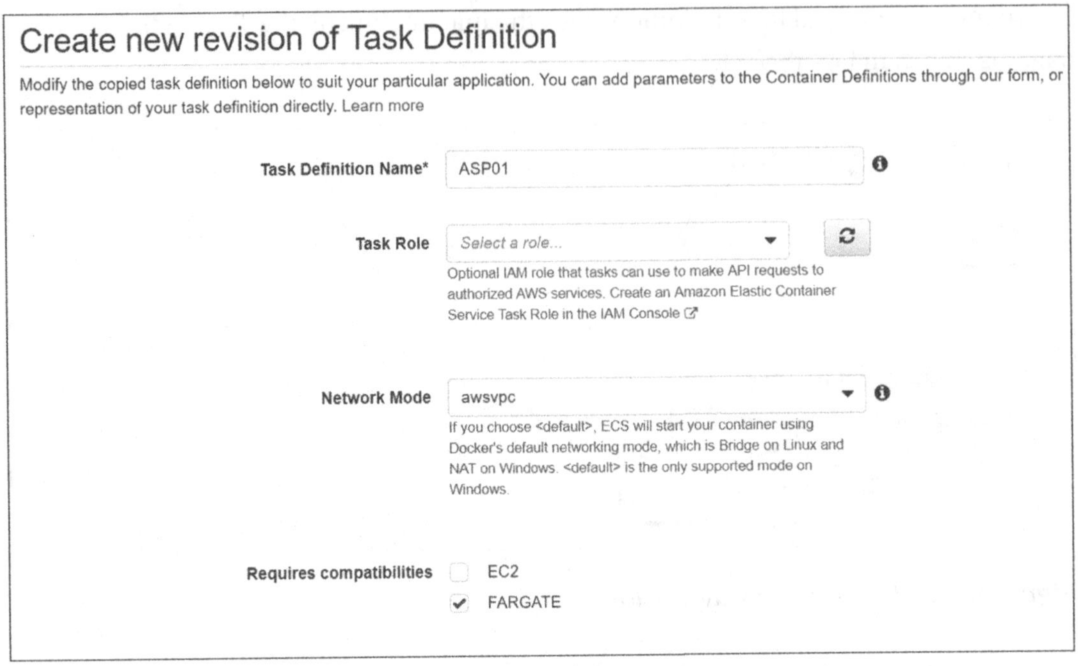

Create new revision of Task Definition

Modify the copied task definition below to suit your particular application. You can add parameters to the Container Definitions through our form, or representation of your task definition directly. Learn more

Task Definition Name*   ASP01

Task Role   Select a role...

Optional IAM role that tasks can use to make API requests to authorized AWS services. Create an Amazon Elastic Container Service Task Role in the IAM Console

Network Mode   awsvpc

If you choose <default>, ECS will start your container using Docker's default networking mode, which is Bridge on Linux and NAT on Windows. <default> is the only supported mode on Windows.

Requires compatibilities   ☐ EC2
                               ☑ FARGATE

Figure 9-23.   Creating a new revision of a task definition

Backing Up Your Amazon EKS Configuration

Because EKS is a cloud service, most of it is managed by AWS; your job for backup and restore is minimal.

The most essential part of Kubernetes is the master node, which is managed and controlled by AWS. You, on the other side, look after the permissions, updates, networks, and worker nodes. The worker node configuration is kept in CloudFormation and can be easily copied in case you need to re-create it.

Note   My recommendation for EKS backup and restore is that you keep your documentation up-to-date and in the case of a disaster you use the same steps to re-create the service.

CloudFormation, like ECS, offers you the option to restore worker node templates using the Filter menu.

Figure 9-24 shows the Filter menu with all the deleted templates.

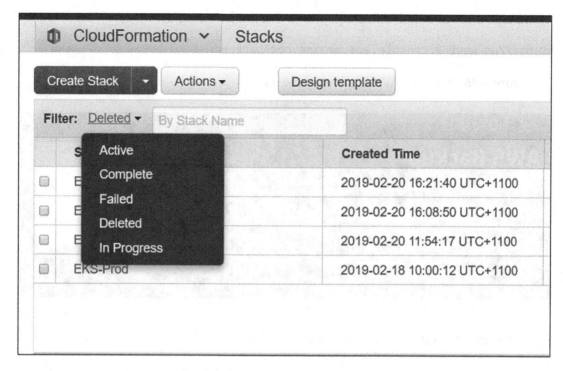

Figure 9-24. *CloudFormation Filter menu*

Using a deleted template, you can create a new worker node group with similar settings. To do so, open a deleted template and use the same settings with a new template.

Using AWS Backup

If your environment is growing and you feel you need more advanced tools to back up your AWS services, you should explore AWS Backup. AWS Backup is a managed backup service that is fully managed by AWS.

With AWS Backup, you can centralize all your backups in one place and fully automate the lifecycle of your data. AWS Backup works across AWS services and can connect to your on-premises environment.

The advantage of AWS Backup is that you no longer need to manage backups per service and can use backup scripts to run automated backups. AWS Backup automates the entire process and saves you time and effort. You can also build backup policies with schedules and retention policies of data.

To read more about AWS Backup, please visit the following URL:

https://us-west-2.console.aws.amazon.com/backup

Figure 9-25 shows the AWS Backup home page.

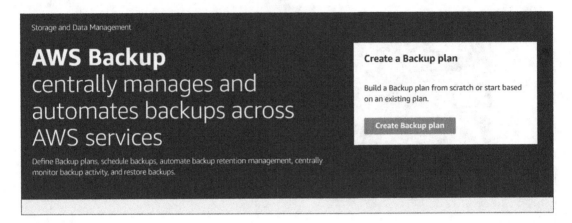

Figure 9-25. *AWS Backup home page*

AWS Backup is based on the number of gigabytes stored; for example, each gigabyte of EBS storage costs $0.05.

Currently, only the following AWS services are supported by AWS Backup:

- AWS EBS volumes

- AWS RDS

- AWS DynamoDB

- AWS EFS

- AWS Storage Gateway

Getting started with AWS Backup is simple, because AWS has automated most of the process for you. When you set up AWS Backup, the first thing you need to create is a backup plan that defines when you are going to back up and for how long you are planning to retain the data. AWS Backup comes with predefined plans that already define the most important details of the backup.

Figure 9-26 shows a predefined plan with data retention configuration.

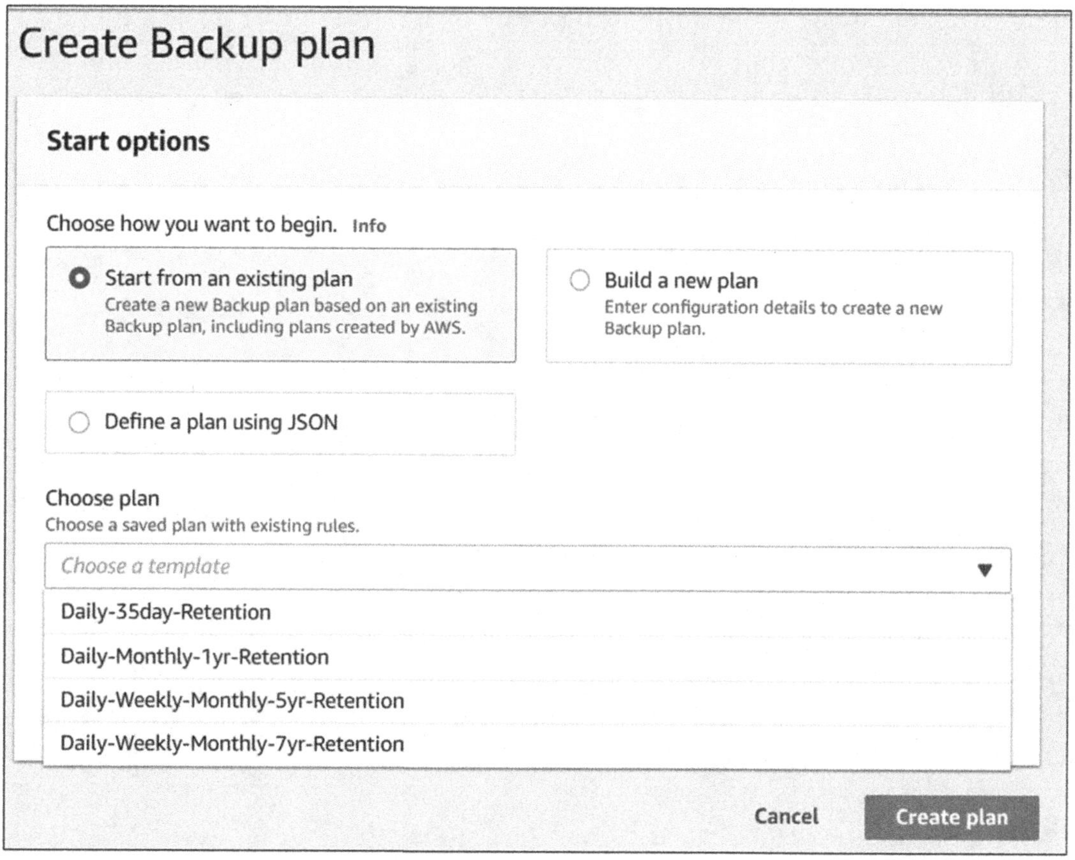

Figure 9-26. *Creating a backup plan*

For more information, visit the AWS Backup home page listed earlier.

Summary

Is this chapter, I covered the main backup and restore offerings for AWS that can help you back up and restore your container services.

My recommendation for this chapter is always to do a restore test to make sure the backups are working and that you are familiar with the restore process and the time it takes to restore a host or a service.

CHAPTER 10

Troubleshooting Amazon AWS Containerized Solutions

Troubleshooting AWS services is something every AWS administrator or engineer should know how to do. In this chapter, I will show you some of the tools and techniques you can use to troubleshoot the services that you are consuming from AWS.

Most of the issues your applications or services will have are probably a result of a misconfiguration. In the last few years, I have seen only a handful of issues where the root cause could be attributed to a cloud provider. Most issues are caused by misconfiguration, lack of documentation, or selecting the wrong service.

Dealing with Common Issues

Most of the issues I have seen over the years in deployments are related to not sizing the AWS resources and services properly. For example, if you select the wrong storage disk type (HDD and no SSD) and the application has a lot of read and write operations, performance will be impacted.

In this case, if the wrong ECS resource allocation is selected, the application will be impacted. The same concept applies to ECR. If the selected region is not in the same region as ECS or EKS, you will experience slowness compared to deploying ECR in the same region.

If you are planning to deploy EKS, make sure you select enough worker nodes to fulfill all the requests and deployments. Under-resourcing any AWS service will impact performance.

© Shimon Ifrah 2019
S. Ifrah, *Deploy Containers on AWS*, https://doi.org/10.1007/978-1-4842-5101-0_10

Troubleshooting Amazon EKS

Troubleshooting AWS Elastic Kubernetes Service (EKS) is something you will definitely need to know how to do.

Troubleshooting any service can be split into two categories.

- Availability issues

- Performance issues

Troubleshooting Availability Issues

Availability issues are issues that cause your application to become unavailable. When applications are not available, the tasks you need to perform to understand the root cause are entirely different than when dealing with performance issues.

When building solutions on AWS, it is always recommended that you build them with enough redundancy. For example, when using EKS in production, make sure you deploy a minimum of three worker nodes.

The same rule applies to EC2 instances that are acting as container hosts.

Troubleshooting Performance Issues

Performance issues are issues that affect existing services and, in this case, EKS. When a service is affected by a performance issue, it is still running; however, the performance goes down. In other words, transactions take longer to complete, or the number of transactions or users handled goes down.

Troubleshooting performance issues is harder than dealing with availability issues because the service is still running and available but is running slowly. When a service is running and suffers from a performance issue, you are limited by the actions you can take.

Taking an action during the troubleshooting process can cause an outage if it's not planned well. It is also essential you know how to use AWS CLI to extract information about your EKS cluster that is not available in the AWS Portal.

In the following sections, I will show you a few AWS CLI EKS commands that will provide detailed information about your EKS cluster.

Note As always, I recommend you maintain some documentation containing these commands, which can be handy in the case of performance or availability issues.

Checking EKS Availability and Configuration

In this section, I will show you how to check the health status of an EKS cluster. The starting point to check essential availability is the EKS console.

In Figure 10-1 you can see my EKS cluster on my EKS home page.

Figure 10-1. *EKS cluster's general configuration page*

The important part is that the status of the cluster is Active, which tells you that there are no issues with the cluster's master node.

Using AWS CLI

The EKS home page offers basic information; however, sometimes you need to extract information that is not available on the home page. In cases like these, you need to use the AWS CLI tool.

Note My recommendation is to have the latest version of the AWS CLI tool installed.

Once you install the tool, make sure you configure AWS CLI with all the security details needed to connect to AWS. Please read Chapter 1 for more information about installing AWS CLI and configuring it.

Using AWS CLI EKS Commands

If your EKS cluster is not in the same region as your AWS EKS cluster, you won't be able to connect to it.

To connect to your EKS cluster, your AWS CLI needs to be configured to use the same region as the EKS cluster. In my case, my default region is us-west-1; however, my EKS cluster is in us-west-2. To change the default region name of AWS CLI, you can use the aws configure command and follow the prompts. If there is nothing to change, type enter.

When I get to the region section, I type us-west-2.

To start the configuration process, type the following command (shown in Figure 10-2):

```
aws configure
```

```
PS C:\1.DevOps> aws configure
AWS Access Key ID [*************
AWS Secret Access Key [*********
Default region name [us-west-2]: ▉
```

Figure 10-2. *The aws configure command*

To list all the EKS clusters, you can use the following command, as shown in Figure 10-3:

```
aws eks list-clusters
```

```
PS C:\1.DevOps> aws eks list-clusters
{
    "clusters": [
        "EKS-Cluster"
    ]
}
```

Figure 10-3. *The eks list-clusters command*

Using the EKS cluster name gathered from the previous command, type the following command (shown in Figure 10-4) to get more detailed information about your cluster:

```
aws eks describe-cluster --name EKS-Cluster
```

```
PS C:\1.DevOps> aws eks describe-cluster --name EKS-Cluster
{
    "cluster": {
        "name": "EKS-Cluster",
        "arn": "arn:aws:eks:us-west-2:852051225911:cluster/EKS-Cluster",
        "createdAt": 1554263591.04,
        "version": "1.12",
        "endpoint": "https://2660073EAFFEF047FFF9ECEF8FA7C117.sk1.us-west-2.eks.amazonaws.com",
        "roleArn": "arn:aws:iam::852051225911:role/EKS_Service_Role",
        "resourcesVpcConfig": {
            "subnetIds": [
                "subnet-06e4a9a04c103710b",
                "subnet-01a6547d5b7bafdf1",
                "subnet-0ee13d81a44a68c15"
            ],
            "securityGroupIds": [
                "sg-04084c7132e38f585"
            ],
            "vpcId": "vpc-0207a37adedf986ef"
        },
        "status": "ACTIVE",
        "certificateAuthority": {
```

Figure 10-4. *The eks describe-cluster command*

To check which updates are associated with your EKS cluster, run the following command (shown in Figure 10-5):

```
aws eks list-updates --name EKS-Cluster
```

```
PS C:\1.DevOps> aws eks list-updates --name EKS-Cluster
{
    "updateIds": [
        "d0800c34-4783-46a1-94a6-ad52c74fc4b7"
    ]
}
```

Figure 10-5. *The eks list-updates command*

You can also use EKS CLI to install updates, delete clusters, and update the cluster configuration.

To update a cluster, use the following command:

```
aws eks update-cluster-version --name EKS-Cluster --kubernetes-version 1.12
```

Troubleshooting EKS Worker Nodes

The next step in the troubleshooting process is to check the EKS worker nodes and their configuration in CloudFormation.

AWS CloudFormation helps to provision infrastructure in AWS using templates and JSON files. You can also automate the provisioning process using CloudFormation. If you remember, in Chapter 4 you created an EKS cluster and used an AWS preconfigured template.

The first step in CloudFormation and the EKS cluster troubleshooting process is to review the configuration of the stack. The stack configuration will appear on the tabs under the stack name after you select it.

Figure 10-6 shows all the tabs.

	Stack Name	Created Time	Status	Drift Status	Description
☑	EKS-Cluster-Node-01	2019-04-03 16:12:53 UTC+1100	UPDATE_COMPLETE	NOT_CHECKED	Amazon EKS - Node Group
☐	EKS-Prod	2019-04-03 14:41:38 UTC+1100	CREATE_COMPLETE	NOT_CHECKED	Amazon EKS Sample VPC

Overview   Outputs   Resources   Events   Template   Parameters   Tags   Stack Policy   Change Sets   Rollback Triggers

To view detailed drift information for specific resources, visit the Drift Details page.

Figure 10-6. *AWS worker node's CloudFormation template*

To check the events that belong to the EKS worker node's stack, you can use the Events tab. The Events tab shows action by action the events belonging to the stack.

Figure 10-7 shows the Events tab.

Overview	Outputs	Resources	Events	Template	Parameters	Tags	Stack Policy	Change Sets	Rollback Triggers

Filter by: Status ▾   Search events

2019-04-09	Status	Type	Logical ID	Status Reason
▸ 16:11:53 UTC+1000	UPDATE_COMPLETE	AWS::CloudFormation::Stack	EKS-Cluster-Node-01	
▸ 16:11:51 UTC+1000	UPDATE_COMPLETE_CLEANUP _IN_PROGRESS	AWS::CloudFormation::Stack	EKS-Cluster-Node-01	
▸ 16:11:49 UTC+1000	UPDATE_COMPLETE	AWS::AutoScaling::AutoScalingGroup	NodeGroup	
▸ 16:11:30 UTC+1000	UPDATE_IN_PROGRESS	AWS::AutoScaling::AutoScalingGroup	NodeGroup	
▸ 16:11:23 UTC+1000	UPDATE_IN_PROGRESS	AWS::CloudFormation::Stack	EKS-Cluster-Node-01	User Initiated
2019-04-08	Status	Type	Logical ID	Status Reason

Figure 10-7. *CloudFormation events*

In the case of a performance issue, you can increase the capacity by selecting your worker node stack and selecting Update Stack from the Actions menu.

Figure 10-8 shows the Update Stack item.

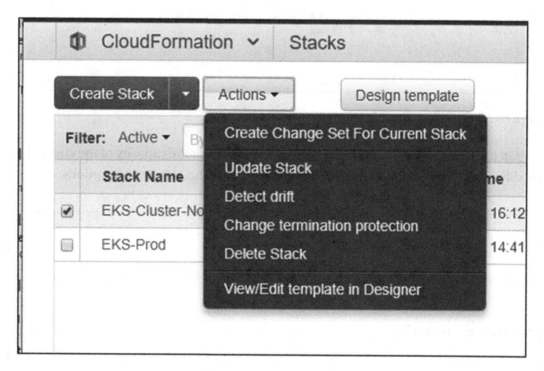

Figure 10-8. *Updating the CloudFormation stack menu*

On the Select Template page, select the "Use current template" option, as shown in Figure 10-9.

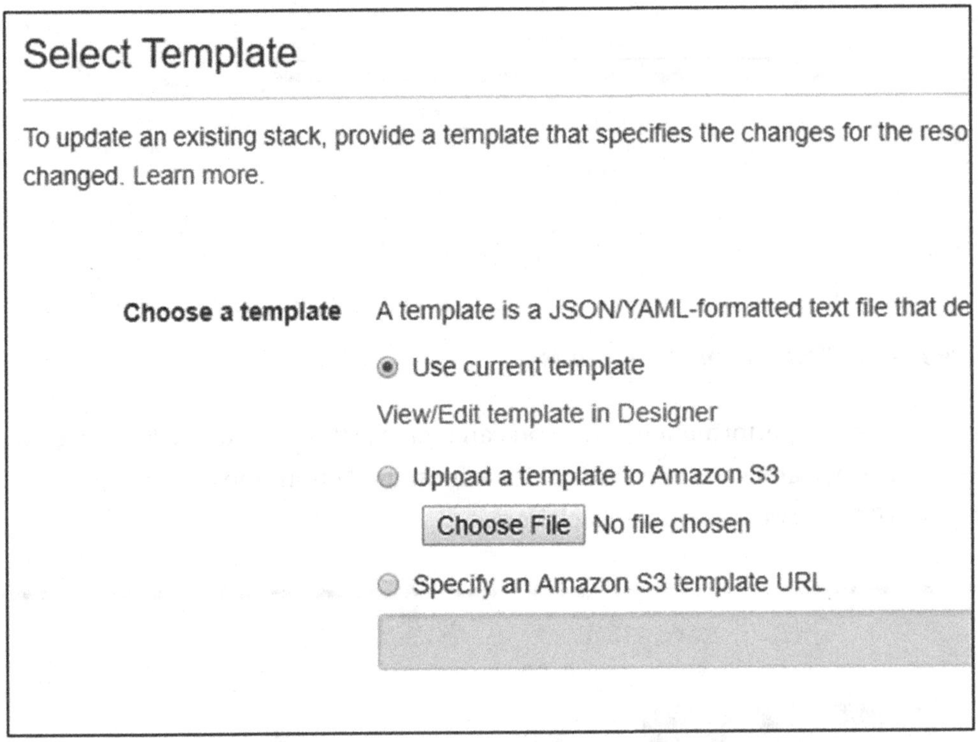

Select Template

To update an existing stack, provide a template that specifies the changes for the reso changed. Learn more.

Choose a template   A template is a JSON/YAML-formatted text file that de

◉ Use current template

View/Edit template in Designer

○ Upload a template to Amazon S3

Choose File   No file chosen

○ Specify an Amazon S3 template URL

Figure 10-9. *Select Template page*

On the template details page, you can quickly increase the capacity of the cluster by modifying the AutoScaling settings. Figure 10-10 shows the AutoScaling options.

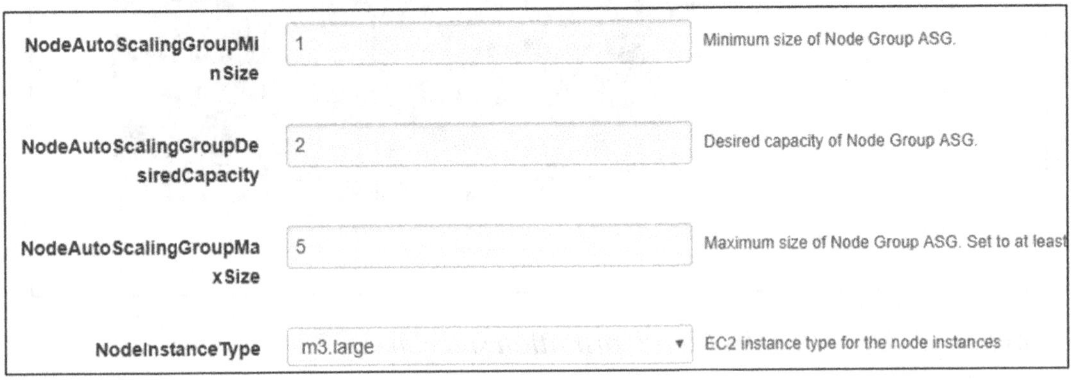

NodeAutoScalingGroupMinSize	1	Minimum size of Node Group ASG.
NodeAutoScalingGroupDesiredCapacity	2	Desired capacity of Node Group ASG.
NodeAutoScalingGroupMaxSize	5	Maximum size of Node Group ASG. Set to at least
NodeInstanceType	m3.large ▼	EC2 instance type for the node instances

Figure 10-10. *AutoScaling options*

Troubleshooting Amazon ECS Operations

In this section, I will cover a few methods that will help you troubleshoot AWS ECS. Troubleshooting an ECS cluster and Fargate is split into two sections. If you are using an ECS cluster with EC2 instances, you will also need to use the EC2 troubleshooting section. For ECS Fargate, you can use this section.

The starting point when troubleshooting ECS is the ECS management console, which is available at `https://console.aws.amazon.com/ecs/`. In the console, you can review what is running and what is not running in ECS. Figure 10-11 shows both ECS Fargate and an ECS cluster.

In my case, I am not running any ECS clusters, so the cluster count is 0. However, because I am using Fargate, you can see that I have two services configured and zero containers running.

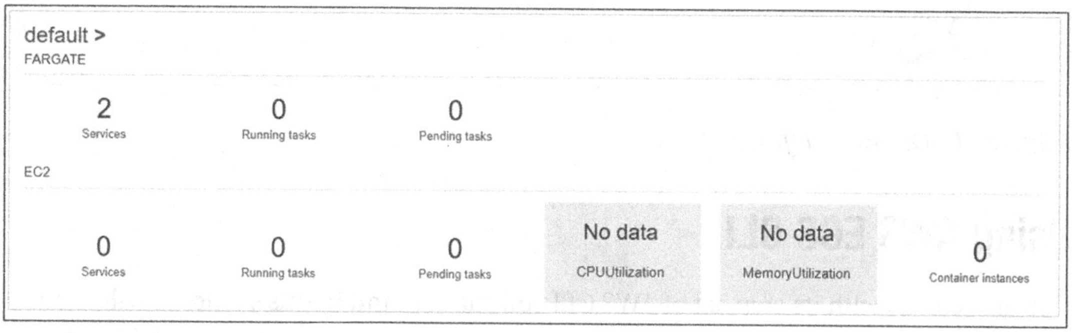

Figure 10-11.   ECS clusters in ECS management console

If you click the Fargate cluster, you can get access to more resources, such as tasks (containers), services, and metrics.

If your ECS service is under load or not performing well, you will find some useful information here. See Figure 10-12.

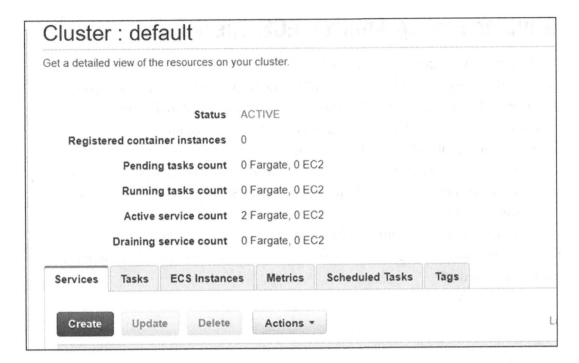

Figure 10-12. *ECS default cluster*

Using AWS ECS CLI

ECS also comes with its own set of AWS CLI commands, and in this section, I will show you how to use some of them. The starting point when using AWS CLI is to change the default region name if the ECS cluster is not located in the default region. In my case, I will switch the region to us-west-1 using the aws configure command, as shown in Figure 10-13.

aws configure

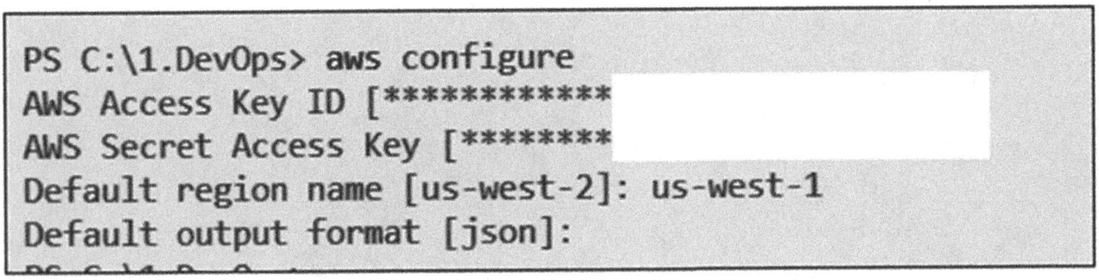

```
PS C:\1.DevOps> aws configure
AWS Access Key ID [************
AWS Secret Access Key [********
Default region name [us-west-2]: us-west-1
Default output format [json]:
```

Figure 10-13. *The aws configure command*

To view all your ECS clusters including Fargate and EC2, use the following command (shown in Figure 10-14):

```
aws ecs list-clusters
```

```
PS C:\1.DevOps> aws ecs list-clusters
{
    "clusterArns": [
        "arn:aws:ecs:us-west-1:852051225911:cluster/default"
    ]
}
```

Figure 10-14. *The ecs list-clusters command*

To view all the configured task definitions, use the following command (shown in Figure 10-15):

```
aws ecs list-task-definitions
```

```
PS C:\1.DevOps> aws ecs list-task-definitions
{
    "taskDefinitionArns": [
        "arn:aws:ecs:us-west-1:852051225911:task-definition/amazonlinux2:1",
        "arn:aws:ecs:us-west-1:852051225911:task-definition/first-run-task-definition:5"
    ]
}
```

Figure 10-15. *The ecs list-task-definitions command*

To view all the configured ECS services, you can use the following command (shown in Figure 10-16):

```
aws ecs list-services
```

```
PS C:\1.DevOps> aws ecs list-services
{
    "serviceArns": [
        "arn:aws:ecs:us-west-1:852051225911:service/Apress",
        "arn:aws:ecs:us-west-1:852051225911:service/nginx-service"
    ]
}
```

Figure 10-16. *ecs list-services command*

ECS comes with five times more commands than AWS EKS; therefore, I strongly recommend you review them using the following command line:

```
aws ecs help
```

Figure 10-17 shows the `help` command output with a description of ECS and all the commands.

```
PS C:\1.DevOps> aws ecs help

ecs
^^^


Description
**********

Amazon Elastic Container Service (Amazon ECS) is a highly scalable,
fast, container management service that makes it easy to run, stop,
and manage Docker containers on a cluster. You can host your cluster
on a serverless infrastructure that is managed by Amazon ECS by
launching your services or tasks using the Fargate launch type. For
more control, you can host your tasks on a cluster of Amazon Elastic
Compute Cloud (Amazon EC2) instances that you manage by using the EC2
launch type. For more information about launch types, see Amazon ECS
Launch Types .

Amazon ECS lets you launch and stop container-based applications with
simple API calls, allows you to get the state of your cluster from a
centralized service, and gives you access to many familiar Amazon EC2
features.

You can use Amazon ECS to schedule the placement of containers across
your cluster based on your resource needs, isolation policies, and
availability requirements. Amazon ECS eliminates the need for you to
operate your own cluster management and configuration management
systems or worry about scaling your management infrastructure.
```

Figure 10-17. *The ecs help command*

Troubleshooting Amazon ECR Registries

In this section, I will cover the AWS Elastic Container Registry (ECR) and how to troubleshoot it. Behind the scenes, ECR is a storage service with a great access control mechanism.

ECR repositories can be created in every region, but it is recommended you create your ECR repositories in the same region as your applications. There is no point in having an ECR repository in Southeast Asia when your applications are in the United States.

Please review Chapter 2 where I covered ECR in great detail.

ECR, like the other services, is accessible from the ECR portal where you can create and manage registries. AWS CLI also includes a module for ECR.

Using the ECR Management Console

The first step in managing and troubleshooting ECR is the ECR management console. The console gives you an overview of how many repositories you have and their URLs.

In Figure 10-18, you can see my ECR console and the one repository I have.

Figure 10-18. *ECR repositories page*

Clicking the repository will show you how many images you have and the size of each one. See Figure 10-19 for mine.

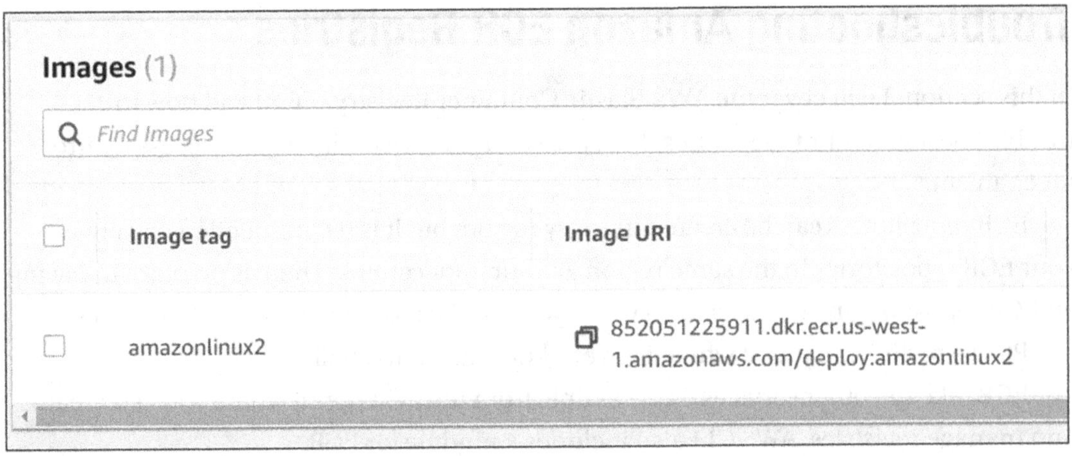

Images (1)

	Image tag	Image URI
☐		
☐	amazonlinux2	852051225911.dkr.ecr.us-west-1.amazonaws.com/deploy:amazonlinux2

Figure 10-19. *ECR images*

If you can access an image using a pull request, I suggest you start there, check that the image exists, and check that it has not been deleted.

I have seen cases where a misconfigured lifecycle policy deleted images that were needed. So, if you start to miss images, check that your lifecycle policies are configured correctly.

If you need a refresher about ECR and lifecycle policies, please review Chapter 2.

Using AWS CLI

AWS CLI offers a set of commands to manage ECR that you can use to automate or script your troubleshooting tasks. To use AWS CLI with ECR, use the following syntax:

```
aws ecr
```

The following command (shown in Figure 10-20) will display all your repositories in your region:

```
aws ecr describe-repositories
```

```
PS C:\1.DevOps> aws ecr describe-repositories
{
    "repositories": [
        {
            "repositoryArn": "arn:aws:ecr:us-west-1:852051225911:reppository/deploy",
            "registryId": "852051225911",
            "repositoryName": "deploy",
            "repositoryUri": "852051225911.dkr.ecr.us-west-1.amazonaws.com/deploy",
            "createdAt": 1554424325.0
        }
    ]
}
```

Figure 10-20. *The ecr describe-repositories command*

The following command (shown in Figure 10-21) will display all the images I have stored in my deploy repository:

```
aws ecr list-images --repository-name deploy
```

```
PS C:\1.DevOps> aws ecr list-images --repository-name deploy
{
    "imageIds": [
        {
            "imageDigest": "sha256:fe1f25a3ebb2a736c04ea3a522b1eff9c315539604a534d519c787b277e94b9e",
            "imageTag": "amazonlinux2"
        }
    ]
}
```

Figure 10-21. *The ecr list-images command*

To view all the available ECR commands, type the following (shown in Figure 10-22):

```
aws ecr help
```

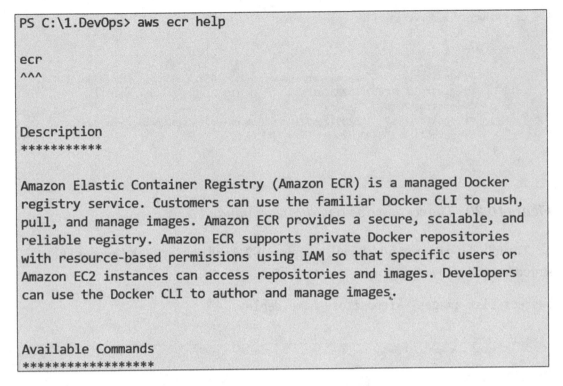

```
PS C:\1.DevOps> aws ecr help

ecr
^^^


Description
**********

Amazon Elastic Container Registry (Amazon ECR) is a managed Docker
registry service. Customers can use the familiar Docker CLI to push,
pull, and manage images. Amazon ECR provides a secure, scalable, and
reliable registry. Amazon ECR supports private Docker repositories
with resource-based permissions using IAM so that specific users or
Amazon EC2 instances can access repositories and images. Developers
can use the Docker CLI to author and manage images.


Available Commands
*****************
```

Figure 10-22. *The ecr help command*

Troubleshooting Amazon EC2 Container Hosts

In this section, I will cover some troubleshooting points about EC2.

EC2 is one of the major services in AWS, along with the associated services for storage, network, and security. EC2 provides the backbone infrastructure for running containers.

Each one of these services is like an island, but AWS has done a great job of integrating them and enabling you with tools and command lines to configure them. However, let's say you are having trouble logging in to your EC2 container host.

The issue can be related to a network problem, user permissions, or an unresponsive VM.

Note   My recommendation is troubleshoot each layer and eliminate each layer one by one.

To be on the safe side when working with EC2 instances, make sure you don't block the management ports when modifying your security group.

Using AWS CLI EC2

It is recommended that you get familiar with the AWS CLI EC2 commands. AWS CLI EC2 has the largest number of commands out of all the CLI modules.

If you type the following `help` command, you will see how many commands are available (see Figure 10-23):

```
aws ec2 help
```

```
PS C:\1.DevOps> aws ec2 help

ec2
^^^



Description
**********


Amazon Elastic Compute Cloud (Amazon EC2) provides secure and
resizable computing capacity in the AWS cloud. Using Amazon EC2
eliminates the need to invest in hardware up front, so you can develop
and deploy applications faster.

To learn more about Amazon EC2, Amazon EBS, and Amazon VPC, see the
following resources:

* Amazon EC2 product page

* Amazon EC2 documentation
```

Figure 10-23. *The ec2 help command*

To view how many instances you have in AWS, you can run the following command:

```
aws ec2 describe-instances
```

The command offers a detailed view of the instance and its configuration. Figure 10-24 shows the output.

```
PS C:\1.DevOps> aws ec2 describe-instances
{
    "Reservations": [
        {
            "Groups": [],
            "Instances": [
                {
                    "AmiLaunchIndex": 0,
                    "ImageId": "ami-0ec6517f6edbf8044",
                    "InstanceId": "i-01eab6eb3bf564a48",
                    "InstanceType": "t2.micro",
                    "KeyName": "EC2WindowsHost",
                    "LaunchTime": "2019-04-24T00:15:09.000Z",
                    "Monitoring": {
                        "State": "disabled"
                    },
```

Figure 10-24. *Viewing EC2 instances*

If you want to see all the AWS regions that have EC2 services available, you can run
the following command (shown in Figure 10-25):

```
aws ec2 describe-regions --output table
```

```
+----------------------------------------------------------------+
||                          Regions                             ||
|+-----------------------------------------+--------------------+|
||              Endpoint                   |     RegionName     ||
|+-----------------------------------------+--------------------+|
||  ec2.eu-north-1.amazonaws.com           |   eu-north-1       ||
||  ec2.ap-south-1.amazonaws.com           |   ap-south-1       ||
||  ec2.eu-west-3.amazonaws.com            |   eu-west-3        ||
||  ec2.eu-west-2.amazonaws.com            |   eu-west-2        ||
||  ec2.eu-west-1.amazonaws.com            |   eu-west-1        ||
||  ec2.ap-northeast-2.amazonaws.com       |   ap-northeast-2   ||
||  ec2.ap-northeast-1.amazonaws.com       |   ap-northeast-1   ||
||  ec2.sa-east-1.amazonaws.com            |   sa-east-1        ||
||  ec2.ca-central-1.amazonaws.com         |   ca-central-1     ||
||  ec2.ap-southeast-1.amazonaws.com       |   ap-southeast-1   ||
||  ec2.ap-southeast-2.amazonaws.com       |   ap-southeast-2   ||
||  ec2.eu-central-1.amazonaws.com         |   eu-central-1     ||
||  ec2.us-east-1.amazonaws.com            |   us-east-1        ||
||  ec2.us-east-2.amazonaws.com            |   us-east-2        ||
||  ec2.us-west-1.amazonaws.com            |   us-west-1        ||
||  ec2.us-west-2.amazonaws.com            |   us-west-2        ||
|+-----------------------------------------+--------------------+|
```

Figure 10-25. *Viewing all regions with EC2 in a table output*

According to the output, AWS EC2 is available in 16 regions.

You can also review all your EC2 volumes using the following command (shown in Figure 10-26):

```
aws ec2 describe-volume-status
```

```
PS C:\1.DevOps> aws ec2 describe-volume-status
{
    "VolumeStatuses": [
        {
            "Actions": [],
            "AvailabilityZone": "us-west-1a",
            "Events": [],
            "VolumeId": "vol-00335d78067abf6bb",
            "VolumeStatus": {
                "Details": [
                    {
                        "Name": "io-enabled",
                        "Status": "passed"
                    },
                    {
                        "Name": "io-performance",
                        "Status": "not-applicable"
                    }
                ],
                "Status": "ok"
```

Figure 10-26. *Viewing the EC2 volumes' status*

Summary

In this chapter, I covered a few methods and tools that can help you troubleshoot your AWS container services.

If you follow the AWS best practices covered in this book, you can achieve great availability and redundancy without spending unnecessary funds.

Index

A

AKS Cluster configuration
  AWS IAM authenticator
    Linux, 145
    macOS, 145
    Windows, 146
  Kubectl
    Linux, 144
    macOS, 144
  Kubectl, Windows
    download command, 140
    environment variable, 143
    system properties, 141, 142
    testing, 143

Amazon AWS
  Free Tier accounts, 13
  running containers, 40
  sign up, 12

Amazon ECR
  components, 42
  cost explorer, 71, 72
  create report, 74–78
  creating IAM account (*see* IAM
    account, ECR)
  definition, 41
  delete images, 80, 81
  lifecycle policies
    apply policy, 67, 68
    creation, 63
    image counter, 66

    match criteria, 66
    testing, 67
    test rules, 64, 65
    view results, 68, 69
  pricing structure, 42
  pull images
    authentication, 62
    Docker pull request, 62, 63
  push Docker images
    authenticate AWS ECR, 57, 58
    build command, 55
    nginx, 57
    publish image, 59, 61
    repository, 54
    tagging, 57
    upload/push, 58, 59
    URI, 55
  S3 Storage bucket, 73, 74
  tagging, 69, 70
  view report, 79, 80

Amazon ECR registries, troubleshoot
  describe-repositories command, 353
  ECR Console, 351
  help command, 354
  image, access, 352
  list images command, 353

Amazon EKS, troubleshoot
  availability issues, 340
  performance issues (*see* Performance
    issues, Amazon EKS)

© Shimon Ifrah 2019
S. Ifrah, *Deploy Containers on AWS*, https://doi.org/10.1007/978-1-4842-5101-0

Amazon Fargate, 86

Amazon Linux Container image, 22

Auto scaling, 100–101

AWS backup

  advantage, 335

  home page, 336

  plan creation, 337

  services, 336

AWS CLI, 352–354

AWS CLI, installation

  access keys, 19–20

  Amazon Linux Container image, 22–25

  configuration, 18

  download, 14

  help command, 16, 17

  Linux and macOS, 15

  Nginx, 25, 26

  Python download, 16

  security credentials, 19

  setup, 15

  usage, 20–22

  on Windows 10, 14

AWS CloudWatch

  AWS CLI, 118, 124, 125

  AWS ECS CLI

    Linux, 122

    MacOS, 122

  AWS ECS CLI, Windows

    code, 119

    Edit environment variable, 121

    system properties, 119, 120

    variable, 120, 121

  ECS CLI, 118, 122–124

  EC2 dashboard view, 117

  home page, 116, 117

  monitoring service, 116

Windows containers

  ECS cluster, 125

  ECS container, 126

  EC2 instance, 126

  EC2 task definition, 128, 129

  external IP address, 131

  IIS server page, 132

  JSON, 129

  key pair, 128

  run task, 130, 131

  security groups, 127

  storage, 127

AWS configure command, 342

AWS Container Services

  Amazon ECS

    ECR Commands, 314

    Fargate task, 308–312

    Run Task option, 307, 308

  EKS cluster

    EKS-Admin user,

      creation, 293, 294

    Heapster, 290–292

    Influxdb, 291, 292

    install Web UI (dashboard), 290

    monitor cloudwatch EC2

      (*see* Cloudwatch)

    monitor Nodes, 298, 299

    monitor Pods, 297, 298

    opening Dashboard, 295, 296

    retrieve authentication token, 295

    Web UI Dashboard, 296, 297

  monitor Docker Container hosts

    CloudWatch metrics, 315, 316

    create alarm, 316, 317

    EC2 monitoring view, 314, 315

AWS EC2 regions, 21

B

Backup and restore ECS container
    ASP01 task, 333
    Fargate task, 332
    inactive task, 333
    new task creation, 334
Backup EC2 instance,
        EBS Snapshot, 320

C

CloudFormation, 335, 344
CloudWatch
    AWS resources, 235
    bucket size, 242, 243
    CPU metric, 305
    Dashboards, 240, 302
    definition, 300
    disk information, 307
    EC2 monitoring, 300
    graphed metrics, 242
    graph options, 242
    logs screen, 238, 239
    matric page, 241
    network packets, 301
    network usage, 301
    overview screen, 238
    resource misuse, 235
    security, 235
    select metrics, 303, 304
    widget type, 241, 302, 305, 306
Code and applications protection
    rotate security keys, 230–232
    trail creation, 232
        logging, 234, 235
        name screen, 233
        storage, 233, 234
Command line interface (CLI), 13, 118

Containers and Docker hosts
    AWS CloudWatch (*see* CloudWatch)
    AWS configuration
        resources, 248
        role, 248
        rules, 248, 249
        started screen, 247
    billing alerts
        account menu, 243
        alarms, 244–246
        Billing Dashboard menu, 243
        email address, 246
        limit, 245
        preferences, 244
    navigation menu, 236, 237

D

Docker container host
    deletion, 200, 201
    deployment, 198–200
    downloading images
        Docker images, 197, 198
        pull request, 196, 197
        search images, 195, 196
    EC2 host, security group
        actions menu, 202, 203
        adding rules, 204
        configuration, 206, 207
        copy, 204, 206
        creation, 205
        details page, 202
        inbound rules, 203
    storage volumes
        Data Lifecycle
          Manager, 211
        Elastic block, 207, 208
        snapshot, 210

Docker container host (*cont.*)

    volume page, 208

    volume size, 209, 210

    Windows server, 193, 195

Docker Desktop, installation

    channel selection, 4

    download, 3

    hello-world, 11

    on Linux, 9, 10

    on macOS, 8, 9

    PowerShell console, 8

    screen, 5

    version command, 6

    version selection, 4

    virtual machine, 6, 7

    for Windows 10, 3

Docker Host

    on Linux EC2

      Amazon Linux AMI, 176

      Docker installation, 182, 183

      EC2 container host, 184

      public DNS (IPv4), 176, 177

      Windows 10, SSH, 177

    on Windows

      auto-assign Public

        IP address, 186

      credentials window, 191

      Docker version, 191, 192

      EC2 instance, 189

      hello-world, 192, 193

      instance size, 185, 186

      Key pair, 188

      password, 190

      Remote desktop

        file, 190

      security group, 187, 188

      storage, 187

      virtual machine, 185

E

EBS Snapshot, 320

ecs-cli configure command, 123

ECS cluster, 85

ECS EC2 cluster, 84

    AWS console, 102

    configuration, 103, 104

    deployment status, 104, 105

    ECS console, 102

    options, 102, 103

    scaling, 113–115

    task and clusters, 112

    task, creation

      external link IP, 111

      launch type, 109, 110

      nginx page, 111

      Run new Task, 108, 109

      view, 110

    task definition, creation, 105

      container, 107

      ECR image, 107, 108

      network mode, 106

      task size, 107

    task definitions, scaling, 112, 113

ECS Fargate and ECR, container

    deployment

    auto scaling, 100, 101

    container definitions, 91

    container page, 91, 92

    ECR image, 91

    ECS service

      configuration, 98, 99

      creation, 97, 98

      load balancer, 99, 100

      update, 101

    ECS workflow, 97

    Fargate task, 93, 94

    launch type, 88, 89

nginx screen, 96

run task, 92–95

task configuration, 89, 90

task definition, 87, 88, 92, 97

task size, 89, 90

task status, 95, 96

VPC, 94

EC2 Container Host troubleshoot

AWS EC2 help command, 355

EC2 regions, 356, 357

issues, 354

View EC2 instances
command, 355, 356

volume status, 357, 358

EKS cluster list update command, 344

EKS cluster, manage and secure

AWS CLI commands, 170, 171

CoreDNS, 168

Dashboard version, 168

deployment, 167

Kubectl commands, 168–170

namespaces, 165, 166

nodes, 166, 167

persistent volumes, 166

service limit, 173

services, 167

worker nodes, 171, 172

EKS configuration, backup, 334

EKS list clusters command, 343

EKS worker nodes
troubleshoot, 344–346

Elastic Block Storage

Block device details, 322

confirmation page, 326

description, add, 326

instance, 321

menu, 324

monitor snapshot process, 327

select volume, 325

Snapshot, 320, 325

volume ID, 323

Elastic Container Registry (ECR), 38, 351

Elastic Container Service (ECS), 38,
39, 83, 86

Elastic Container Service for
Kubernetes/Elastic Kubernetes
Server (EKS), 39, 135, 340

architecture

control panel components, 138

DNS server, 139

Web UI, 139

worker node components, 139

building blocks, 137

domain, 136, 137

service role, 147

services, 136

EKS networking

deploy application, 158, 159

EC2 Key pair, 152, 153

EKS cluster, 150–152

join worker node, 156–158

Kubectl configuration file, 152

VPC and security group

CloudFormation stack, 148, 149

stack output, 150

template page, 149

worker node

acknowledge box, 156

configuration, 155, 156

EKS cluster setup, 154

network configuration, 156

stack creation, 153

F

Free Tier account, 13

G

Git init command, 33
Git show command, 34

H

Heapster, 290
Hyper-V Linux container host, 10
Hyper-V virtual machines, 7

I, J

IAM account, ECR
    access key for AWS CLI, 50, 51
    AWS login screen, 49
    AWS services, 49
    create Group page, 46
    IAM administrators
        group, 47
    managed policies, 46
    MFA, 50
    recommendations, 43
    repository, 51, 53, 54
    set permission, 45
    users, 44
    user screen, 48
IAM policies, 217, 218
    add user, 219, 220
    attach policy, 223
    create group, 221
    IAM user, 218, 219
    password policy, 225, 226
    policy usage, 224, 225
    S3 admin user, 222
    S3 policies page, 222
    usage view, 222
    view policy, 223, 224

Identity Access Management (IAM)
    grant least privilege, 216, 217
    groups, 215, 216
    MFA, 227, 228
    policies (see IAM policies)
    roles, 228, 229
Influxdb, 291–292

K, L

Kubernetes Web UI
    admin service account, 161
    app page, 164
    create service, 164
    Heapster, 160
    home page, 163
    installation, 159, 160
    nginx page, 165
    services, 165
    sign in page, 163
    token, 162

M, N, O

Multi Factor Authentication
    (MFA), 50, 227

P, Q

Performance issues, Amazon EKS
    AWS CLI, 341
    AWS CLI EKS commands, 342–344
    CloudFormation
        auto scaling, 346
        events, 345
        template, 344
        update stack item, 345
    EKS Cluster status, 341

Pods, 297, 298

Powershell cmdlets, 10

PuTTY Key
    configuration, 180
    EC2 Key, 179
    generator, 178
    installation, 177
    Linux EC2 instance, 181, 182
    private key, 178–181
    PuTTYgen notice, 179

R

Restore EC2 instance
    attach EBS volume, 330, 331
    block device status, 332
    detach EBS volume, 330
    detach old volume, 329
    EBS volume status, 331
    stop EC2 instance, 329
    volume attach, 328
    volume creation, 327

S

Scale Amazon EKS
    acknowledge, 270
    CloudFormation, 268
    create cluster
        configuration file, 262
        IAM role, 256, 257
        menu, 259, 260
        networking, 261
        VPC, 257, 258
        worker node, 263–268
    EC2 running instances, 272
    Fargate service
        active services, 276
        Task Definitions page, 273, 274

        tasks tab, 275
        update service, 275
    Linux-Cluster, 278, 279
    registry limitations, 281
    repository, 281, 283
    scaling down, 272, 273
    select template page, 269
    Task Definition, 276, 277, 279, 280
    update cluster version
        confirm update, 285
        Docker Container Host, 286–288
        Kubernetes, 284, 286
        view, 283
    update stack, 268
    worker node, 270, 271

T, U

Task definitions, 85

Troubleshoot Amazon ECS
    AWS configure command, 348
    AWS ECS help command, 350
    ECS default cluster, 348
    ECS list clusters command, 349
    ECS list task definitions
        command, 349
    ECS management console, 347
    List ECS services command, 349

V

Virtual Private Cloud (VPC), 87, 148

Visual Studio code
    ASP.NET Core razor app, 32
    clone/download repository, 32
    Docker extension, 27, 28
    Docker registries, 28
    file deletion, 34

Visual Studio code (*cont.*)

    Git

        home page, 30

        init command, 33

        show command, 34

    GitHub

        files upload, 36

        home page, 31

        login, 36

        usage, 31

        view files, 37

    home page, 27

    installation, 27

    new repository creation, 35

W, X, Y, Z

Web access control list (Web ACL)

    page, 251

Web Application

    Firewall (WAF)

benefits, 249

creation

AWS console, 250

CloudWatch, 251

conditions, 252, 253

rules, 253, 254

Web ACL page, 251, 252

pricing, 250

Printed in the United States
By Bookmasters